THE CRETAN WAR, 1645–1671

The Venetian–Ottoman Struggle in the Mediterranean

Bruno Mugnai

'This is the Century of the Soldier', Falvio Testir, Poet, 1641

Helion & Company

Helion & Company Limited
Unit 8 Amherst Business Centre
Budbrooke Road
Warwick
CV34 5WE
England
Tel. 01926 499 619
Fax 0121 711 4075
Email: info@helion.co.uk
Website: www.helion.co.uk
Twitter: @helionbooks
Visit our blog at http://blog.helion.co.uk/

Published by Helion & Company 2018
Designed and typeset by Serena Jones
Cover designed by Paul Hewitt, Battlefield Design (www.battlefield-design.co.uk)
Printed by Henry Ling Limited, Dorchester, Dorset

ISBN 978-1-911628-0-40

British Library Cataloguing-in-Publication Data.
A catalogue record for this book is available from the British Library.

For details of other military history titles published by Helion & Company Limited, contact the above address, or visit our website: http://www.helion.co.uk

We always welcome receiving book proposals from prospective authors.

Contents

List of Illustrations & Maps

Illustrations

(*Further information is available for images marked *, pp.256–266*)

Part II: Venetian Crete

Appendices

Maps

Preface

The great conflicts between the Christian powers and the Ottoman Empire are a remarkable part of 17th century military history. There are several studies concerning the political reasons and the campaigns resulting in the 1683 siege of Vienna and the defeat of the Sultan's army at the Kahlemberg. While, until now, there are relatively few studies on the almost 27-year conflict between the Venetian Republic and the Porte. One of the main reasons of this lack of studies is that Italian historiography for a long time disliked discussing a defeat.

Apart from some studies by German authors, made on the basis of the memories by professional officers in Venice's service, Italian sources remained almost inaccessible till now. Only recently this conflict has been considered with a more critical approach, especially related to the contemporary economic transformations in the Mediterranean area. The long duration of the conflict was underlined to be a clear evidence of the economy structural change in both the States, because if maritime trade was still their main source of income, neither Constantinople nor Venice could continue to fight so long for Crete. It has also been remarked the multicultural vocation of the 'Most Serene' Republic and the significant help – however alternating – received by the other Italian states.

In this context, the great 1986 exhibition in Venice, 'Venice and the defence of the Levant', provided a glimpse into the sources about these facts. It recovered eyewitness accounts by those who were involved in that long struggle and it also put a new light on the Venetian 'military': a topic still seeming almost unknown to 20th century historiography. Eleven years later, a conference of Italian and Greek scholars held in Heraklion debated on the centuries-old relationship between Crete and Venice. The conference brought new contributions to the studies about the sieges of the city. However, after these initiatives, the contributions to the military history of the Cretan war continued to be rare and, except for the studies of Guido Candiani about the fleet, and Luciano Pezzolo about the military policy of Venice, our knowledge about Venetian warfare and the history of the Italian contingents fighting in the epic defence of Crete appeared desolately empty. The equally poorly investigated sources were also useful to deepen our knowledge on the war effort of the Ottoman Empire.

Apart for the research by Daniel Panzac and Rhoads Murphey about the fleet, studies on the Ottoman army were mostly focused on the confrontation with Austria in Hungary and the Balkans. They cared about the struggle for Crete focusing only on naval strategy, whilst it should be clear to everybody, especially in Vienna, that the lessons learned during the siege of Candia pushed the Porte very close to achieve a victory, with incalculable consequences for the history of the Western world. Therefore, the Cretan war appeared relegated to a peripheral context, like the eastern Mediterranean. Besides, the importance of this event can be easily realised just listing the State chanceries involved in the war, no matter whether committed on the ground or simply involved in as diplomatic or financial supporters.

There are many reasons making this conflict a major interesting one. Just remember that, in the last years of war, on a personal level, soldiers from almost all the European countries concentrated in Crete, as well as soldiers on the Ottoman side came from Asia and Africa. Had the war lasted longer, it would possibly have involved also other States, because Venice tried many times to organise the largest possible anti-Ottoman front.

Moreover, this work fills a gap in the recent military historiography and is also the first book in English on this topic. It provides also an insight into the technical evolution in military equipment, warfare and weapons. Lastly, concerning pictures: the different kinds of soldier involved in that struggle have been accurately reconstructed, according to the most significant examples and using many unpublished sources, also if the interpretation of the known iconography present many interpretation problems.

Ciro Paoletti

Acknowledgements

I conducted a considerable part of this book on archive documents and contemporary printed sources who engaged me, even with several pauses, since 2002. In this long travel, I had the good chance to meet a few and glorious rank of specialists and friends. To everyone goes my special thanks.

I would like to thank Ciro Paoletti for his critical reading and commentaries, Alberto Secco for having introduced me to the sources preserved in the Venice's State Archive, and Dr. Jacopo Marcello for his help in the search of the iconographic sources. I would also like to thank Prof. Kahraman Şakul and Dr. Yener Emir, who introduced me to the Ottoman sources and documents, arousing great gratitude and admiration.

Bruno Mugnai
Florence, 26 March 2018

Introduction

Empire power means sea power, and both are bound together,
so that one cannot exist without the other.

(*Obrist* Wilhelm von Bigge, *Der Kampf um Kandia in den Jahren 1667–1669)*

In the afternoon of 19 July 1657, from the rampart of the fortress of Çanak-Kalaasi, Grand Vizier Köprülü Mehmed meditated on what he had witnessed in the battle began three days earlier between the Ottoman and the Venetian fleets. Now, he was resigned to a new defeat. The aged Grand Vizier recalled the main phases of that crucial campaign and perhaps he returned to 6 June, when Sultan Mehmed IV had called him to confer the command of the operations in the Dardanelles. He remembered the solemnity of the event, underlined by the court ceremony and the young Sultan who attached to his turban two heron plumes set on a diamond brooch. Then he had received two silk kaftans, the first without fur and the other lined with sable, and finally the Sultan had entrusted to him the *uqab*, the sacred Prophet's banner. Maybe, he thought to the next day, when he had marched to Çerpegy and from where he had reached the Dardanelles following the path on the mainland with one janissary *orta* and six *sipahy kapikulu* and *toprakli* cavalry squadrons as escorts. At the first stop, in Karakaldürün, he had review the troops in the places assigned by the *çavus* who preceded him. After five days, he arrived at Gelibolu to cross the channel, then he landed on the Asian side and established his headquarter in the nearby castle. Now, faced by this new problem, he thought of his destiny. Now, his adversaries at court could easily exclude him and ask for his head.

On the same day, some hours before sunset, the flagship of the "young and brave" captain general Lazzaro Mocenigo, with all the insignia of the various states that had sent their squadrons to the fleet, passed sailing in front to the castles followed by another 11 galleys. The Venetian commander might also come back with the memory. Perhaps he thought of the hundreds of days lived on the sea; to the sustained battles; the fallen friends; the sacrifices required; the wounds received. Possibly, for a while, he also remembered what he had told the Duke of Brunswick before departing from Venice: "Your Highness will soon hear something of great, or ..." However, that day really seemed to be the day of victory: to advance into the channel for imposing peace on the enemy with the galleys' guns, now that the capital was defenceless and a few miles away. Only the strong forts erected on the two banks of the channel

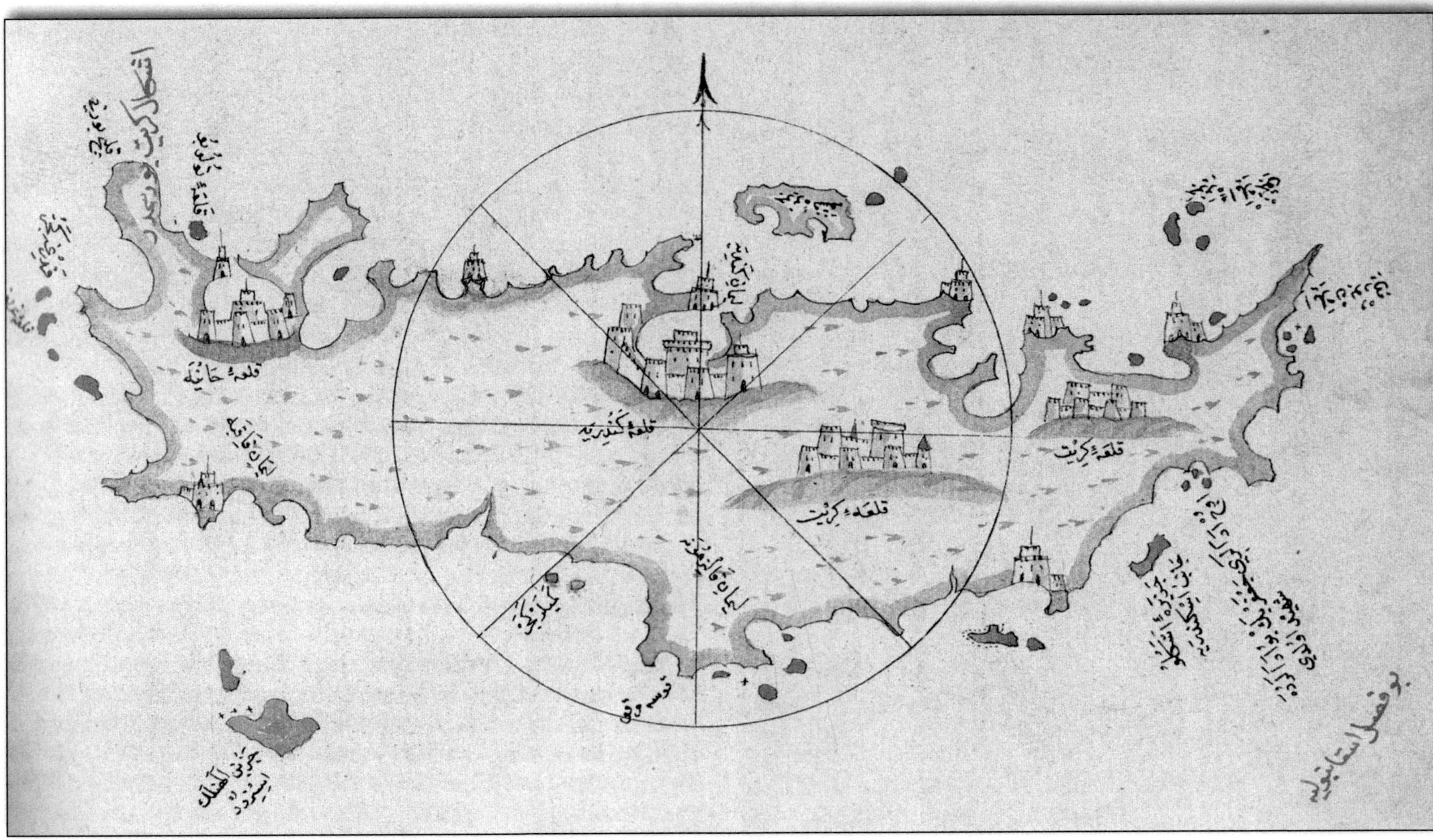

1. Crete in a 17th century Ottoman naval map

2. The Ottoman landing at Gognà beach in front of Chaniá, on 24 June 1645. (*Theatrum Europeum*, Frankfurt am Main, 1670)*

were to be overcome. The agile ships sailed in front of the coastal batteries almost at a gunshot's distance. The Venetian squadron passed the first three batteries without damage, but in front of the Koumtourni Castle a galley was hit on the rudder and another lost a mast.

On the gun emplacement of the fortress, a gunner, named Kara Mohammed, pointed one of the great guns to the larger flagged galley and fired. The projectile hissed in the air and hit the powder deposit of the galley. The explosion broke the mainmast in two and hit Mocenigo by killing him with the blow. For nearly an hour the channel was obscured by a dense cloud of smoke, and when it dissolved the debris of the galley was seen scattered in the channel. What recently seemed like an irreversible defeat, now appeared to be a great and undreamed of achievement: the Venetian squadron was about to return to the West suspending the action; the capital was saved and the challenge for the conquest of Crete could again be reopened.[1]

Despite the favourable outcome, a direct attack on Constantinople was not so obvious, and even the possibility of imposing an immediate peace would be considered; the presence of the Venetian fleet in the Marmara Sea could surely have caused a new crisis in Ottoman politics, with certainly negative consequences on the Porta's ability to continue the struggle, because the strategic war's goal was the island of Crete, but the gravitic centre of the conflict was the sea and without the control of the routes for supplying the army there was no chance of success. The war took place entirely in this strategic context: in order to complete the offensive, the Ottomans had to provide supplies to the troops on the island; conversely, the main priority for the Venetians was to interrupt the connections between the besiegers and their bases. Given these premises, it is obvious how the decisive confrontation took place in the Aegean, in the Ionian and in the Libyan Sea. Each year, the outcome of the campaigns in Crete and Dalmatia depended on the encounters on the sea. The conflict did not always reach the same level on the mainland, while naval duels did not know much about rest periods. The fleets of both contenders were called to support a struggle of an ever-recorded intensity, conducting campaigns lasting many months, protracted even in the winter season.

Although the Venetians had succeeded in gaining dominance over the seas, the strategic initiative was always in the hands of the Ottomans, who, notwithstanding enormous sacrifices, were able to ensure the survival of

1 This version of Mocenigo's death had been credited by the Ottoman historian Mustafa Naima and cited by Josef von Hammer-Purgstall in his *Geschichte des osmanischen Reiches* (Pest, 1827–33), vol. XI, p. 22. The same tale appears also in Nani-Mocenigo: *Storia della Marina Veneziana* (Rome, 1930), pp. 202–203. Some contemporary sources related a different version, namely that the Venetian captain general was killed while he was engaging seven Ottoman ships anchored under the protection of the costal forts. The attempt to penetrate the Marmara Sea is, possibly, a reconstruction of posterity, but in the following years the Venetian government continued to consider the plan designed by Lazzaro Mocenigo as real. See also Guido Candiani, *Vele, remi e cannoni: l'impiego congiunto di navi, galee e galeazze nella flotta veneziana, 1572–1718*, in 'Mutazioni e Permanenze nella Storia Navale del Mediterraneo – secc. XVI–XI' (Milan, 2010); p. 148, and Anastasia Stouraiti: *Una Storia della Guerra, Pietro Garzoni e il suo Archivio*, in: Mario Infelise and Anastasia Stouraiti (eds.): 'Venezia e la guerra di Morea. Guerra, politica e cultura alla fine del '600' (Franco Angeli, Milan 2005), p. 242.

their army in Crete despite the many defeats suffered on the sea. In such a situation, it was almost a miracle for the Porte to have maintained an occupation corps on the island, isolated for long periods and often lacking supplies. However, they were helped by the attitude of the Venetians, who chose the option of passive resistance in the hope of provoking the depletion of the enemy and forcing him into peace talks.[2] To be decisive for the Ottoman side was the peculiar structure of its military structure, strategically set up for the offensive, therefore intrinsically more agile and subordinate to a supreme command with absolute powers. Instead, the Venetians, resolute to oppose an indefinitely defence, remained conditioned by their intricate state apparatus, retarded by the internal dynamics that always underwent the appointment of commanders and the formation of fleets.

The Ottoman aggression was the result of a clear expansionist policy, which left no space for manoeuvre for Venice. Despite the attempts made to avoid the war, the conflict broke out, and surrender the island without fighting was inconceivable if Venice wanted to maintain the prestige and freedom of its institutions. Freedom, a valour often referred to in the speeches of the Senators, reported in the narratives of the conflict by the contemporary historians, constitutes one of the founding points of the myth of Venice during the Cretan war.

Scholars have not sufficiently focused on, or have even avoided, Venetian attempts to expel the Ottomans from Crete.[3] The myth of the heroic resistance has overshadowed the three campaigns launched in 1650, 1660 and 1666. These actions were very important efforts planned with large employment of means and resources, and if the first attempt had been conducted with clearly insufficient forces, the campaigns of 1660 and 1666 involved several thousands of men and sailors. Meanwhile, the Venetian naval strategy aimed at causing material depletion of the enemy through the naval blockade and the implacable hunting to the Ottomans supplies, which sailed to Crete. Although Venice did not consider immediately the hypothesis of defeating the enemy expeditionary corps in Crete, it is unfair to affirm that the Republic conducted just a defensive strategy. Surely, the indecision caused loss of valuable time, allowing Constantinople to find other ways to refuel the army on the island. When Venice understood that the flow of supplies from the ports in Southern Anatolia and North Africa had consolidated, the war moved closer to the shores of Crete.

From a strategic point of view, three different fronts can be identified: the island of Crete with the capital Candia-Heraklion; the eastern Mediterranean from the Dardanelles to Corfu; Dalmatia, Albania and Bosnia. In these latter

2 This assumption is accredited by Kenneth M. Setton's 'Venice, Austria, and the Turks in the Seventeenth Century', *Memoirs of the American Philosophical Society, vol. 192; Philadelphia, 1991*, pp. 104–203.

3 Concerning the evasive attitude of certain historians about the Venetian passivity, see David Brewer, *Greece, the Hidden Centuries: Turkish Rule from the Fall of Constantinople to Greek* Independence (London: I.B. Tauris, 2011). Notwithstanding the good quality of the work, in Chapter 12: 'The Turks take Crete', the author does not make any mention of the Venetian operations in Crete to expel the Ottomans, and explains the Venetian defeat as the result of a sterile and passive defence.

3. Ibrahim I (r.1640–48). **(*Theatrum Europeum*, Frankfurt am Main, 1670)***

regions minor clashes occurred, but were destined to have a significant strategic importance, especially because the war profoundly altered the ethnic pattern of these regions.

Finally, when we approach the national sphere, the war created a phenomenon of great historical interest, as it caused the mobilisation of soldiers from all Italian states against a common enemy two centuries before the Risorgimento.

The conflict of 1645–71 also marks a point of passage of great importance in European history. The Ottoman conquest of the island not only changed the history of the eastern Mediterranean, but returned to the Sublime Porte confidence in its offensive means by opening new channels in the expansionist policy, materialised by the challenge under the walls of Vienna. This event has been considered as the extreme organisational effort of the Ottoman warfare, overpowered by the victory achieved in a long and complex struggle, as had been the war for Crete. From a certain point of view, the Cretan war represented a kind of general proof for the subsequent campaigns against the Christian states. This view altered the specific meaning and conditioned the point of view of certain historiography. Compared to the conflict of 1570–73 – fought between two states in full strength – the clash has been described as an exhausting duel fought by two states in severe economic crisis and took place in a theatre – the Mediterranean – that had lost its secular centrality. Several scholars agree in their judgement that the two powers, far from engaging in empty sabre-rattling and vainglorious attempts to recall and, if successful, restore their faded 16th century imperial glory,[4] actually fought for more tangible and immediate material rewards. In the view of these scholars, both sides were seeking to establish an exclusive control over eastern Mediterranean markets. One scholar[5] in particular concludes that the much-discussed rise of the Atlantic economies based on control of the transatlantic trade did not materialise nearly so suddenly nor as completely as is often supposed, and that the Mediterranean remained the most important destination for the goods of northern Europe well into the 17th century. The analysis which follows, will be framed as a cost–benefit assessment of post-1650 Ottoman investment in the maritime sphere, and an estimation of what they gained or stood to gain in return.[6]

4 Rhoads Murphey, 'The Ottoman Resurgence in the Seventeenth-Century Mediterranean: The Gamble and its Results'. In *Mediterranean Historical Review*; n. 8 – 1993; p. 187.

5 Richard T. Rapp, 'Unmaking of the Mediterranean Trade Hegemony', *Journal of Economic History*, n. 35, 1975, p. 504.

6 R. Murphey, cited work, p. 188.

4. Crete with the four Venetian administrative provinces in an early-17th century print. (Author's archive)

Moreover, the long duration of the conflict is the clear proof of the structural economic change of the two states involved in the struggle, because if the maritime trade had still been the main source of income as in the previous century, neither Constantinople nor Venice could have continued to fight so long for Crete. Also concerning the means employed and the technical development of armaments, the fact that the conflict opposed two states now in irreversible crisis, has insinuated the suspicion that the lack of innovations depended on the state of prostration and technological backwardness of both the parties. All this revolves around the naval question, or the lasting coexistence of sailing and oar, so much so that – even today – resist the conviction about the significant use of rowing units, to the detriment of modern sailing ships, would be the most evident sign of the technological delay of the two contenders. This assumption is reiterated also by historians of great fame and has become a commonplace difficult to eradicate.

The conquest of Crete – *Candia* for the Venetians and *Kandye* for the Ottomans – was an option that has long been carefully considered by the Ottoman Porte.[7] With the possession of the island, Constantinople would have not only consolidated its rule in the Levant, in which Venetian Crete was a foreign body, but would be able to influence the economy of Southern Europe and the Mediterranean in its favour. In the half of the 17th century, the empire

7 The hypothesis about an attack on Crete had already been assessed during the reign of Sultan Selim II, shortly after the conquest of Cyprus, but the heavy defeat at Lepanto in 1571 had changed the Ottoman plans. See also in Svat Soucek, 'The Ottoman Conquest of Rhodes, Cyprus and Crete', in *Studies in Ottoman naval History and Maritime Geography* (Piscaway, NJ: Gorgias Press), 2009.

5. The remains of the fortification on the island of Agios Theodoros a few miles from Chaniá, on which now lies a small church with a few houses. (Author's photo)*

faced a crucial turning point in the economy and needed to strengthen internal policy. The results achieved by the *vezir i-âzam* (grand vizier) Kemankes Kara Mustafa in economic affairs were slowly returning a solid financial base to the empire, but prosperity concealed some dangerous pitfalls. Two parties faced each other in Constantinople with the aim of controlling the feeble Sultan Ibrahim I (1640–48): the faction led by the grand vizier oriented to the internal political balance achieved by gradually abolishing the power of the janissaries, the powerful professional soldiers; opposed to the other represented by the military, under the Anatolian *kazasker* (military judge) Cinci Hoca Hüseyin.[8] This latter was able to gain the favour of the *valide* (the Sultan's mother) Kösem.[9] She was the only member of the Imperial family with a remarkable political

8 Cinci Hoca Hüseyin, is the epithet of Karabaşzade Hüseyin Efendi, a 17th-century Ottoman spiritualist whose influence on the Sultan caused many problems in the government. He was born in Safranbolu (in the modern province of Karabük, Turkey). He claimed to be a descendant of Sadrettin Konevi, a 13th-century Sufi. However, unlike his famous ancestor, he made a name as a witch doctor and *valide* Sultan Kösem invited him to the palace to cure the unbalanced Sultan İbrahim. In 1643, İbrahim appointed Cinci as the *kadı* of Galata and in 1644 as the *kazasker* of Anatolia, an appointment which caused a great reaction among the *ulama*. Cinci used his increasing power to increase his wealth by accepting bribes. When İbrahim was dethroned in 1648, the new grand vizier Sofu Mehmet Pasha faced the problem of bonus salaries (Turkish: *culus bahşişi*), the traditional salary paid to soldiers upon the enthronement of the new Sultan. He confiscated Cinci's earnings and expelled him to Damascus. During his journey, Cinci fell ill in Mihalcık (now Karacabey, Bursa). While staying in Mihalcık, he criticised the Grand Vizier and consequently was executed. See von Hammer-Purgstall, cited work, vol. 10, pp. 231–241.

9 Kösem Sultan (*c.*1589–1651) – also known as Mahpeyker Sultan. She was one of the most powerful women in Ottoman history. Kösem achieved power and influenced the politics of the Ottoman Empire when she became *haseki* Sultan as favourite consort and later legal wife of Ottoman Sultan Ahmed I and *valide* as mother of Murad IV and Ibrahim, then as grandmother of Mehmed IV. She was one of the prominent figures during the Sultanate of Women. See also

skill, and in a short time, the *valide*'s faction had the better of the Grand Vizier's faction, obtaining as the seal of its victory the elimination of Kemankes in January 1644. The new scenario required that the military class would retake the power lost during the government of the hated Kemankes, their centrality in the court and society, and possibly the promise of a war of conquest along with the treasures gained through an easy victory. A new expansive jump was also a useful escape for the political turmoil, always lurking in the unstable Ottoman scenario. However, at court, no one had thought about who to turn the forces on. In Hungary, the Habsburgs appeared more prepared than in the past to withstand an assault. Further east, the animosity and the raids of the Cossack communities were not a qualified target. Moreover, it was necessary to operate on a front where to also mobilise the navy. The choice was limited to two options: Malta, or the Greek islands still under Venetian rule, and in this case, Crete was the most craved for goal. Only the *mufti* spoke out against the decision to engage the state into a war whose outcome was – in his opinion – uncertain, but he paid his opposition with deposition and arrest.

Thus, in the autumn of 1644, the Porte accused Venice of having allowed to land in Crete Ottoman subjects captured by the Knights of Malta while on the *caravan* of Alexandria – the rich commercial convoy that annually sailed between the Bosphorus and the Egypt – as well as allowing the Order's ships to repair after the action in a bay on the island. Giovanni Soranzo, *Bailo* of the Ottoman Porte – as the Venetian ambassador to Constantinople was officially called – tried to prove the falsity of the charge and thought he was able to overcome the threat, when he was informed that the Ottoman fleet would leave to fight the Maltese Knights. On 30 April 1645, the fleet took off, without actually knowing whether Malta or Crete was the target. Just off Navarrino (today Pylos, Greece), the Ottoman commander Mascovich Yusuf received the order to sail to Crete. With the Ottoman landing, which took place on 23 and 24 June 1645, began the 26-year-long war fought between the Republic of Venice and the Sublime Porte for the possession of Crete.

The conflict had a huge echo all over Europe. Crete was the place of confrontation for two different military models, the western and the Ottoman, and in the imagination of the 17th century, the island became the 'Campo di Marte' of the European continent. Today, these campaigns show us a specific peculiarity, as they represent the first 'war of materials', namely a conflict fought far from the involved states. The decisive strategic duel involved the belligerents in the control of the supply routes, and the metropolitan territory of both sides remained almost excluded by military operations. It was a conflict where logistical organisation and the ability to supply the armies made the difference, very similarly, to provide an understandable example to everyone, to the campaigns in the southwestern Pacific during the Second World War. It could be said that the Cretan War was the first conflict of the contemporary age, but fought by 17th century means.

Gabor Agoston and Bruce Masters, *Encyclopedia of the Ottoman Empire* (New York: Facts on File, 2009), pp. 263–269.

Chronology

1644

September 28	St John Maltese Knights capture two Ottoman ships off Rhodes; among the prisoners there are some members of the Sultan's court. On the way back to Malta, the Knights' galleys stop in Crete.
October 16	Venetian ambassador in Constantinople rejects the insinuations of complicity with the Maltese Knights.

1645

April	Ottoman fleet is joined at Navarino in the Peloponnese, officially ready to sail against Malta.
June 26	Ottomans land on the Cretan beach of Gognà and seize the Venetian fortress on the island of Saint Theodor.
June 29	Ottomans lay siege to Chaniá; the city surrenders after 54 days.
July 12	Venetian fleet bombards the port of Patrasso.
Sep 28–29	Venetian fleet, reinforced by Italian auxiliary galleys, attacks the port of Chaniá, but is repulsed.

1646

January 3	Death of Doge Francesco Erizzo; Francesco Molino succeeds him.
January 30	Sultan Ibrahim I removes the commander in Crete, Mascovich Iussuf, who is sentenced to death; *beglerbeg* Baltaoğlu Hüseyin is appointed as new commander; he will hold the position for 11 years.
March 30	Venetian sailing ships under Tommaso Morosini anchor in front of the Dardanelles to impose the naval blockade.
May 26	Venetians repulse the Ottoman attempt to overcome the blockade of the Dardanelles.

Spring/summer: First plaque epidemic in Crete, which lasts until 1648.

June 15	Ottomans conquest Gramvousa Island a few miles off Crete.
November 21	Venetian garrison of Réthymnon surrenders after 24 days of siege.

1647

January 27	Naval encounter off Chalkis between the Venetian sail ship squadron commander Tommaso Morosini and 46 Ottoman galleys. With the arrival of the rest of the squadron, the Venetians prevail, but Morosini is killed in action.
February 28	Ottomans conquer the Venetian fortified port of Novigrad in Dalmatia.
March 19	Ottoman fortress of Zemunik Donji in Bosnia surrenders to Lunardo Foscolo.
March 31	Venetians retake Novigrad in Dalmatia.
June 28	Field battle of Messarea, the Ottomans repulse the Venetian assault on their encampment.
August 12	Inconclusive encounter between the Venetian and Ottoman fleets off Chios.
August 26	The Ottomans lay siege to Šebenik in Dalmatia, but leave on 16 September.

1648

March 7	Storm off Psarà in the Aegean Sea; Captain General Giovanni Battista Grimani is drowned.
March 18	The Venetians under Foscolo siege Klis in Bosnia; the fortress surrenders on 1 April.
May 1	The Ottomans lay the siege at Candia; after heavy casualties, the operations end on 10 November.
Augus 18	Sultan Ibrahim I is deposed and killed; his 12-year-old son Mehmet IV succeeds him.
Autumn:	First rebellions in Anatolia.

1649

May	With a successful landing, the Ottomans conquer the fortress of Palocastro at Crete, but fail at Suda Island.
May 12	Venetian fleet defeats the Ottomans at Foça.
Spring–summer	**New rebellions in Anatolia.**
Jul 8–Oct 2	Ottomans siege unsuccessfully Candia for the second time.
September	Venetians fail to conquer Sinj in Dalmatia.

1650

April 7	Venetian galleys under Giovanni Battista Barbaro assault the Ottoman port of Monemvasia in the Peloponnese, where they capture 20 enemy merchants.
May–June	Venetians defeated in their attempts to expel the Ottomans from Ierapetra and Sitia in Crete.

July 14	Venetians reconquers the fortress of Agios Theodoros and Turluru at Crete. Some days later they leave both places, after destroying the fortifications.
Summer	Ottoman raids against Zadar in Dalmatia.

1651

June	Venetians unsuccessfully siege the fortress of Zadvarje in Bosnia.
July 10	Venetians win naval engagement off Paros Island in the Cyclades.
August 2	Captain General Lunardo Foscolo conquers the island of Leros.
October	Negotiations are opened between Venice and Constantinople.

1652

February 21	Venetians conquer the fortress of Zadvarje in Herzegovina.
Summer	Venetian Senate sends Ambassador Giovanni Capello to the Porte to negotiate a truce.

1653

Spring–summer:	**Lootings and reprisals between Ottomans and Venetians in Dalmatia, Bosnia and Herzegovina.**
August 20	Venetian fleet assaults the Ottoman port of Monemvasia.

1654

March 25	Venetians defeated at the siege of Knin in Herzegovina.
April 21	Maltese galleys defeat an Ottoman sailing squadron off Rhodes.
May 16	Ottoman fleet under Murad Paşa prevails over Venetian vessels led by Giuseppe Dolfin in the First Battle of the Dardanelles.
September	Ottomans fail to conquer Tinos in the Aegean Sea.

1655

February 27	Carlo Contarini is elected as new Doge.
May	Venetian fleet under Francesco Morosini destroys the port of Volos in Thessaly and plunders Aegina Island in the Aegean Sea.
June 21	After six hours of fighting, the Ottoman fleet abandons the attempt to force the Venetian blockade in the Second Battle of the Dardanelles.
July	New peace negotiations are opened between Venice and the Porte.
July 23–Sep 27	Bombardment of the Ottoman port of Nauplia in the Peloponnese by Venetian galleys under Antonio Barbaro.

1656

Spring	Uprisings and rebellions in Syria, Anatolia and Egypt.

April 30	Doge Carlo Contarini dies; on 17 May, Francesco Corner is elected as new Doge, but he dies after 20 days; Francesco Valier succeeds him on 14 June.
May	Riots in Istanbul caused by the devaluation of the new currency.
June 26	Third Battle of the Dardanelles, Venetians triumph over the Ottoman fleet; Captain General Lorenzo Marcello is killed in action.
July–August	Venice conquers the islands of Bozcaada and Limnos in northern Aegean Sea.
September 14	Köprülü Mehmed is appointed as grand vizier.

1657

April–June	Great rebellion in Syria and Anatolia led by the *paşa* of Aleph, Abaza Hassan.
May 18	Venetian landings on the Anatolian coast under Lazzaro Mocenigo, who conquers the Ottoman fortress of Sığacık.
June 3	Venetian sailing ships destroy off Chios the supplies for Crete, sailing from Egypt.
June	Ottoman raids against Venetian domains in Dalmatia and Albania.
July 17–19	Fourth naval battle of the Dardanelles and a new Venetian victory. Venetian galleys led by Lazzaro Mocenigo enter the straits and engage the enemy forts, but the explosion of the Captain General's galley puts an end to the operation; Captain General Mocenigo is killed in action.
July 30	Ottomans besiege Castelnuovo of Kotor, but leave after two months.
Sep 23–Oct 1	Ottomans reconquer the islands of Bozcaada and Lemnos.
Autumn	New peace negotiations opened in Constantinople.

1658

April 8	Election of Giovanni Pesaro as Doge.
May 1	Francesco Morosini is appointed as captain general.
May 3	Punitive expedition against Transylvania ordered by Köprülü Mehmed.
July	Venetian and Maltese landings in Anatolia; plundering of Çeşme and Kastelorizo Island.
September 23	Maltese and Papal galleys destroy the Ottoman pirate port of Lefkada.

1659

May 3	Venetians reconquer Gramvousa islands.
June 12	Venetian fleet, under Francesco Morosini, assaults and destroys the Ottoman port of Chios.
September 30	Domenico Contarini is elected as Doge.
October	Plague epidemic in Candia.

1660

Feb–March	Ottoman incursions in Dalmatia.
May 6	Fire in Constantinople destroys the Galata arsenal.
June 11	Venetians land on Skiathos in northern Aegean Sea.

Summer–Autumn: Plague epidemic spreads to Crete.

Aug–Sep	Venetians and Allies land near Chaniá but fail in their attempt to conquer the city; the following assault on the Ottoman encampment of Yeni Kandie is another failure, which ends with heavy casualties.
September 1	Venetians conquer Butrint in Albania.

1661

Spring	Plague epidemic in southern Aegean Sea, which lasts until 1664.
August 27	Venetian galley fleet, reinforced by Maltese Knights, defeats the Ottomans off Milos Island.
October 30	Death of Grand Vizier Köprülü Mehmed; succeeded by son Ahmed.

1662

Spring	Negotiations for an armistice reopen in Constantinople.
Autumn	Growing tensions between Austrian Habsburgs and the Ottoman Empire following the Transylvanian crisis.

1663

April	Ottomans reconquer Butrint.
June 2	War between the Emperor and the Porte.

1664

February	Peace negotiations between Venice and the Porte are interrupted.
August 1	Imperial General Raimondo Montecuccoli defeats Köprülü Ahmed in the battle of Szentgotthárd-Mogersdorf; nine days afterwards the Imperials and Ottomans sign the Peace of Vasvár.

1665

Spring–summer: Ottoman raids in Dalmatia, followed by Venetian reprisals in Bosnia and Herzegovina.

1666

Summer	Plague epidemic in Crete.
August 24	Allied contingent lands on Crete under the Marquis Francesco Villa and lays siege to Chaniá; the operation is interrupted after 14 days.
September 12	Venetian attempt to expel the Ottomans from Crete fails after the unsuccessful assault against Yeni Kandie.

1667

May 22	Death of Pope Alessandro VII; Clement IX succeeds him.
May 28	Grand Vizier Köprülü Ahmed reopens the siege of Candia.

1668

Autumn–winter:	**Venice renews the offer of peace to the Sultan, but the Grand Vizier opposes the continuation of talks.**
December 18	French volunteers under Marquis de la Feuillade are defeated in the sortie from Candia.

1669

June 19	French relief corps sent by Louis XIV arrive with the fleet at Candia.
June 25	Great sortie of the French contingent led by Duke of Beaufort is repulsed with heavy casualties.
July	Allied fleet bombards the Ottoman trenches at Candia; the action is unsuccessful.
August 19–21	French contingent leaves Candia.
September 6	Captain General Francesco Morosini signs the surrender of the city.

1671

July 27	After months of negotiations for the establishment of the border in Dalmatia and Bosnia, the peace is officially signed between Venice and the Porte.

1

Oars, Sails and Soldiers

The Military Strength of the *Sublime Porte*

In 1645 the Ottoman Empire was still proving to be an evenly matched opponent for any major European power. It was the only state in Europe to maintain a considerable number of professionals for both a permanent army and navy. The Porte[1] maintained superiority over the Western European states also in terms of territory, population, and natural resources. At its height in the 16th and early 17th centuries, the Sultan ruled over nearly 7,000,000 square kilometres, with a population of approximately 25,000,000. His domain linked three continents: Asia, Europe and Africa. The Empire stretched from the southern borders of the Holy Roman Empire through Hungary and the Balkans to Yemen and Eritrea in the south, controlling much of North Africa and western Asia, and encompassing an array of cultures, languages, peoples, climates and social and political structures. This varied ethnic composition made the empire a melting pot of cultures and religions. There were not any restrictions for Christians and Jews, and in this aspect the empire ruled by the successor of Othman was possibly the most tolerant in 17th century Europe.

The Ottoman court had been established in Constantinople after 1453 and based in the Topkapy Palace. A picturesque crowd of pages, eunuchs, concubines, and employers for the various tasks required by the Imperial protocol resided in the luxurious rooms of the palace. Officials and servants occupied the two branches of the *seray*, the imperial court: the *enderun* (internal service) and the *birun* (external service). In the first service operated the members of the *has oda* (the Sultan's private secretary), the *hazine-yihassa* (treasurer), *silihtar* (esquires), *terçuman* (dragoman or interpreter), the white eunuchs and finally the first Sultan's attendants, his cousin and the school for the princes. In the *birun* were registered the court Imam, physicians, eye medics, surgeon and astrologer. The medical–religious service was followed by the *müteferrika* (the household horsemen), *bostangi* (gardeners), room guardians with their

1 The Sublime Porte, also known as the Ottoman Porte or High Porte (Ottoman Turkish: بابعالى – *Bab-ı Ali* – from Arabic: باب, *báb* 'gate' and عالي, *alī* 'high'), is a metonym identifying the central government of the Ottoman Empire, by reference to the gate giving access to the buildings that housed the principal state departments in Constantinople.

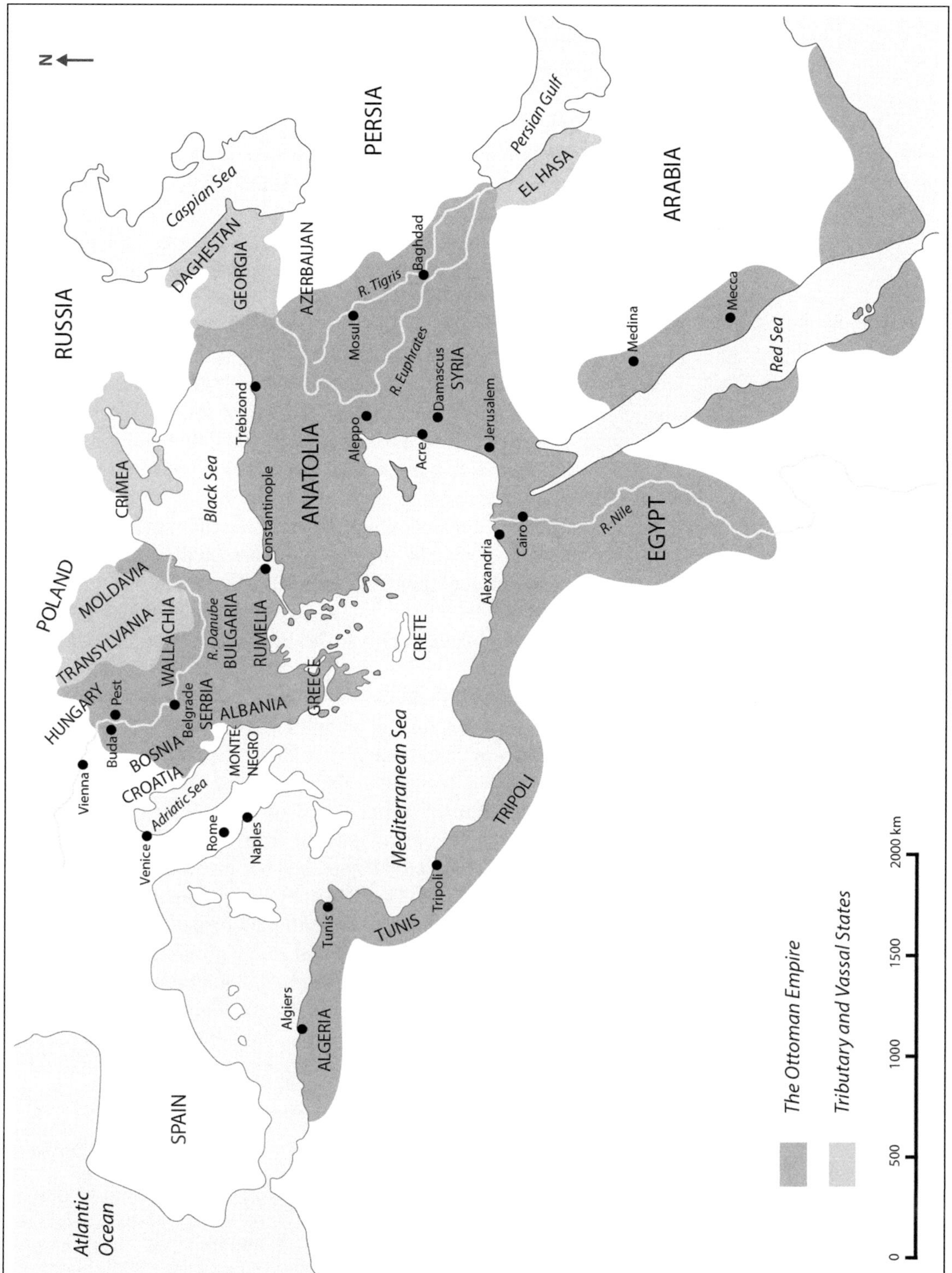

Map 1 The Extent of the Ottoman Empire

6. The ***kapudan paşa*****, the chief admiral of Sultan's fleet. (M. la Haye,** ***Recueil de cent estampes representant differentes nations du Levant*****, Paris 1714)***

commander, workers and other personnel. Next to the court was located the *divoan*, the government of the state directed by the Grand Vizier. In the *divoan* operated the *defterdar paşa* (finance minister) with the other ministers, the major army and navy officers, religious judges, caliphs, province governors and the chief of ceremonies. Naturally the Sultan participated in the *divoan* too, and observed government meetings behind a grate window. Each political decision would depend on the Sultan, who issued a *firman* (imperial decree).

The empire was divided in provinces, *vilayet*, each governed by a *beglerbeg*, governor of a *beglerbeglik*, numbered four until 1687: Rumelia (Greece), Hungary, Anatolia and Egypt. The hierarchy continued with the *paşa*, governors of *paşalik*, with 19 in 1645. *Beglerbeg* and *paşa* occupied the high places of the imperial structure of power and their political authority was considerable; indeed, in the *divoan* they followed just after the *vizir*. Each *vilayet* was divided in *beglik* with a *beg* or *sancakbeg* as chief. The last provincial partitions were the *zeamet* and *timar*, appointed to modest territories or beneficiaries of rural areas and cattle breeding.[2] In any case, the attribution of the charges and relating income was entrusted only temporarily: the ownership of the land remained with the Sultan, who could remove the curators and approve new allocations.[3] The close relationship between civil society and military organisation was often the cause of changes in territorial divisions. In 1660, for example, was established the *pasalik* of Várad on the border with Transylvania, in order to better control the turbulent political situation of the tributary princedom. In a similar way, minor land appointments following the military campaign may be noted at Crete, when the island was divided in 17 *zeamet* and 15,130 *timar*. The system of power based on the military conquest had its legal base on the *vakif*. The terms derived from an ancient Muslim law, which established that half of the land conquered became the Sultan's property, leaving the remainder to the army. The hierarchy established on the territorial division also constituted the military leadership structure of the empire. Each governor had command over the troops raised in his province. The Ottoman Empire resembled in this regard to a military dictatorship, as outlined by some scholars.[4] The Ottoman regime conformed to the pattern of the military

2 Originally, the Ottoman provincial structure had affected elements of the existing system of Byzantine pronoia and more directly from the itqà of the Seljuk. See Alessio Bombaci: 'Gli Ottomani dalle origini alla conquista di Costantinopoli', in Bombaci-Shaw, *Storia dell'Impero Ottomano* (Turin: UTET, 1981), pp. 215–216.

3 In the Western sources, the Ottoman provincial offices were compared to those of the feudal aristocracy, while in reality the differences were significant. The concept of nobility, in the sense of belonging to a privileged class, was not provided for in the Ottoman culture. The appointments were not transmissible by inheritance and theoretically any Muslim subject could ascend to the rank of Grand Vizier. The concept of nobility applied only to the Sultan's family.

4 D.E. Streusand, *Islamic Gunpowder Empires: Ottomans, Safavids, and Mughals* (Philadelphia, PA: Westview Press, 2011), p. 31.

patronage state. The entire governmental machinery, civil administration and military forces, and even religious functionaries were treated as part of the military establishment. The Ottomans defined them as *askeari* literally meaning 'military' though frequently translated as 'ruling class'. The subject population was the *raya* (common people). The *askeri* received taxation, and the *raya* paid it. The circle of justice defined the proper relationship of the *askeri* and the *raya*.[5] Justice involved reasonable and predictable tax demands, the maintenance of order, and, for the Ottomans, the maintenance of the distinction between *askeri* and *raya*, the most fundamental social division within the Empire.

One of the greatest difficulties encountered in defining the size of the Porte's armies derives from the scarcity of reliable sources made by Ottoman officials. As rightly stated by John Stoye,[6] the military history of the Ottoman Empire in the 17th century still waits to be written. Despite the heroic attempts of some historians, a huge number of documentary texts preserved in the Turkish archives still need to be explored. Nevertheless, even when these sources are accessed, the cultural and political tradition of the Ottoman Empire made dignitaries and military leaders little inclined to draw up state documents and instructions for the army on the Western model, or write memoirs to explain or justify the actions taken. In this way, certain episodes and decisions remain in a mysterious and ambiguous context. Even men of culture who accompanied the armies in campaigns left only succinct reports about the events to which they assisted. Yet, no one better than them was in the best position to observe and judge certain episodes. Fortunately their Austrian, Hungarian and Italian enemies registered much precious information regarding the Ottoman military strength. In order to learn the numerical strength of the Ottoman army and navy, it is enough to refer to the most experienced scholar of that age, Count Ferdinando Marsigli, who worked as secretary of the Porte's Bailo.[7] He had the opportunity to consult the military administration registers, the so-called *kanun-name*. In 1670, based on his knowledge, Marsigli established an overall force of 248,440 men in the army and another 50,572 in the navy, comprising a balanced force of 142,000 soldiers and 35,000 sailors and rowers immediately available.[8]

The Cretan War represented a very interesting test for Ottoman military power in the crucial age of its incoming decline. Few historians have focused on this age for investigating the actual importance of this turning point for the Ottoman 'military' faced the Western world. In the debate about the 'military revolution' several scholars have tried to explain in different ways the radical change both in tactics and technology that gradually gave significant advantage

5 Naima Mustafà, the aforementioned 17th-century Turkish chronicler, wrote significantly at this regard. Ottoman society was separated in classes: the mass of the subjects at base, producer of the state wealth, maintained the military class at the top of power, conforming to an 'equity cicle': *1. State or government cannot exist without the army; 2 .The maintenance of the army requires wealth; 3. The wealth is produced by the subjects; 4. The subjects can prosper only in a condition of justice; 5. Without state or government cannot exist justice.* Various Authors: *Islamic World Atlas*, p. 72.

6 John Stoye, *The Siege of Vienna. The Last Great Trial Between Cross & Crescent* (New York: Pegasus Books, 2008), p. 28.

7 Term indicating the Venetian ambassador to the Porte.

8 Luigi Ferdinando Marsigli, 'Stato Militare dell'Imperio Ottomanno' Den Haag, 1721, pp. 148–150.

to the West over various non-Western powers, the Ottoman Empire included. Some authors appropriately note that the definition of "the nature and chronological location of Military Revolution" has become a scholarly obsession in recent times.[9] Other historians have previously tried to give technocentric explanation for the rise of Western European power, however recent works challenge these theories, focusing on the crucial importance of the economic and social-political factors in these changes.[10] The success of the West against the Ottoman Empire had usually been credited to various factors, such as new tactical discipline, effective military leadership, better equipped and trained troops and higher standard of artillery above all, while in recent studies some authors underline the significance of the economic domination of Europe in the creation of its political hegemony. It seems to be a consensus that military technological superiority alone cannot be accountable for the Ottoman military decline.[11] Amongst more recent studies, there are numerous scholars who are less inclined towards "an inexorable stagnation and decline" of the Ottoman Empire.[12] Some of the blame for this decline has been attributed to the vagaries of a patrimonial households directed by useless and ruthless sultans who were unable to take their role seriously. Even though the Ottoman state lasted from the beginning of the 14th century until 1923, few scholars have acknowledged or explained its longevity. Instead, conventional accounts have argued for a long decline, starting at the end of Süleyman the Magnificent, as if everything after his reign was a form of failure. The later history of the Empire has been viewed through a negative lens of centuries of weakness and loss, rather than interesting and resourceful adaptation and reconfiguration of rule.[13]

Under several aspects the term 'decline' itself reflects a judgment passed by Europeans convinced of their superiority, rather than an accurate assessment of Ottoman military capabilities in the 17th century.[14] According to some recent studies which employ the *Krause-model* in order to locate capabilities on the scale of the international production hierarchy, included arms production,

9 See John Childs, *Warfare in the Seventeenth Century* (London: Harper Collins, 2006), p. 16.

10 John A. Lynn, in *The Military Revolution Debate* (Boulder: Westview Press, 2015), pp. 185-6; C.J. Rogers: 'The Military Revolution in History' and Jeremy Black, *A Military Revolution? Military Changes and European Society, 1550–1800* (Basingstoke: Macmillan, 1998).

11 In the debate on the 'military revolution' it is possible to note that most of the authors fail to examine the Ottoman case. Jeremy Black, for instance, complains that Geoffrey Parker treats quite impressively even the non-European theatre and subsequently he neglects the Venetian–Ottoman warfare. Cited work, p. 99.

12 See Jonathan Grant, 'Rethinking the Ottoman Decline: Military Technologies diffusion in the Ottoman Empire, 15th to 18th centuries', in *Journal of World History*, 10 (1999), p. 176. According to Grant, the word 'decline' always suggests a kind of comparison and in the case of the Ottomans, this comparison may be measured against either other states. On the following pages, Grant makes a good point when he tells us that the comparison of the Ottoman Empire with England, France or the United Provinces of the Netherlands, for instance, is a dubious proposition since the Ottoman armies operated mainly in Eastern Europe and Eastern Mediterranean and not in Western Europe.

13 On the decline thesis, see also the interesting contribute of Karen Barkey, *Bandits and Bureaucrats: The Ottoman Route to Centralization* (Ithaca, NY: Cornell University Press, 1994).

14 *Ibid*., p. 180. It is interesting to read that the authoritative Inalcik Halil, who always speaks about Ottoman decline in the late 16th century, is rather convinced that this issue cannot be narrowed down only to technological inferiority. See Halil Inalcik, *An Economic and Social History of the Ottoman Empire, vol. I; 1300–1600* (Cambridge: Cambridge University Press, 2006), p. 22.

arms transfer and technological diffusion, the Ottoman Empire belonged to an intermediate position between the second and third category or 'Technology II and III'.[15] The Ottomans were obviously able to copy and reproduce existing technology, but they could not have mastered the underlying process of innovation or adaptation; thus, they were essentially third-tier arms producers. Based on the aforementioned model, there was not an actual Ottoman technological decline. Indeed, in its third-tier producer category from the end of the 15th century to the early 18th century, the Ottoman Empire maintained its original military technological position. In other ways the general constraints under which the Ottoman army operated are often neglected or underestimated. Five contributory factors influenced in diverse proportions Ottoman military performance in actual deployments: 1) technological constraints; 2) cost constraints; 3) physical barriers and environmental constraints; 4) motivational limits; 5) limits of the state power and coercion. Considering this scenario, Ottoman military thought acted for centuries in an immutable context,[16] where several factors determined choices and mistakes too. Some authors rightly consider political crisis and economic stagnation as the most important factors of the 'Ottoman decline'.

7. **The European revisers of these mid-17th century Ottoman miniatures identify the top figure as a janissary from Cairo, while probably, this is a marine *azab*. Above: a *levend*. (Ottoman mid-17th century miniatures from the Rålamb collection, Stockholm)***

The Ottoman Navy

Establishing the force levels of the Ottoman navy in this age is not an easy task. Because to the very different record keeping traditions of the Ottoman bureaucracy, rationalised lists and tables of organisation do not exist in the Ottoman Empire until the 19th century. Therefore, research has to rely largely on reports of the foreign travellers, spies and embassies.[17]

---

15 This classification differs slightly respect Keith Krause's book *Arms and the States. Pattern of Military Production and Trade* (Cambridge: Cambridge University Press, 1992), p. 19. Krause places the Ottomans in Technology II. The four categories are Technology I: just enough skills to operate and maintain different kinds of weapons. Technology II: sufficient scientific and engineering skills to reproduce or copy basic weapons belonging to the first category. Technology III: appropriate skills through various military and economic organisation to adapt and refine existing weapons for particular battlefield conditions. Technology IV: proper economic, social and political structure to create new weaponry utilising advanced technology.

16 See R. Murphey, *Ottoman Warfare, 1500–1700* (London: UCL Press, 1999), in the chapter entitled: *Material constraints on Ottoman warfare: the immutable context*.

17 Fortunately, in recent years a series of studies about warships and shipbuilding industry of the Ottoman Empire changed this situation. Based on the Ottoman archives and especially emphasising the second half of the 17th century, these researches allow us to draw a more-or-less accurate picture of the Ottoman navy in the Cretan War. See Yusuf Alperen Aydın, *Sultanın Kalyonları* (Constantinople, 2011), and Ali Rıza İşipek, *Cezayirli Gazi Hasan Paşa* (Constantinople 2009), pp. 392–393. Special thanks to Emir Yener for noticing these works.

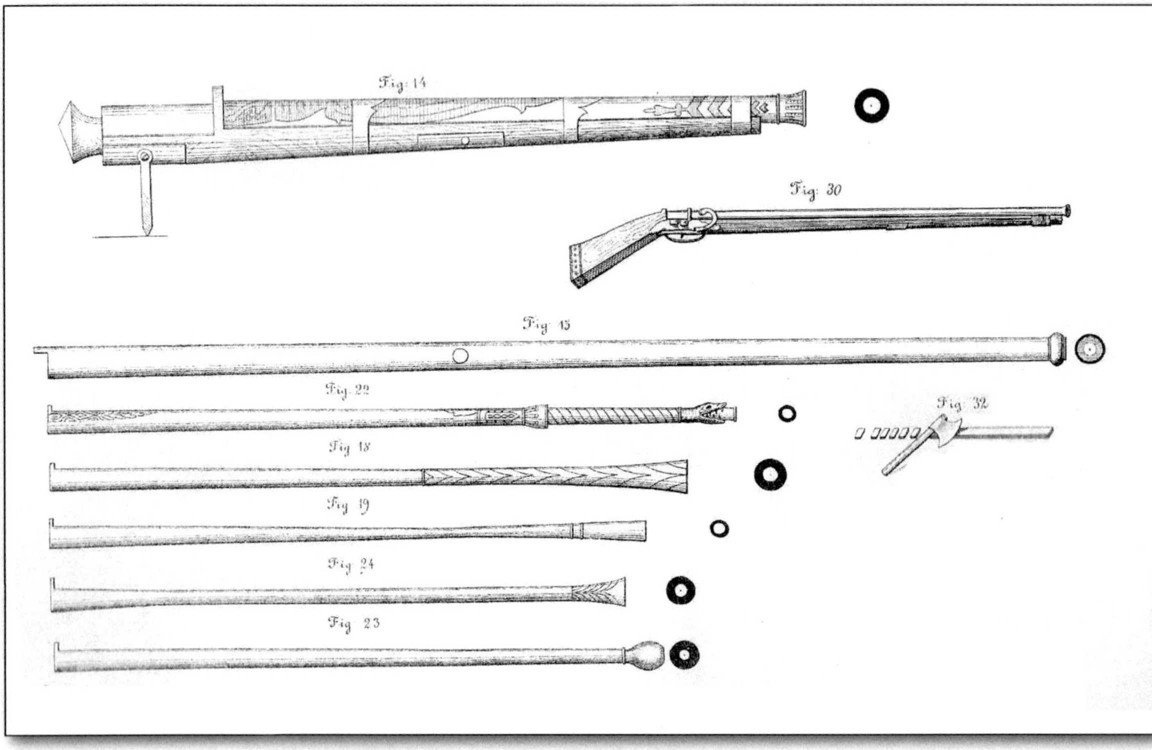

8. On board ship the Ottomans employed a variety of firearms, including portable guns like these depicted. (Illustration from *Cevad Ahmed Beg, Etat Militaire Ottoman depuis la Fondation de l'Empire jusqu'à nos jours*, **1892)***

The Ottoman navy was divided into one stable fleet administrated by the central government and another set up at the expense of provincial governors.[18] From an organisational point of view, the first group depended by the arsenal of Kasimpaşa in Galata, a suburb of Constantinople, where the dockyard facilities were located, and workers and sailors were operating. The Italian traveller Pietro Della Valle visited the arsenal in 1615 and in one of his letters described it as "great as a city" and populated mostly by Francs or not Turkish people, "…located on the other side of the merchant harbour, with the roofs of the houses of Pera and with the towers of the walls surrounding the haven, it is a very beautiful perspective."[19] The arsenal was the junction point of the Sultan's marine sourcing system. Along with the resources to fuel the activity, every year the shipbuilding material was assigned to each province according to a predetermined scheme: 21,000 tree limbers from Izmit and neighbouring provinces; 12,050 *kantars*[20] of ropes from Smyrna and Thessaloniki, and from this last place 2,000 swatches of fabric for sails, until the rowing poles with all the other necessary accessories gathered in the furthest village of the Empire.[21]

18 Some contemporary Italian texts often speak about this definition, pointing to the latter with the term 'feudal', but this title represents an easier explication, without link with the original term used in Western Europe. See Marsigli, pp. 67–69.

19 Pietro Della Valle, *Viaggio in Turchia* (Rome, 1630), p. 123.

20 One *kantar* is equival to 100 lb or 45,359 kilograms.

21 Marsigli, p. 138.

According to the Ottoman source, the Sultan's fleet consisted of 150 large units.[22] This figure is the one presented during the invasion of Crete in June 1645.[23] Of these, some 50 ships were oar-powered units built in the arsenal of Galata. Ottoman warships consisted of galleys, in Ottoman Turkish known as *giktere*, and the *mavuna* or *maona*, the Ottoman version of the galleass; but during the Cretan War, the Ottoman navy began to introduce a significant number of sailing ships. These ships were vessels of about 30–50 cannons, with some defects according to the contemporary commentators, but they still posed a significant threat and were known in the West with the name *sultana*. Although technologically inferior to contemporary vessels of northern Europe, Ottoman sailing ships were comparable to Venetian ones. From the technological point of view, the Ottoman and Venetian vessels mirrored each other, especially in producing sailing ships: an achievement that the Ottomans claimed to have reached before the Venetians. Shipbuilding traditions of both countries were inherited from their predecessor, the Byzantine Empire. This shipbuilding tradition, called the 'single frame system', produced very lightly built and thinly planked hulls; optimised for speed but problematic when it came to withstand a sustained fight.[24] The Ottoman sailing ships were usually armed with bronze guns, but iron guns were also issued, turning to England and the Dutch Republic through intermediaries and smugglers.[25]

Although some historians place the introduction of an actual sailing ships squadron in the Ottoman fleet after 1680, in August 1650 two vessels of 300 tonnes were in construction in Galata.[26] Their dimensions were not comparable to the great northern European sailing ships such as the Swedish *Wasa*, which displaced 1,210 tonnes, or the English *Sovereign of the Seas*, with 1,546 tonnes, but large enough for the Mediterranean theatre. In the spring of 1651, the first sailing ship left the arsenal of Kasimpaşa, followed by four more before the end of the year. The debut was unfortunate, because on May 1651 one of these ships, a two-deck with 60 guns, overturned in the sight of the Sultan and his court, who participated at the launch ceremony. Despite some setback, the confirmation that the Ottoman achievements performed well is proved by the fact that some of these vessels captured by their adversaries were immediately placed in the sailing squadrons and entrusted to important captains. In 1656, at the Third Battle of the Dardanelles, Lazzaro Mocenigo sailed on the Ottoman *sultana* renamed *San Marco*. In November 1665, one of the ships captured off Chios – two decks with 58 guns – was renamed *Sol d'Oro* and immediately integrated into the Venetian fleet. This was the seventh sail ship produced at Galata to be taken into service by Venice during the Cretan War.[27]

---

22 R. Murphey, 'The Ottoman Resurgence in the Seventeenth-Century Mediterranean', p. 188.

23 Venetian historian Battista Nani in his *Dell'Istoria della Repubblica Veneta*, Vol. IX p. 39, increased this number to the improbable figure of 378 ships of different sizes.

24 See also the article of Yener Emir about Ottoman sailing ship technology, 'Ottoman Seapower and Naval Technology', in *International Naval Journal*, 2016, Vol. (9), Is.1, 9.

25 Bruno Cianci, *La Marina dell'Impero Ottomano, 1299–1923* (Bologna: Odoya, 2015), p. 188.

26 *Ibid.*, p. 176.

27 Another Ottoman sail ship, renamed *Sant'Alvise*, was fully analysed by the Venetians and described as manufactured "of finest wood and studded with the better iron, with well-designed junctions to tail and join at the best"; cited by G. Candiani in *I vascelli della Serenissima. Guerra,*

After 1650, one large section of the Kasimpaşa arsenal was intended for the construction of sailing vessels, but it is unclear how many of the existing 135 covered basins for galleys at the end of the century had been demolished to accommodate the larger ships. According to some testimonies, the Ottomans preferred not to build the vessels in covered dockyards – as the Venetians did, to extend production throughout the year – but outdoors, favoured by the milder climate. Other dockyards were converted for building sailing ships in the Black Sea at Sinope, Samsun, Varna and Batum, where in the years before 1655 were launched 10 new vessels.[28] Throughout the war, the Ottomans always followed closely the western 'Masters', copying the innovations,[29] and when they could, availed themselves of foreign workers and consultants. The last of these, and possibly even the most important for the history of the Ottoman navy, was the renegade Mustafa, born in Venice as Nicolò Furlan,[30] the father of the *sultana*.

Other types of warship built at Galata were the *fricate*, *bergende*, *galiota* and the *orta*, respectively comparable to the contemporary frigate, brigantine, *galeotta* and large galley of the western Mediterranean fleets, which in the 17th century much differed from the more familiar units with the same name of the following centuries. These ships were in fact of mixed propulsion; besides the sails, the *fricate* had 10 or 12 oar banks, the *bergende* had 18 or 19, then 19 to 24 the *galiota*, and finally 27 to 32 the *orta*. The latter, similarly to the Venetian *galea bastarda*, was usually the flagship. The classic Ottoman galley, the 42-metre unit, was manned by 180 oarsmen and according to contemporary sources it could be built in less than a year in Galata, for an overall capability of 60 galleys each year.[31]

Further warships and crews were provided by the governors of the maritime provinces, from which the name of *beylere* (issued by *sançakbegs*), which belonged to the *paşalik* of Caffa, Gelibolu, Trabzon, Cyprus and more 27 *sancakbegs* distributed in the Peloponnese, Aegean Islands, Egypt, Syria, western and southern Anatolia. At the beginning of the war, their number was up to 70 galleys.[32] In these ports other galleys could be armed with sailors, oarsmen and naval infantry recruited in the respective provinces, this latter totalled 6,336 men and was known as *levend*.[33]

All this complex structure converged under the supreme admiral commander, or *kapudan paşa*, the highest position of the navy; it was also one

---

politica e costruzioni navali a Venezia in età moderna, 1650–1720 (Venice: Istituto Veneto di Scienze, 2009), p. 35.

28 Daniel Panzac, *The Geostratégie de l'Empire Ottoman (des origins à l'apparition de cuirassé)*, in. Candiani and L. Lo Basso (Editors), cited work, p. 105.

29 B. Cianci, cited work, p. 187.

30 Obviously, for Venice, the betrayal of one of its captains was an unpardonable fault, but Furlan was doubly hated because he had become an esteemed expert in navigation for the Ottomans. However, when he was captured, Furlan was not executed because the Porte had informed the Senate that his death would be avenged by the killing of the Venetian merchants and war prisoners. Moreover, the Ottomans demanded that Furlan be treated with respect and paid with a substantial salary. Venice, however, knew how to eliminate its enemies and after 1654 Furlan disappeared forever in the *Piombi* jail.

31 R. Murphey, *The Ottoman Resurgence in the Seventeenth Century Mediterranean*, cited work, p. 192.

32 *Ibid.*, p. 188.

33 Marsigli, p. 139.

of the most important in the Empire, as his power extended beyond the fleet and included port governance, merchant trade, as well as the governorate of the island of Rhodes, his official place of residence, although his activity has long been held between Constantinople, Galata and Gelibolu. Under his direction there was one lieutenant, with the title of *terzane agasy*, one *terzane kiaja*, deputy admiral and inspector of the whole fleet, and one *serdar*, another lieutenant of the *kapudan paşa* based in Rhodes. The lower ranks were occupied by officers with administrative functions, divided according to the duties performed in the typical Ottoman practice. So, the *terzane katibi* was responsible for calculating all arsenal expenses and arrears, the *kindane katibi* performed the same functions for the convicted oarsmen, and the *iliman katibi* supervised the administration of timber and fabric for the construction of ships.

On board of the galley, the first officer was the *beg* or commander, the *reis* or pilot, and one *odabaşi* every 20 sailors, included a quote of or *mukaddems* (novices). There were also a *guardianbaşi*, keeper of the rowers, and six or more craftsmen with carpenters, caulkers and blacksmiths.

Along with these forces, other units became available thanks to the contributions of Barbary squadrons of Algiers, Tunis and Tripoli, which increased the Ottoman fleet to several dozens of galleys and sailing ships, considering that the main activity of their captains lay in corsair actions. The North African corsairs were particularly concerned to give a further impulse to the use of the sailing ship. Many corsairs, especially the renegades, had perfected sailing navigation techniques in the Mediterranean, and thanks to their contribution, the *kapudan paşa* could deploy dozens of good units, commanded by prepared captains and served by good crews.

However, in the mid 17th century the backbone of the Ottoman fleet was still galleys, which were divided into two categories only to identify their membership of the stable fleet or the provincial one; in the first case, they were called *zakale* galleys, in the other – already mentioned – *beylere* galleys. In peacetime, the Ottoman fleet normally deployed 40 galleys and six *mavunas*; a further 20 galleys were maintained by the provincial fleet, for a total of 16,400 men, of which 11,330 were oarsmen.[34] These latter were usually convicted men or state-property slaves, known as *miri forsalan*. Later, facing the shortage of oarsmen, the Porte resorted to war prisoners and also volunteers enlisted with high salaries.

The fleet had a stable guard corps called *azab* based at Galata, rising to 1,364 men in 1670, divided into 650 *oda* (chambers), each of two or four men in charge of presiding over the arsenal, escorting wagons or convoys that transported the materials for the dockyards; the oldest among the *azabs* also provided surveillance in the harbour area, others controlled the prison of the convicted oarsmen, while about half of their force could be used for carpentry work under the masters. The command of the whole corps was entrusted to a *reis*, with an *odabaşi* as lieutenant and an *ascybaşi*, the cook chief, as second junior officer. The various positions taken by the *azab*

34 *Ibid.*

included gendarmerie, craftsmanship and naval duties, considering that they also knew the use of compass, nautical cartography and explosives.

Alongside the Imperial *azab* corps, the infantry embarked on warships were represented also by the aforementioned *levend* and *mensugat*. While the first corps was recruited by *paşa* and governors of the major provinces, the second was formed with non-professional naval soldiers in the minor departments, namely *beg* and *zeamet*, and mainly used as reserve troops. Both these categories of soldiers also provided personnel for naval artillery, as well as for landing troops, garrisons in the ports and coastal fortifications.

The Ottoman Army

It was estimated that in the years between 1630 and 1650, the Porte could deploy 75–80,000 professional soldiers,[35] and even considering that at least one third were enrolled in honorary or non-combatant roles, the remainder still constituted one of the major military force of the time. This corps of permanent troops, known as *kapikulu*, literally 'slaves of the Porte', had an autonomous administration structure and therefore could in reasonably short time participate in a campaign of war. The main components of the *kapikulu* were the infantry with the *yeni-tcheri* (janissaries) and the cavalry with the *sipahy ulufely*.

In 1660, from a total of 98,342 employers in the court apparatus, the janissaries were 53,849 of which 14,379 quartered in the main towns of the Empire and formed the standing infantry garrisons in the principal fortresses in Europe, Asia and Egypt.[36] Each garrison was known as an *ocak*. The remaining were headquartered in Constantinople and consisted of about one third registered as honorary members. In fact, the major dignitaries too usually belonged to the janissary corps. Another contemporary source related a slightly different figure: in the same year the Ottoman treasury paid salaries to 54,222 janissaries.[37] In Istanbul and Edirne were stationed 32,796 janissaries, including the honorary members. In the mid 17th century there were a further 5,000 janissaries distributed between Cairo in Egypt and Damascus in Syria.

In the mid 17th century there were 196 janissary *ortas*. Each *orta* numbered a variable strength between 100–600 men, divided in *oda* (chambers) under the *odabasi* as non-commissioned officer, while each *orta* was under the *çorbaci* officer leading a minor staff composed of one *bayrakdar* (ensign), one *vekil-harçi* (fourier), one *asci* (the cook), and one *başeski*: the oldest member of the unit. Each *orta* was identified by an ensign and a number. However, this bore no relation to the rank of the unit. In hierarchical order the first *orta* carried the number 19, while the second had the number one and the third carried the number 111. The *ortas* belonged to three classes in order of rank. The first rank was the *cemaat* or *yayabeg*, with 101 *ortas*, which represented the ancient original janissary corps. The second rank was the *bölükler* composed

35 Robert Mantran, 'L'Evolution de l'Armée Ottomane aux XVI et XVII siècles', in *16a Settimana di Studio dell'Istituto di Storia Economica Francesco Datini* (Prato, 1984), p. 128.

36 Ahmed Cevad Beg, *Etat Militaire Ottoman Depuis la Fondation de L'Empire Jusq'a Nos Jours* (Istanbul–Paris, 1882), pp. 138–149.

37 Marsigli, p. 7.

of 61 *ortas* and finally there was the *segmen* corps with 34 *ortas*. The last class originally represented the reserve, and its members could carry out commercial activities as well as other additional jobs. Significant differences in salary existed between the three classes. All the janissary *ortas* marched on campaign irrespective of their traditional historical function. Each janissary unit was originally formed to provide a specific duty, such as the *orta* 35, known as the *Avcilar*, who accompanied the Sultan in the hunt, while the number four unit was known as the *Deveci* or camel drivers, because they originated to escort the baggage train. Except for the following: the *orta* 99, *Mehter*, made up of the musicians of the corps, and the *ortas* 61, 62, 63 and 64, *Solak*, who formed the infantry Sultan's bodyguard, all the janissaries were trained specifically as musket-bearing soldiers. The janissaries were primarily trained as light infantrymen; traditionally carrying muskets, as well as individually carrying a variety of personal weapons, such as the classic Ottoman curved bladed sword, the *kilic*. They were also known to be equipped with other smaller weapons, such as daggers and dirks, to use in close combat. These were the only weapons personally carried by janissaries, because their muskets and ammunition were held, until action, by a special corps of the *kapikulu*, the *cebeci*, who served as ammunition sellers and smiths. This corps accompanied the janissary on campaign and single detachments quartered in each garrison.

9. The Janissaries' ceremonial dress comprised special ornaments to be applied to their *ak börk* headgear. (Illustration from the *Codex Vindobonensis*, late 16th century, Vienna)*

The cavalry was represented by the prestigious corps of *sipahy ulufely* and in 1650 amounted to 35,000 men, of whom probably 20–25,000 were ready to enter in campaign in a few days. Although the total cost was lower compared to the janissaries, the daily pay of a *sipahy* was the highest in the *kapikulu* and almost one and a half times that issued to a janissary.

Moreover, the Sultan deployed further corps of specialist belonging to the *kapikulu*, like the *topçu* (artillerymen) and the *humbaraci* (bombardiers) and the whole logistic structure for maintaining the army in campaign, included the water seller for the troops, the *sakka*. Besides this permanent force, the Porte could turn to the troops collected after the mobilisation of the governors' contingents, and also to the ones provided by tributaries and other states subject to the Sultan. This manpower could be mobilised with the call of arms of the *zeamet* and *timar* holders in the regions close to the war theatre, as established by the government after the enactment of the *ösür*: the quote of recruits assigned to each province. This mounted force was known as *sipahy toprakly*. The provincial governors themselves, *beglerbeg* and *paşa*, also had to mobilise other contingents that further enhanced the army of thousands of other men, without considering the possibility of using the general call to the armies of the *serhaddkulu* militia, which also included the contingents of pioneers, engineers and miners necessary

10. and 11. (overleaf) The Ottomans disposed a composite military structure, including several special corps such as the dely raiders of the *serrhadkulu* cavalry. (Hyeronimus Beck's *Exaratae turcarum imperatorum, capitaneorum. Immagina, habitus, ludos, caerimonias*... Österreichische Nationalbibliothek Vienna, early 17th century)*

for the siege of trenches and mines, as well as other infantry and artillery corps to be used as a reserve for the *kapikulu* janissaries and *topçu*.

The Ottoman war strategy had always been aimed at a rapid and violent offensive with as many forces as possible, anticipating the opponent's moves and then gaining the initiative. Therefore, success was proportional to the Porte's capacity to supply large contingents for enough time to complete a campaign. In this aspect, the Ottoman commanders enjoyed an extremely efficient logistical organisation, whereas in the rest of the 17th century, supplies were often a big problem for conducting a military campaign.

To this end, the supply network was entrusted to the care of the *defterdar*, a kind of commissioner-administrator of supplies. However logistical staff, just as skilled and at the head of an extensive network of warehouses, had to deal with several problems to supply a large army in campaign, especially if it included the hard-to-please professional soldiers. For instance, an active member of the *kapikulu* received daily 100 *dirhem* (320 grams) of bread, 50 *dirhem* of biscuit or hardtack, 50 *dirhem* of rice, 60 *dirhem* of mutton and 25 *dirhem* of butter; a fully-fledged food treatment that can provide the 3,000 daily calories needed to ensure the livelihood of an active man.[38] All *kapikulu* members also benefited from special protection against speculation and, in case some supplies were unavailable, their statute recognised them as the equivalent of money. Indeed, it was impossible to effectively use the professional soldiers without providing them with fine treatment assured by their statutes. During the campaigns in Crete it was normal for janissaries, *cebeci*, *sipahy* and *topçu* to suspend their service in trenches or batteries waiting for the tea or water ration, which they were constantly being supplied by the *sakka* carriers. All the janissary rations were highly regulated, including clothing allotments and special funds for equipment. Individual *oda* often had a provisions fund, contributed by the members themselves, which served the common good. The provincial *toprakly* contingents were expected to feed and outfit themselves, but were often given food rations, or its cash equivalent, at the beginning of a campaign.[39] A gratuity often preceded a major battle, and certainly rewarded the especially valorous afterwards. Complaints about the lateness or non-arrival of these 'fringe benefits' were used as excuses for failure to show up on the battlefield, universal problems in all early modern military contexts.

38 R. Murphey, *Ottoman Warfare 1500–1700*, cited work, p. 89.

39 V. Aksan, cited work, p. 95.

The logistical effort for supplying an Ottoman army required an operative staff of relevant dimension. Included in the army on campaign were not just the soldiers, but members of all the guilds of the empire, as part of their service to the war endeavour. The countryside, too, expected – and dreaded – to be mobilised: peasants provided manpower, food, transport, pack animals and the like. Already in the previous century, one observer compared the Ottoman army to a wedding party, while another eyewitness complained that grand vizier headquarters resembled a grand bazaar, with more camp followers than combatants.[40] Making war was simply part of the scenery of early modern empires, and military headquarters just another venue for the small entrepreneur.

For obvious reasons, a logistical effort of these proportions could not be maintained for a long time, and then it was necessary to achieve the objectives in the shortest time possible. Though the Ottoman forces appeared to be of considerable size, it was equally true that this effort could only be maintained at high levels for short periods. They were not just the huge figures needed to support troops to influence the duration of campaigns, but also the fact that many non-professional soldiers were serving for a limited period, like many of the auxiliaries, such as miners, diggers and conductors. They were hired year after year, often negotiating engages with communities in Greece, Bosnia or Armenia. Like the provincial troops, the larger part of them returned to their ordinary occupations once the campaign ended. Even though on many occasions the Ottoman commanders yielded prizes and wages to the soldiers, the availability of money was not always unlimited. The shortage of money concerned the Ottoman commanders in Crete, who each year had to wait for the arrival of the fleet from Constantinople, when it had been able to avoid the scourge of the Venetians and their allies. If the resources could arrive on Crete from the sea a little at a time, the concerns did not disappear, especially during the severe financial crises that had collapsed the Empire between 1653 and 1656, which actually could cause the failure of the war plans.

The Porte could deploy powerful and well-armed armies, but the weak points of its military effectiveness resided in the poor preparation of the officer class. Apart from the many who had obtained command positions in the *kapikulu* thanks to the aid of some important court member, others – more deserving – could not raise to higher degree due to the malevolence of ministers or because they became victims of recurrent internal riots. Although the war acted as an accelerator to remove the worst subjects, the internal situation of the officer corps remained critical and the knowledge of the larger part of the commanders remained at mediocre level. Many of the *beglerbeg* and *paşa* had been soldiers before becoming governors, but – in addition to gaining office due to the aberrant dynamics of nepotism and corruption – they were almost leaders capable of leading a raid than modern officers able to lead composite corps, coordinate the activities of subordinates, take care of logistics and oversee the many tasks required by a campaign of war. The command structure did not facilitate the tasks of the commanders, as this did not follow the classic pyramidal structure, but was rather a vertical one, and this resulted in a poor number of subordinate

40 *Ibid.*, p. 88.

11. (See previous caption)

officers. This was more common in the irregular units, but at the *kapikulu* level the command structure was often insufficient to ensure the correct direction of the forces. At the lowest levels, the hierarchy reflected all the negativities that afflicted the Ottoman state, with the result that the key posts were occupied by officers in close relation of some protector or the commander in chief. The commander's authority was always absolute, while the subordinate officers had limited autonomy to make decisions. Despite the choice of simple and easy-to-implement strategies, each time the action took on a more complex address, the offensive power was fading and the whole army entered in crisis. For this reason, small but tactically well conducted Venetian contingents in Dalmatia almost always prevailed against the large but ineffective formations commanded by the local *paşa*. In September 1645 the Ottomans assembled in Sarajevo a force of 20–25,000 men for an attack against the territories of the Republic, but the two local commanders, Ibrahim Paşa *beglerbeg* of Bosnia and Haly Beg *sançakbeg* of Lika, each acted on their own, through mutual distrust avoiding collaboration to develop a common operational plan. In Bosnia, Ibrahim's prudence generated the suspicion of secret intelligence with the Venetians. Sporadic raids were launched by Halik Beg, "implacable enemy of the Christian name",[41] along with his son Durac as a lieutenant; but apart from the destruction

41 Girolamo Brusoni, 'Historia dell'Ultima Guerra tra Veneziani e Turchi' (Venice 1673), *Libro* III, p. 61. Together with the works of Battista Nani and Andrea Valiero, the 'Historia' of Brusoni is the most important printed source on the Cretan war. The 28 Libri of the work deals in detail the events happened during the 27 years of war, though returned from a Venetian perspective. While the works of Nani and Valiero are more focused on political and diplomatic conflict, Brusoni devotes much of the narrative to the military operations, often accompanied by official reports from Venetian and Allied commanders.

12. Köprülü Mehmed was appointed as grand vizier on 15 September 1656, in the middle of the severe economic and political crisis aggravated by internal rebellion and external threats, which were dividing the Empire. (Mid-17th century Austrian print. Author's archive)*

of some wooden forts, cattle slaughter and crop fires, no important strategic result was achieved, and it was only because the Venetians – fearing an incursion in Friuli – did not send troops that the Ottomans could operate undisturbed. Before the end of the year, a reinforcement of 3,000 janissaries and *sipahy* arrived in the Skopje area to support local forces, together with a new commander, Tekeli Mustafa, in charge as new *beglerbeg* of Bosnia. The Ottoman offensive was directed against Novegradi (today Novigrad), conquered in July 1646, but after this success, before the end of the year, all the achievements came back to the Venetian side. The Venetians repeatedly defeated Ottoman commanders using their fortifications, the strategic support of the fleet and the territory conformation, which was unsuitable for cavalry, namely the main Ottoman war instrument in that theatre. For Constantinople, the scenario worsened the following year as a result of the flight of the Bosnian population, frightened by the cruelty of the irregulars in Venetian service and the sudden fall of the fortresses defending the region. In 1647 Zemonico and Dernis surrendered, while an attempt by Haly Beg and the *beglerbeg* against Šibenik resulted in disaster. In 1648, the fall of Clissa, considered to be the door of Bosnia, was paid by Tekeli Mustafa with his destitution. Nevertheless, if the overturns suffered by Ottoman leaders on a secondary front could be considered strategically irrelevant, in the early years of war the conduct of operations in Crete was not crowned by decisive successes. The assault on the island was led by Mascovich Yussuf, considered a talented man as a politician, but completely devoid of military preparation. His story is in some respects emblematic and represents very well how military careers in the Ottoman army could be fast, but also fragile. Yussuf, also known as *silihtar* (esquire), had become army commander after climbing the internal court hierarchy, in which he had been enlisted very young as a gardener. He was a clever and much appreciated servant. Sultan Ibrahim I chose him as a trusted adviser, gave him a daughter to marry, and on the eve of the war against Venice appointed him as *kapudan paşa*. From many points of view, the *silihtar* was not worse than the average court officers were, and despite his military unpreparedness, he managed to lead the army to Crete, to land on the island and to give course with unusual speed to the siege of Chaniá. The city surrendered after 54 days of siege, but at the cost of nearly 8,000 men dead and wounded, and despite the initial gratitude of the Sultan, who celebrated his enterprise by ordering three days and three nights of festivities and luminaries in the capital, the price in casualties was considered too high. At court, his opponents acted and spread more details to Yussuf's account, until they alienated the Sultan's favour, who ordered the execution of Yussuf in January 1646.

The command of the operations passed to Sultanazade Mehmed, who was dismissed a few weeks earlier by the order of the grand vizier and sent to Crete to rectify his mistakes. Nevertheless, fearing to do the same end as the predecessor, he became ill, until he was replaced by *beglerbeg* of Egypt Baltaoğlu Hüseyin.[42] In July 1646, Sultanazde Mehmed died, ironically, of fever. It was under the leadership of the new commander that operations in Crete resumed with the siege at Réthymnon and the following years with the conquest of the rest of the island, except the capital and main port Candia. Hüseyin had begun his military career as *sipahy* and had received his first appointment as general commander having completed the Crimean campaign against the Russians and the Cossacks in 1642. It was during the Egyptian governorship that Hüseyin earned the title of *deli* – mad, but in his case bold – with which he became famous also in Crete, demonstrating in every case a courage out of the ordinary and exposing himself several times in person to the dangers of a battle. In July 1648, while leading an assault against a bastion of Candia, he was injured by a shot in his face, but continued to carry out operations, binding the wound with the band of his robe and urging on the soldiers with his example. Hüseyin avoided the campaign failure on the island in the crucial years between 1650 and 1658, when the Ottoman garrison remained isolated for a long time because of the Venetian naval blockade, facing a revolt of unpaid troops and managing to maintain control over the territory despite the many problems that afflicted her soldiers. In order to keep open the threat on Candia, in 1650 the *serasker* ordered the construction of a fortified encampment near the town. This large camp was named *Yeni Kandie* (New Candia), providing a winter quarters to the besieging troops and counteracting the sortie of the defenders. In the spring of 1658, Hüseyin was finally removed and appointed as commander of the fleet, but before the end of the year, he paid for his opposition to the new grand vizier Köprülü Mehmed: in his memory, folk songs and poetic compositions were composed, for centuries keeping him alive in the memory of his compatriots.

42 Baltaoğlu Hüseyin (1605?–1659), known as *Deli*, or *Ghazi* (warrior) and also *Sari* (blonde) Hüseyin, was born near Bursa, in Anatolia and was of Turkish origin. Little is known about his early days in Constantinople. During the reign of Murad IV, he was a member of the palace court's personnel. Hüseyin attracted the attention of his superiors for his skill as archer. After winning Sultan's appreciation, he was promoted to various posts: chief stable man and then *sipahy* cavalry officer, participating in the war campaigns at Baghdad and Yerevan. Promoted as *paşa* of Silistra, in Bulgaria, he became *beglerbeg* of Egypt in 1635. From the very first day of his arrival in Egypt, when he confiscated his finance minister and advisors' properties for his own, Hüseyin began a series of reforms that made him widely disliked by the local populace. He brought with him to Egypt a large number of Druzes who committed robberies in Cairo, and extorted money from the locals for an upcoming feast celebrating the *beglerbeg*'s arrival. Hüseyin also often reportedly rode a horse through crowds of people and animals, swinging a sword, for recreation. Each month, he forced locals to trade in their bullion coin for adulterated metal and sent bureaucrats and officials to remote locations without explanation. During his rule, he had over 1,200 people executed, not including those that he killed by his own hand. Despite his cruelty, Hüseyin was an able commander and leader of the local troops, which was a particularly difficult task in Egypt. He was attentive to government details and successfully decreased robbery and burglary in Egypt. See Mevlüt Uluğtekin Yilmaz: *Osmanlı'nın Arka Bahçesi* (Ankara, 2007), pp. 162–164.

The *Invittissime Armate*[43] of the *Serenissima* Republic of Venice

Although Venice did not show any tendency to follow a military policy in the modern sense, the Republic could deploy a remarkable army, and could set up a fleet that had few rivals in the Mediterranean. All this made the military power of the Republic decisively asymmetrical, which, according to many observers, seemed too unbalanced at the expense of the field forces. Scipione Pannocchieschi, Papal nuncio to Venice between 1647 and 1652, tried to give a personal explanation of the particular Venetian military structure:

> The Armies (of Venice) are regularly composed by Italians who are not subjects, Germans and Slavs, and even captains are foreign. And this happens to maintain people untrained for war. Of course, the people feel always little friendship for the nobles; and Venice did not need nobles to the command, because it wants to preserve the government from the tyranny, fearing more the condition of its subjects than the foreigners'.[44]

Other commenters, more maliciously, attributed this trend to the poor warrior attitude of the 'avid merchants of the lagoon'. In 1675, the historian Gregorio Leti even offered a more drastic judgment. He argued with some truth, but also with harshness and undeserved criticism, that "in Italy, the Republic (of Venice) is the poorest state in the profession of arms. Admittedly, the Venetians can be invincible on the sea ... but in campaign they value very little or nothing."[45] In another sentence, Leti also deplored the employment of foreign officers, "who subtract resources from the Country".

Historians have long considered the Venetian 'military' as an obsolete model, neglecting the innovative tactics and weaponry introduced in the campaigns on the sea. Even when they investigate the naval strategy focusing on tactical and technical improvements, historians have assumed some not completely correct common views,[46] or they consider the matter as a mystery just to avoid it. In effect, the Venetian 'military' represents a singularity in the

43 'The Invincible Armies' of the Venetian Republic, as they were denominated in several late 17th century sources.

44 *Relazione delle cose di Venezia di Monsignor Francesco d'Elci Pannocchieschi, nipote e coadiutore di monsignor Scipione, Nunzio Apostolico in Venezia* (Pisa, 1656); Libro I, p. 276.

45 Gregorio Leti, *L'Italia regnante o vero Nova descritione dello stato presente di tutti prencipati e repubbliche d'Italia* (Rome, 1675), p. 318.

46 It is remarkable to observe how modern knowledge on the military history of Venice is based especially on outdated stereotypes. The studies of John Hale and Michael Mallett opened a window to investigate the Venetian military structure, but unfortunately, their contributions have stopped at the 16th century. The accurate works of Jeremy Black, *Warfare – Renaissance to Revolution 1492–1792* (Cambridge: Cambridge University Press, 1995) and John Childs, *Warfare in the Seventeenth Century*, have both neglected the Venetian wars. The same oversight occurred in the excellent book of John Glete, *Warfare at Sea* (London: Routledge, 1999), closing his work just before the Cretan War and the development of sea warfare in the Mediterranean. The 17th century military history of Venice remains, then, *Terra Incognita* outside Italy and although there have appeared important contributions by Piero Del Negro, Pietro Marchesi, Guido Candiani, Luca Porto, Alberto Prelli, Guido Ercole, Pier Luigi Tamburrini, Luciano Pezzolo, Sergio Perini, Marco Morin, Virgilio Ilari, and Riccardo Caimmi, these works are yet

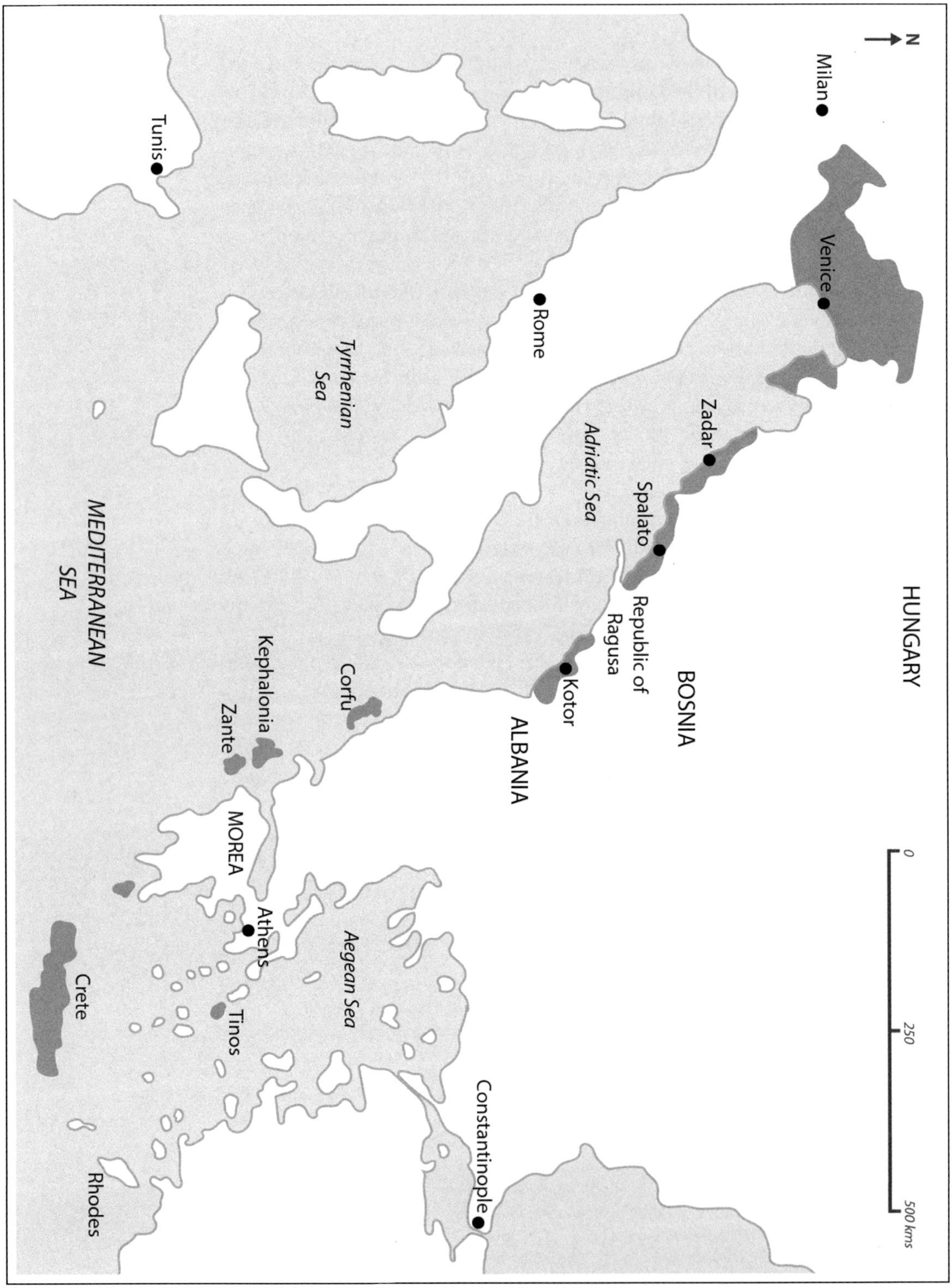

Map 2 Venetian Domains

European scenario of the 17th century. Despite the gradual increase of war engagements on the sea and on the land, Venice continued to consider 'fleet' and 'army' as a single military force. The result was the creation of an entirely original instrument of war unlike any other European armies: a model which was probably not the best possible one to defend the state, but surely the most appropriate way to face political contingency and war emergency. In this context, the aristocracy's atavistic conservationism contributed to slow the development of armed forces in the modern meaning, but even more decisive was the attitude derived from the 'garrison system'[47] to influence the Venetian military policy. The resistance against the modernisation of the army was nourished by the 'state-city' ideology. Moreover, the government continued to pursue the goal of managing the mosaic of peoples and military corps in a rather conservative way. These choices seem to suggest what a French contemporary policy writer has called "the double paradox of Venice", unable to free themselves from the state–city role to become the capital of a territorial state, but also to rule its territories beyond the traditional schemes of domain.[48] Notwithstanding this attitude, the Venetian Republic represented the only multiethnic state of Italy, where different languages and religions coexisted until its dissolution in 1797.

Because the Republic of Venice based its political organisation of on the principles of collegiality and polyarchy that characterised all the power relations,[49] the military mirrored the state's structure. The elected Doge represented the highest 'dignity' of the State, but he had to act in concert with the government affairs, balancing his power with the Republican institutions.[50] As a result, power was shared with the Senate. This institution was the actual core of the political and administrative life of the state, and in case of war, the Senate discussed and addressed to the commanders the strategic objective of each campaign. The Senate comprised the elected representatives from the noble families, the members of the technical magistrates and the exclusive and secret *Consiglio dei Dieci* (Council of Tenths), in charge of foreign affairs. The larger part of the Senate was represented by the *Maggior Consiglio* (Major Council), which elected the Doge and decided the appointment of all other councils and magistrates, with unlimited and sovereign powers on

---

scarcely diffused outside Italy. Recently, Mario Infelise and Anastasia Stouraiti have been the editors of further important contributions about the Venetian wars.

47 See P. Del Negro, 'Il Leone in Campo: Venezia e gli Oltramarini nelle Guerre di Candia e di Morea', in *Mito e Antimito di Venezia nel Bacino Adriatico – secoli XV–XIX* (Rome: Il Calamo, 2001), p. 331.

48 Jean Claude Hocquet, cited by P.L. Tamburrini in *L'Organizzazione Militare di Venezia nella prima metà del Settecento* (collana SISM – Società Italiana di Storia Militare, Rome 2014), p. 9.

49 Instituted in 1229, the Venetian Senate was originally composed of 60 members, soon increased with 60 additional members. At the beginning of 16th century, the Senate numbered 200 members. In the modern era, the Venetian Senate assumed the direction of several affairs, including political, military, legislative, administrative, and ecclesiastical ones. Since the 12th century, the aristocratic families further diminished the Doge's powers by establishing the *Minor Consiglio* (Minor Council), and the *Quarantia* as a supreme civil and administrative tribunal.

50 As noted by some contemporary historians, Venice claimed to be a Republic but it actually followed a mixed government model, combining elective monarchy in the Doge, aristocratic oligarchy in the Senate, and 'democracy' in the Major Council.

13. The *Capitano Generale da Mar* was the most important military position in Venice, being the Doge's lieutenant in the navy and army. (Engraving after the Doge's portrait by Bernardo Strozzi, Author's archive)*

any matter. As the historian Marin Sanudo declared: "He (the Doge) could do nothing without the Major Council and the Major Council could do nothing without him". The Senate appointed also the *Minor Consiglio* (Minor Council), composed by six strict advisors of the Doge. All these institutions were combined into the *Signoria*, which consisted of the Doge, the Minor Council and the three leaders of the *Quarantia* (the Forty). Then, the *Signoria* was the actual Venetian government, representing the continuity of the Republic as shown in the traditional expression: "the Doge is dead, but the Signoria is not". Other important members of the Venetian power were the *Procuratori di San Marco*. They were the highest dignitaries after the Doge and preserved their title for life. The Doge himself was normally elected among them. Usually the *Procuratori* managed key functions, including expertise on public and ecclesiastical affairs and, naturally, fleet and army.

Because the Venetian political doctrine obeyed to a principle of balanced power, the command structure of the army and navy followed a rigid regulation, as well as the offices appointed to the administration and inspection of the troops, sailors, gunners, rowers, vessels and galleys reflected the political scheme. Moreover, lacking a true ministry of war, every aspect of the military machine came to have its magistracy, more or less independent and superimposed on the work of further officials.

In the Venetian power system, the *Consiglio dei Savi* (Council of the Elders) had a special importance in both army and navy affairs. This council was the operative core of the Senate, organised in a collegial branch composed of elected magistrates, inspired by the ancient Roman Republic institutions. There were 16 *Savi* in all, and among these there were five *savi agli ordini* or *savi da Mar* (Elders to the Orders or to the Sea) who managed the matters regarding trade and navy, including the war fleet. Together with them, another five *savi di Terraferma* (Mainland Elders) had specific competencies in the army and navy, including sailors, gunners and oarsmen. Each Council's members had to submit to the Senate the strategic considerations, including those relating to the continuation of a conflict or debate for the war resolution. The first *savio di Terraferma* was also identified as *Savio alla Scrittura* (Elder to the Writings):

14. The captain general's carmine red ensign, after an illustration of Giovanni Grevenbroch, published in 1757. *

the Venetian variant of the War Secretary.[51] He supervised the standing troops, fortresses and artillery, and had the direction of a six-member 'conference' in charge of military affairs. In peacetime, the *savio alle Scritture* held the direction of the administrative affairs for the army, but in case of war the Senate appointed further offices to better coordinate the whole military forces, considering the need of taking urgent decisions in any upcoming campaign. The *Savi* also managed the work of the *inquisitori di Stato* (State Inquisitors, namely inspectors, in charge of controlling the strength of the corps in the campaign or in garrison, like the contemporary army commissars), and the personnel employed to control the supplies for the army, fleet and militia. Other inspectors were appointed to control cavalry, military chancellery, marine arsenals, equipment and ammunitions.

15. Girolamo Foscarini, captain general in 1655, had passed through the internal hierarchy before becoming general provveditor in Dalmatia. Although he had any special qualities as a naval commander, his appointment – as often in other cases – was influenced by venetian politics, always concerned to maintain the balance of power in the aristocratic class. (Print after an engraving by an anonymous artist. Author's archive)

The Venetian military hierarchy summoned the *capitano generale da Mar* (sea captain general) who in fact was the head of the fleet – which in Venice was identified with the word *Armata* – and he assumed the strategic direction of all the operations carried out in the overseas war theatres, including those involving the field troops.[52] Like the other state leadership positions, the captain general was appointed by the Senate, and as everyone undertook the highest dignity of the state, namely the *Doge*. Surely, the authority of the

51 The military policy and the conduct of the conflicts was decided within the *Consulta dei Savi*, which included the *Savi del Consiglio*, the *Savi di Terraferma* and the *Savi agli ordini*. The matter deliberated by *Consulta* had to be approved by the Senate even though it was often a more formal than substantial passage. Specifically, in the Council, the Savio was responsible for the regular army, while the Savio alle Ordinanze dealt with the latter and in general with the militias. According to the Republican statute, the Savi lasted only six months in their office, followed by another six months of absence, in which they could not participate in the Consulta. Although this rule was not always respected or in other cases, especially with regard to the Mainland's Savi, they systematically alternated their assignments on a six-monthly basis for several years, it was difficult to maintain a precise military policy with this continue change of offices.

52 The constitution of the Venetian Republic, in which power was theoretically shared in equal parts between all members of the aristocracy, attributed functions as 'prince-commander' to the captain general: it is a very special case in which the captain general was at the same time an exponent of the class power and servant of the same power. In respect of his power over army and fleet, the functions of captain general appeared to some contemporary commenters as very limited. The aforementioned Papal nuncio Scipione Pannocchieschi wrote: "He (the captain general) is master only of ships subject to inconstancy of the waves and winds, and his command is so limited that ends once the troops have been landed." Other authors do not fully confirm this statement, while claiming that the captain general carried a function comparable to that of a ruling prince. Amelot de la Houssaie, the French contemporary political writer, and secretary in the French embassy in Venice, stated: "His power is absolute on all other generals and officers, so much so that he seems to be a dictator or at least a sovereign. His authority extends not only to the fleet, but still on all ports, islands and fortresses, where everyone obeys his orders without question."

16. The Arsenal of Venice was considered "the heart of the State", where shipbuilding and armament would converge with all related activities. During the Cretan War the arsenal worked at full strength as related by the *Savio agli Ordini* Bertucci Trevisan, who until 1669 registered the launch of 138 galleys, 10 *bastarde* and 18 galleasses, in addition to minor ships. (Author's photo)

captain general depended much on influence and prestige with which he held the office. His authority could be relevant, assuming he served the Republic positively. It was not by chance that to further raise his dignity, the Senate instantly gave him the rank of *procuratore di San Marco*, and naturally his performance in campaigns conditioned any further appointments. Over the years, the influence of certain commanders had grown up, especially during the period in which the command was held by Lazzaro Mocenigo, in 1657, and Francesco Morosini, captain general from 1658 to 1660, and again from 1667 to 1669. Notwithstanding personal qualities, the captain general constantly had to manage the Venetian policy. Possibly, in no other country in Europe, did civil power influence the armed forces so directly. Throughout the 17th century and also later, it is interesting to note that the presence of a war department or council composed only of military professionals was always opposed by the Venetian aristocracy and even an actual military code was never instituted, preferring to judge officers and soldiers in the civil tribunals.[53]

The Senate exercised its control over both the army and the fleet through the *provveditori generali* (general provveditors – superintendants): characteristic offices of the Venetian state. They usually managed civilian tasks and as happened for the captain general, their appointment was assigned with a limited mandate, generally renewable with a subsequent election. After the *provveditori generali*, there were the provincial *provveditori*,[54] who managed the double task of civil governor and major staff chief. They were equally prestigious and more experienced, such as the *provveditori generali*, closely linked to local institutions and jealous of their prerogatives. Many of the responsibilities for military operations fell on the *provveditori* and, according to a classical scheme of that age, the *provveditori* to be appointed as Captain-General or even to the election of the office of Doge, as was to happen in 1656 to Lunardo Foscolo, general provveditor of Dalmatia. This official played a very important role when, starting from 1646, he directed war operations in Dalmatia, obtaining a series of extraordinary achievements by leading his troops to the conquest of strategic sites like Zemunik Donji and Klis for an overall 40 fortresses and villages in Ottoman Bosnia and Herzegovina. In the course of the conflict, many Venetian aristocrats alternated in the office of captain general and *provveditore*, but both functions

53 See Sergio Perini, *La Difesa Militare della Terraferma Veneta nel Settecento* (Il Leggio, Chioggia, 1998), p. 81.

54 These directional and administrative charges had been instituted in 1467, during the first war against the Ottoman Empire and in the early 16th century, they became stable appointments.

were always assigned to subjects belonging to the most important families. Alongside the *provveditori* of the provinces, in the last year of 17th century there were 35 other superintendents, each provided with specific functions. The three *provveditori all'Armata* (provveditors of the navy) managed arsenal activity, namely the production of galleys, galleasses and vessels. In wartime, one of the provveditors became part of the war council as first lieutenant of the captain general. Alongside the major *provveditori*, in wartime the government appointed also a *provveditore straordinario* in each office: another clear sign of the obsessive balancing of power at all stages.[55] Though the number of ships to build and maintain every year was deliberated by the Senate, the office of provveditor represented the executive office with competencies similar to a contemporary Admiralty. They supervised the service of the *capi da Mar* (navy officers), including the recruitment of sailors, gunners, rowers and *fanti da mar* (marine soldiers). The appointment lasted three years, but they could be reappointed after a year of absence. Each *provveditore all'Armata* participated in turn to the war campaigns as a regular member of the commander's council with the title of *provveditore generale all'Armata*. In peacetime, this office was the highest of the fleet, and in campaign, he automatically became the vice-admiral. When resident in Venice, the provveditors the navy presided, in turn, over a college composed of three *savi* (advisers), one high counsellor and service personnel. The college included three other superintendents: the *provveditore all'Arsenale* (superintendent for the Arsenal of Venice); the *provveditore sopra il biscotto* (superintendent to the food supply for the Navy), the *provveditore all'Artiglierie* (artillery provveditor), *provveditore dei cavalli* (provveditor of the cavalry) and even the *provveditore dei forzati* (provveditor of the convicted oarsmen). Further superintendent with military tasks were the *provveditore generale in Terraferma* (provveditor in the Venetian Mainland), with control over the militia, and the *provveditore sopra le fortezze* (provveditor for the fortifications). This latter controlled and directed the affairs concerning forts, fortified outposts, and urban walls, as well as bridges and storages for food and ammunitions. His action was considerable in keeping the extended Venetian defensive system as efficient as possible and therefore he had four adjutants. His office worked in coordination with the *provveditore all'Artiglierie* when the artillery was active in the fortresses. Generally, some of these offices were permanent, while others were appointed in case of war.[56]

55 As in the case of other extraordinary offices introduced in the course of the war, some office of extraordinary provveditor was not occupied for the entire duration of the conflict. For instance, this was the case of the extraordinary provveditor in Dalmatia. In fact, between 1650 and 1654, when the shift of the Republic's strategic focus to the Levant directed majority of its forces to the Eastern Mediterranean battlefields, the post was left vacant. However, increased Ottoman corsair activity in the Adriatic prompted the Senate to renew this command post. Accordingly, in April 1654, Alvise Civrano was elected as the extraordinary provveditor in the Gulf with the main task of facing Ottoman corsairs and keeping the Adriatic safe for navigation.

56 Government officials, military and technical personnel, formed a typical command centre of a Venetian province at the beginning of the war. In 1645, the office of *provveditore generale* of Crete belonged to Andrea Corner; during the siege of Chaniá there were the *provveditore straordinario* Antonio Navagero with the Governor of the Troops Giovanni Domenico Albano, Sergeant Major Niccolò Fossa and the cavalry commander Francesco Vizzamano, alongside

Finally, the commanders of the Allied troops and fleet also participated in the war councils, which made these meetings very crowded. During the Cretan War, and even later, these councils turned into endless, almost inevitable, discussions and quarrels with Allied commanders. Rivalry and suspicion existing between the Allies more than once caused delays to the beginning of operations, setbacks and failures, as happened very visibly in the first phase of the war. Matters of precedence of the complicated ceremony regulating diplomatic relations between the states were used whenever the prestige of an ally was undermined. The Senate and the captain general complained often about such miserable rivalry between the Allies, getting in several cases the support of some Italian sovereign; however, even among Venetians, harmony did not always reign and sometimes incomprehensible conduct occurred, explainable only by the fear of offending the sensibilities of such important families.

The Venetian Fleet

The fleet was exclusively allocated to members of the Venetian aristocracy because its command possessed a strong political value, as the fleet itself had for the nobility a very particular meaning as compared with the field army. Despite the fact that, in the 17th century, Venetians began to lose confidence in the sea, the long naval tradition was exalted in the symbolism of the state and cultivated in the tradition of all the most important aristocratic families, where there was no one who did not regard the service on a galley as a merit. For the Venetian aristocrats, the apprenticeship in the fleet began very early, probably also in comparison to the policies of the time, if we consider that at the Third Battle of the Dardanelles took part as *nobili sulle galee* the brothers Andrea and Antonio Muazzo, respectively aged 12 and 13. The 'genius' for the sea, innate in the Venetians, was outlined by the aforementioned Cardinal Scipione Pannocchieschi, who explained it by comparing the different scenario existing in the field army: "In the matters of the sea, the Venetians proceed otherwise. All-important ranks are occupied by the nobles, not by foreigners. Among aristocrats, the government elects a general, the captains of galleys, galleasses, and vessels; and subjects are also the sailors, the oarsmen, and almost all the soldiers on board."[57]

The Venetian native presence in the fleet was in fact considerable – including many noblemen from the Mainland – but the ethnic variety was very extensive too. Apart from the captains, pilots and crews of the northern European sailing vessels, the presence of 'national' Greeks and Slavs and even of foreign volunteers was very strong. Finally, in several campaigns the Venetian squadrons were strengthened by the Knights of Malta's galleys, Papal and Tuscan galleys, and occasionally by galleys and other ships from Naples, Sicily, Spain and Portugal.

If sailors and oarsmen came from the cosmopolitan Venetian rule, the officers were usually Venetian aristocrats, included on the sailing ships, but the galleys from Istria, Greek islands and Crete were commanded by

with the chief engineers Agostino and Carlo Alberti, Jan De Wert, Christopher Mollwitz and Pietro Leoni. See Brusoni, *Libro* II, p. 37.

57 Pannocchieschi, cited work, p. 278.

17. Carpenters and other craftsmen building vessels, from a Venetian 18th century panel of a carpenter's workshop.*

alternative captains. In wartime, the Senate appointed navy officers in specific functions which usually lasted three years. In the sailing fleet, the *capitano delle navi* (captain of the vessels) was also appointed. He was tasked to direct the vessels' squadron, known in Venice as the *Armata Grossa* (Heavy Fleet), while the galleys were joined in the *Armata Sottile* (Light Fleet), under the direct command of the captain general with the *capitano delle galeazze* as second in charge, but only for the Light Fleet. The war council included the aforementioned *provveditore generale all'armata* (provveditor of the Fleet), the chancellor (also appointed by the Senate), the commissar and the *sopramasser* (the maritime version of the quartermaster, in charge of administrative and logistical affairs). This war council operated like a typical general staff of the baroque age, including further officers depending on the strategic scenario.

As for any command, the Venetian government controlled the ranks of the fleet through the Senate, electing all appointments from the major officers to the simple noble apprentice, namely the young volunteer who trained to be officers on the ships. As discussed before, the captain general was the supreme commander and his office lasted for up to three years. When the new election was made, the outgoing captain was excluded. However, in the course of the Cretan war, the career of Francesco Morosini was a significant exception. He held the captain general's rank twice, though not consecutively. Other important officers were the *capitano della guardia in Golfo* (captain of the Gulf squadron of the Adriatic Sea), who directed the galley squadron of the Adriatic

18. For Venice, the galley was not just a warship but also a symbol of state power. (Captain general's galley, oil painting by anonymous artist, dated 1680; private collection, Venice)*

Sea, and finally the captain of the galleasses; all these tasks were entrusted to experienced officers and were the starting point to become captain general.

The intensive administrative work required to maintain the fleet effectively was run by the three *provveditori all'armar* (armament provveditors). Every two months this trio received relations from the *capi da mar*, namely the commissars in charge of inspecting the fleet's units, concerning role and number of the crewmen and the state of armaments, oarsmen, ammunition, expenses, and other matters relating to the fleet's administration in concert with the *inquisitori di Stato*. Under the *savio alla scrittura* supervision, the three provveditors managed the recruitment of sailors, rowers, and gunners. They also appointed non-commissioned and subordinate officers.

At operational level, the galley commander's responsibilities for his ship resembled those of an infantry or cavalry captain for his company. Both the *sopracomito* and the *governatore* commanded a galley or *galleass* and each led a composite major staff consisting of a *comito, sottocomito*, pilot, *padrone* (the sailors' senior NCO), *capo dei provisionati* (infantry picket commander), *capo bombardiere* (artillery senior NCO), secretary, chaplain, and *eccellente* (physician). The presence of other ranks depended on the ship's characteristics. For example, the *sopramasser* served on the captain general's galley. Other tasks and duties aboard the galleys and galleasses were appointed to other non-commissioned officers and specialists such as the *maestranze* (caulker, smith, carpenter), the *titolati* (senior sailors), and the *agozzino* (executioner). The *scappoli* (the onboard infantry detachment), and obviously the oarsmen completed the galley and galleass crews. Sailing vessels included different functions and ranks, and the captain usually exercised his authority over a smaller number of subordinates, whose denominations were often borrowed from foreign naval terminology. Over time, the increasing presence of vessels increased the number of high-level commands. In 1657 the rank of *almirante delle navi* and *patron delle navi* were set up, because the number of sailing ships had grown so high that it was necessary to subdivide them into three squadrons.

In time of peace, the Venetian fleet deployed 23 or 27 galleys: eight were at anchor between Corfu, Zakynthos and Kefalonia, to which four more were added during the summer months. A squadron of seven galleys was in Venice and, together with Istria's squadron – formed by four galleys – crossed the northern Adriatic and known as the *Guardia in Golfo* (Gulf's Guard). Finally, four more galleys belonged to the Candian Guard and were located in the island of Crete. In case of a conflict, the naval force could increase up to three or four times, and this was allowed by the wide availability of reserve *arsili* (galley hulls) preserved in the Venetian arsenal. This number was consistently maintained over 50 units, of which 25 were armed and ready to be employed. On the eve of the Cretan War, the arsenal produced seven galleys a year and even though far fewer than the figures produced in the previous century, they represented significant results, also because the quality of the Venetian light ships was superior to the ones deployed by their Ottoman opponents.

Since 1633, as part of the war disposition, Venice also had six galleasses, of which three were already armed and with the assigned crews.

In July 1645, just a few weeks after the start of the war, the Venetian fleet deployed a total of 40 galleys and four galleasses, not included the Cretan squadron. In the following years, the number of oared ships decreased, while that of sailing vessels grew, and for a long time constituted the second fleet of the Republic, known as *Armata Grossa* (Heavy Fleet). From the early 17th century, Venice had introduced an increasing number of sail units, which although penalised in the Mediterranean with regard to the galleys, possessed a remarkable firepower. Generally, the acquisition of these large ships, mostly converted merchants armed with 20 or 30 cannons, had been possible through contracts signed by the Republic with private ship owners and enlisting one or more pilots with a small crew of sailors. The government completed these crews enlisting other sailors in their own domains and providing gunners and soldiers. Originally, the vessels had to carry out the task of transporting large corps of troops, which otherwise would have to cross the sea on board the galleys. This did not mean that the oared units did not transport soldiers, but in any case, the greater capacity of the vessels was a remarkable advantage and above all allowed a less uncomfortable navigation for the troops during the journey from Venice to overseas domains. Contrarily to the Ottomans, in Venice the production of sailing ships began later. The Venetian arsenal started the production of vessel in late 1660s. These ships, owned by the state and generally with mixed crews, were also called *navi pubbliche* (public ships), and differed from the units chartered by private captains or directly loaned by friendly governments such as the United Provinces of the Low Countries. These latter represented the core of the Venetian sail fleet in the first phase of the war and they were actual warships, with 40 or more cannons, served by foreign crews and gunners, where the only Venetian on board was the commander.

19. A vessel built in Venice leaves docks propped on *camelli*, the ideal solution to the shallow waters of the lagoon. The disparity between English and Dutch counterparts became more apparent in merchant ships than war vessels for various reasons: the main one being that materials and technology alike were absorbed chiefly by the war fleet, but also because availability of wood and oakum (tarred fibre) had diminished dramatically since the end of 16th century. (Illustration from *Mario Nani-Mocenigo, Storia della Marina Veneziana*, 1930)

These ships had higher sailing quality than the armed merchants, and this was the cause of various problems during fighting.[58] After much delay, the first vessel entirely built and armed by the Venetian Arsenal, *Giove Fulminante* (*Lightning Jupiter*) with 62 cannons, launched in September 1667. Like the Ottomans, Venice never passively suffered this technological gap. While acquiring large vessels and hiring crews abroad, the government divided the sailing vessels into three homogeneous classes as early as 1660. During the Cretan War, the Arsenal never stopped experimenting with new armament solutions for sailing ships and, naturally for galleys, and galleasses. Between 1668 and 1699, Venice launched 18 first class, 14 second class and 10 third class vessels.[59]

After the Dutch Republic, England and France were the main suppliers of vessels. However, Venice also entered into agreements with other states, exploiting the network of relations in its possession to contain the high costs of war which involved the state, hiring sailing ships in the *Hansa* Republics of North Germany and even in Denmark. This latter provided three sailing ships and one admiral in the two-year period 1658–59 sent to the Mediterranean for professional advancement.

58 As rightly outlined by Luca Lo Basso, the coexistence of galleys and ships in the Venetian fleet has been interpreted in different ways. Today, scholars no longer consider old theories valid. Instead, they describe the transition from rowing to sailing – and then to steam – like a kind of Darwinian evolution applied to navigation. This traditional view originated from an alleged Mediterranean backwardness with respect to the northern European naval scenario, where sailing vessels occupied an undisputed primacy in the war fleets. The actual situation was very different. The Mediterranean, with its irregular winds, presented serious problems for large vessels, at least until ship and sailing technology overcame these limitations. Even the Venetian Arsenal's seemingly backward vessel designs withstand the light of recent investigations, which on the contrary, demonstrate a scenario of fruitful experiments in all fields of shipbuilding and armament production. See *Introduzione – Mutazioni e Permanenze nella storia navale del Mediterraneo*, secc. XVI-XIX (Milan: Franco Angeli, 2010), pp. 7–12.

59 Each class was identified by dimension and armament. A first class vessel carried 62 guns and 10/12 *petrieri* (guns firing stone ammunitions); second class had 48 guns and 10 *petrieri*, and third class 44 and 10 respectively. Despite the initial investment was very high compared to the cost of a galley, subsequently a vessel required much lower funds in campaign respect the oared ships. Apart from the smaller number of crew members, the vessels offered major advantages for loading of troops and war materials. A second-class ship could load up to 506 soldiers – including officers and 13 musicians between drums and fifes – plus 165 sailors, gunners, and picket of sentinels. Recent studies have revealed an original Venetian tradition of large sailing vessel designs which started in the early 17th century, see Candiani, cited work and Guido Ercoli *Vascelli e Fregate della Serenissima. 1652–1797* (Trento: Gruppo modellistico trentino di studio e ricerca storica, 2011).

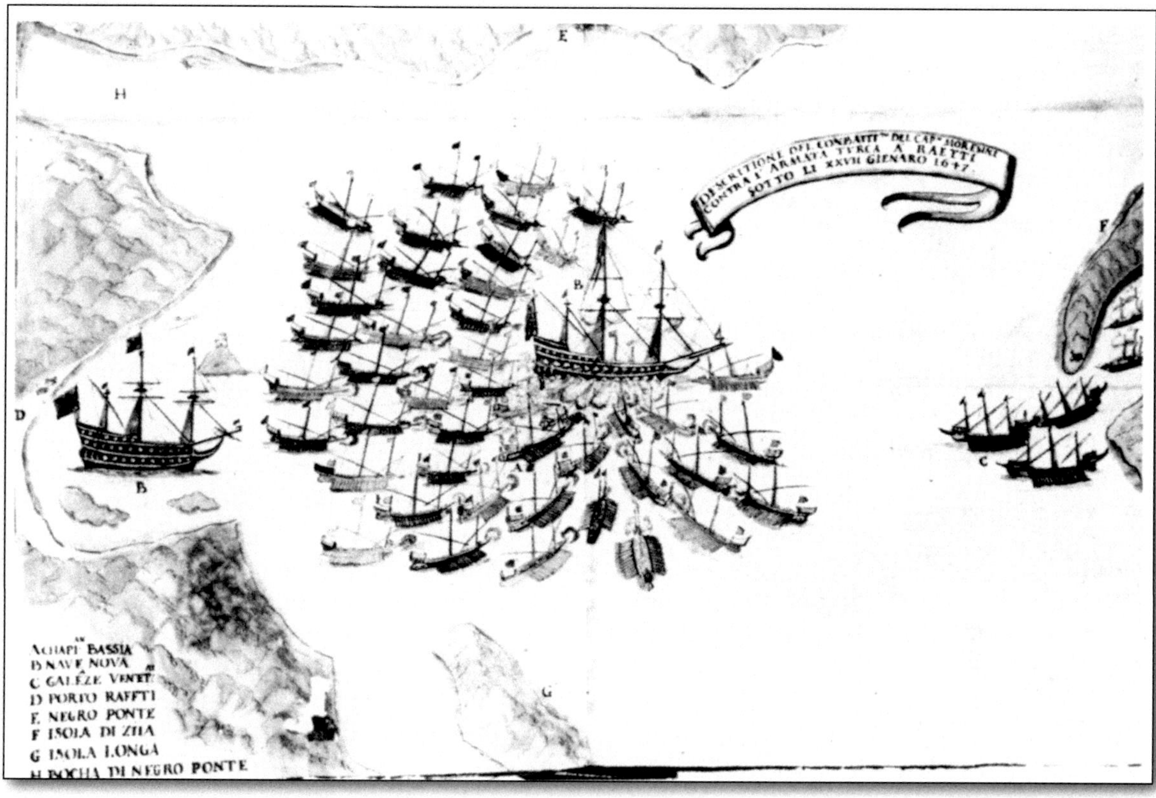

20. The defensive quality of vessels became evident off Chalkis in Eubea, on 27 January 1647, when a single sailing ship commanded by Venetian squadron commander Tommaso Morosini bested 46 Ottoman galleys. The Venetian sailing ship, although surrounded and isolated by the opponent, fought strenuously for hours allowing the arrival of reinforcements to its rescue, but losing Morosini's life in action. (Drawing by anonymous, Marciana National Library, Venice)

In addition to the types discussed, Venice employed a large number of small units, especially in the war theatre of the Adriatic Sea, where the morphology of the coast and the seabed represented an obstacle to the employment of larger units. If the galleys formed the squadron's core, the bulk of the Venetian naval forces in the Adriatic Sea consisted of smaller warships: *fuste*, *galeotte*, *barche armate* (armed boats) and brigantines. Such units were the direct result of the need to provide armed ships for each of the many guard posts along the coast. All these units belonged to the category of small, oar-propelled warships, armed with a varied number of guns and heavy firearms. Brigantines and armed boats were the smallest, and consisted of a single deck with between 10 and 12 benches with one oar each and one sail. Each ship carried crew of one company of *scappoli* marine infantry with strength of up to 40 men, and was usually armed with two spingards, two nine-pounder *petrieri*[60] and one three-pounder falconet. *Fusta* and *galeotta* represented smaller versions of the galleys – with a *galeotta* being slightly bigger than a *fusta* – with 14–18 benches and a single triangular sail.[61] Armament of these ships varied, but usually consisted

60 *Petriere* or *periere* were gunpowder weapons of a smaller calibre loaded with replaceable gunpowder cartridges, commonly used to arm *fregates*, *fuste* and *galeotte*. See: Marco Morin, *Artiglierie navali in ambito veneziano: tipologie e tecniche di realizzazione*, in: 'Quaderni di Oplologia' 23 (2006), pp. 3–28.

61 Domagoj Madunić, *The Adriatic Naval Squadron (1645–1669): Defense of the Adriatic during the War for Crete*, in 'Dalmacija' (UDK; Zagreb, 2013), p. 227: "*Galeotte* were perfectly suited to the task of facing Ottoman *fuste*: slightly larger, they could match *fuste* both in speed and in strength. Thus, a task force of *galeotte* could operate either independently or as a support to the galleys without significantly slowing them down. Over the years and following the advice of general

of six *petrieri* of different calibres: mainly nine and 12 pounders, and six heavy muskets. Their crews were larger than those of armed boats or brigantines, numbering between 60 to 100 men and thus requiring two full companies of marine infantry to arm them.

Notwithstanding the relevant foreign presence in the fleet, the cosmopolitan Venetian domains remained the greatest recruitment pool for sailors, gunners and oarsmen, and overwhelming numbers of Venetian aristocrats served as ship commanders. Throughout its history, the Republic constantly exerted control through the work of its officials not only over crews and ships, but also over local inhabitants. Sailors were recruited mainly in the *Dogado* territory, namely Venice, Chioggia and Laguna islands, registered as militia and established in the *Ordinanza da mar*, the compulsory service on the fleet instituted in 15th century. All sailors aged 18 and over were registered into categories as provided by the *Ordinanza da mar*. Alongside them, enlisted and reservist *bombardieri* (gunners) were trained in Venice and Chioggia. All able male subjects were classified according to their respective characteristics, so that, in case of need, fleet replacements could be found and assigned in a short time. The *Ordinanza da mar* had established also a levy of oarsmen, which included both the city of Venice and the peasants of the *Dogado*. This system meant that, in the event of war, the communities provided 10,000 oarsmen aged 18 to 45. However, it seems that in the 17th century the Venetian *sopracomiti* had little consideration for the oarsmen enlisted among the peasants of the *Terraferma*, who were particularly refractory for serving on the galleys. Generally, the oarsmen were drawn up among unmarried or children of large families, provided they offered someone as a volunteer, since the candidate could be exempted by paying a tax or procuring a substitute. Although there are numerous studies on the Venetian fleet, there is no comprehensive information on this phenomenon, especially on the implications of the substitutions and the methods used by the subject to avoid service on the galley. Although, during the Cretan war, the government turned again to the enlistment of Italian subjects, from 1647 it was decided to abolish the levy in the Venetian Mainland. After this date, the main recruitment pool of rowers became the territories of the overseas domains, both through compulsory conscription and voluntary service. The provveditors of Istria, Dalmatia and the Greek Ionian Islands had to update lists of subjects who could be employed as oarsmen, and therefore the fleet could complete the galleys' crews in a relatively short time. Among the overseas subjects, the Greeks provided the largest number of men for the service on the galleys' benches, due principally to the condition of most poverty of the population of the islands, which more easily accepted hardness and risks of a naval campaign, as well as for the better attitude of the Greeks to serve in the navy. Recourse to convictes was also practiced, including those delivered from other Italian states. To find more volunteers, the Venetian government offered a reduction of punishment in exchange for one or more years on board a galley. For instance, the death sentence could be avoided by agreeing to 10 years as

---

provveditor Corner, the Republic reconfigured the Adriatic squadron. At the end of the war, in addition to seven galleys, 21 Venetian *fuste-galeotte* served widely in the Adriatic Sea."

an oarsman.[62] Less common than on the Ottoman galleys, the employment of war prisoners was adopted especially at the end of the campaigns, when the number of rowers often became insufficient. The Venetians repeatedly resorted to the recruitment of rowers in the Aegean islands under Ottoman rule. Recruiting campaigns were carried out in order to retrieve deserters who had found refuge on some Aegean island. The vastness of the sea must make it a difficult task to escape the fate of the benches, and in fact the Venetian captains promised to save the communities from plundering if the escaped oarsmen were returned to them. In April 1656, the galley fleet turned to Andros and after an intimation by the captain general to the elders of the community, 64 *falliti*, namely deserters, were delivered to him. Before the end of the month, the fleet recovered in this way 240 oarsmen, "who were of great service, being all disciplined and experienced people."[63]

The Venetian Army

With the mobilisation of all the forces available, Venice could deploy a number of soldiers far below the Porte. Since the first half of the century, Venice used its field troops exclusively for passive defence and internal surveillance, as it clearly appeared from their deployment into the fortified places in the Mainland and overseas. After the war against Austria in 1615–17, the *Serenissima*'s field army had decreased from 26,000 to 24,000 of all the specialties employed to counteract the riots in Valtellina in 1625–27, until the 6,900 *provvisionati* (commissioned, or salaried) sent to Parma during the war against the Papal State, for a final mobilisation increased to more than 20,000 regular soldiers and militias at the end of the conflict.[64]

In time of peace, the permanent army deployed about 9,000 regulars of foot, including 2,200 infantrymen in the Mainland, divided between 15 major cities and fortresses of the state, and a further 7,500 in Dalmatia, Corfu, Zákynthos, Kefalonia, Tinos, Cerigo (today Citéra, in Greece) and Crete.[65] In the latter island, there was the larger garrison, with 3,500 regular infantrymen replaced every five years.

The cavalry was represented by the *corazze* (cuirassiers), whose number ascended at the end of the 1630s to about 15 companies, for an overall of 600 men, and by the light cavalry, the *cappelletti* (after the cloth headgear worn by these horsemen) who in the same period deployed 20 companies of 1,600 men in all.[66] After 1640, a couple of dragoon companies were formed, modelling the infantry formations on horseback deployed by the Austrians during war of Gradisca. In the sources, cuirassiers and dragoons were also indicated as *Cavalleria Grossa* (heavy cavalry).

---

62 Antonio Parente, *Quando il carcere era galera e bagni erano penali* (Dipartimento dell'Amministrazione Penitenziaria, Rome 2002), p. 55.

63 Brusoni, *Libro* XIII, p. 309.

64 Between 1616 and 1644, Venice hired 27 infantry regiments through various capitulations. Almost half of these – 13 regiments – came from Switzerland, 5 regiments were hired in the Netherlands, four were *Alemanni* (Germans), three from the Grisons, one from France, and one English regiment under Colonel Patton. This latter appeared only in the battle order of 1620.

65 ASVe, *Senato Mar*, R. 102, c. 90.

66 Alberto Prelli, *L'Esercito Veneziano del Primo Seicento*' (Venice: Filippi Editore, 1993), p. 56.

21. Portrait of Moukios da Roma, captain of Zakynthos, 1660. The Greek noble was the commander of the galleys provided by the three islands: two galleys from Zakynthos and one each from Kefalonia and Corfu. The Greek population of the Ionian Islands, much more than occurred in Venetian Terraferma, participated actively in the war on the sea with officers, sailors and rowers. (Author's archive)

Finally, the Republic's permanent war machine was completed with 400 gunners, bombardiers, and engineers with other specialists and assistants. These figures represented a considerable force, one of the largest in Italy, even though constantly subject to decrease for economic reasons.

Alongside with this core of professional soldiers and officers under contract, the government associated, if necessary, to hired foreign troops, and eventually resorted to the mobilisation of militias – ordinances[67] or *cernide* in the Italian mainland, *craine* in Dalmatia and *proli* in Crete and Archipelago – with a level of physiologically unequal efficiency. However, they could increase the army to thousands of men and in fact, in 1645, on paper the militia totalled 20,000 men in the Mainland and another 18,000 in the archipelago and in Dalmatia, trained and ready to support the country's defence.[68]

Unlike the Ottomans, who distinguished more-or-less clearly field troops from those embarked, no distinction was made in Venice, and therefore all the infantry could be at the same time landing, garrison or field force.[69] This was a direct consequence of the unconventional military structure of the Republic and of the substantial unity of the Venetian *Military*, which for the overseas Levant did not conceive an autonomous land strategy from the naval one. As the commander in charge of the fleet held the supreme command on the seas or in the field, the infantry could therefore be regarded as a component of the *Armata da Mar* in all its aspects.

---

67 In 1593 were promulgated the rules called *Ordinationi et Regole in materia di Ordinanze*; this document, except for a few changes, continued to be adopted for almost two centuries. Even amid lights and shadows, the militia absolved their tasks admirably in the war against the Habsburgs in 1615–18. The basic unit of the ordinances was the *centuria*, formed by 100 men. The required obligations were represented by five annual *mostre* (reviews) and a preliminary training of one week. The age limits were initially set from 16 to 40, but the family heads were released from service and the government avoided mobilising more than one man per family. Seasonal workers were also excluded, because "due to the poverty they change home every year." Alberto Prelli, *Sotto le Bandiere di San Marco. Le Armate della Serenissima nel '600'* (Bassano: Itinera Progetti, 2012); p. 67. See also John R. Hale, *The Military Organization of a Renaissance State* (Cambridge: Cambridge University Press, 1984), pp. 241–247.

68 In 1642, the Venetian disposed in the Ionian Islands, Dalmatia and Albania 12,187 regular soldiers and *craine*. This figure included 892 Italian infantrymen, 921 *Oltramarini*, 702 *Schiavoni* (Slavics), 28 'others, 60 professional artillerymen with 593 *scolari* (assistants and apprentices), and 8,991 *craine* and Greek militiamen'. ASVe, *Senato Mar*, R 346, cc. 23–27, June–August 1642.

69 The only actual Venetian naval infantry was the picket of *Scappoli* embarked on the galleys and galleasses. See also in Del Negro, 'Il leone in campo; Venezia e gli oltramarini nelle guerre di Candia e di Morea', in *Mito e antimito di Venezia nel bacino adriatico – secoli XV-XIX* (Rome: Fondazione Giorgio Cini, 2001), pp. 323–344.

22. Count Achilles de Remorantin entered in Venetian service in 1646 as a colonel of an infantry regiment he recruited in France. (Author's archive)*

The complex network of balanced power contributed ultimately to maintain separate the field forces in a classification according to their composition, origin and economic remuneration. At the beginning of the 17th century, the division of the troops according to their nationality had become definitive, as already clearly defined in the cavalry, where the *cappelletti* light horsemen were mostly Slavs and Albanians, while the cuirassiers filled their ranks with Germans and Italians.

The infantry was divided into three major categories: the Italians, the subjects of the Mainland as well as those enlisted in other states of the Peninsula; the *Oltramontani*, namely Germans, Swiss and Dutch, with the French who were added as a category apart; the *Oltramarini*, the subjects from the eastern coast of the Adriatic and Greece. These latter appear sometimes in the sources as *Nazionali* (Nationals), while Italians and *Oltramontani*, when they were not hired or auxiliary contingents, qualify themselves in the sources as *truppe particolari* (special troops), *provvisionate* (salaried) or even *Marcoline* (of Saint Mark). A similar prescription of 'military policy' concerning the "division of nations, and of each one separately forming a regiment" was proposed in 1647 by general commander Camillo Gonzaga, when he took the command for the defence of Crete. The nationalities in Venetian service already garrisoned in the island were French, Italian, Corsican and *Oltremarini*, a term that in this case would identify the Greeks.[70]

On the eve of the Cretan war, the army of the Venetian Republic had very little upgraded structure and ordinances set up in the early 17th century, and despite having supported a war against the Austrians in 1615–17 and another against the Pope in 1641–44, it was still in a transitional phase between the late Renaissance model and the modern arrangement assumed at the end of the 17th century. Considering that political power controlled every civil and military activity, even the army officers were subject to the balance of power, which was typical of Venice. In fact, the subordinate commanders had limited authority in the war theatre involving the Venetian overseas domains, where the *governatori delle armi* (governors of the land troops) directed the garrison and the militia of their respective province. Above them, the prominent figure in the Venetian high command of the field army was the *governatore generale delle armi* (general governor of the field troops), appointed by the

70 *Ibid.*, p. 326–327; cited after S. Anticano (A. Santa Croce); 'Frammenti istorici della guerra di Candia' (Bologna, 1647), pp. 286–287 and 305.

Senate to lead the field army in campaign. This supreme officer was chosen from among the candidates expert in western warfare techniques and he extended his command to all the infantry and cavalry in the Mainland theatre in wartime. This high general was usually appointed among foreign captains, as evidenced by the long series of commander who served the Republic in the 17th century, like the Italian princes Giovanni de' Medici and Luigi d'Este, or experienced veterans as the Corsican Pompeo Giustiniani. The functions of these commanders were regulated by a contract setting salaries, duration of the engagement, and authority over the militias and other clauses, such as the obligation to reside in the territory of the Republic for the duration of the service. The work of these commanders often generated tensions with the administrators, who tended to extend their control over any activity in the territory managed by them, while the military maladapted themselves to acting in a subordinate status. During the Cretan War, the government occasionally appointed a general, always trying to assess the political opportunity of choices. In 1645, the Senate conferred the rank upon don Camillo Gonzaga Prince of Bozzolo, a professional soldier who had been in the service of France. In 1653 was elected Prince Orazio Farnese of Parma, formerly commander of cavalry in the Spanish army, while in 1660 the nomination went to another exponent of the French party, Prince Almerico d'Este, the Duke of Modena's young brother, the same general who directed the unfortunate expedition to Crete. Two years later, Prince Philipps von Pflaz-Sulzbach, a former captain at the service of the King of Sweden, was in charge for the same office for a short time.

In addition to these officers, the government could enlist a number of captains such as the *governatore delle armi* (governors of the troops), *sergente generale* (major general) or simply *generale*, who were responsible of regional or subordinate commands under the high general. In this context there was also the *generale degli Oltramontani*, who directed the German and Swiss troops in Venetian service. Regarding the nationality of the troops, during the Cretan war new offices were established. In July 1648, the Senate sent to Dalmatia an experienced and proven officer, *Cavaliere* Niccolo Delimarcovich (Nikola Delimarković), with the title of *Colonello della natione Crovata* (Colonel of the Croatian Nation). Although his title referred to him as the colonel of Croats only, Delimarcovich was in charge of all infantry aboard the fleet, Croat or Albanian. After he was killed in action in July 1653, he was succeeded by Vuco Cernizza-Orlandich, whose title was adjusted – to reflect his actual authority – to that of *colonnello delle Nationi Crovata, et Albanese*.[71] Obviously, commanding and coordinating the actions of several dozens autonomous companies would be very difficult, especially during wartime. In order to address this issue, even before the war a special command post above the level of infantry captain, with the title

71 The appointment took a place upon the Colonel's arrival in Dalmatia in July 1648, yet two years later the Senate had still not confirmed it, so the Colonel, through the mediation of general provveditor Foscolo, sent a petition to the Senate. See ASVe, *Provveditori da Terra e da Mar*, b. 470, c. 726, in Zadar, dated, 25 July 1650. The arrival of Colonel Delimarcovich coincided with the introduction of the office of sergeant-major of the armed boats, a post to which Foscolo appointed the Colonel's nephew, Captain Zorzi Delimarcovich.

of *governatore di Militie Albanesi et Crovate* (governor of the Croatian and Albanian troops) was established. The 'ethnic' title denoted a commander in charge of several companies of marine infantry serving aboard the armed boats. Often the commander himself recruited these companies. In addition to social prestige, and military rank, this title usually (but not always) brought also a small income, depending on the merit and status of the individual.[72]

Since the beginning of the Cretan war, the *generale dello sbarco* (general of the landing forces) had become a particularly important figure, also appointed by the Senate. He held the command of landing troops during amphibious operations. Apart from rare exceptions, this rank was always assigned to foreign mercenary officers, mostly Italian. Even in this case many of these assignments were issued to foreigners, and this trend did not change during the war, with commanders such as the Tuscan Alessandro del Borro, the Italian of Austria Rodolfo Colloredo, the Walloon Gilles De Haes, or the French Alexandre de Saint'André-Montbrun, just to name a few.

There was a further rank usually appointed in wartime when the Republic faced an enemy on the Venetian Mainland. This officer received the title of *maestro di campo generale* (general field captain), however it was a function more apparent than substantial, because Venice no longer had to confront opponents in Italy, and then this charge remained vacant after 1645.

Unlike the aforementioned quotations, the native Venetian presence in the army was not a minority as claimed by certain sources and even though senior officers and many of the subordinates were foreign mercenaries: those from the *Terraferma* (mainland), the colonies, or from Venice itself were such a large group. The Venetian decision to enlist mercenary commanders was a calculated price to ensure political stability, avoiding the formation of a class of professional soldiers who would change the state's internal balance. Dissatisfaction with this rule meant calling into question the political and social order of the state. Moreover, appointments to prestigious military posts were useful for managing the network of diplomatic relations to which Venice had always attached great importance. In this context, in 1647 the Marquis Jacques de Gremonville, brother of the French ambassador to the *Serenissima*, was appointed with the rank of lieutenant general of the infantry. Venice was, however, able to secure the service of good officers, capable of achieving considerable results despite the inconclusive strategies imposed by the supreme command and the inconstant efforts of the government in the conduct of the war. Alongside the foreign officers, mercenary captains came from all Italian regions, mostly from Marche, Abruzzi, Umbrian and Romagna, while some were originally from Corsica and others from the ducats of Parma and Modena.[73]

---

72 See the decrees granting the title of *governatore* in ASVe, *Senato Mar*, R.104, f. 242, dated 15 September 1646; b. 106, f. 80, dated 2 March 164, b. 113, f. 53–54, dated 13 March 1652, and b. 113, f. 102–103, dated 19 April 1652.

73 According to the estimates formulated after some biographical encyclopedias of the 1930s – quoted with the benefit of the doubt by Gregory Hanlon in his *Twilight of a Military Tradition* – between 1600 and 1670, in the Venetian army there were at least 600 Italian 'foreign' officers, included significant aliquots from Tuscany, Rome, Puglia and even officers coming from states historically unrelated to the Republic, such as the Milanese and Genoa.

23. Alexandre de Puy, Marquis of Saint'André-Montbrun, was the last *governatore delle armi* of Crete, assuming the position aged 60, but always demonstrating great courage and determination. Before the surrender of the city the Marquis was wounded several times, but always returned on the ramparts to encourage his men armed with spontoon and helms. (Engraving by Antoine Masson after Gilbert Seve, Gabinet des Etampes de Musée de Louvre, Paris)

At the beginning of the war, the basic tactical-administrative unit of the Venetian army was the company of infantry or cavalry, placed at the orders of a captain or a lieutenant when it was associated with others to form larger corps, namely regiment, normally consisting of five to 10 or more companies. The number of men could also vary from many dozen men between one company and another. Only in 1662, the Senate established that an Italian infantry regiment should be composed of eight companies of 84 private infantrymen with six corporals, four musicians, one *furiere* (paymaster), one *scrivano* (secretary), one sergeant, one ensign, one lieutenant and one captain.[74] In 1648, the heavy cavalry companies consisted of 40 soldiers and officers, while the light cavalry deployed 50 men in all.[75]

As happened in other armies of the 17th century, even the Venetian one, the term 'regiment' was still a vague concept and represented a not always defined group of companies assembled for tactical necessity – especially in campaign – and then dissolved when the soldiers were divided between garrisons or fleet. For a long time this aspect still interested the Italians and the *Oltramarini* while the contingents hired outside Italy were usually already structured in actual regiments. A state of the force of the Venetian infantry in the mainland, dated February 1641, issued to the *provveditore generale in Terraferma* Andrea Corner, distinguishing between Italian independent companies and others assembled into regiments, implicitly confirmed the persistence of a double organisation of the military corps. In 1645, a part of the *Oltramontani* companies garrisoned in Italy were not regimented, which indicates the persistence of these dynamics even among foreign contingents. Conversely, in 1646, the militia of Zara, Split and Šibenik were amalgamated in four 'regiments' under the cavalry provveditor Vendramino Francesco Georgio.[76]

Naturally these dispositions had an exclusively administrative function, and in the following years the regiments in the service of Venice continued to deploy different strengths and numbers of companies. A clear demonstration of the difference existing between theory and practice appears in the order of battle of the army under the Marquis Francesco Villa de Ghiron, who, in spring 1666, was preparing to land in Crete to besiege Chaniá. Among 11 Italian infantry regiments, none deploy eight companies as established.

74 Ten eight-company Italian regiments had been formed in Crete in late autumn 1662 by the *Provveditore Generale delle Armi in Candia*, See ASVe *Senato, Rettori*: b. 45, c. 124; Nicolò Corner's relation dated 12 December 1662.

75 A. Prelli, cited work, p. 51.

76 Brusoni, *Libro* V, p. 99.

Furthermore, in the same battle order there are still independent companies, classified as *compagnie franche* (free companies).[77]

Examining other cases is possible to guess different explanations. In the garrison of Candia there are companies assembled in regiments but with two different origins. There were regiments recruited in the country of provenance and the ones formed directly in Candia, assigning a certain number of companies to a single colonel. This is the case of the regiments garrisoned in 1659, almost all assembled from reforms carried out by the commanders and divided by nationality into three *Oltramontani* regiments, five Italian regiments, one Corsican regiment, three regiments of Greeks and one regiment of oltramarini. In addition, there were four independent companies, three Italian and one Greek.[78]

At the end of the 16th century the government prescribed that the permanent infantry force in the Venetian Mainland would consist of only 2,000 men under four senior colonels, eight colonels, 12 *governatori*, and 40 captains who held long-term contracts for a further enrolment, if needed, of further 6,000 Italian footmen. The custom of enlisting entire foreign regiments had long existed. In 1616, Count Johann Ernst of Nassau signed an agreement for recruiting a regiment of 3,000 Dutchmen infantrymen, including 600 English soldiers under his lieutenant Sir John de Vere.[79] A year later, still from the Netherlands, Colonel Vassenhoven arrived in Venice with 1,000 infantrymen; then in 1625 the Venetians sent the Duke of Candalle, recently arrived in the service of the Republic, to Valtellina with his French infantry regiment of 1,500 men. The needs of the war led to the standardisation of contingents and by the end of the 1650s the 'regiment' began to assume the modern meaning we know. However, until the end of the century the Venetian infantry regiments continued to present quite different strengths.

24. Prince Philipp von Pfalz-Sulzbach, one of many foreign commanders who served as general for Venice. He received the office of governatore delle armi of Crete in 1662. Unlike the larger part of the captains in Venetian service, the Prince was a Lutheran who had fought in the Swedish Army. On several occasions at Candia, officers and soldiers who had been enemies a few years before fough under the same flag. (After *Theatrum Europeum*, Frankfurt am Main, 1670)

In 1647, for instance, when Count Achilles de Remorantin signed with the *Serenissima* the capitulation of one infantry regiment for Crete, the total strength increased to 20 companies, for 4,000 men in all.[80] One year later, the cantons of Zurich and Bern granted the recruitment of a 2,000 men strong regiment consisting of 10 companies of 200 infantrymen each fielded into two battalions. A third capitulation, signed in early 1648, fixed the enlistment

77 *Les Memoires du Voiage de Msr le Marquis de Ville au Levant, ou Histoire Curieuse du Siege de Candia*, Amsterdam, 1670, pp. 69–83.

78 ASVe, *Provveditori da Terra e da mar*, b. 551, c. 98.

79 Hale-Mallet, cited work, p. 504.

80 *Il Mercurio ovvero Storia dei Correnti Tempi – Anno 1647*, Lyon, 1649, p. 329.

25. Venetian *corazza* (cuirassier), mid 17th century. All contemporary sources relate that the Venetian heavy cavalry employed metal plates more than did their foreign colleagues. (Author's illustration)*

of one Walloon infantry regiment of 3,000 men with 15 companies.[81]

Often, these arrangements were determined by the contingency of the period and Venetian demand, but a decisive factor also resided in the entrepreneurial capacity of the capitulations' holders. Forming a regiment was a remarkable commercial undertaking and in those years, there were many colonels who acted as real entrepreneurs specialised in setting up military contingents. The commander's reputation, especially when dealing with a good number of campaigns in Flanders, Germany or Hungary, conditioned the capitulation of regiments as a result of their strength and, of course, the cost of their employment. For this reason too, many foreign colonels in Venetian service could consider themselves veterans over their native counterparts, thus finding them in a condition of privilege, causing sometimes the deterioration of internal relations.

However, regarding the composition of the infantry regiment, Venice was always careful to update troops with modern weapons and tactical discipline, so that both in the Italian infantry and in the foreign too, as well as in the militia, the ratio between firearms and pikes was even higher than in the Swedish army, with 33 percent of pikemen against 66 percent of musketeers.[82] This percentage, certainly high but fully in tune with the defensive attitude of the Republic, did not undergo major changes during the conflict. Moreover, the utility of pikes and other polearms was never questioned, and, at the end of the war the Venetian infantry was still equipped in the same proportion as 20 years ago. Even inside the besieged Candia, pikemen represented the tactical reserve for supporting the firearms to counter the feared Ottoman assaults. The use of

81 The contract signed by *sergente generale* Gritti, represents an excellent example in several aspects. The regiment, recruited by count of Longueval, wasa composed by Walloons, Flemish, and other recruits from Liège, for a total of 3,000 infantrymen, distributed over 15 companies of 200 soldiers each. The regiment had to concentrate in Anvers within 15 March, to be boarded and transported to Venice. The engagement established that weapons and equipments would be supplied by Venice, but reimbursed with a monthly deduction from the soldiers' salaries. The only exception was when the equipment was lost for a shipwreck or damaged or lost in combat, in this case, every expense was assumed by the Venetian government. It is also interesting to note that the contract was valid for only one year, after which Venice could, at will, renew the firm or license the men. In the latter case, the regiment would have received the one month's pay, both soldiers and officers, for the return journey. Contracts released for the levy in foreign countries normally included several thousand men at a time. See Roberto Vaccher, 'L'esercito veneziano e la difesa di Candia, 1645–1669 (Master's degree thesis) (Università Ca' Foscari, Venice, Academic Year 2013–14), pp. 61–62.

82 Prelli, cited work, p. 18.

half-pikes, *brandistocchi* and *corsesche* polearms produced in large numbers and always registered in the Venetian arsenals until 1669, proves the persistent use of cold steel weapons on the ramparts of Crete. The proportion between pike and muskets was reiterated by the provisions issued by the government and concerned all infantry except for the *Oltramarini*, although, for budgetary reasons, militiamen received a more heterogeneous armament.

Naturally, the full regulations implied that the soldier or non-commissioned officer presented himself with his full equipment, something that rarely happened, despite the capitulations establishing what should be the equipment provided for the various specialties.[83] Although the State tried to obtain a homogeneous standard, many details and particularities introduced by captains tended to make the equipment between one company and another very different. This tendency diminished through the years, especially when entire regiments were capitulated, but effective regularity was never achieved and differences of various kinds continued to exist between the units.[84] The many nationalities present contributed to making the equipment so varied, especially the troops belonging to the Allies, equipped according to the use of their countries of origin.[85]

Though several differences existed in the field army units, the artillery corps benefited from significant homogeneity. In fact, when compared to other sectors of the Venetian armed forces, the artillery received more attention in organisation, equipment and training. Even before the Cretan War, the *Provveditore Generale del Terraferma* proudly stated that the Venetian artillery was "the best equipped among those of any prince."[86] For

83 Since the war of Gradisca the Venetian infantry was armed with musket called *Modello Chinelli*, manufactured in Brescia with a length of 25 onze (132 cm), and a total weight of 6.25 kilograms including the forked musket rest. Each musketeer received a bandoleer with pre-measured charges contained in wooden cartridges. The number of cartridges was 10 or 12, while inside a leather bag, always hanging on the bandoleer, were transported the lead balls and other accessories. The armament of the Venetian musketeer was completed by a shoulder strap for the sword, which was universally used throughout the conflict, even though during the siege many soldiers preferred not to use them, to be more agile, both in the landing operations and in the narrow spaces on the rivellini and in the ditches. Regarding the pike, in 1641 the infantry captain Fabio Gallo, over five years in the service of the Republic, in his *Forgia di Marte, ovvero Disciplina Universale dell'Arte Militare* (Forge of Mars or Universal Discipline of Military Art) described the pike which had to be at least 15 feet long (5.20 metres), with the tip of laurel or lozenge-shaped iron, fixed to the ash wood rod and provided with two metal side bars to prevent the sword blows from breaking the rod. See Prelli, cited work, p. 14.

84 At the beginning of the century it was established that at least 20 percent of pikemen wore the corselet, so that the first rows were armoured, while the remaining were *picche secche*, namely without armour. Although the availability of corselets was increased over time, some evidence would confim that the infantry in Crete had forgone metal protection, except for helms, which instead continued to be worn by infantry soldiers. It seems equally evident that the Venetian heavy cavalrymen, on the contrary, preferred for a long time to retain armour. This characteristic had already distinguished them during the war of Gradisca, when the wide use of helms, protection for arms and armour with front and back earned the nickname of *padelloni* (iron pots) for the Venetian cuirassiers.

85 For instance, in 1666, the soldiers of the Tuscan landing battalion in Dalmatia, were equipped with pike of 3.5 metres, and muskets partly still with the rest, along with lighter arquebuses. SeeArchivio di Stato di Firenze (State Archive of Florence) ASFi, *Mediceo del Principato*, F. 2129, *Milizie in Levante*, cc. 224.

86 ASVe, *Savio alla Scrittura*, b. 11 cc. 178–179.

service in the artillery were selected candidates coming from the militia who aspired to become *bombardiere*, completing the training in special schools active in all the major cities of the Venetian domains.[87] To receive the status of *bombardiere* and to be able to aspire to a rank as salaried, it was necessary to pass a specific exam. Once they passed the exam they were sent to the garrison, where the artillerymen would serve, receiving a monthly salary. The pupils were those who had not yet taken the exam but could serve under the supervision of an NCO. As assistants, they received no salary directly from the state and their livelihood depended on the artilleryman to whom they were entrusted. The artillerymen were estimated to be very important for their abilities and the death of one of them was considered more harmful than that of a much greater number of soldiers. However, the skills with which *bombardieri* and assistants handled the pieces could vary and was often the cause of complaints from the Venetian commanders in Crete. In 1649, Baron Nicolò Theodorico Spesseiter reported how the state of the artillery of Candia was bad, also because of the lack of master builders and artillerymen assigned to the garrison.[88]

The clear distinction between the militia and the regular army, composed of mercenaries, is clear at the financial level. The militia was attended by a *savio all'Ordinanze*, who differed from the official who was in charge of economic issues for the regular army, namely the *savio alle scritture*. Similarly, there was a commander in chief, with the rank of *governatore delle Ordinanze* (Governor of the Ordinances). Because the relationship between civil society and 'the military' had always been a sensitive nerve of the Venetian policy, the militia assumed a particular meaning in the state. Although contemporary commentators exaggerated the alleged mistrust of the Venetian subjects of military service, the government's decisions regarding the militia were often hesitant and conditioned by conflicting factors. First, there was certainly the desire not to turn the civilians to regular and continues military exercises, but only that necessary for the formation of a force not merely representative, so turning civilian manpower away as little as possible from its activity. This concerned especially the mainland population, because Venetian citizenship was excluded from service in the field militia, and alongside the one of Chioggia they were interested only in the service in the navy. In addition to these economic precautions, the government was also pressed by the need not to endanger the consensus between the dominant centre and the periphery.

The level of preparation of militiamen was obviously not comparable to that of professional soldiers, but their maintenance also involved considerable spending. In order to restore efficiency, careful direction and systematic training were needed, and something was tried on the eve of the war, but in fact it was too late to produce appreciable results.

---

87 In Italy, there were schools in Brescia, Bergamo, Crema, Orzinuovi, Pontevico, Asola, Peschiera, Verona, Legnago, Padua, Treviso, Rovigo, Palmanova, Marano, Vicenza, Bassano, and Udine. In Dalmatia schools were active in Split, Zadar, and Koper and in the Greek islands there were one school in Corfu. Venice and Chioggia provided gunners only for the fleet, destined to handle the guns aboard of galleys and sailing ships.

88 ASVe, *Senato, Dispacci, capi da guerra*, b. 9, 7 December 1649.

II

Venetian Crete

Venice held Crete for four and a half centuries, much longer than any of its other possessions among the islands of the Mediterranean or on the mainland of Greece. In the division of territories in 1204 after the fall of Constantinople to the Fourth Crusade, Crete had gone to Boniface of Montferrat, Lord of Thessalonica, who sold the island to Venice. But Genoa too coveted Crete, and in 1206 the Genoese fleet seized the unfortified town of Iráklion (Candia) and other Cretan territory. After several unsuccessful attempts Venice finally ejected the Genoese in 1211, the start of continuous Venetian rule of Crete.

In the first two centuries of Venetian rule barely a decade passed without a Cretan revolt of some kind. Some Greek historians tend to lump these together, seeing them all as struggles for an unspecified freedom, and as expressions of national consciousness, a concept that acquired meaning only in the 18th century. As rightly outlined by David Brewer: "their argument can even become circular: the leaders of revolts had nationalist sentiments, therefore the revolts must have been inspired by nationalism, and therefore, the leaders must have had nationalist sentiments".[1] None of the revolts achieved any lasting result, and they were sometimes followed by Venetian reprisals. Many, however, ended with Venetian grants of privileges to the Cretans, or confirmation of existing privileges.[2] There were some benefits for the people of Crete. The different classes – nobles, their children and so on down the scale – were recognised and made permanent, so that nobody could be deprived of his own status. It was also promised that a Greek Orthodox

1 D. Brewer, *Greece, the Hidden Centuries: Turkish Rule from the Fall of Constantinople to Greek Independence* (London: I.B. Tauris, 2011), p. 219.

2 A significant long revolt occurred in 1282–99, led by the wealthy landowner Aléxios Kalléryis. The revolt was centred on the district of Milopótamos between Réthymnon and Iráklion, but spread to most of western Crete. In previous risings, Kalléryis had sometimes supported rebels against the Venetians, sometimes Venetians against rebels, and his aim now was not to expel the Venetians – they were preferable as rulers, he believed, to Genoese or Catalans – but to carve out a semi-independent principality for himself under Venetian rule. The Kalléryis revolt dragged on inconclusively until 1296 when a Genoese fleet attacked western Crete, captured Chaniá, and invited Kalléryis to join them. Kalléryis refused and this paved the way for the agreement of 1299, known as the *Pax Alexii Callergi*, which ended the revolt. He was later referred to as the *avthéntis* (ruler) of Crete, and his name was inscribed in the *Libro d'Oro* of Venetian nobility, a unique privilege for a Cretan.

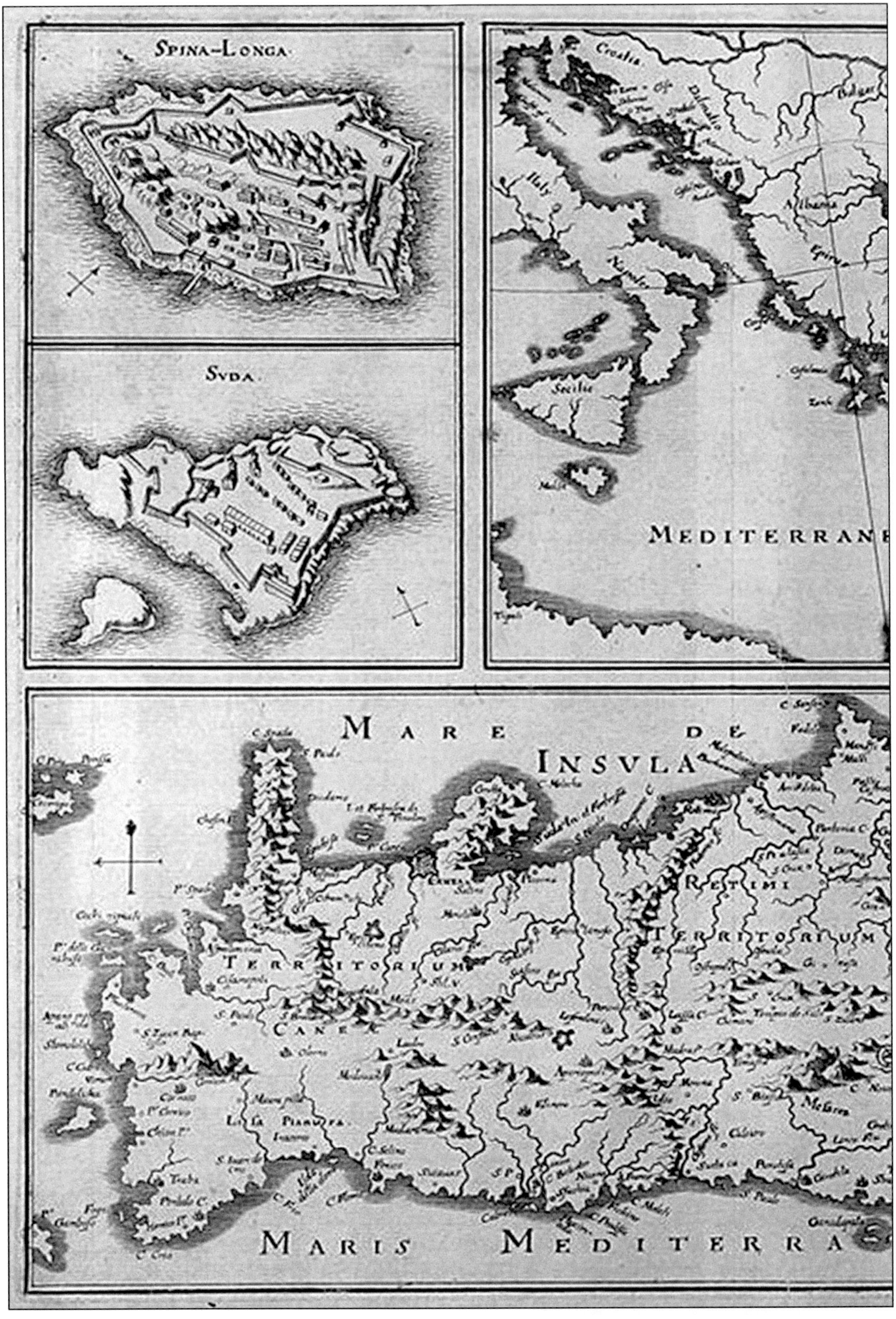
SPINA-LONGA
SVDA
MEDITERRANE
MARE DE INSVLA
RETIMI
TERRITORIUM
TERRITORIUM
CANEA
MARIS MEDITERRA

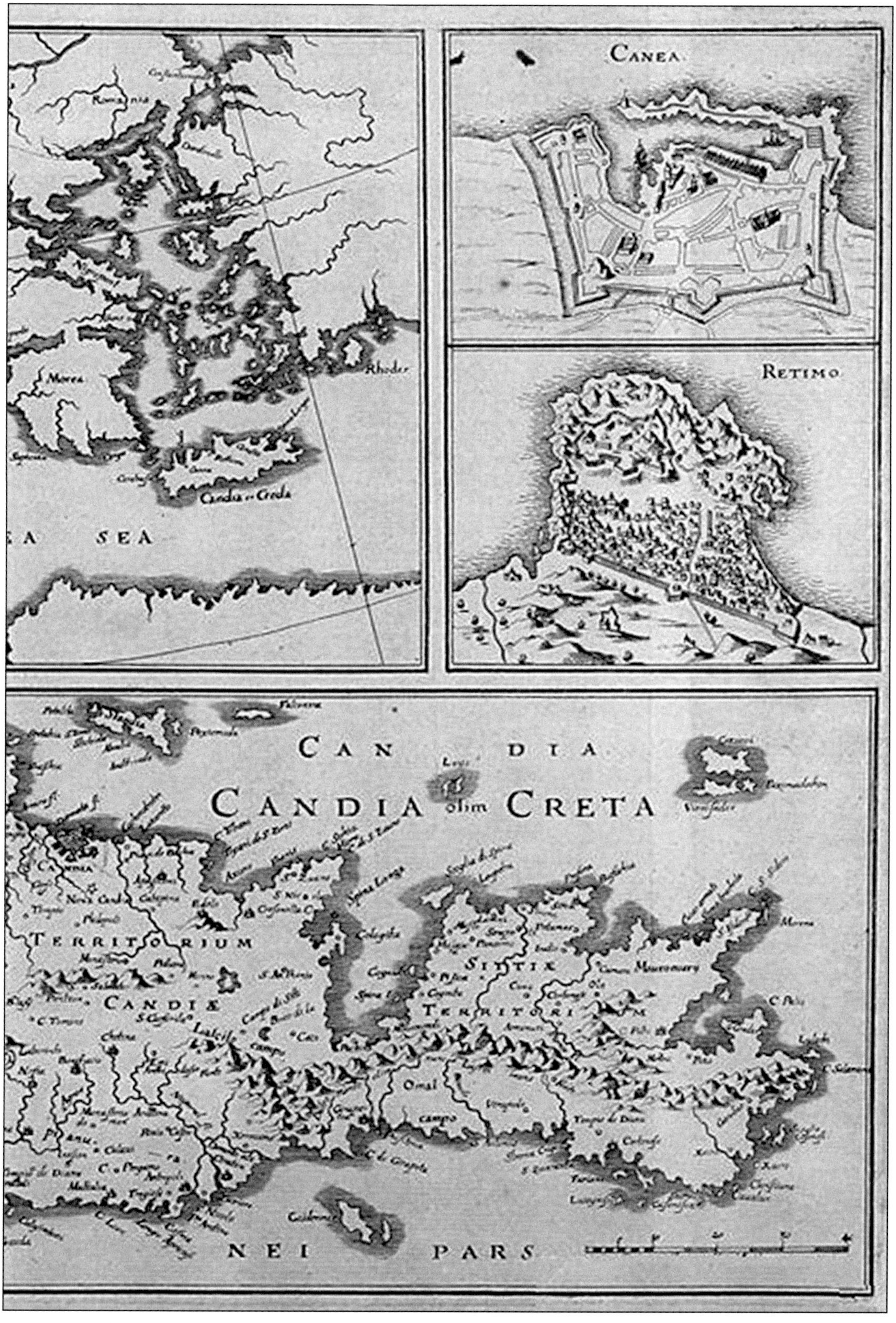
CANEA
RETIMO
SEA
Rhodes
Morea
CAN DIA
CANDIA olim CRETA
TERRITORIUM
CANDIÆ
SITTIÆ
TERRITORI
NEI PARS

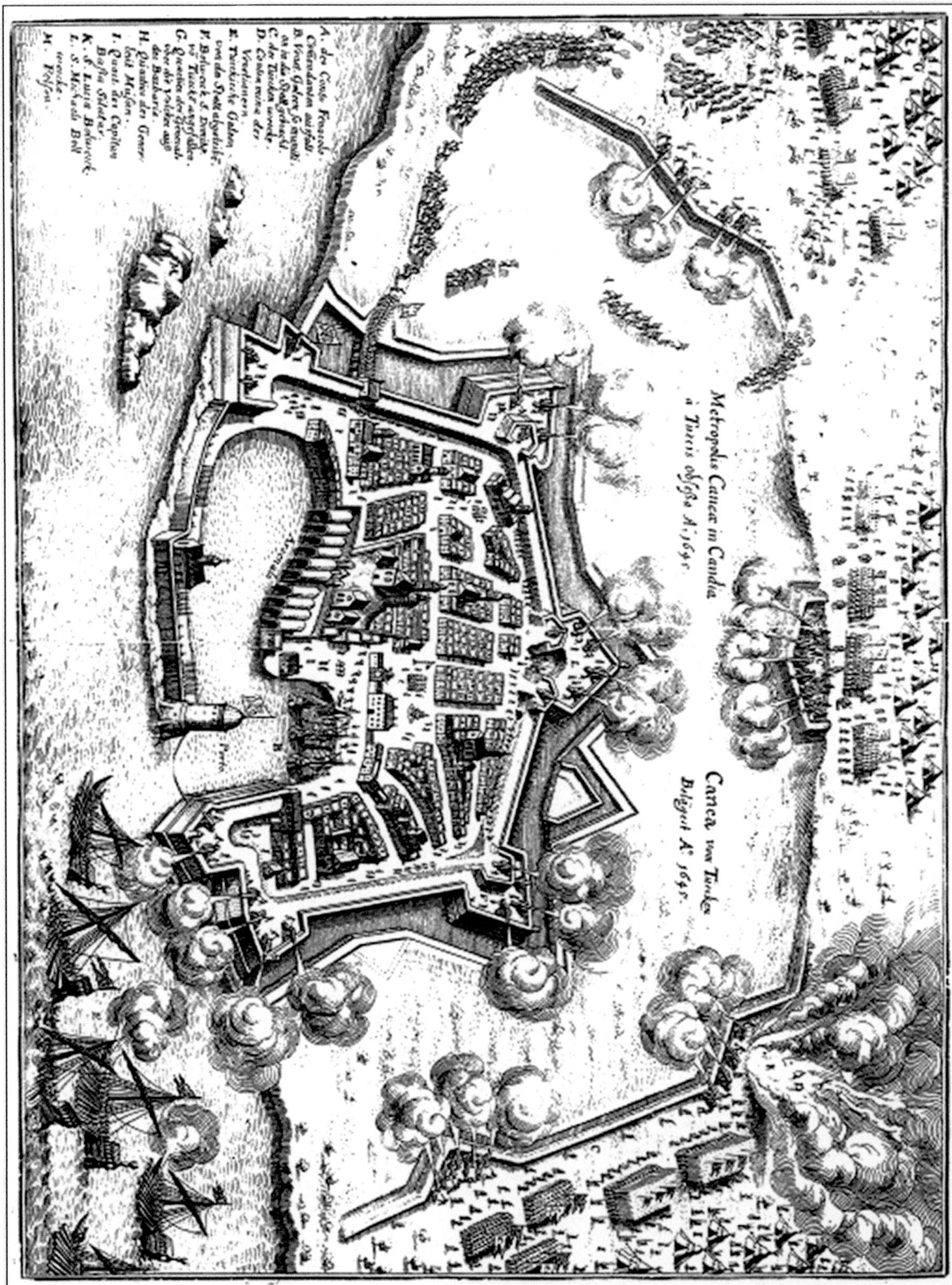
Metropolis Caneae in Candia à Turcis obsessa A. 1645
Canea von Türcken Belägert A° 1645

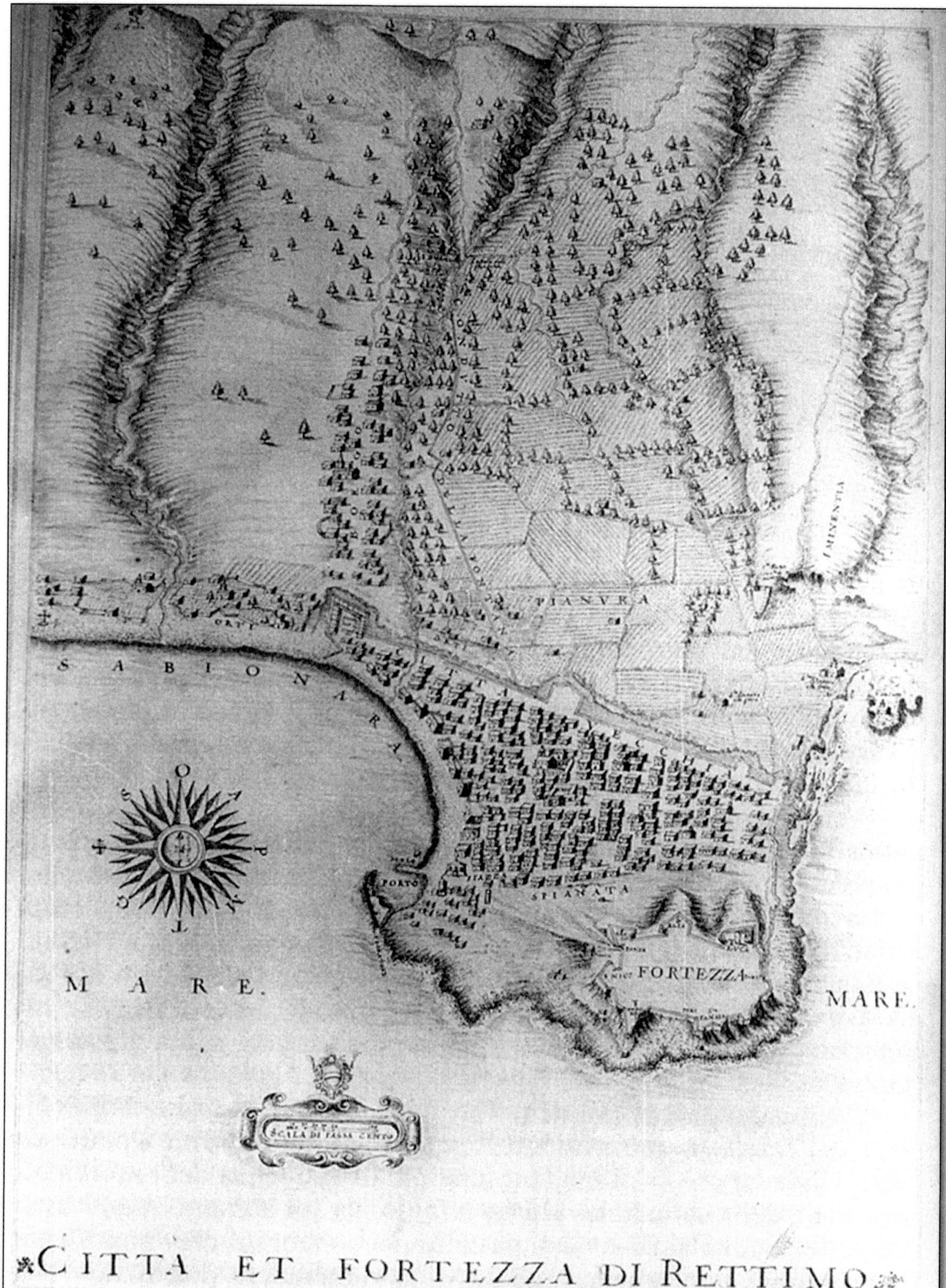
SABIONARA
PIANURA
SPIANATA
PORTO
FORTEZZA
MARE.
MARE.
CITTA ET FORTEZZA DI RETTIMO

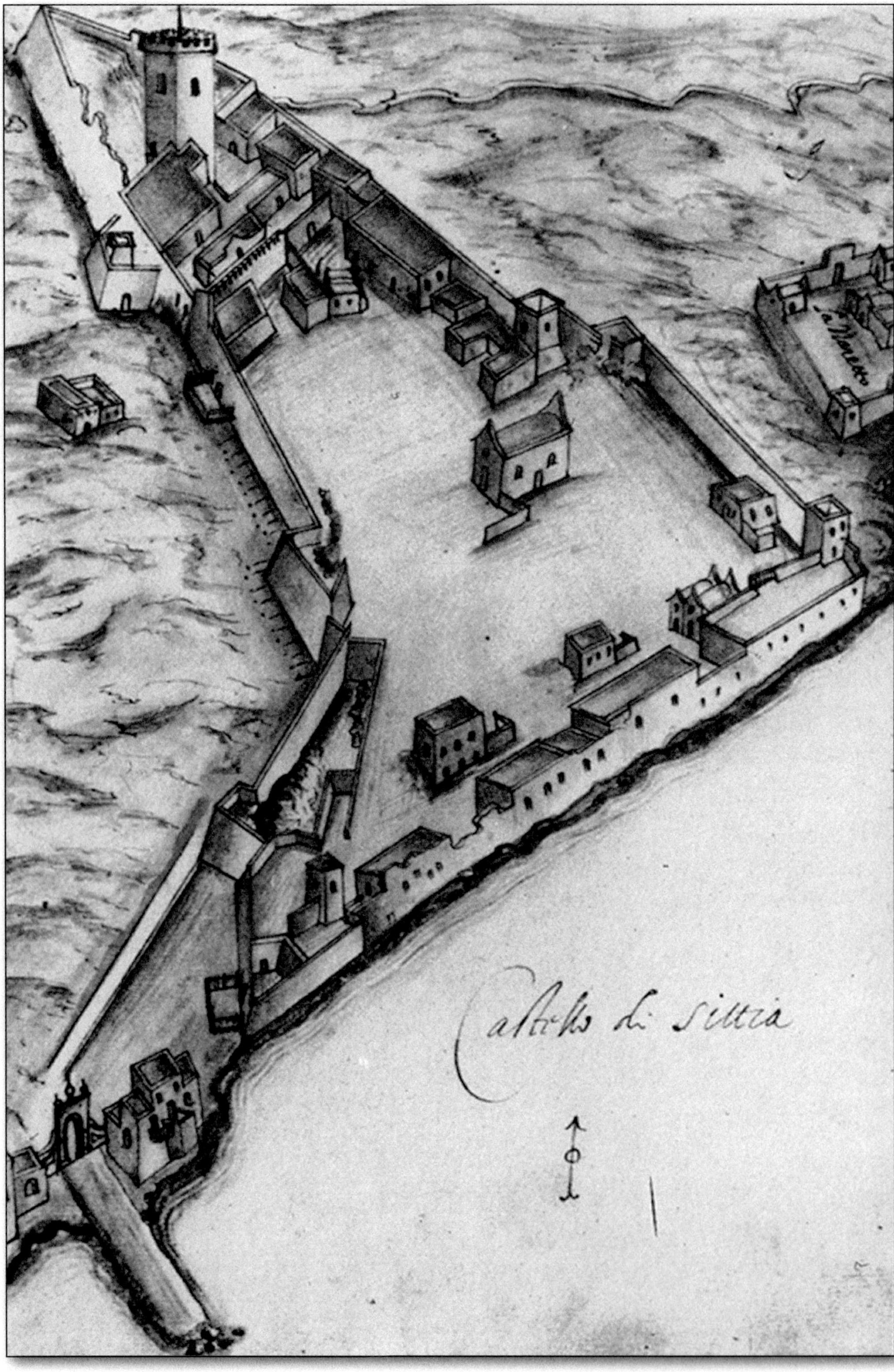
Castello di Sittia

Illustrations 26–29, pp. 70–74

26. Map of Crete with the islands of Suda, Spinalonga, with Gramvousa, the only bases remained under Venetian control at the end of the war. These ports represented useful terminals for the Venetian strategy and a constant treat for the Ottomans communications. Suda Island was besieged three times between 1649 and 1663, but the Venetians repulsed all the assaults. (*Theatrum Europeum*, Frankfurt am Main, 1670).

27. The fortifications of Chaniá were built around the medieval castle on the highest point near the port. The perimeter followed the outlines traced in 1540 by Michele Sanmicheli, characterised by short and not very thick curtains. The harbour with the arsenal, although several flaws, was considered as one of the major ports all over the Eastern Mediterranean. In 1645 the garrison numbered 800 Italian and *Oltramontani* footsoldiers with hundreds of militiamen, who were later joined by another 270 men and 100 armed monks. The city surrendered on 22 August 1645, after 54 days of siege.

28. Réthymnon was the third Cretan town per number of inhabitants, however in the early 17th century provveditor Luca Michiel described it as "a miserable and desolate city". Réthymnon suffered considerable damage during the incursion conducted by Ulug Ali in 1571, and after two years it was necessary to build a new curtain. The project for new fortifications was designed in early 17th century by Sforza Pallavicini. The defences were strengthened before the siege of 1646, but the city resisted for only 24 days. The garrison consisted of about 600 Italian, French, Corsican and Dutch soldiers. (Author's archive)

29. Described as open space, weak, old and ruined and without a port, Sithya lay distant from the major Cretan cities and nearly isolated, indefensible and exposed to raids by privateers. Before the Ottoman occupation of 1651 the Venetians decided to slight Sithya to prevent enemies surprising the place "away from relief".

bishop would be appointed for the first time, the choice to be agreed between the Cretan nobles and the Catholic archbishop. But though the agreement of 1299 is sometimes presented as a great advance for the people of Crete, the main beneficiary was undoubtedly the native aristocracy.

The Venetian officials administering Crete were, from the beginning, essentially the same as those that Venice later established in Cyprus, and reflected the power system of Venice itself. The head of the administration was a Venetian noble governor based in Candia/Iráklion with the title of 'Duke of Crete', assisted by two counsellors. This office remained in charge, even with several interruptions, until 1668. Subordinate to the governor were the captains of each of Crete's province, initially six and later reduced to four. Military command was exercised by the *governatore delle armi* sent from Venice, and each of Crete's fortresses had its own commander. Superior to all of these, including the Duke of Crete, was the *provveditore generale del regno di Candia*, at first appointed only intermittently in times of crisis but from 1569, when the Ottoman threat to Cyprus had become obvious, the office became permanent.

Both the general provveditor and the Duke of Crete were appointed in Venice and sent out to Crete for only two years. Venice persisted with this policy in both Crete and Cyprus in spite of its obvious drawbacks. Probably this was in part because Venice was afraid that long-standing colonial administrators would build themselves a threatening power base, partly because candidates would not want to neglect for too long their political careers in Venice. In fact, several general provveditors later became Doge.

But the inevitable problems caused by the short term of the arrangement is clear from the protests of the inhabitants.[3]

In the European trading system Crete represented the natural port for the trade from northern Europe with lead, tin, metal, wool, and the one which from the *Levante* exported wax, spice, grapes, silk, olive oil and, above all, salt, the most important product of the island, and for which Venice has been an actual monopoly for more than a century. Crete was the largest salt mill in the Mediterranean, whose production was able to support the island's economy, especially after the reforms introduced by Girolamo Foscarini in the late 16th century, which had reduced the dependence from Venice and strengthened the political bond between the capital and the Greek-Venetian aristocracy. As a dominant class, in a short time the Venetian-Cretan nobility extended its dominance over the countryside and the means of production. The political and economic set-up on the island strongly influenced the attitude of the rest of the population, maintained in a state of subjection by powerful landowners, thereby compromising the loyalty of the lower classes to the Republic. In spite of this intrinsic fragility, Crete represented for Venice the crown of its colonial empire, the royal dignity able to give to the *Serenissima* (the 'Most Serene') the same prestige as the great European powers, the last important domain remained in the eastern Mediterranean after the loss of Cyprus in 1573.

Venice had secured possession of Crete and in the following years established control of the island through granting military fiefs to Venetians. These fief-holders were granted land that had been taken from local landowners or the Church, and in return had to provide troops, cavalry if the fief-holder was of a noble Venetian family and infantry if not. In the first century of Venetian rule an estimated 10,000 Venetians were settled in Crete. From about 1500 this system began to break down. Cretans were displacing Venetians by buying fiefs or subdivisions of them, and they began to occupy posts in the island's administration. By 1600 only 164 of the 964 fiefs in the Candia region were held by Venetians, the remaining 800 by Cretans.[4] This scenario, from initial Venetian dominance to later fusion of Venetian and Cretan interests, also happened in the relations between the Venetians and the Orthodox Church. At the start, Venice abolished the Orthodox bishoprics, and the bishopric promised in 1299 had a short life. Orthodox priests had to go abroad to be ordained, either to the Venetian possessions in the Ionian Islands where, curiously, Orthodox bishops were permitted, or to Ottoman territory. However, there was no ban on Orthodox churches, and by the 17th century there were 113 Orthodox churches on Crete and only 17 Catholic ones.[5] In 1602 the provveditor Benedetto Moro wrote that Catholics and Orthodox often went to each other's churches, and that Venetian officials should make a point of attending Orthodox services to show solidarity with

3 In 1629, citizens of Iráklion protested against a proposed new water supply. Besides claiming that it was impractical and unaffordable, they objected that the time left for the current provveditor was too short to finish the scheme, and that no provveditor ever completed the project of his predecessor, but each one preferred to prestart his own. See ASVe *Senato Mar*, R. 96, c. 38.

4 *Ibid.*, R 93, cc. 11–12.

5 *Ibid.*, *Collegio, Relazioni*, b. 80, Moro's relation dated 24 May 1601.

30. Alongside the engineers van Wert and van Bor, active in Crete from 1645, the Republic of Venice recruited other specialists in the Netherlands to direct restoration and modernisation of its fortresses. The engineer Henrik Ruse (1624–1672) played a very important role in Dalmatia, where he strengthened the defences of Split, Zadar and Sibenik, and later became member of the Venetian staff under Lunardo Foscolo during the sieges of Novigrad, Klis and Risano. (Amsterdam History City Museum, Collection of Prints)

the Cretans.[6] He also ordered that Catholic priests must not preach against Orthodoxy. In many ways the island had become a shared world.[7]

The Catholic Church was the main instigator of education in Crete, but frequently harried it. Cardinal Vissaríon, a Greek converted to the Catholic Church, founded a Greek school in Iráklion in the mid-15th century, but the Cretans distrusted it because the school propagated Vissaríon's support for the unification of the Catholic and Orthodox Churches. Schools to train Cretans as Catholic priests were established in Iráklion in 1592 and later in Chaniá and Réthymnon. The Jesuits established in Iráklion in 1585, but their extreme views scandalised the Cretan Orthodox, and 20 years later the Venetian authorities expelled them. A worse fate befell the Calvinists, champions of the Reformation, who started a school at Iráklion in the same period. The Catholic archbishop of Crete called for the public burning of their books, and the three teachers of the school were arrested and sentenced to imprisonment in Venice, the principal for life.

As schooling was uncertain, there was a demand for private tutors, and troops of the Venetian garrison were often employed to teach Cretan children. Only in the last century of Venetian rule was higher education properly established, with the founding of academies at Réthymnon in 1562, Iráklion in 1590 and Chaniá in 1637. This not only contributed to the Venetian-Cretan renaissance but produced a steady flow of Cretan students to universities in Italy, principally Padua. There, in the decades before the fall

6 *Ibid.*, b. 81, 1 August 1602.

7 A remarkable expression of these shared values was the so-called Veneto-Cretan renaissance of the last century of Venetian rule. In literature, the most famous figure was Vitséntzos Kornáros, author of the *Erotókritos*, a romance in verse of nearly 10,000 lines from an Italian source but with the action transferred to ancient Athens. Anachronistically the poem contains a fight between a Cretan and a Turk, perhaps a reference to the battle of Lepanto. Of the Cretan artists of the period, even the more prominent are little known outside Greece, with one exception: Dhoménikos Theotokópoulos, known as El Greco. Further reading: D. Brewer, cited work, pp. 219–227 and Molly Greene, 'A Shared World: Christians and Muslims in the Early Modern Mediterranean' (Princeton Modern Greek Studies), Princeton University Press, Princeton (NJ) 2001.

of Crete in 1669, 234 Cretan students are recorded as attending the medical school and 290 the law school, and other Greeks studied the same subjects.[8]

This idyllic shared world was not without friction, and one cause of it was Venetian recruitment of oarsmen for the galleys. Until the time of Lepanto enough free oarsmen could be recruited, for a limited period and for pay, but as the number of Venetian galleys grew and as service on them became increasingly unpopular there were not enough free oarsmen. Venice tried to solve the problem in various ways: by recruiting oarsmen abroad, in Dalmatia and in the mainland itself by using convicts. In Crete they drew on the pool of Cretan peasants who were registered for a period of compulsory labour as a form of taxation. The pool was large, some 40,000 men in 1629, but it was difficult to recruit even the 400 men needed for the peacetime galleys. Recruitment was brutal, as related in an anonymous report written in 1594:

> The provveditor gave the order for all those who were to be enlisted to come forward and present themselves. So, the men of the village aged between 15 and 50 came along, and all those who seemed to be the most suitable for service were enlisted in the usual way. Then they were rounded up in the barns or churches and when fifty or sometimes a hundred had been gathered they were chained up to each other in pairs so that they could not get away, and in the custody of the local noble and some horses they were promptly escorted to the galleys.[9]

Some villagers fled to offshore islands to escape galley service, some ruined themselves paying substitutes to replace them, and a recruit from Anópolis on the south coast hanged himself rather than serve in the fleet.[10]

Another cause of friction between Venetians and Cretans was the question about the agriculture of the island. In the 15th century Crete produced plenty of grain, especially on the fertile plain of Messarea in the centre of the south coast. There was enough to feed Crete and to export large quantities to Venice. But the same century saw a massive increase in vine-growing at the expense of grain, and Crete soon came to depend on imports of grain for three or four months of the year. These imports at first came from Ottoman territory until they were banned in 1555, and Barbary corsairs made grain shipments from any source dangerous. In the following decades vine growing became increasingly profitable. The troops stationed on Crete after the fall of Cyprus drove up wine prices, and pirates, especially English ones, came to Crete, "and bought up all the wine they could, paying fancy prices because they were so rich."[11]

The Venetian authorities tried a forcible solution to the problem. In 1575 they ordered vines to be ripped up to encourage grain cultivation instead, and there were more such orders in 1584 and 1602, which suggests that the policy was not working. Even when it did force a change of crops this was not necessarily to grain but often to olives, and in 1589 the provveditor confessed the failure of the reform, because olive tree cultivation was intruding on the

8 D. Brewer, cited work, p. 233.

9 Theocharis Detorakis, *History of Crete* (Iraklion: Detorakis, 1994), p. 196.

10 *Ibid.*

11 D. Brewer, cited work, p. 223.

growing of wheat, just as has happened with viticulture. The destruction of vines provoked an outcry that was a warning for the Venetians; the landowners declared that they would make "no distinction between being subjects of Venice or of the Ottomans"[12] that is that Venice's harsh measures risked losing Cretan support against any Ottoman invasion. But there were still advocates of Venetian rule by force. In 1616 the priest Paolo Sarpi, adviser to the Venetian state, addressed the Senate on how Venice could keep perpetual dominion over Crete. His ferocious polemic read, in part:

> For your Greek subjects of the island of Candia, the Greek faith is never to be trusted; and perhaps they would not much stick at submitting to the Turk, having the example of all the rest of their nation before their eyes. These therefore must be watched with more attention lest, like wild beasts, as they are, they should find an occasion to use their teeth and claws. The surest way is to keep good garrisons to awe them. Wine and bastinadoes ought to be their share, and keep good nature for a better occasion.

Regarding the Cretan nobles, Sarpi added:

> You must be very watchful of them; for besides the natural ferocity of the climate, they have the character of noblemen, which raises their spirits. If the gentlemen of these Colonies do tyrannize over the villages of their dominion, the best way is not to seem to see it, that there may be no kindness between them and their subject. It will not be amiss likewise to dispute all their pretensions to any particular jurisdiction; and if at any time their nobility or title be disputed, it will do well to sell them the confirmation of it at as dear a rate as possible: and, in a word, remember that all the good that can come from them, is already obtained, which was to fix the Venetian dominion; and for the future there is nothing but mischief to be expected from them.[13]

Venetians on the spot saw things differently, and were well aware of the need for Cretan support against an external attack, which was becoming ever more probable. In 1639 the provveditor wrote that the Cretan people:

> … must always be treated well so that they will remain faithful and devoted. Because when they are oppressed and used too much in forced labour by the fief holders and sometimes even by the representatives of the state, and subjected to extraordinary harshness, they are driven to despair. Then they abandon the kingdom and go to the Turks. They incite the enemy and open the way toward attacks, which perhaps the enemy would not otherwise have thought of.[14]

However, it was very late in the day for the Venetians to adopt a conciliatory policy towards their Cretan subjects, and too late to win their general support against the imminent invasion.

---

12 M. Greene, cited work, p. 64.

13 *Opere di F. Paolo Sarpi, servita*, Vol. V (Venice 1783), pp. 345–46.

14 M. Greene, cited work, p. 58.

In Crete on the eve of the war there were major garrisons in Candia, Chaniá, and Réthymnon, and in the forts erected on the islands of Suda, Gramvousa, Agios Theodoros and Spinalonga (Kalidon). In the early 17th century the regular forces were garrisoned in the following places:[15]

Candia	3,000 men
Chaniá	1,200 men
Rhéthimnon	800 men
Spinalonga	400 men
Suda	400 men
Gramvousa	400 men
Agios Theodoros	40 men

All over the Kingdom of Candia the regular army could be joined by other 10–12,000 *proli* (Cretan militiamen) in a relative short time, recruited from a total population of 220,000 inhabitants. It was believed that, after the general call of arms, at least 78,000 armed men could protect the island against an enemy threat. Possibly, some traditional judgement about the Cretan islanders could have motivated the government's disinterestedness for reforming the local militia. In 1602 the Venetian general provveditor described the military quality of the male inhabitants of Sphakiá:

> They surpass all the other (men) of Crete. This is not only because they are manly in appearance, competent and agile with muscular bodies, robust, proud, daring and courteous in manner. What most distinguishes them is their keenness of spirit, their greatness of soul, and their unrivalled ability to handle arms, whether bow or musket, in which they are exceptional. That ultimately is why they are without doubt the most daring, the most virile and the noblest of the men on this island.

Unlike this optimistic vision, already at the end of the 16th century the *provveditori* sent from Venice had revealed defects and the inefficiency of the local militia. Maintenance of the relationship between the population and the government in a critical condition was affected by the fact that the *Proli* remained under the leadership of the Creole aristocrats who, overriding feudal rights, privileged cavalry service and held all the command posts, relegating the population of the countryside to the infantry and subordinate functions, which made many Greeks reluctant to serve in the militia.

Though Venice treated its domain like a colony, Crete represented the crown of its royal dignity and the major overseas possessions. In late 16th century, the provveditor Luca Michiel noticed again to his compatriots that the Kingdom of Crete was not only one of the most beautiful and powerful states in Europe: "the major pillar of the strength and reputation of the whole Christian Republic". To assure the safety of their kingdom, the Venetian provveditors acted several improvements to the old fortifications. The most important renovation was managed by Giacomo Foscarini after 1577, who received from the Senate the

15 ASVe, *Senato Mar*, R. 102, c. 91, 3 April 1610.

31. Spinalonga was the main Venetian garrison in the Cretan islands. Control of a harbour such as this allowed Ottoman provisions to be kept under constant threat and permitted easy sailing in the Aegean sea. Ottoman attempts to seize this and other islands close to Crete were thwarted thanks also to the excellent state of fortifications and in spite of the small number of soldiers manning them. Venice possessed many more harbours like Spinalonga on the Aegean, Ionian and Adriatic seas, an example of which was Pago island, a little fortress on the Dalmatian coastline, manned only by 24 soldiers. (Author's photo)

32. The island of Gramvousa, a few miles off the north-west coast of Crete, was one of the countless harbours under Venetian control. The military system of the Republic shows a great interaction between naval forces and strongholds of the ***Dominio da Mar*** (overseas domains). It is not by chance that Cristoforo da Canal's 16th-century treatise on the Venetian military fleet had as its cover image a galley enclosed into a quadrilateral, whose corners are depicted with four fortresses. The idea of Venice strong at sea but weak on land must be interpreted under a different perspective, one which saw field army and navy as one. (Author's photo)

funds to improve the defences of the three major cities: Candia, Chaniá and Réthymnon. The provveditor found in the engineer Michele Sanmicheli a skilled and devoted specialist, who redesigned most of the fortifications and proposed many others works to ensure the defence of the major cities. Largest resources were allocated to Candia. The ancient city walls were improved between 1538 and 1539 by Michele Sanmicheli, as already proposed in 1518 by another skilful engineer, Giacomo di Campofregoso. Despite the work already undertaken at the end of the previous century, at the beginning of the war many of the defences were still incomplete. Technical delays and chronic lack of money had prevented improvements to the fortifications on the sea sides while many aspects remained obsolete compared to the cannons introduced by the Dutch engineers: the corner bulwarks were too small and distant from each other; the curtains too long; the ditches are not wide enough and flattened to conveniently repulse an assault: "... because a bastion can neither see nor defend the forehead of the other, and this is a fatal error."[16] The works continued until the eve of the 1648 siege with new platform for the artillery, the enlargement of the ditches and the provision of large amounts of land to erect elevated platforms, cover the casemates and fill the embankments.

Sanmicheli turned his attention also to Chaniá, but due the shortage of funds, the improvement was minor. Here the fortifications had been built around the castle on the highest point in relation to port. The walls around the city followed the new outlines traced in 1540 by Michele Sanmicheli, characterised by short and not very thick curtains. The three sides of the walls to the mainland were connected to the four bastions: San Salvatore to the north-west; San Dimitri to the south-west; Saint Lucia to the south-east; Sabbionera or Mocenigo to the north-east. Halfway across the southbound curtain, a large pentagonal platform was placed. Four elevated platforms were built about halfway up each curtain and two other great circular platforms provided the entrance to the bastions of Santa Lucia and San Dimitri. In 1645, outside the fortifications seems there were two half-moon redoubts to defend the gate of Réthymnon and the western curtain. Many observers described the fortifications pointing out the flaws, such as the bastions too narrow and acute, the undefended sides and especially the fact that the surrounding land was at a level above the town. On the opposite side facing the campaign lies the harbour with the arsenal, which – although with several flaws – was one of the major ports in the Eastern Mediterranean. In 1645, the garrison numbered 800 Italian and *Oltramontane* foot soldiers with hundred *feudati*, who they were later joined by another 270 militiamen and 100 armed monks.

Unlike Candia and Chaniá, in Réthymnon there was a major contrast between civilian buildings and military installations. The place was described by the provveditor Luca Michiel as "miserable and desolate city" that had developed around a rocky hill on which stood a castle of Byzantine origin, transformed into a fortified citadel around 1540 following the proposal of the engineer Michele Sanmicheli. Réthymnon suffered considerable damage during the invasion led by Ulug Ali in 1571, so that after two years it was necessary to build a new curtain. The project for new fortifications, designed by Sforza Pallavicini, followed a very simple scheme with four main bastions, three angular projections, a main gate to the east and two other minor gates in the west and north side. The works continued until the siege of 1646, but the city held out for only 24 days. In 1646, the garrison consisted of about 600 Italian, French, Corsican and Dutch infantrymen.

16 ASVe, *Provveditori alle Fortezze*, b. 56 (n.d), relation of Michele Sammicheli.

III

Judith versus Holofernes: Diplomacy and Strategy in the Cretan War

The image of Venice, with the semblance of the brave Jewish girl opposed to the Sultan, represented like the ruthless Assyrian general, became an icon that lasted long in the Western Baroque imagination as an idealised representation of the struggle for Crete. For the Ottomans, the conquest of the island represented a further step in the formation of the universal empire, the fulfilment of which was required by the Koran, at least according to the most credited interpretation of that age.[1]

At different times of the long war, the Venetians gained a position of advantage. Between 1649 and 1651, again in 1656, 1660 and finally in 1663–64, the *Serenissima* could play good cards on the green table of the war, but the Republic was not able to play it at its best because of concomitant factors, first of all the shortage of forces. In 1656, after the triumphal victory achieved in the Third Battle of the Dardanelles, the Venetians could easily turn their force to expel definitively the Ottomans from Crete. Instead, war council and Senate decided to conquer the islands in front of the channel, in order to continue the strategy of the blockade, without considering that the Porte would find other ways to supply his army.

After the failure of the assaults on Candia in 1648–49, the Ottoman army at Crete seriously risked being abandoned, deprived of supplies and without a leadership in Constantinople capable of formulating a new strategy. In Venice many people believed that, sooner or later, the Sultan would have agreed to the peace, and in the following years many others fell victims to this conviction. Such certainty was supported by previous experiences capable of convincing most of the observers. An assertion of Italian politics argued that the Sultan, while possessing powerful armies, was unable to keep his achievements for a long time, and news of revolts across the Empire

1 The *Serenissima*, according to a long series of eschatological theories, embodied the nascent Universal Empire at the service of the second coming of Christ on the Earth. A myth opposed to the Ottoman Empire, in which there was not much imagination needed to guess the Antichrist.

33. The Third Battle of the Dardanelles was fought on 26 June 1656 and ended with a catastrophic defeat for the Ottoman side, who almost lost the entire fleet, against the loss of only three vessels and 207 men on the Venetian counterpart. The defeat created a wave of panic in Constantinople, causing the court's flight from the Topkapi, fearing of an imminent enemy landing. (17th century German print)

seemed to confirm the predictions of an imminent retreat. To facilitate it, Venice tried to get in touch with the states interested in countering the Porte. After the outbreak of the war, Venice tried to obtain the support of the powers which faced Ottoman expansion, such as the Austrian and Spanish Habsburgs. Contacts were also established with the Black Sea Cossacks and the Croatian *banus* Miklós Zrínyi,[2] who openly challenged the Porte from his domains in Croatia and Hungary. More diplomatic missions and exchanges took place with Poland, Transylvania and with Moscow and the Cossacks too, but the chances of coordinated action never gained credibility and even the hypothesis of forming an alliance with Safavid Persia failed. From the beginning, the human and material costs of the war were becoming unsustainable for Venice, so the attempts to find an agreement with the Porte began in 1646 and continued uninterrupted until 1648, especially after the deposition of Sultan Ibrahim I thanks to French mediation. Despite the efforts, the negotiations failed and the French ambassador De La Haye paid for the consequences, being imprisoned in May 1649. The unstable Ottoman political situation of those years provoked serious problems to Venetian diplomacy. On 6 June 1652, Giovanni Cappello was appointed as extraordinary ambassador to the Porte and the instructions received from the Senate on 26 October had been granted the permission to show Venice's availability to pay a large indemnity and an annual fee to the Sultan, but any assumption for a cession of Crete was strictly ruled out. But as soon as this position became apparent, for Cappello also the Ottomans opened the terrifying prisons of the Seven Towers. The belligerents' positions remained for a long time: Venice was willing to return its achievements in the Balkans, but demanded the total withdrawal of the Ottomans from Crete. On the other hand, the Ottomans were determined not to leave the island. New negotiations were opened in the fall of 1657, just few months after the Fourth Battle of the Dardanelles. The historian Andrea Valiero reports on the outcome of the meeting:

> The *bailo* Ballarino, who was in Constantinople with the utmost restriction of avoiding any interruption of the negotiations, presented his proposals. He avoided of talking about the cities of Candia and Chaniá, so as not to irritate his interlocutor. Nevertheless, the grand vizier replied: "If the Republic wanted to buy with all the gold of the World a single stone or even a blind dog in the kingdom of Crete, the Grand Lord will never give it; rather he will prefer to lose the empire!" And the *mufti* added: "Candia will be ours, when we will and in the meantime, we will turn to another goal." Ballarino tried to answer, but he was interrupted by the grand vizier who said: "You know our requests: we want Candia, Clissa and all the fortresses in Bosnia; if you have the power to accept it, I will intercede with the Sultan, otherwise you can return to Venice."[3]

In 1658, facing the difficulty of maintaining the naval blockade at the

2 Andrea Valiero, *Historia della Guerra di Candia* (Venice, 1679), p. 56.
3 *Ibid.*, p. 457.

34. Reports from Crete nourished the ideal of crusade against the Ottomans, causing the mobilisation of volunteers and collection of funds to support the defence of Candia. However, there was also a practical aspect in this mobilisation, which resulted in the opportunity to gain experience, sending officers and crews to participate in the conflict: as did, for example, the King of Denmark in 1658, sending three ships in the Levant to join the Venetian fleet. The command of the squadron was assigned to Admiral Cort Adler, who participated in the naval campaigns until 1659, when Denmark withdrew its ships because of the ongoing war against Sweden. (Author's archive)

Dardanelles, the Senate was deliberately debating, and this time Venice was about to accept the Ottoman demands to completely surrender the island. It was a shattering dilemma, on which the Senate split into two factions. It was to determine whether, losing Candia, Venice would still be herself, even with a piece less, or lose her identity. Moreover, the exorbitant price required to defend the island was obvious to everyone. Doge Bertucci Valier was convinced, and not without reason, that finding an agreement with the Porte was inevitable. Despite the defeats inflicted to the Ottoman fleet, the blockade could be considered as failed and the senators took note of it. It was advisable to surrender the island now, with an agreement between two antagonists in which no one could proclaim as winner, rather than lose it after a bitter defeat. However, reasoning in terms of convenience was not enough, and without considering what it meant in terms of international political relevance. To persuade the senators to peace, it was to be shown that, even though Crete was surrendering, the role of the *Serenissima* in the European scenario did not diminish, and the Doge Valier sought to do so, arguing that Venice could wisely lighten a weight, "a burden" without any discredit. The Republic renounced to the island, only to this, but not to royalty. It was impossible to not consider that the conflict had already cost a fortune, much more than the famous arm amputated in Cyprus. The economic importance of Crete resided more than anything else in its ports, since the tax revenue of the island did not even cover the maintenance of its defence in peacetime. The mercantile traffic was increasingly shrinking, making clear how much the patriciate was now much more oriented towards land rents than to trade with the Levant. Yet, it was not enough to reason in economic terms when the prestige of the state was the main topic, and perhaps even its kingship. Because this was one of the cornerstones of the question: with Cyprus lost, the Kingdom of Candia was the only possession able to guarantee prestige in Venice. After all, the Doge continued, it would only be a matter of yielding "a shadow" because now, since the beginning of the invasion, "nothing is obtained from Candia but everything is sacrificed for Candia". Beyond the Kingdom, beyond the crown there was the 'royalty' and 'nobility' and these – according to the Doge – Venice has for itself without needing any piece of land to justify them.

However, the Doge did not succeed in convincing the majority of senators, who were represented by the position of the *savio* of the council Giovanni Pesaro. For him, the war was to be pursued to the utmost and all bargaining agreements rejected: "If we want to maintain the crown on our heads, we do not throw it at the ground, otherwise it will be said that we have lost the kingdom and the soul too!"[4]

Venice could not hope to prevail with its forces, and then the obligatory choice was to turn to other states, equally interested in rejecting the Ottoman offensive in the Mediterranean, or at least sign an alliance with the Republic. It is only by observing the Venetian policy, and the European scenario in general, that is possible to understand the motives of this exhausting indeterminacy and the passive defence strategy pursued by Venice. Although the Peace of Westphalia had been signed in 1648, at the western borders of the Venetian state, France and Spain remained belligerent until 1659. Getting concrete help from either of the two powers proved to be impossible, if not compromising the position of the Republic in the strategic context of northern Italy. To make the picture even worse, unexpected complications occurred, such as the uprising of the Fronde against the French monarchy in 1648 and 1649. Spain seemed less likely to help Venice at such time. Examples are the case of the viceroy of Naples, Duke of Arcos, who refused to send the galleys of Naples to the rescue of the Republic in 1646. At the grievances of the Venetian ambassador, the Spanish prime minister answered:

> ... (his Majesty) well recognised the prejudice that from disobedience to his orders resulted in the service, but this malpractice has become so common and the insolence in disobeying so widespread, that not a Duke of Arcos only, but a hundred of his ministers would have their heads cut off to remedy this disorder. But the conjunctures of the times do not allow it and persuade his Majesty to a disguised connivance, because the remedy was not worse than evil.[5]

Eventually a letter from the King addressed to Don Juan of Austria succeeded in unblocking the situation and the galleys joined the auxiliary fleet in front of Candia. The war between France and the Habsburgs also caused difficult to the viceroy of Naples, considering that in the two-year period 1647–48, the capital of that kingdom had become a battlefield after the uprising led by Tommaso Aiello, better known as Masaniello. As is easily understood, neither Philip IV nor his successor Charles II had any interest in opening a new front in the Mediterranean against the Ottomans, to help the Venetians.

---

4 *Ibid.*, p. 334.

5 *Relazioni ambasciatori veneti al Senato*, edited by Luigi Firpo, Vol. X Spagna, 1635–1738 (Turin: Bottega d'Erasmo, 1979), *Relazione di Spagna di Girolamo Giustinian ambasciatore a Filippo IV dall'anno 1643 al 1649*, p. 135. In this regard, it is enlightening a Senate's report written by Giacomo Querini, who was ambassador to the Spanish court between 1653 and 1656. He clearly emphasises how the frictions generated by the will of Venice, to maintain several relevant towns close to the state of Milan, in addition to prevent the Spanish expansion in Italy, it makes the Republic more an "enemy by nature" for Spain than a possible ally.

It was unthinkable to put at risk the Italian domains and exacerbate the already tragic situation of the state finances to help a state which was, in the end, a competitor in the Mediterranean trades, and both the Venetian ambassadors and the Senate were well aware of this situation.

Only in the second half of the 1650s did shadows on the European political scenario began to disappear, and at that point, to continue the war and find a capable ally for changing the strategic context, the choices were almost obligatory. After years of mutual distrust, relations between Venice and Paris became more cordial and, as a sign of willingness to sign an alliance, a grandson of Cardinal Mazzarino was welcomed in the Venetian nobility. Previously, from France had come some private help and for the rest only vague promises of more troops and ships, diplomatic pressure in Constantinople, and the promise to allocate contributions: too little for the expectations of Venice. The possibility of a French intervention alongside the *Serenissima* began to be considered in 1657, and then – through the mediation of the Duke of Modena – Paris' interest in a military alliance with Venice became more and more concrete. It was proposed that a contingent of 20,000 infantrymen and cavalrymen would be created between Modena and the Venetian Mainland, supplied by the Duchy of Este and the *Serenissima* and commanded by a captain to be nominated among a set of candidates proposed by Modena and Venice. The Senate examined the proposal, considering any possible reaction at international level. It appeared that the presence of French troops in northern Italy was a concrete threat to the *Estado de Milan*, which would then be encircled between the domains of Savoy, Modena and Venice. In view of a division of Milan, France was ready to cede to the Republic Cremona, the left bank of the Garda and other territories of the Milanese. The offer was naturally subordinated to a direct military commitment by the Venetians against the Spanish forces, and this circumstance had to be carefully examined, considering that Spain deployed strong contingents protected by remarkable strongholds, without taking into account that Madrid would certainly have fought with all its forces before surrendering to the aggressors. Venice need first to win in Crete, and only after begin the invasion of Milan. Turning to the French side immediately would have exposed Venice to the retaliation of Spain's allies, with all the attendant risks.

Moreover, Spain could influence the Holy See for not supporting the Republic in Crete and acting against the Venetian interests for a possible strategic collaboration with the Habsburgs of Austria, in case of the Vienna's involvement in Transylvania and Hungary against the Porte. Lastly, it was to be considered that as a retaliation for the alliance with France in an anti-Habsburg league, the Emperor could allow free access to the Ottomans through Croatia and Slovenia for an incursion into Friuli, as had happened in 1499 when the *akinçy* raiders had crossed the border to plunder the Mainland up to the province of Treviso. However, the support offered by a strong French contingent could represent the yearned opportunity to defeat the enemies and force the Porte to open a peace talks. At the end of several exhausting meetings, with great sense of responsibility, in 1658 the senate rejected the offers and disposed of the departure of the emissary sent by Mazzarino.[6] Despite this failure, a channel remained open with Paris to ensure the flow of aid promised by the Cardinal. In the winter of 1659–60, thanks to the mediation of the Duke of Modena, the French court had consented to the recruitment in France of volunteers for a Venetian landing in Crete planned for the following summer. When young Louis XIV began to move his first steps in the European political scenario, Venice had already realised that the goal was Continental supremacy and therefore his help seemed no less interested than Mazzarino's. With the French involvement in the Mediterranean, following the expedition against Algerian corsairs of 1664, Louis XIV began to consider the usefulness of maintaining the Venetian possession of Crete. However, the long awaited help materialised in 1669 did not change the bitter outcome.

35. Though intermittently, the Pope was the major ally of Venice, collecting aid in the form of money, troops, and ships. The drawing by Quinto Cenni presumably depicts a Papal officer and pikeman dated 1665–1670, showing the features of the military dress of those years. The coats, in red cloth, have a shape and typical size that was maintained into the next century, while there remain some differences in the breeches, in grey-azure: *Rhingraeve*-style for the officer on the left and broader and less fashionable for the soldier on the right. (Author's archive)

After the 1660s began the slow rapprochement with Vienna too, but the Austrian Habsburgs were in serious distress, and unlikely to help a state against which they had fought in 1617, and which had always prevented free access to the harbour of Trieste to trade in the Adriatic, without considering that a Venetian weakening was an event that Austrian chancellery did not despise at all. If the opportunity to get relief from the major monarchies seemed difficult and remote, not even the help of a great republic like the Netherlands was at hand. In 1648 the 'Seven Provinces' were victorious from the long conflict against Spain, but from 1652 to 1654 and then from 1665 to 1667 they had to support a series of challenging wars against England, while simultaneously they faced the Portuguese in the Indian Ocean and South America. From the Netherlands came to Venice technicians and sailors, but they were limited and very costly. Ultimately, though the relations between the *Serenissima* and the United Provinces remained friendly, in the mid 17th century, the enterprising Dutch merchants were beginning to represent fearsome competitors in the Mediterranean, capable of undermining the Venetian trade monopoly on those routes. Therefore, an even more significant presence of Dutch ships in the *Levante* was likely to turn into economic damage with catastrophic consequences for Venice.

Venice considered England too as possible source of help, but the mission appeared as difficult. In fact, the Cretan war aroused only a small impression across the Channel.[7] Yet, the English merchants were involved in the Mediterranean markets and it was precisely on this that Venetian ambassador tried to open a negotiation with London. An official appeal to the King of England emphasised the commercial interests that England had in

6 Brusoni, *Libro* XVI, p. 24.

7 In the English archives there are few official documents containing more than simple references to the conflict. The only impressions that left significant traces go back to the outbreak of war in 1645, and the final months from 1668 onwards.

36. In 1660, Duke Charles Emanuel II of Savoy recruited soldiers for the war in Crete to help Venice, as a result of their rapprochement. Previously, the Duke and the Republic had long been divided by the dispute for the title of King of Cyprus. Nevertheless, Turin and Venice continued to contend for a domain that, from 1571, had become a permanent Ottoman possession. (Duke of Savoy by Pietro Mignard; villa della Torre Valsassina, Ziracco, Turin)

the Mediterranean, fearing damage suffered to traffic, in the event that Crete turned into an Ottoman base, used by pirates and corsairs. In reality, for the English merchants, the Ottomans represented one of their main commercial partners and their presence in Crete did not pose particular problems to the transit of goods, if anything the contrary. Helping the Venetians and alienating the Sultan's benevolence was not a risk that could be run lightly and without directly considering the extraordinary gains that could be made in such a conflict.[8] British ships were hired indifferently to both the Venetians and the Ottomans, and many captains, if properly paid, were willing to transport supplies to Crete at their own risk. Not only ships but also gunpowder, weapons – the well-known English iron guns – and food supplies were bought and sold to both sides. In 1661, exasperated with the umpteenth case of the genre, Venice presented an official petition addressed to the King of England through its ambassador Francesco Giavarina. The ambassador complained that "for the transport to Candia of militias and munitions, the Turks had employed two English merchant ships" and underlined "the inconvenience is so great and considerable and if such abuses continue, the prejudice that would be affected not only by the Republic but by whole Christianity."[9]

In the following years, the presence of northern European ships decreased, especially with the outbreak of the first Anglo-Dutch war (1652–1654). The friction between the British and Dutch crews, who remained in service in the Venetian navy, was another direct consequence of the conflict. In December 1652, an English envoy arrived in Venice with the order to leave for Leghorn with all ships flying the St. George's jack.[10]

The international situation was so intricate that even conflicts in distant regions from the Mediterranean could have major repercussions. The war begun in 1655 between Sweden and Poland caused the intervention of the House of Austria, Denmark and Brandenburg and eventually involved the Ottoman Empire, which intervened to take into obedience the Prince of Transylvania, engaged in the war against Poland, a state that – like the Transylvanian prince – paid a tribute to the Sultan. Even minor disputes, such as the short wars of Bremen, Münster and East Frisia, fought between

8 R. Vaccher, cited work, p. 21.

9 *Ibid.*

10 ASVe, *Senato, Rettori*, f. 36, document dated 26 December 1652. There were 11 English ships in Venice and the Senate released seven, holding only the four which were in the dock for work.

1653 and 1666, contributed to making difficult any negotiations for signing agreements or receiving aid from the outside, especially as these conflicts tended to catalyse the professional soldiers in less inhospitable regions than the ones where Venice disputed the possession of Crete.[11] Even when the Venetian Senate allocated significant figures for aid with regards soldiers and war material, it was not always able to find the forces needed to conduct an offensive campaign and to drive out the Ottomans from Crete. Recruiting abroad also clashed with regional crises, as in Switzerland with the peasant revolt of 1653 and the First Villmergen War in 1656, which set Catholic cantons against Protestants. In practice, external aid, both in the form of military support or money, arrived mostly from Malta, France, some princes of Germany and the Italian states. Despite the religious difference, Venice with its heroic resistance gained considerable sympathy and admiration in

37. "Recruitment of a thousand infantrymen of Modena to help the Republic of Venice". The recruitment of soldiers for the Republic involved many Italian states, who agreed the capitulation of complete regiments or recruited volunteers in their own territories. Among the most eager Italian states to provide soldiers for Venice were Parma and Piacenza, the Pope, Savoy, Modena, Tuscany and even the small Republic of Lucca. (Illustration from *L'Idea di un Prencipe et Heroe Christiano*, **Modena 1659)**

11 Venetian ambassadors related also the negative propaganda, which hampered the effort to find recruits for Crete. A dispatch by Battista Nani, dated 3 July 1645, then just at the beginning of the war, warned the Senate that in France ran rumours of all kinds concerning the horrible situation of the Venetian troops in the Levant. Plague, disease, food shortages and generally bad conditions of life afflicted the soldiers who served there. Nani mentioned how such insistent rumours could seriously damage the *Serenissima* that just than was trying to enlist, in France, new mercenaries: "people tell of many thousands of deaths for hunger and illness, who are reduced to biscuit and water and without straw to lie down." These rumours came also to Cardinal Mazzarino who spoke with Nani: "the Cardinal told me something about Crete and because the sufferings and death reigning fiercely in the Levant "bewildered any thought of going there". ASVe, *Senato, Dispacci di Francia*, 3 July 1645, ff. 102–103.

38. Ferdinando II de' Medici, Grand Duke of Tuscany, here portrayed in Turkish dress. (Painting by Justus Sustermans, Palazzo Pitti, Florence)*

Protestant Europe and even in pro-Ottoman France.[12] Venice resorted to every means available to feed the flow of aid. Carnival festivities, which lasted for weeks in Venice, attired the nobility and crown princes from all over Europe, attracted by the extraordinary festivals celebrated in the Lagoon: opera, banquets and courtesans could be useful to convince some powerful state to support the Republic in the war against the Porte.[13]

Among the Italian states, the Pope's support was not always unconditional and its level fluctuated. Innocent X Pamphili's pontificate was not favourable to Venice, who had fought against the Ecclesiastical State in the Castro war of 1641–44, so that only with the pontificate of Alexander VII, begun in 1655, did political support and military aid become more consistent. In 1667, the new Pope Clement IX promoted a league to which France also adhered, and actually collected useful aid in ships, men and materials. The Pope's participation in the last two campaigns of the war was underlined by the appointment of his nephew, Vincenzo Rospigliosi, as general admiral of the allied fleet.

The demands of the war pushed the Senate to resort to extraordinary measures and diplomatic compromises, which contrasted the traditional Venetian foreign policy. Pope's concessions for the appointment of Venetian bishops and the return of Jesuits to the Republic served to proceed with the alienation of part of the treasure of St. Mark and to appropriate the annuities of the disbanded religious orders. Ultimately, the support of the Pope meant for Venice the renunciation of the ancient prerogatives of autonomy and much more. The Ottomans took advantage of Venetian secularism, influencing the decisions of the Constantinopolitan Archbishop in matters of religion, including with regard to the Greeks living under Venetian rule. In 1655, the religious question provoked an earthquake in Crete, when the Porte

12 The open support to Venice endangered a trickle of direct and indirect help, but never official, because most governments wanted to be on good terms with the Porte. Fleeting and partial exceptions were Oliver Cromwell, aflame with crusading zeal, and Robert Blake, his admiral in the Mediterranean. Blake was allowed to take action against the Tunisian corsairs in order to prevent them from joining the Ottoman fleet in the Aegean Sea, and on 4 April 1655, his squadron destroyed the Tunisian ships in the harbour of Ghar al-Mihl. See Julian S. Corbett, *England in the Mediterranean: a study of the rise and influence of British power within the Straits, 1603–171* (London: Longmans, 1917), v. I, pp. 258–266.

13 In this address, Venice sent to Paris the most famous of her composers of melodrama, Francesco Cavalli, who, despite his lack of enthusiasm, in 1662 composed the opera *L'Ercole Amante* to celebrate the wedding of Louis XIV and Maria Teresa of Habsburg. Further reading: *La circolazione dell'opera veneziana nel Seicento*, edited by Dinko Fabris (Naples: Turchini Edizioni, 2005).

39. Abaza Hassan Aga, *paşa* of Aleppo. He was the major troublemaker of the revolts in Syria and Anatolia against Köprülü Mehmed. Like other contemporary portraits of Ottoman personalities, this also is imaginary, but many details are represented accurately, such as the turban with a couple of feathers, distinctive for *paşa* and *beglerbeg*. (*Theatrum Europeum*, Frankfurt am Main, 1670)

pushed for the appointment of an Orthodox bishop on the island, an event that in the past Venice had opposed with all its strength and which now became a tool for obtaining the consent of the native population.

Without the anguish and the uncertainties of the Venetian diplomacy, the Porte could enact its strategy with little concern. After all, it was usual for a new Sultan to inaugurate his rule with a military conquest, and territorial expansion was at the root of Ottoman politics as a stabilising factor. For Sultan Ibrahim I and his counsellors the plan for conquering Crete appeared simple. The priority was a rapid establishment of a bridgehead, to be obtained after securing a port to set up a logistic base to supply the troops. Therefore, Constantinople was interested in landing as many men and materials as possible, and for this reason it was necessary to escort the troops between Constantinople and Crete avoiding the enemy and returning to the Bosporus as soon as possible. In order to succeed, the Porte sent spies and informers in the archipelago's islands who kept the Ottoman commanders informed, and on occasion spread false news about ships' movements to deceive the Venetians. The Porte was confident it would conquer Crete in two or three years at least, addressing no more than 65,000 soldiers and auxiliaries.[14] However, At the beginning of the hostilities, the Ottoman war machine had fallen foul of its poor preparation in completing the conquest of the island, especially when it was unable to secure supplies to the troops, and though after three years the Ottomans became masters of almost all Crete, with poor supplies and isolated by the Venetian naval blockade their possessions on the island represented little more than a bridgehead. Moreover, the Porte had to deal with its problematic political scenario.

The 17th century was a very turbulent and problematic period in Ottoman history. While the sultans consolidated its domains in Hungary with the peace of Zitvatorok in 1606, the Empire had lost several provinces in western Iran and most of the northern Caucasus. The political climate within the Empire was increasingly deteriorating. In 1640, the death of Murad IV caused a power vacuum that opened the way to the intrigues of the *valide* Kösem Sultan, who supported his son Ibrahim I's claim to the throne. The short reign of this sultan (1640–48): "magnified and exalted so much the ills of the state, (that) … none of the princes after him dared to give his name to their children".[15] The outrageous conduct of *dely* Ibrahim (mad Ibrahim) provoked the intervention of the janissaries, who deposed and assassinated him after the repression of the *sipahy* with the massacre of At Meydan, the ancient Byzantine hippodrome of Constantinople. The war against Venice

14 Von Hammer-Purgstall, Vol. X, p. 93.

15 Stanford J. Shaw, *History of the Ottoman Empire and Modern Turkey*, part one, p. 441.

reopened the ever-increasing spiral of inflation which led to the beginning of frightening economic chaos. The uncontrolled court extravagances of Ibrahim I and his unwise foreign policy against the Venetians, of blocking foreign trade from the ports of Constantinople and Izmir, paralysed whole sectors of the Ottoman economy. The currency was devalued repeatedly, and the Treasury resorted to collecting taxes two years in advance. Anatolia was crossed again by the bands of *celali*,[16] to which was added a local population exasperated by fiscal measures. Riots and revolts exploded in Constantinople too. As a result, the title of sultan passed to Ibrahim's teenage son, Mehmed IV, who was destined to remain on the throne for 39 years. Grand viziers were replaced with bewildering rapidity and the instability of the political situation resulted in internal chaos. A succession of 18 grand viziers held the post in less than 12 years. Internal conflict within the palace and civil unrest became the norm, fomented by the *haseki* (the sultan's first concubine), the *valide*, the janissaries and the major governors.

In 1656 new civil unrest broke out with political instability exploding initially in Egypt and Anatolia, and then extending into Syria. This insurgency was led by the governor of Aleppo, Abaza Hassan. Politically, the situation appeared desperate. In Western Europe several political observers reported that the Ottoman Empire was on the verge of collapse. But the deposition of Sultan Ibrahim I was not enough to restore order in the empire, and the following years were marked by a chronic political instability that heavily influenced military operations in Crete, almost causing the failure of the plan. This scenario resulted in frequent shift of strategy and change of campaign targets. All this had a detrimental effect on the overall Ottoman war effort.

By the end of 1650s the Porte had to face the Transylvanian crisis, which absorbed a significant part of his military forces, using almost three years to bend the resistance of an opponent whose strength seemed insignificant when compared to its armies. In the autumn of 1656, the task of appointing the new grand vizier fell to the *paşa* of Damascus, the former janissary and ultra-septuagenarian Köprülü Mehmed. Thanks to the efforts of this aged vizier, the empire stabilised and returned to be the menacing power of past centuries. Palace intrigues were repressed with energy, army discipline restored, and every dissent harshly eliminated. The *celali* revolts resumed their intensity, but soon crushed, with the execution of all the rebel leaders. By 1656 renewed disorders in Anatolia, the major Venetian victory over the Ottoman fleet outside the Dardanelles, and food shortages, led to panic in the capital and Mehmed turned to Köprülü Mehmed to rescue the situation. He had spent his life in the sultan's service, holding a wide variety of posts in the palace, central and provincial administration, the janissary corps, and on

16 The term *celali* is probably a misnomer. The misunderstanding begins with Ottoman court historians of the 17th century who referred to the rebellions as *celali* revolts after a certain Sheikh Celal, who raised a popular rebellion in Eastern Anatolia against the Ottoman authorities in 1519. Historians differ over the reasons for the *celali* rebellions. Some researches cite evidence of severe economic and social pressure in rural Anatolia caused by half a century of consistent population growth. Others point to the economic upheaval caused by the influx of cheap silver from the Americas; the drop in the real value of silver destabilised prices and led to rapid inflation.

campaign. He was living in retirement, aged almost 80, when his supporters at court persuaded Mehmed IV and his mother that he could succeed where all others had failed. He took office as grand vizier, with complete authority, on 14 September 1656. Essentially, Köprülü Mehmed Pasha, who remained in office until his death in 1661, and his son *Fazil* Ahmed Pasha, who served as grand vizier from 1661 until he died in 1676, reprised Sultan Murad IV's program. They made the system work by dismissing or executing those who abused it, tightly controlling expenditure, and increasing income. On land, Köprülü Mehmed faced challenges in the east and the west. In Anatolia, the weakness of the government had spawned a new uprising, led by Abaza Hasan Paşa, who sought to become the ruler of an independent Anatolia. The grand vizier defeated the rebels, who had reached Bosporus in 1658, and drove Abaza Hasan eastward. The revolt ended when Köprülü Mehmed Pasha offered the rebel leaders a truce, invited them to a banquet, and had them slaughtered. Some 12,000 rebels and sympathisers were executed before the grand vizier returned to the capital in 1659.

Köprülü Mehmed returned to the sultan a cohesive state and an army capable of expanding its empire on all fronts. Uniquely in Ottoman history, Mehmed also assured the succession of the post of Grand Vizier to his equally able son Ahmed. The action of both Köprülü permitted the Porte to regain power in the European political scenario, restoring the Ottoman military prestige. However, internal revolts and corruption had undermined the institutions of the Empire, and even though with the advent of the Köprülü government the disorder and excesses had been severely repressed, the political balances remained uncertain for a long time and the mechanism of the administration required many years to return to optimal efficiency. Moreover, the Porte had to face several menaces on other fronts, such as Cossacks raids on the Black Sea, the threat of Safavid Iran to the east, and the already mentioned crisis in Transylvania. The next, crucial, confrontation with the Austrian Habsburgs in Hungary, concluded with the defeat of Szentgotthárd-Mogersdorf on 1 September 1664. All these commitments contributed year after year to postpone the achievement of the Cretan conflict.

IV

Campo di Marte dell'Europa

In 1668 the general of the *Oltramontan* Friedrich von Spaar wrote: "... all good soldiers should go to Candia to refine themselves in the art of war",[1] exalting the valour of the defenders over a powerful and aggressive enemy like the Ottomans. The impressions provoked by descriptions and reports of the battles aroused in contemporaries the desire of emulation. This epic contributed to the rebirth of the chivalrous virtues and the crusading spirit. In this climate the Baroque mythology of the exaltation of the Christian faith transfigured in a heroic sense, destined to radiate throughout Europe until the Holy League war of 1683–99. The war's events caused a profound change in forms of communication too: treatises; novels; pictorial works and sonnets began to appear from the restricted circle of the European courts to influence a wider range of people, to form a kind of public opinion, propagating the desire to take part in the struggle. For this reason, the Cretan War attracted hundreds of volunteers who, at their own expense, arrived on the island to fight in defence of the *Serenissima* republic, pushed by heroic exaltation, but also by the opportunity to acquire war experiences that, once they returned to home, would be a merit for obtaining a prestigious military assignment. Participation in the conflict of a large number of soldiers from all over Europe led to the spread of a wide variety of combat disciplines and tactics, as well as the introduction of more up-to-date military organisation, all elements and novelties that would constitute a wealth of unmatched skills.[2] The mobilisation was so vast that it would bring to Crete soldiers who would never normally be involved in that theatre: alongside Greek, Slav, Italian, French, Swiss and German mercenaries, English, Irish, Dutch, and even

1 Valiero, p. 228.

2 Among the foreigners who went to Candia to watch the fighting was also Thomas Lynch, sent to Crete by Lord Arlington, demonstrating the attention of the English government to the Cretan situation. Thomas Lynch wrote a letter from Crete describing two of the most representative episodes of the last months of the siege: the failure of the great French sortie of 1669 and the bombardment of Ottoman positions by the whole fleet. After about twenty days he left for Venice, judging, rightly, that the end of the city was near. Lynch became famous as governor of Jamaica; he was the organiser of the Jamaican buccaneers movement as well as their dissolution. See Kris Lane, *Blood and Silver: A History of Piracy in the Caribbean and Central America* (Oxford: Signal Books, 1999), pp. 128–129.

Danish sailors also fought for Venice. On the other side, a *koiné* of equally diverse nationality was deployed: Turks; Armenians; Egyptians; Syrians; Circassians; Kurds; Bosnians; Bulgarians, without forgetting the case of the Albanians, who, together with the Greeks and the Slavs, fought on both sides.

The Maintaining of the War Machines

With extraordinary effectiveness, the historian and economist Carlo Maria Cipolla classified the war as a 'negative economy' in which soldiers represent the workforce, while weapons are the capital. The conflict between Venice and the Porte for the possession of Crete is perfectly declined in this representation, since it was a conflict that involved the whole war apparatus of both the contenders and dilated exorbitantly the logistical effort, catalysing every economic and financial resource. According to 19th century historian Carlo Botta, in Venice the war consumed every year between four and five million French Francs 'in numbered coin'[3] and three times as much in ammunition and other resources, while between 1645 and 1669 the Venetian State's revenue remained around three million ducats and in any case it never exceeded four million. In 1668, the Venetian ambassador to Rome calculated that the war had cost the Republic 4,392.000 ducats a year. When some years later at the end of the conflict it tried to estimate the total spent, the figure that emerged was around 125 million ducats,[4] which increased the Republic's debt to 64 million in 1671.[5]

It was a very considerable financial effort, whose dynamics have recently been focused in the contest of the general Mediterranean crisis on the 17th century, in which, however, the Venetian state represented a laboratory of economic transformations.[6] After the crisis culminating in the plague of 1630, the Venetian economy was able to see signs of recovery after 1650, confirming a tendency that emerged in the previous years.[7] However, the existence of the expenses forced the Venetian government to resort heavily to credit to finance the war. After 1645, Venice continued the custom of financing military spending through the contributions of the richest families, and this practice was practiced until the end of the conflict. Initially, this system provided that citizens would voluntarily donate money and later the government would commit itself to return the sum paying a small interest. Nevertheless, with the

3 Carlo Botta, 'Storia d'Italia continuata da quella del Guicciardini sino al 1789', vol. 27, p. 97.

4 Luciano Pezzolo, 'Stato Guerra e Finanza nella Repubblica di Venezia fra Medioevo e Prima Età Moderna', in *Navies and State Formation*, Volos, 9–12 September 2004, p. 108.

5 Some Toronto University students have tried to calculate the war expense incurred by the two sides in relation to its contemporary economic value, suggesting 15 billion dollars for Venice and maybe double for Constantinople. Thanks to Chun L. Wang for noticing this research.

6 The most decisive signals came from agriculture, as evidenced by the technical improvements introduced on the Venetian Mainland. The demographic growth that occurred after the plague, though not exceptional and more evident in the countryside than in the cities, is more evidence of the flow of capital to the Mainland. See Luciano Pezzolo, *Il fisco dei veneziani* (Verona: Cierre Edizioni, 2003), p. 213.

7 *Ibid.*

beginning of hostilities this practice was no longer capable of dealing with the huge expenses needed for the war campaigns, so the practice was introduced of requesting forcible interest loans on all citizens based on their economic wealth. The war accelerated the consolidation of a crucial financial innovation that ended up transforming these deposits into long-term debt, reimbursed by allocating some of the tax revenue. In 1645, a few weeks before the war, the Senate had granted seven percent interest to the meritorious people who had signed a 60,000 ducat loan for the annual nourishment of a regiment of 1,000 Italian infantrymen. This financial policy provided the government with large amounts of money at relatively low cost and without excessive pressure on citizens, but on the other hand it deprived important resources to the civilian economy, condemning the state to remain debtor to its subjects for many years. In addition to the financial effects, debt consolidation contained important political implications, because Venetians themselves became creditors involved in the war. The government maintained rigid taxation in order to obtain money from business transactions and freight rates. The appointments to *procuratore* too were charged with a tax of 10,000 ducats, and the number of *procuratori*, increased by only three members in 1643, grew by another 40 during the war. From 1646, in the desperate attempt to find money to fuel the resistance in defence of the kingdom under siege, the government introduced the sale of the nobility license at the price of 100,000 ducats. This was a considerable figure, albeit relative to the general war costs, as the purchase of the aristocratic status permitted the yearly maintenance of a 1,000 *Oltramontani* infantry regiment. Practically anyone, through the payment of the sum, could enter with his family into the Golden Book of the nobility and therefore aspire to a government office. In the course of the conflict, the Republic cashed in this way 8,000,000 ducats. In 1647, to encourage the offer, it was even decided to set up a lottery to which 10 families at a time could subscribe paying 10,000 ducats each.[8] Soon, the war did raise beyond all expectations the costs necessary for the defence of the kingdom, and with this the search for money to finance the conflict increased dramatically. The economic effort represented a tremendous blow for the public treasury. According to a report dated 1650, the ordinary costs for the maintenance of the troops grew to 500,000 ducats, to which were added further 200,000 ducats only for the troops in Candia.[9] Fourteen years later, the three State Treasury Deputies estimated a state budget deficit of one and a half million ducats, a huge sum if one considers that ordinary entrants amounted to 3,600,000 ducats.[10] A decisive aid to the financing of the war was materialised by the gains obtained with the monopoly of the currency exchange rate. Monetary control proved to be an excellent remedy to keep under control the economic situation in the besieged city. In addition

8 *Ibid.*, p. 213. Another measure had bitter consequences for the communities, namely the sale of public land to private individuals. This act provoked an authentic drama for the families of peasants who had exploited this land. Instead, it constituted a real deal for the Venetian patriciate who, having money to spend, obtained large lots of land. This is one of the many contradictions of a patrician who, while supporting the continuation of the conflict to the end, proved unable to victoriously conclude it.

9 ASVe, *Miscellanea Codici*, I, *Storia veneta*, 117, c. 51.

10 *Ibid.*, *Senato, Rettori*, f. 61, 6 February 1664.

to the fact that the troops in the Levant were paid with the currency in use overseas, which had a lower value than the one used in the Venetian Mainland, the government also authorised the issue of a 'siege currency'. It was a small copper coin minted specifically to pay the garrison. Since this coin circulated essentially to pay the soldiers, in a short time it began to devalue until it lost almost a third of its original value. In this way, the *Zecca* of San Marco could nominally pay the troops at the nominal value of the Mainland's currency, but at the real cost of the one coined for the siege. All this produced every month a saving of almost 30 percent on soldiers' salary expenditure. This measure, beneficial to the Venetian government, had dramatic effects on the soldiers, who found themselves with a coin that was worth practically nothing outside of Candia. This effect afflicted above all the officers, who, already damaged by the delay with which the salary was paid, became indebted and reduced themselves to only bread or garrison biscuit.[11] The lack of cash for paying the officers and the consequent delay of the salaries reduced them practically in poverty and caused severe desertion among their ranks. When it was no longer possible to find loans or credit, or to defer payments, Venice resorted to every possible expedient it could find. In some cases, it was from within the garrison that some funds for the continuation of resistance came. In February 1657, the provveditor Andrea Corner informed the Senate: "Having disposed of every substance of the suppliers and of others, I was helped by divine providence by ways never devised before." The divine ways, of which the provveditor refers, had the features of two French aristocratic *venturieri* who fought in Candia. Corner persuaded both to lend 15,000 ducats "with the obligation to return it immediately as soon as I received the public subsidies." This money was immediately spent to pay a third of the salary to the garrison.[12]

If Venice somehow managed to fuel the flow of money required for financing the war through the growth of its economy, debts and other expedients, in 1645 Constantinople was in a situation that today we would define as stagnation, if not actual economic crisis. Although the Ottoman sultans ruled over a vast empire and had considerable resources, corruption and bad administration had favoured the decline in the efficiency with which the state previously found the capital for financing its war of conquest. Traditionally, before any campaign, the Sultan and his high dignitaries calculated and evaluated the costs of war, supplies and requisitions to ensure the logistics of the army in the field, before embarking on a large-scale expedition. The Ottoman divan also reviews the financial benefits of territorial conquests with, notably, the development of fiscal resources, the military garrison, the exploitation of servile labour, and the construction of buildings for a strategic purpose.[13] Wars of conquest were the main political goals of the sultans, who based their prestige on victorious campaigns and a good outcome could be useful for hiding drawbacks in state affairs.

---

11 *Ibid., Senato, Dispacci di Provveditori*, b. 550, relations dated 30 November 1656 and 1st February 1657.

12 *Ibid.*, b, 549, *Relazione* of Andrea Corner, 24 March 1655.

13 See J. Strauss, 'How Cyprus Came Under Turkish Rule: A Conquest and the Historians', in *Wiener Zeitschrift für die Kunde des Morgenlandes*, vol. LXXXII, 1992, pp. 323–34.

When the conquest of Crete was planned, and the war began, the immediately available solution for financing the campaigns consisted in the increasing of fiscal policy on sources of income that could not escape taxation, namely trade and agricultural production. The result was the paralysis of the economy of whole provinces. The sultans has contributed to worsen the scenario, being responsible for the enlargement of the court apparatus. The *Topkapy*'s staff, established by Süleyman the Magnificent, fixed the overall staff to 350 employees. In addition to the administration staff, the personnel included a large number of clerks, who carried out all the tasks of the complex court ceremonial, from the most important to the bizarre, such as guardian of the peacocks' feathers, the guardian of nightingales and parrots, or the servant in charge of carrying an icy water pitcher during the great lord's walks. In addition to these often well paid employments, the sultans managed a crowd of pages who, being 40 established by Süleyman, had become 70 under Ibrahim I. He added other expenses for maintaining the exorbitant number of concubines, which reached the record number of 270, and some of them benefited from an annuity equal to that of a provincial governor.[14] Obviously, such administrative disorder led to an uncontrolled rise in expenditure, which triggered a financial crisis with a catastrophic outcome. The devaluation of coins and the increase of taxes fed the protest, forcing the government to send troops to repress the riots which exploded in many provinces. In 1648, even the population of the capital rose up. The unexpected halting of the Cretan conquest plans caused a violent military and political crisis, and resulted in a new wave of violence. On the other hand, the Janissaries instigated a fierce struggle against the military leaders who were hostile to them. The government demonstrated its inability to face the situation and as prisoners of rivalry and favouritism, the ministers turned to the old sultan mother Kösem, who turned to play a deplorable political role.[15] Venality spread to all ranks, so much so that even the governorship and ministerial offices were sold. The government's action, conducted through the work of complacent officials, contributed to making the scenario even worse. In response to the blockade of the Dardanelles channel by the Venetian fleet, the sultan – poisoned with rage – ordered the suspension of trade licenses to all Western commercial companies; then, faced with the risk of a paralysis of commerce, he revoked the order, confining it to the Venetian trade alone. The dramatic situation was expressed in clear letters by a court official:

> The sultan is hostage of brigands, the harem women command and everything is sacrificed to their whims; all this while the Venetians have penetrated into Bosnia and hold the access to the Dardanelles. The population is ruined, the empire can no longer bear such a state of affairs.[16]

In August 1648 Ibrahim I was deposed and strangled, and his son Mehmed IV, just 11 years old, was placed on the throne: a docile instrument in the hands of factions in a struggle for power. The devaluation and speculations ruined

14 Von Hammer-Purgstall Vol. X, p. 456.

15 Bombaci-Shaw, cited work, p. 439.

16 Von Hammer Purgstall, vol X, p. 222.

the monetary system and the government was for a long time unable to put finances in order. Many historians agree that it seems almost impossible that the Porte managed to continue the war in such a disastrous financial situation and in the most total political chaos. In 1652 began a brief period of good political management, thanks to the government of the grand vizier Tarhonçu Ahmed, a man of integrity and great character, but the rigorous measures taken by him were not appreciated by the regime's profiteers, who ultimately made him destitute in March 1653. Rebellions and mutinies in the army had shaken the empire to its foundations and a few people thought that the Porte would have continued the war against Venice.

Already before the war, the government became conscious of the need to modernise both army and navy and stored resources for the objective of achieving closer parity between the oared and the sailing ships. Fiscal constraints delayed the full achievement of this goal, but the realisation of the need was the product of its wartime experience three decades earlier. In general, the educational value of defeat for Ottomans should not be underestimated. The loss endured by their forces on land and sea strengthened the resolve of Ottoman military leaders to impose a higher standard of discipline. However, for supporting these objectives the government had to reform its economic policy. In 1630 military expenditure formed 77 percent of the Ottoman budget, and in 1670 this had decreased to 62.5 percent.[17] The salaries for these troops amounted to 133,424,896 *akce* per year,[18] equal to 46.6 percent of the overall court personnel expenditure. This proportion seems even more relevant if we consider that after 1648 many of the expenses necessary to maintain the huge apparatus created by Sultan Ibrahim I had been cancelled. The biggest expenditure item was, as stated above, military salaries, usually paid quarterly but in fact often in arrears.[19] These demands had been exacerbated by the price revolution of the last century and subsequent coinage devaluations. Since the military received quarterly wages, every three months the government had to hand out massive amounts of silver coin. But most taxes were paid on an annual basis, and because of the discrepancy between the solar and lunar calendars, every 33 years there was a lunar year in which payments had to be made but no taxes were assessed; in times of financial difficulty the resulting deficits were carried over from year to year. Moreover, many taxes were traditionally paid in kind.

---

17 Linda T. Darling, 'Public Finances: the role of the Ottoman centre', in *The Cambridge History of Turkey*, vol 3; (Cambridge University Press, Cambridge, 2006), p. 118.

18 Marsigli, pp. 195–201. The *akçe* was a conventional currency calculated to the silver value. An annual revenue of 2,000 akçe was considered as a good income; a *kapikulu* high officer earned in one year about 8,000 *akçe*.

19 Arrearages of pay were always dangerous during wartime, when soldiers might refuse to fight if unpaid, or in the capital, where unpaid soldiers could and did threaten high officials, and even the Sultan himself: "The chroniclers record numerous pay revolts by the standing army or the army in the field. The first serious one being in 1586 when the government attempted to pay the soldiers in newly debased coinage worth only half of its former amount. A revolt in 1600 protested against the granting of tax farms to wealthy civilians instead of cavalrymen as well as the payment of salary arrears in debased coin. Similar complaints, together with Sultan Osman II's plans to reduce or eliminate the standing military forces, ignited the revolt of 1622 that ended in the Sultan's deposition and death." LT. Darling, cited work, p. 122.

In the first half of the 17th century, the Porte faced and met the challenge of altering the taxation system to a cash basis. Traditionally, tax levels were more or less fixed, but changes in the relationship between gold and silver allowed the government to raise nominal tax rates set in silver *akçes* while keeping them fixed in terms of gold. By this means the *cizye* (head-tax payable by non-Muslims) was raised from 50–80 *akçe* in the mid sixteenth century to 240 *akçe* in the mid seventeenth; the latter figure was supplemented by sheep and wine taxes and salaries for the collectors to a total of 325 *akçe*. For financing court and army, the government introduced a new system of taxation on an annual or extraordinary basis. As the incidence of occasional taxation increased, provincial officials began to collect their own version of the extraordinary levy, which was illegal but tolerated because of the ancient Ottoman tradition of allowing governors to collect their own revenues. Another locally collected tax which had a clear link with the war expenditure, was the *imdad-ı seferiye* (campaign assistance), collected by provincial officials and notables to reimburse themselves for wartime loans to the government or to pay for additional *toprakly* provincial troops.[20] Special taxes were paid also by the *timar*-holders, like the *Timar bedeli*, paid by *timars* who did not serve on campaign.

After 1630, however, many taxes began to be collected by agents of a provincial finance supervisor, but even in the 17th century, most taxes had been collected by soldiers, either *timar*-holders or members of the standing army. Assigning tax collection to members of the permanent army augmented their salaries in a period of severe budgetary deficits and provided the central government an effective, if temporary, enforcement arm in the provinces. The 17th century also saw the creation of new taxes, some legal and some illegal. As the extraordinary levies became ordinary, new 'extraordinary' taxes were introduced in times of extraordinary need. In the meantime, the financial bureaucracy had adapted in an ad hoc fashion to the needs of the period. As the centrally controlled taxes gained in importance, the central bureaucracy grew to accommodate its increased workload. From about 65 salaried members, the staff expanded to approach 200 by the mid 17th century. Moreover, the presence of other collectors for tax revenues besides the treasury and the military forces made it more difficult for the central government to meet its expenses. Tax-collectors making their rounds were entitled to bed and board from the villages they visited, but their entourages tended to grow and their stays to lengthen. Discharged military men, such as *timar*-holders who failed to appear at muster or men enlisted only for a single campaign, took up lives of banditry, either stealing tax revenues outright or imposing extra levies on peasants and villagers.

The spiral of the tax system, increasing fiscal demands, and catastrophic administration, forced the Porte to licence extreme and unpopular measures. In 1655, in order to meet the primary expenses and to pay the salary to the troops, the government resorted to new extraordinary taxes, confiscation of

20 Halil Inalcik, 'Military and Fiscal Transformation in the Ottoman Empire, 1600–1700', *Archivum Ottomanicum* 6 (1980), 283–337, at pp. 318, 323–7.

goods and low-value coinage which has remained famous such as 'tavern coin' or 'Bohemian coin'. The introduction of this coin immediately gave rise to a rebellion by the janissaries in the capital itself. Paid with the new currency, they soon discovered that no one wanted to accept it, because it was too devalued. The consequences were brutal and in order to appease the janissaries, the sultan ordered, on their request, the death sentence for 30 dignitaries of the court, considered mainly responsible of the crisis.[21]

The economic situation remained precarious for a long time. In 1648 the Imperial treasury had recorded revenue of 362,000,000 *akçe* but, had sustained expenses for 550,000,000. The deposition of Ibrahim I failed, immediately, to change the situation and in 1653 to face an increase in revenues to 532,000,000 *akçe* there was a further increase in expenditure which came to 677,000,000 *akçe*.[22] The only way to reduce public spending would be to cut military spending, which would reduce the number of soldiers. With the war in progress this was not possible, indeed, in order to end a revolt in Anatolia the grand vizier was forced to legitimise the acquisitions of the rebels and to incorporate them into the army, resulting in an increase in military spending.

Finally, on 15 September 1656, at the head of government was designated the elder Köprülü Mehmed, a personality with remarkable energy and animated by the feeling of greatness of the Empire. The new grand vizier succeeded in obtaining full powers, which he used with ruthless and sometimes cruel rigor, but he was the master of the Ottoman rebirth. After restoring the order and authority of the government in Constantinople and in Anatolia, Egypt and Syria, the grand vizier resumed the fight against Venice. After him, his son Ahmed, who succeeded after his father's death in 1661, would gain the mark of victory by completing the conquest of Crete. Under these grand viziers the Porte realised a number of tangible and intangible benefits from its experience of war.

As a comparative instance, it should be interesting to compare the economic resources required for launching and maintaining one of the main instruments of the Cretan War: the galley. For purpose of easy comparison, it will be most convenient to use the classic Ottoman galley of 24 benches and the similar Venetian *galera sottile*. In 1650, the coast of building and operating an Ottoman galley resulted in 1,280,000 *akçes*. Production and armament accounted for 45 percent, while the cost of crew's salary for six months of campaign represented 38.75 percent. Finally, the provisions add the remaining 13.25 percent.[23] For the Venetian counterpart, in 1660

21 Von Hammer-Purgstall, Vol. X, p. 344.

22 Geoffrey Parker, *Global Crisis: War, Climate Change and Catastrophe in the Seventeenth Century* (New Haven, CT: Yale University Press, 2013), p. 197. However, these figures resulted in large part from revenue rights paid in advance. This system provided for the stipulation of a contract with a private person to whom the levy of taxes of a given province was contracted. The person who received the contract had to pay immediately to the royal treasury a pre-established sum. The convenience for the central power was to transform a future, uncertain, entrance into a pre-paid income. In practice, in 1653 the Ottoman Empire, thanks to this system, had already received the future income of several taxes.

23 Murphey, *The Ottoman Resurgence in the Seventeenth-Century Mediterranean*, cited work, p. 189.

the overall cost was 17,076.7 ducats for the production and weapons and 16,854 for crews' salary and provision.[24] Considering the difference between the cost of life in the Ottoman Empire and in Venice, this figure suggest that for Venice the production was less expensive but conversely crew and maintenance resulted in a major cost.

It is difficult to identify the different elements, which produced these results. Without doubt, for the Ottoman case, the easier explanation is speculation and fraud. Probably certain captains tried to enrich themselves as much as possible at the expense of the public, almost to avenge themselves in advance of the inquisition, to which, inevitably, they were subject at the end of their tenure. Definitively they acted in a similar way as their enemy. The captain general as well as the *kapudan paşa* exercised the right to reserve for themselves part of the war booty or the prisoners for ransom; the same rights were demanded by Maltese and Italian auxiliaries, but during the war many other enrichment systems were pursued. Though there were suspicions about the legitimacy of the fortunes accumulated by the commanders in Venice, only Constantinople had certainty about the illegal origin of the fortune accumulated by certain commanders, but the corruption was so widespread that few noted this. Possibly, one of the factors that contributed to the extension of the conflict, should be sought not only in the belligerents' strategic options and contingencies, but also in the accumulation of capital generated by the war itself. The Ottoman military class had a strong interest in obtaining the greatest gains as possible from a conquest war, and despite the occupation of Crete not materialising in a few years, as hoped, the pursuit of wealth ended up moving towards other opportunities. These were risky choices, however practicable in the context of the corruption and mismanagement into which the Empire had fallen. These dangers, associated with the prolongation of the conflict, were not just the ones relating to the speculation and malpractice that could affect the officers: rather, the heavy defeats suffered on the sea and the loss of territory in Bosnia were not taken into account, in any case, the hypothesis of a defeat was never considered by the government and this attitude guaranteed the continuation of the war. As indirect confirmation, there are the huge fortunes accumulated by many profiteers, as well as the anomaly in the Ottoman Empire's history of a long-lasting conflict like the Cretan war. Many commanders were enriched with confiscations and looting, or speculating on military supplies. It was enough to suspect violent reactions, as happened in 1656 to the janissaries' *defterdar* Divici Mehmed, pursued and targeted with stones by the soldiers of the Cretan garrison who had not received their salary. Opportunities to accumulate fortunes were numerous and invested the army and navy at all levels, pushing many officers to take advantage of the continuation of the war for personal purposes. There were innumerable cases of enrichment,

24 ASVe, *Collegio da Mar, Relazioni*, b. 57 (1670): *Nota distinta di tutto quello che costa una galea redotta in stato d'ogni perfettione, cavata da polizze dell'Arsenale*. In details, the production imported 9,827 ducats for the hull, 262 ducats for the mast and the rudder, 328,14 ducats for rows, benches and accessories. 2,382.8 ducats for sails, ropes and anchors, 3,615.19 for ammunition and guns, and 660,14 for various weapons, lead and matches. The overall cost for building one galleass was 76,940.21 ducats.

more or less collected thanks to the war, which involved personalities at all levels. In 1648, vizier Kovanoz Ibrahim was condemned for having diverted the money for the recruitment of volunteers in Anatolia. Seven years later, the government discovered the enormous fortune accumulated by the chief engineers who directed the construction of the forts in the Dardanelles, obtained by oppressing the local inhabitants. The inhumane hardness with which they treated the population who had to deal with them provoked fierce hate and the aversion of the people to the government.[25]

Conversely, in the opponent's field the speculation followed different path. Historians have focused on the possibility of enrichment – as well as of political advantage – offered by the war to the Venetian commanders, and some of them have subscribed the opinion of Battista Nani. In 1720, the historian declared that, during the Cretan war, corruption had assumed a quite structural character.[26] The command of a ship required a considerable financial commitment, as the recruitment and maintenance of the crew demanded a concerted economic effort, especially when the commander had to anticipate the necessary funds. As in any other Western army and navy of the time, Venetian captains and *sopracomiti* were the owners of companies or crews, and as a result, they practiced more or less lawful speculations. The gains came from paybacks on salary, clothing, or weapons – as it was unlikely that they would be delivered at a cost price – or with the remuneration received from authorised food retailers, especially when the officers themselves or their clients were the owners of the business. In turn, the state sought with various means to recover the money spent for capitulations of regiments and crews, and as a result the captains did the same with soldiers and sailors before they became ill, deserted or fallen in battle. It was not uncommon for recruits to repay the officers in a few months, pushing the soldiers to plundering to compensate the cutback of their salaries. This phenomenon, which distinguished both the Christians and the Ottomans, led to catastrophic outcome, as happened in 1660 following the Venetian landing at Chaniá. When the troops advanced to the city, whole companies scattered for campaigns in search of booty, contributing to the failure of the siege campaign. Three years earlier, General Lazzaro Mocenigo, aware of the discontent of the crews and troops embarked on the fleet, had allowed the looting of villages around the fortress of Sığacık in Anatolia, only for the benefit of soldiers and sailors. The enlistment of the crews, the setting up of the fleets and their maintenance acted as capital multipliers but drained the state treasury. In fact, the Venetian Senate can also be considered like an administrative board of the Republic. From the very beginning of the Republic, the senate included aristocratic members with wide interests in maritime commerce, therefore it was obvious that the Senate's decisions were strongly influenced by the interest in commerce of the merchant class. The naval war strategy was therefore strongly conditioned by this typically mercantile approach, which in the past had brought great benefits, but which in all likelihood represented one of the causes of defeat. In other words, investment in military spending by

25 Von Hammer-Purgstall, Vol. X, p 159.

26 Battista Nani, *Dell'Istoria della Repubblica Veneta* (Venice 1720), vol. X, pp. 66–69.

the Republic was split, with the goal of achieving the greatest result with the least effort. Possibly, if Venice had invested in more men and weapons with the greatest decision when the adversaries were in difficulty – an event occurred several times during the war – the outcome could be different and eventually the huge accumulated debt to be lower.

However, the flow of capital resulting from the war had a very considerable impact both on private fortunes and on the economic development of regions situated near the front. For instance both insular Patmos, favoured by corsairs as a centre for the disposing of captured vessels and redeeming of prisoners, and coastal port of Kusadasi, serving as a kind of labour exchange and centre for the recruitment of replacement crews, owed their prosperity to the war raging in the Aegean. The war favoured above all the Ottoman island of Chios, which served as base of operations for the Ottoman fleet while on manoeuvres, but also as the dockyards and chandlery for the *beylere* fleet in the Aegean. In addition to playing a role in the provisioning and preparing of the Ottoman fleets for campaigns at sea, Chios also absorbed a large share of the proceeds of war, in the form of both slaves and captured enemy vessels.[27] Specularly, Candia became the most profitable emporium for West European tradesman in the Mediterranean Sea, especially after 1657, when the port was open to free commerce. Although isolated from the rest of the overseas colonies, the assiduous work of Francesco Morosini – in his role of provveditor between 1655 and 1657 – granted access to international trade with dispensation of fees in favour of merchants and encouraged privateers to sale stolen goods on site. In the same period, new galleys were built in the local arsenal, something that had not occurred since 1648.

Mobilisation and Recruitment

The Cretan war demanded a large number of soldiers, sailors and specialists from all corners of Europe and, in the case of the Ottomans, from Asia and Africa too. Because Constantinople conducted an offensive war, the balance of strength was consistently in its favour, never less than three against one, mobilising in the three-year period 1667–69 more than 70,000 men of the army and 40,000 of the navy for the final assault at Candia. Also on the Venetian side the mobilisation of men reached new heights. At several points the Republic deployed more than 30,000 professional soldiers, 25,000 sailors and oarsmen, 20,000 militiamen and other irregulars: a war device divided over the multiple fronts of the Italian mainland, Dalmatia, the fleet and Crete. Even before the war began, devising an Ottoman attack in the Aegean Sea, Venice sent reinforcements to Crete and to the other islands of its domain. In the spring

27 The Ottoman historian Evliya cites the case of Ak Mehmed Paşa, a retired Ottoman official and nephew of the one-time grand vizier Receb Pasha, whose estates in Chios, composed mostly of vineyards, employed 2,000 slaves, acquired in part, it may be presumed, during the course of his governorship in Tunis. At the conservative rate of 8,000 *akçes* per head for his slaves alone. Evliya further describes Chios as a flourishing and populous place whose equal he had not encountered during 31 years of travels in the Empire. See R. Murphey, *The Ottoman Resurgence*, cited work, p. 195.

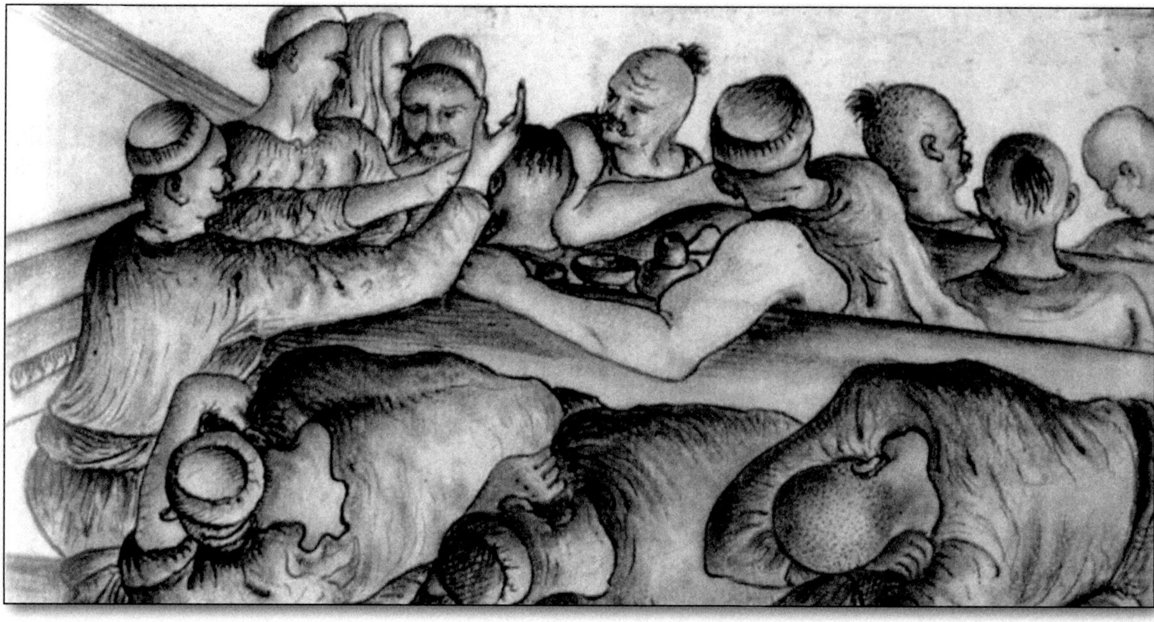

40. Oarsmen received harsh treatment, although they were a human engine, and therefore of capital importance for the conduct of naval campaigns.*

of 1645, several infantry companies began landing hurriedly on the island. On 20 March there came to Chaniá four companies of *Oltramontani*, and three days later two other companies of 48 and 52 infantrymen. On 11 May, the Cretan galleys were sent to Tinos to upload ammunitions; in addition, four other infantry companies arrived in Crete, one assigned to Candia, one in Réthymnon and two in Chaniá. On May 22, the captain of the ship Giovanni Cappello arrived with eight vessels in Suda. Seventeen days before the Ottoman landing, came to Suda nine companies of *Oltramontani* and *Oltramarini* infantrymen. They were the last, and insufficient, reinforcements to arrive in Crete before the invasion began.[28]

The Senate issued instructions and funds to its diplomats for enlisting further experienced foreign troops already in the first months of 1645. Alongside German, Swiss and French soldiers, Venice contacted also an English mercenary who served in France, Colonel Sidney Atkins, for recruiting one regiment of 1,200 experienced soldiers. The Venetian ambassador in Paris, Battista Nani, accorded to Colonel Atkins a monthly salary of 150 ducats for five years' service in Crete. The agreement waited just for the signatures, instead the parties left the contract unachieved and the opportunity for recruiting an English regiment vanished.[29]

When the news of the Ottoman landing on the island arrived in Venice, the government sent missions to all the ambassadors to negotiate more aid in terms of soldiers and weapons. In the spring of 1645, the Senate had decided to increase the ground forces to 25,000 men, and another 7,000 for the following year. The Venetian army strengthened its manpower in

28 ASVe *Senato, Dispacci di Provveditori* b. 543.

29 *Ibid., Collegio*, b, 123, c. 12–13. This source is a particularly interesting document, because it contains the accurate description of the company major and minor staff. They were composed of one captain, one lieutenant, one ensign, two sergeants, four corporals and one secretary.

41. Ottoman sailors and oarsmen, after the *Codex Vindobonensis*, presented to the Emperor Rudolf II of Habsburg in the late-16th century. *

the years between 1646 and 1649, deploying 6,500 troops in Crete and in the Archipelago, 15,000 embarked on the fleet, or in Dalmatia, Istria and the Greek Islands, plus another 10,000 in the Mainland as reserve. In the 1650s, the force deployed to Crete never dropped below the 4,000 men who were garrisoned in Candia and in the islands of Suda, Spinalonga and Gramvousa, this latter returned under Venetian control in 1659.[30] A year later, 11,200 infantrymen and 1,200 horsemen, in addition to about 5,000 in Candia, were concentrated in Cerigo in prevision of the greatest military effort ever made by the Republic to liberate the island.[31] In 1666, during the last Venetian attempt to expel the Ottomans from Crete, 8,328 infantrymen and 860 horsemen were recruited, soon reduced to 8,586 at all when they landed near Chaniá under Marquis Francesco Villa de Ghiron. In the last three years of war the mobilisation continued using all the available methods to find men for defending Candia, a place transformed into a furnace that continually consumed hundreds of soldiers. Between 1667 and 1669, the Republic sent no less than 20,000 men to Candia, in order to prevent the garrison from falling under the figure of 4,000 soldiers, considered as the minimum to continue the resistance. Alongside the infantrymen, the garrison included engineers, pioneers, miners and artillerymen. The number of *bombardieri* increased with the progress of the conflict, especially in conjunction with major operations. In 1650 there were about 150 artillerymen in service, including assistants, but in February 1656 they had become 215, and 259 in January 1657.[32] In 1666 the number was 240, including 35 'pupils' but in the last months of siege it well exceeded 300 men. In April 1669 there were 273 *bombardieri*, of which 236 "able for the factions" and 95 among "boys" and sick, which by June had become 362, including 64 assistants.[33]

In Crete were concentrated ultimately the greatest efforts of both the contenders and, compared to the other fronts, these figures confirm how the island was the strategic centre of gravity of the war, however in Dalmatia the Republic tried to strengthen its forces for rejecting the Ottoman assault and subsequently for launching the counter-offensive into enemy territory. In 1649 between Split, Zadar, Šibenik, Trogir, the recent conquests of Zemunik

30 See Crete's complete garrison strength in the Appendix.

31 Brusoni, *Libro* XVII, p. 75.

32 ASVe *Senato, Dispacci di Provveditori*, b. 563.

33 *Ibid*. It is noted that the contribution, even numbers, of the unpaid 'pupils' or assistants was far from unimportant for the functioning of the artillery present in Candia.

Donji, Dervis, Klis and other places conquered in Bosnia, the Venetians deployed 5,000 regular soldiers, 2,000 irregulars, 500 *corazze* and *cappelletti*, and some 4,000 *craine* militiamen.[34] One year later the overall force available in Dalmatia and Albania was 5,390 regular infantrymen, including 1,019 Swiss and 400 Papal soldiers, and 407 cavalrymen.[35] During the war, this figures remained more or less unchanged, except in 1658, when the renewed Ottoman pressure forced Venice to deploy 6,167 foot soldiers among *Oltramarini nazionali*, Italians and Germans, 1,046 Swiss infantrymen, 660 Papal auxiliaries of foot, 1,575 militiamen from Istria and 91 horsemen.[36]

In 1654, in an attempt to conquer the Ottoman stronghold of Knin, the Venetian army entered into a campaign under Lorenzo Dolfin with 2,000 infantrymen and 250 regular cavalrymen, 1,600 irregulars on foot and another 300 on horseback, alongside 1,140 *craine* and *cernide*. The Ottoman menace to that area, represented by the raids continued more or less violently until 1662, did not allow the Republic further to diminish its forces before 1666, when 3,542 regular foot soldiers are registered in the reviews.[37]

Because the Venetian subjects were mainly enlisted in the militia and in the fleet, recruitments were mostly outside the territories of the Republic, but often there were cases where, after extraordinary decrees, soldiers were also recruited on the Venetian Mainland, especially at the end of the conflict, extracting volunteers from the Mainland's *cernide* militiamen. In 1668, facing a shortage of men to send to Crete, the Senate authorised the method of 'decimation', namely a form of compulsory military service extracting one volunteer for every 10 militiamen.[38] It was an extreme and very unpopular measure, but the urgent need of men to defend the 'Kingdom's bastions moved the traditional political cautions into the background. From 1660 more and more soldiers were recruited in the Venetian provinces of Lombardy, Veneto and Friuli, at first a few hundred, then 3,000 volunteers in total in 1665. Also in the domains of Dalmatia, Albania and Greece, the recruitment of *Oltramarini* volunteers experienced an increase between 1645 and 1650, mainly after the desertion of the Morlachs and Albanian-Cimariote communities to the Venetian side, as well as the recruitment of about 4,000 Greeks in the Mani peninsula, through a formal agreement signed with the leaders of the fierce community established in that region, over which the Porte did not exercise any authority. Venice had always been very active in searching for troops to hire in distant countries. In the summer of 1645, the extraordinary Venetian ambassador to the Westphalia peace conference, Alvise Contarini, hired officers and soldiers from the disbanded regiments in southern Germany. Other contracts were awarded for the capitulation of regiments in Switzerland and in the Graubünden, countries in which the Republic had consistently held permanent agents for recruiting mercenaries since the early years of the century. In the same period, Venice

34 *Ibid.*, *Libro* IX, p. 220.

35 ASVe, *Provveditori da Terra e da Mar*, b. 470, cc. 755–768.

36 *Ibid.*, b. 483, cc. 181–220 and b. 484, c. 2.

37 *Ibid.*, b. 496, c. 165 and b. 497, c. 249.

38 Brusoni, Libro XVII, p. 277.

also claimed 4,000 men to the United Provinces of the Netherlands, to travel to Venice by sea along with four warships, but negotiations broke up without result, except for the arrival of engineers and other specialists for improving fortifications and sailing ships. In the 17th century the reputation of northern European soldiers was very high, it was nothing more than the knowledge accumulated in the Thirty Years' War campaigns, and for this reason the salary accorded to the *Oltremontani* was higher than the one paid in Italy, and twice the amount issued to the *Oltramarini* recruits. This disparity appeared more relevant also by the different value of the currency circulating in the overseas domains. Before the beginning of the war, Venice had a single German infantry regiment, to which two more were added in 1645, after the contracts with mercenary commanders in Bavaria and Swabia. Until 1648 new agreement were signed with the Swiss cantons for two infantry regiments and a third was recruited in the Graubünden. Swiss and Grison troops were always welcomed because the contingents arrived already organised in large companies of usually 200 men with their officers and NCOs, and ready to enter in service after receiving arms and equipment.

The contracts signed between Venice and the Swiss canton are interesting sources to find several details regarding organisation and equipment. The contract signed on 6 May 1648 with Zurich and Bern for one infantry regiment of 11 companies for the Italian mainland, specified that one third were of pikemen and the remaining two thirds musketeers, for 2,200 men in overall. Regarding the pikemen, half of them was equipped with armour issued in Venice. "All weapons must be delivered, as necessary, from the depots set up in Zurich and Berne, with no other obligation than keeping them clean and replacing them after the dismissal of the regiment."[39]

In the early years, the emergency prompted the Republic to seek troops out of Germany and Switzerland too, as happened in 1647 with Colonel Longueval's Walloon foot regiment, and one year later with the Frenchman Count Achilles de Romorantin. While contracts with the Swiss cantons and the Graubünden were governed by contracts signed with local government authorities, in Germany the 'market' presented a scenario that we would now call of actual 'deregulation'. This scenario favoured negotiations which could be conducted directly with the colonel-entrepreneurs who were fully autonomous not only concerning the recruitment of the men, but also their equipment and all other aspects related to the formation of contingents. This option appeared less problematic from an organisational point of view, and even with implied higher costs, helped the Republic avoid unpleasant inconveniences, such as those with some Swiss "levies" arrived in Venice, as reported by the *Mercurio* of 1653, "... exhausted and ripped, almost naked". Private negotiations with mercenary commanders also ensured the continuation of those relations between politics and the military that, in the 17th century, constituted a characteristic feature of the exercise of power.

39 Bern Staatsarchiv V.B.A. p. 529, Bundesarchiv Bd. 61 p. 446 f. *Kapitulation* for the regiment Wertmüller, formed by five companies from Bern and six from Zurich, dated 6 May 1648.

During the conflict, private negotiations and direct enlistment increasingly opened the way to specific agreements with the ruling houses, which moved complete and fully equipped regiments with major staff ready for renting. Institutional relations, however, made the contingents slower to obtain. Furthermore, after 1655, the availability of mercenary soldiers in Germany and Switzerland decreased considerably because of the other European conflicts. However, relying on Princes or even representatives of important European states never completely protected the Republic from frauds and speculations against it. The acceptance of the mediation by other states for assembling the contingents was one of the causes that provoked the disastrous outcome of the Cretan campaigns of 1660. The Duke of Modena and Cardinal Giulio Mazzarino sponsored this enterprise, but the troops put together for the operation to liberate the island from the Ottomans were of very poor quality, probably enlisted with deceit and commanded by officers with little or any experience, engaged at a high price thanks to the pressure of some clientele or powerful protector.

Good troops and skilful officers required high salaries. Moreover, these recruits, even if paid at a high price, always took place after exhausting negotiations. In 1649, the Bavarian prince elector allowed the Venetian diplomat Girolamo Cavazza to hire one infantry regiment licensed after the Westphalia peace and assign it to Baron Johann Stephen von Crossen.[40] In that case, the fatigue and the time spent were well repaid, because the regiment served positively in the sorties from Candia in 1652 and 1653, the last of which caused the loss of the skilled and valiant Colonel von Crossen. In 1660, the Venetian delegate Girolamo Giavarina obtained permission to recruit more infantry in Bavaria and in the same year the Habsburg Emperor granted the passage of two regiments in Venetian service. Then in 1661 one infantry regiment arrived from Ansbach-Bayreuth and finally, in 1668, a capitulation was signed with the Duke of Braunschweig-Lüneburg Celle for sending to Crete 2,400 infantrymen, divided into four regiments under Colonel Count Josias von Waldeck. In the last year of the conflict, another regiment was hired in Bavaria, and 600 infantrymen (for other sources 800) were issued by the Austrian Habsburgs. Even when the troops were obtained, the rental clauses or the special privileges granted to colonels made them sometimes difficult to use. Generally, Germans and Swiss were reluctant to serve on the fleet and every sea transfer caused continual problems with them. In the autumn of 1650, when the senate decided to license the Swiss regiment of Colonel Johann Rudolph Wertmüller, among the various clauses there was one that restricted service to some theatre of war. The regiment numbered 2,000 men and had cost a lot of money, but it could be employed only in Dalmatia, and this permission was granted by courtesy of the Colonel, because the capitulation signed with the cantons of Zurich and Berne did not oblige him to serve outside Italy.

In effect, the eventuality of going to fight in Crete was not an incentive. As consequence, Count Rüdiger von Stahremberg, colonel of the infantry

40 *Ibid.*, *Senato, Dispacci di Provveditori*, b. 546, 18 May 1650.

regiment sent to Naples in 1668 by the Emperor, strongly refused to accept the order to transfer himself and his men to Crete in Venetian service. The news about the war was known to many, and the reports provoked ambivalent reactions, such as the poor attitude of the *Oltramontani* to serve in the Archipelago, a feature remained a constant for a long time. In May 1648, in Dalmatia, the false news spread among the troops marching to Split about their departure for Candia was enough to provoke the mutiny of the German cuirassiers with all their officers, who threatened "to pass at the service of Caesar".[41] But the repulsion for Crete was strong also among other nationalities. In the summer of 1664, the soldiers recruited in Savoy and embarked to Crete on the vessel *San Simeone* mutinied when they discovered their destination, then killed the officers and forced the crew to unload them in Sicily. On other occasions, the opposition of the troops to serve in Crete caused the fault of ambitious projects, as learned from the caustic pen of the Venetian historian Valiero. He wrote that, in the spring 1668, Duke Charles IV of Lorraine offered to Venice his son, Count Charles de Vaudemont with 4,000 infantrymen and 500 horsemen recruited at his own expense: "...wishing only some testimony of honour for the count his son".[42] Nevertheless, practical considerations – namely, the poor utility of the cavalry in a besieged city and the high maintenance costs of the horses – alongside other political difficulties such as the appointment of the young prince to a command rank, caused the offer to fail. Charles IV, however, wished to contribute with 1,500 infantrymen, "... and he would have sent them of his own troops, if they did not oppose to the Duke's will with a mutiny and refusing to march." In order to meet the commitment, the Duke obtained from Louis XIV permission to recruit 800 infantrymen in Provence, and sail them to Crete under the Count of Harcourt. The growing demand for recruits pushed Venice to turn to illegal sources of supply, with the risk of affecting relations with other European states. In this context, Venetian agents also turned to the Corsican clans, recruiting between 1645 and 1660 at least two infantry regiments. In Genoa, the authorities did not tolerate these trades, but volunteering recruitment took place through intermediaries operating outside the island to bypass the restrictions of the Genoese government. Throughout the century, Leghorn and Civitavecchia were active as the main clandestine centres for recruiting volunteers in Corsica, who – through the link with native mercenary colonels and other agents – sought fortunes in the army of some European state or chose the military career to escape the recurrent bloody factions of the island. In the 17th century the Corsicans were known to be ruthless soldiers, able to withstand many deprivations and to be content with austere treatment. One Corsican regiment remained in Venetian service for over 10 years under Colonel Giacinto Peri, a veteran of the campaign in Dalmatia, the Archipelago and Crete. Other troops came from the Italian states that had received the request for help from Venice. The Duke of Parma, in honour of the alliance with the

41 Brusoni, *Libro* VII, p. 178.

42 Valiero, p. 388.

Republic in the Castro War, before the end of 1645 accorded the levy of 2,000 men who "...very well assembled alongside 300 dragoons", offered lead them personally himself against the Ottomans. At the beginning of the new year, the Pope twice sent to Dalmatia 2,000 recruits and financial aid, and in 1647 consented to his infantry colonel Innocenzo Conti entering Venetian service. Also the Republic of Lucca issued licenses for the enlistment of 1,000 men to be sent to the Levant.[43] Year after year, Venetian ambassadors made similar demands at all European Courts. In 1651, the Queen of France authorised the recruitment of 2,000 infantrymen and promised a subsidy of 70,000 *scudi*. One year later, Prince Orazio Farnese entered into the service of the Republic with 3,000 infantrymen from Parma and Piacenza; while in 1653, some 1,000 foot soldiers arrived from Modena. In the following years, the Ecclesiastical State provided the most extensive aid. In 1655, Alexander VII granted a levy of 2,000 men; two years later he issued licenses for recruiting in his state 4,000 infantrymen, while the major Roman aristocratic families contributed economically to equip the contingents and the ships for transporting them. Finally, in 1665, the Pope sent to Dalmatia a regiment of 1,000 infantrymen, embarked the following year for Crete. Papal diplomacy contributed to aid the *Serenissima* with the formation of a league of Christian states. In early 1660, in anticipation of the planned landing at Chaniá, the Duke of Modena sent 300 infantrymen to Venice, joining them with the 3,500 French soldiers supplied by Mazzarino. The same did Charles Emanuel II of Savoy, who hired two infantry 'regiments' of 500 men each.

Between 1658 and 1669, the knights of Malta also several times sent their galleys' battalion to Crete or out to sea campaigning, sometimes even in autonomy, as occurred in September 1658, when the Maltese, alongside with the Papal galley squadron, destroyed the Ottoman pirates based in Lefkada Island. In 1668, Lucca agreed to Venice new licenses to enlist other volunteers and finally collected 50,000 lb of gunpowder, while the archbishop of Salzburg sent to Venice another 60,000 lb. In 1664 the Duke of Savoy re-established his contingent in Venetian service of 1,000 infantrymen; while between 1662 and 1666 he had signed permission for the recruiting of 4,000 men in his domains. In 1666, the Grand Duke of Tuscany sent 400 infantrymen to Dalmatia under the Marquis Filippo Pistolozzi. The Tuscan battalion departed two years later to Crete. Further aid and permissions of this type continued to exist until the last, as in the case of the 2,000 men infantry regiment of the Prince of Mirandola, recruited by cooperation of the Pope with the Dukes of Mantua, Modena and Parma. The regiment landed at Candia two weeks before the surrender of the city.[44]

The most significant exception regarding the enlistment of Venetian subjects for the army was represented by the contingents coming from Dalmatia, Albania and the Greek islands. During the war, Venice used its Slavic subjects on all war fronts. Since 1645, ad hoc units of *Oltramarini* infantry were formed in Dalmatia and Scutari in Albania, joining four or more

43 Archivio di Stato di Lucca (Lucca State Archive), f. *Deputazione sopra leMilizie*, f. 244, c. 93, *Leva di truppe per il Levante*.

44 Brusoni, *Libro* XVII, p. 313.

42. Lunardo Foscolo, general provveditor in Dalmatia until 1651 and captain general from 1652 to 1653. Under him the Venetians gained remarkable successes in the Balkans, conquering many towns and fortresses and subduing many local communities. Years later, Foscolo told the historian Girolamo Brusoni that after the campaign of 1649 he could have entirely conquered Bosnia, but he had not, due to an excess of caution and shortage of forces. Lunardo was an ancestor of the Italian Romantic poet Ugo Foscolo. (Author's archive)

companies in temporary regiments, sometimes composed of both Croats and Albanians. During the successful campaigns in Bosnia, several of these units are often mentioned alongside their commanders, such as the *eccellente capitano* Michiel Angelo Crutta, colonel of the *Oltramarina* nation,[45] who gained prestigious achievements and prizes under Lunardo Foscolo.[46] Naturally, even in the Greek islands of Corfu, Zákynthos and Kefalonia, Venice recruited soldiers, employed both as landing infantry and for garrison service in Crete, especially during the last three years of the war. The Republic recruited volunteers in the Greek islands also to form units of pioneers and miners. In 1668, Venice recruited 2,000 Greeks only for these tasks, and sent them to Crete to counter the enemy mine works.

For Venice, enlistment mainly concerned infantrymen, but despite the relative utility of the troops on horseback for the defensive strategy, in the early years there were also regiments of cuirassiers and dragoons. In his *History of the War of Candia*, Girolamo Brusoni records two regiments of 320 horse each sent to Dalmatia in 1646; the first consisting of four companies of Italian mercenaries under Colonel Giovambattista Degna and the other formed by four German companies under the Count of Longueval.[47] With them, one dragoon 'regiment' – commanded by Colonel Alceste Campagna – fought in Dalmatia from 1646 to 1651.[48] As in Crete, also in Dalmatia there were special problems in the maintaining of the heavy mounted troops, who required more training and, above all, war-horses, which were not available in the region and had to be shipped from Italy. As the Republic went on the defensive after the early campaigns, the need for a large cavalry force was less urgent, and in order to cut down on the military expense by 1649, the number of these units was reduced to five companies, included two companies of *corazze crovate*, one German company and one Italian company, known as *corazze Bresciane di Banditi*, namely formed with outlaws serving their sentences in the army.[49] In 1656 and 1657 the size of the heavy cavalry in Dalmatia was maintained to six companies, and after 1658 it was reduced to just two companies. Finally, in the last decade of the war, Venice renounced to deploy heavy cavalry in Dalmatia.

45 That is, Croatian, Dalmatian, Albanian or Greek soldiers.

46 *Ibid.*, *Libro* III, p. 64. Crutta was killed in action in 1649 at the siege of Risan.

47 *Ibid.*, p. 63.

48 *Ibid.*, p. 65.

49 ASVe, *Provveditori da Terra e da Mar*, b. 470, c. 685. The Italian company was disbanded in late April 1653.

43. A view of the fortified town of Klis, dating from the late 17th century. This strategic place, located on high hills and defended with good walls, was considered to be "the key of Bosnia". The Venetian conquest occurred on 1st April 1648, and was celebrated as the major success of Lunardo Foscolo. (*Theatrum Europeum*, Frankfurt am Main, 1670)

Units of light cavalry also followed a similar trend of steady decline: by 1653, the Senate had reformed the whole *cappelletti* light cavalry to six companies;[50] in 1658, following the pressing request of general provveditor Antonio Bernardo, the government agreed to supplement the light cavalry with two more companies, one to Zadar and one to Split, with the duty of escorting supply convoys. In the last years of the war the mounted Morlachs, some 800 men, represented the only actual cavalry in the area.

However, in this war theatre the cavalry played an important role, especially the heavy cavalry, considered as the only effective instrument to face the Ottoman *sipahy* and other irregulars on horseback in open field. Some companies of *corazze* formed the garrison of Candia, where they participated in the fights of 1647 and 1648, both in reconnaissance and in combat role, on foot and on horseback. In 1649, the Senate established in Crete a whole regiment of heavy cavalry, joining the companies of *corazze* already present in the island with others arrived from Venice. The regiment fought at the orders of Colonel Felice Simone, claiming a prominent role in the encounters that took place during the second Ottoman assault on Candia.

In 1666, another regiment of Italian cuirassiers was sent to Crete under Count Sforza Bissaro, in prevision of the Venetian landing to Chaniá. The regiment performed very poorly and after the failure of the campaign, the survivors were garrisoned inside Candia. Throughout the conflict, the main component of the Venetian cavalry were the light horsemen known as *cappelletti*. They were Slavic and Albanian horsemen, sometimes mentioned in the sources as *stradiotti* or *schiavoni* (Slavic). This light cavalry was

50 *Ibid.*, b. 470, c. 685 and *Senato, Rettori,* b. 24, f. 10.

employed in large numbers in the war theatres of Dalmatia and Bosnia, but also in Crete in 1645 there were already two *stradiotti* companies, in this case formed by Greeks, involved in the encounters with the Ottoman cavalry at Apicorno and Cladissà, in the vain attempt to slow the Ottoman landing operations during the first Ottoman campaign in the island. In 1648 a whole regiment of *cappelletti* under the colonel Marko Sinosich was formed with 400 Croatian recruits and sent to Candia, where remained for almost five years. Sinosich was in Crete since the early stages of the war, taking part in the defence of Chaniá as an officer of one light horse company. He was captured by the Ottomans at the surrender of the city, and then released the following year after an exchange of prisoners. Sinosich returned immediately to fight for Venice, and the Senate rewarded him with a colonel's license. In 1651 his regiment still numbered 381 officers and private *cappelletti*.[51]

Venice was able to increase its light cavalry thanks to the arrival of a large number of *zadruga* – extended families, or clans – of the Morlach communities, which after 1649 allowed the formation of one light horse regiment and two foot regiments.[52] Other inhabitants of the region swore allegiance to the Republic, as happened with the community of Makarska in August 1645 on the eve of the inconclusive Venetian assault to Zadvarje: its whose leaders received as a sign of friendship gold rings with the image of the lion of Saint Mark. Then, one year later, the Albanian *Cimarioti* crossed in large numbers to Venice's side.[53] The Albanian connection opened other links with the native communities who wished to back out of Ottoman rule. In the spring of 1648, Venetian agents, in concert with general provveditor Lunardo Foscolo, contacted the majority of Durrës for planning an insurrection against the Ottoman garrison. The Albanians assured the Venetian emissaries that they could supply 10,000 men in arms, but at the decisive moment the uprising was discovered, and all the conspirators executed. Other volunteers came from states with a precarious independence from the Porte, such as the 1,000 Montenegrin volunteers present at the siege of Risan of Kotor in 1649.[54]

Faced with Ottoman pressure, the Venetian Senate immediately resorted to the mobilisation of the militia. The fear of raids that could penetrate into the Mainland, as it happened in 1499, pushed in 1645 to the mobilisation of the *cernide* in Friuli and Istria. The militia was again mobilised in the two-year period 1657–58, persuading the government to double the number of men in the companies. Even greater was the call to arms of the *craine* in Dalmatia, which allowed them to take part in the first defensive battles and then the actions carried out by the Venetians against the Ottoman strongholds in Bosnia. In 1630s there were more than 5,000 Dalmatian militiamen in arms and their number never dropped below the 3,000 men

51 G. Brusoni, cited work, *Libro* IX, p. 211.

52 ASVe, *Provveditori da Terra e da Mar*, b. 467, c. 23–30.

53 The term *Cimarioti* was used in Venice for identifying the Christian Albanian speaking communities settled in the Epiriote region south to Valona. They were mostly Orthodox Chistians and before the end of the century became a fully recognised nation of the Venetian overseas domain. In 1735 the Cimarioti formed two regular infantry regiments of the Venetian army.

54 G. Brusoni, cited work, *Libro* IX p. 224.

who ordinarily needed to take over the major places of the domains.

Generally, local militias demonstrated sufficient reliability when employed to defend their territory, better if supported by regular troops. In the spring of 1657, the *craine* of Bonkovići, on the island of Hvar, defended themselves effectively during the Ottoman assault on the fortress. On that occasion women took up arms too, and despite the unfavourable outcome, the resistance of the militiamen clearly demonstrated how these troops, if protected by solid fortifications, could sustain a siege for a reasonable time. On the contrary, the employment of the *cernide* and *craine* for offensive operations revealed the defects and their lack of enthusiasm when they were forced to fight far away from home.

44. The German Christoph Martin von Degenfeld was one of the most valiant mercenary commanders under Lunardo Foscolo in Dalmatia. He directed the successful defence of Šibenik in 1646. One year after, Degenfeld was awarded the title of *generalissimo delle armi* of Dalmatia and Albania for his excellent service, and as special recognition to his family, which provided many officers to the Republic of Venice. His son, Georg Christoph, served as an infantry colonel and died in the summer 1669 at the defence of Candia. (Museo Correr, Venice)

Already in June 1646, the Senate had given its consent to allow the grant of half-pay and a portion of food (biscuit) to the mobilised *craine*, in order to improve combat effectiveness, and prevent the population from leaving their villages. This measure was proposed by general provveditor Lunardo Foscolo, who asked the Senate that monthly pay should be granted to the militiamen in arms for the whole duration of the war.[55] Similarly, the pay for the Dalmatian nobles acting as officers were also increased. However, these measures proved to be very short lived. In October 1647, faced by the chronic shortage of money, and judging that after the destruction of the Ottoman strongholds in nearby Zadar the imminent danger had ceased, Foscolo decided to abolish the monthly payment to the *craine*.[56] In 1648, during the campaign that led to the conquest of Klis, the militiamen deserted in large numbers just crossing the border; in this regard the comment of the Lunardo Foscolo was related by the historian Girolamo Brusoni:

> ...It is true that in this siege, we received so much more disturbance than advantage from the local militiamen; because in asking the gunpowder and the biscuit were four or five hundred, according to the review, but when we were looking them for the factions, we did not count that six or seven for banner [company], and sometimes we saw the Ensign go alone without Captain, or soldiers almost lurking for the rocks and often looking for lumber and salad leaves.[57]

At the end, the role in campaign of these units remained limited. The reasons were twofold. First, as discussed before, the militiamen were very hard to

55 ASVe, *Senato, Rettori*, b. 17, f. 132–134 and 174.

56 *Ibid.*, b. 18, f . 96–97.

57 Brusoni, cited work, *Libro IX*, p. 228.

deploy outside their home area, which rendered them effective only for the defence of their homes. Second, the 1649– 1650 plague epidemic and the Ottoman raids regularly destroying crops and villages, caused a heavy depopulation of the costal centres and forced the population to move to the more secure Dalmatian islands.

But much worse was the behaviour of both Cretan *proli* and feudal cavalry, who demonstrated poor quality during the defence of their country. When the first rescue troops were sent to aid the Chaniá besieged, five hundred Cretans from the Candia militiamen formed the rear of the rescue corps under Count Carlo Fenarolo. Approaching the city at night, the regular infantry stopped to wait for the militiamen marching more slowly, but the latter, seeing the glitter of the weapons, thought it was an ambush of the enemy's and after discharging a volley they fled, compromising the action. Not even inside the besieged city did the *proli* prove themselves to be reliable. Needlessly, the *provveditore* Andrea Navagero tried with his example to encourage the militiamen:

> At the end of the siege (1648), he (Navagero) was injured in the stomach following the explosion of a mine and he could not by his example to encourage the *feudati* who accompanied him, who would force them to offer a minimum of trial of honourable service, having them, in the greatest risk, abandoned the battle. It seemed that the nobility and the *feudati* always showed very poor interest in the public service, claiming that they were not obliged to be massacred on the walls until there were soldiers paid by the Republic.[58]

Following the negative outcomes at the siege of Chaniá and in other parts of the island, and considering the unnecessary spending for its maintenance, in 1647 the entire Cretan militia was reduced to two battalions of 800 men each and sent into Candia, while the cavalry was reformed to three companies, joining the best-experienced and trusted *feudati*. After the siege, in 1650, the payments to the *proli* were suspended to save money, and consequently, their number decreased rapidly. In 1656 their number had increased to 519, who "do not perceive anything, nor salary, nor bread and remain therefore exempt from any exercise".[59] The Cretan militia was employed only on extraordinary occasions, as happened in September 1658, when the garrison of Candia had been reduced to only 2,200 infantrymen, and to guard all positions it was necessary to employ 200 *proli*. In 1660, Venice tried to call their Cretan subjects to arms for the incoming landing to Chaniá, but the number of men gathered was lower than expected. Before the end of the war the *proli* from the Aegean Island of Tinos began to be requested for the seasonal sending in the archipelago, to use them in the works on the fortifications and in the mines where, employed in place of the soldiers, they became very useful.[60]

In 1650 there were also two companies of *feudates*, "instituted to bring help to many well-known people than to receive reinforcements to the

58 *Ibid.*, *Libro* VIII, p. 196.

59 ASVe, *Senato, Dispacci di Proveditori*, b. 551, 18 September 1658.

60 *Ibid.*, b. 551, 31 October 1669.

advantages of the garrison; while from the number of 330 there are one third and more who are exempt from the obligation of armed service or by indisposition, by age, or by other legitimate respects of convenience or complacency." In 1653 there were still in Candia 331 *feudati* who received a salary for their livelihood.[61]

Usually counted together with the *feudati*, in the reviews there were also the *venturieri*. They perceived a service that allowed them to survive; in Candia their number ranged around 50 men in 1650. Sometimes, some Venetian nobles who went to serve in the garrison rather than on the fleet are also marked in the rolls. In 1666 there were three Venetian nobles who became more or less regularly paid.[62] The *venturieri* were taken into consideration by the Venetian commanders for their high morale and discipline. In 1647, inside the besieged Réthymnon, the *venturieri* generally behaved better than the paid soldiers, even if due to their small numbers they could not significantly influence the outcome.

Generally the militia, at an operative level, remained subject to the contingency of the war. Over the years, it had become increasingly difficult for Venice to meet the continuous demand for fresh troops in all areas of operations: the Aegean, Crete and Dalmatia. However, lacking sufficient regular troops, the Republic begun to turn to its subjects far from the war theatre, such as the Italian *cernide* from the *Terraferma*, in order to compensate for this shortcoming. The first non-local militiamen marched to Dalmatia in 1651. They were 200 *cernide* from Istria, who were quartered in Zadar.[63] The next year, any militiaman was sent to Dalmatia but rather, the provveditor of Istria received the order from the Senate to keep in arms a corps of 500 men.[64] The next group of Istrian *cernide* sent to Dalmatia was the 500 men 'battalion' dispatched in May 1654, after the Venetian defeat at Knin.[65] Similarly, in 1657, when alarming news about the Ottoman offensive had reached Venice, 500 Istrian *cernide* were conscripted and sent into Dalmatia.[66] Almost simultaneous attacks on Split and Kotor convinced the Senate that the Ottomans had serious plans for these fortresses, and for the upcoming campaign of 1658 it ordered a reinforcement of 4,200 men for Dalmatia and Albania. Out of these figures only 2,200 were regular troops, while the remaining 2,000 consisted of 1,500 Italian *cernide* from the *Terraferma* and 500 from Istria.[67] This also represented the greatest commitment of the Venetian militia in Dalmatia. Although until the end of the war, the Republic continued to send almost without interruption reinforcements to Dalmatia, *cernide* as well as regular troops hired abroad.

The most valuable support to the Republic was offered by France, long negotiated, and regulated in order not to cause disturbance in the European

61 *Ibid.*, *Senato Relazioni*, *Provveditori* 546, 18 August 1650.
62 *Ibid.*, *Provveditori da Terra e da Mar*, b. 502, c. 111.
63 ASVe, *Senato, Rettori*, b. 25, f. 156, dated 31 August 1651.
64 *Ibid.*, b. 26, f. 84, dated 7 May 1652.
65 *Ibid.*, b. 28, f. 56, dated 31 March 1654.
66 *Ibid.*, *Provveditori da Terra e da Mar*, b. 481, c. 89.
67 *Ibid.*, *Senato, Rettori*, b. 33, f. 73, and *Provveditori da Terra e da Mar* b. 483, c. 185.

political equilibrium. In 1659 the young Louis XIV, after the advice of Mazzarino, allowed the formation of a corps of 4,000 infantrymen and horsemen to be sent to Crete for landing and reconquering the major places under Ottoman control. In the following years, the French foreign cabinet was constantly in contact with the Senate to negotiate other aid, always trying to dissimulate its origin in order not to affect the old friendship between France and the Porte. Then in 1667 the Duke de La Feuillade, one of the French generals who had participated in the Hungarian campaign under Raimondo Montecuccoli in 1664, obtained from Louis XIV permission to enlist a corps of volunteers under the banner of the Knights of Malta to be sent to the besieged Candia. The Duke contributed his own fortune to set up the contingent, while the King had authorised his colonels to dismiss anyone who wanted to take part in the enterprise. In September 1667, 600 volunteers were ready to leave France. They were mostly officers and aristocratic adventurers, and among them there were cadets of the most important French families, eager to show their valour and gain reputation. Each nobleman had with him an armed servant who carried the arms and was close to him in battle. Under the powerful suggestion of the war in the *Levante*, the spirit of chivalry returned to be incarnated by these aristocrats who, using von Bigge's words, "adorned with scented laces and with a joking motto on the lip, captivated the whole world with their courage."[68] The Republic paid the expenses for their maintenance and half of the salary, established to a daily of one *lira*, the same pay issued to the *Oltramontani*. After one year of service in Candia, the sumptuous contingent had decreased to 450 men who, together with La Feuillade, insisted on launching a sortie in order to "give them an opportunity to do something of worthy of their name and status" and with that action closed their participation in the war. In 1669, Louis XIV offered a new rescue, sending to Crete a corps of 54 (for other sources 50) infantry companies and five cavalry companies for a total of 6,000 soldiers, alongside 2,000 sailors, under the Grand Admiral Duke de Beaufort and General Annes de Noailles. The contingent also included three companies of the *Gardes Françaises*, two companies of the *Mosquetaires du Roi*, and further 232 reformed officers as volunteers. Many of these men were back from the expedition against the Bey of Algiers, ended the year before in a way was far from positive. For this reason fleet commander de Beaufort had the opportunity to redeem the failure. There was no doubt that without the French aid, Candia would fall before the spring. However, the relations between the French commander and the Captain General Francesco Morosini became more and more nervous, and because they disagreed on many questions regarding the use of these troops, the French contribution served only to delay the surrender of the city for four months.

In the emergency caused by the war, every source for supplying soldiers was held in great consideration by Venice, whether it was regiments of veterans already trained and organised, or volunteers recruited through the most varied methods. With the exception of the French and a few others, in most cases the contingents were fully equipped at the expense of the Republic, which

68 Wilhem Von Bigge, *Der Kampf um Kandia in den Jahren 1667–1669* (Berlin, 1899), p. 99.

45. *Oltramarini* **foot soldiers, second half of the 17th century. 1)** *crovato* **(croatian) or** *scappolo* **of a picket guard on galleys and galleasses. 2) Albanian** *Cimerioto* **irregular of foot. 3) Morlachs. (Author's illustration, with kind permission of the Web Magazine** *History and Uniforms***)***

often had to assume the cost of their transfer from the regions of origin. It was common for some state to take advantage of the recruiting campaigns to expel beggars or criminals. Before each campaign, the government received reports from the *Inquisitori* containing opinions about the men enrolled and more or less frequently several irregularities were found. Between 1662 and 1666, for instance, it was repeatedly outlined by the Venetian officials, that among the recruits sent by the Duke of Savoy there were many beggars and outlaws: "unfit to bear the weapon and also the oar". However, the Savoy contingent was one of the most durable, considering that both regiments and recruits from the Duke's states continued to fight for Venice from 1660 until the last day of the siege of Candia. This is a considerable feature, because in the course of the war it is rare to find units with a service life longer than two or three years. The high turnover was due not only to the outcomes of fighting or to the high mortality caused by the epidemics, which afflicted every theatre of the Cretan war, but especially because the Venetian government preferred not to engage too long with the mercenaries, both for budgetary reasons and because the status of service of certain units could prove unsatisfactory, and then proceed without too much trouble to dismiss the less efficient ones. On the other hand, in the alternate international political context of that age, the states could also exempt themselves from granting recruits and determining the dismissing of the units. Even the communities hostile to the Ottomans, who had sent volunteers to the Venetian army since the beginning of the war, withdrew progressively from the battlefield, as did the Greeks of Maina, who in 1660 reduced strongly the recruits for the Republic. Considering all these premises, it is obvious that the army set up by Venice showed alternately preparation and a degree of efficiency. Some contemporary commentators agree that German and Swiss units were the best, believing them as more capable "in taking places and maintaining them" and being "impetuous and obstinate" in offensive actions. According to Venetian *provveditori*, Italian and Corsican soldiers were considered as loyal, while the *Oltramarini* – especially Croatian, Albanian and Greek light horsemen – were judged quite negatively as "naturally without discipline", and violent against the civilian population. However, different opinions are expressed by Johann Scheither, a captain of the Brunswick–Lüneburg infantry contingent who left a large account on the last months of the siege at Candia he considered positively Greeks, Slavs and, of course, Germans; while expressing little favour to French and Italian soldiers. For the minds of the time, the many existing nationalities served to stimulate the emulation spirit among the contingents. In fact, several times have been mentioned courage trials and other enterprises executed by the German defenders of a bastion, to which the French or the Italians replied with equal valour from another bastion. Often, linguistic babel and diversity of customs led to disadvantages that degenerated into open opposition, with the result that Maltese more than once declared that they did not want to fight with Orthodox Greeks and Protestants, or the Germans did not always like the presence of *Oltramarine* or French soldiers, and the latter did the same with Spaniards and Neapolitans. The poor cohesion of such a composite army could easily cause the loosening of fidelity constraints, with the result that there were many desertions. Although the Venetian print sources mention desertion only sporadically, the units almost always arrived on campaign incomplete. Generally desertion occurred more frequently among the *Oltramarini* than the other nationalities, especially the Albanians. Desertions were often encouraged by the Ottomans, who promised higher incomes, or simply to escape a destiny that did not seem to promise anything good. In 1651 both of these cases forced the Albanian captain of a light horse company in Dalmatia, named Voino Iuanina, to desert with all his soldiers because he was "reluctant to be transferred to Crete".[69] There were some cases of soldiers who fought for one and the other side, like Iuanina himself, who – after received the Senate release – returned to the Venetian army before being captured by the Ottomans in 1657. To escape slavery, Iuanina suggested besieging the Venetian fortress of Herceg Novi near Kotor, offering himself as a scout. The intricate Balkan reality could facilitate unscrupulous behaviours such as this, but even in Crete there occurred desertion to move from one side to another. On certain occasions, the desertion caused the loss of strategic sites, as happened in 1646, when a whole Dutch company with all the officers abandoned the cisterns of the fortified cloisters between Suda and Chaniá and crossed to the enemy camp, where the commander became Muslim, accepting entrance into Ottoman service.[70]

Already during the first siege, escapes within the garrison began to take on a significant size. The scarcity of food quickly reduced the garrison to starvation. Furthermore, delays in payment of salary provoked several cases of mutiny. Some episodes were particularly serious at the end of the summer of 1647, when during an enemy assault a whole company threw down their weapons saying, that "without money they do not want to be killed."[71]

In the contingent situation, the commanders could not even take disciplinary measures and therefore it was necessary to persuade the soldiers with flattery and promises, since a punishment could have caused much more serious upheavals. The phenomenon of desertion remained very serious, because it also involved officers and NCOs. In March 1649 a sergeant escaped from Candia "flags in the wind", together with 10 soldiers and also the ensign of the company.[72]

Hunger as cause of desertion is systematically repeated in the dispatches, while there is no mention of desertion as acts of cowardice: "the dispersions

69 Brusoni, cited work, *Libro* X, pp. 237–238.

70 Von Hammer-Purgstall, vol X, p. 233.

71 ASVe, *Senato, Dispacci di Proveditori*, b. 545, 31 August 1648.

72 *Ibid*., b. 546, 28 March 1649.

and the escapes of unpaid people who do not have to sustain and feed themselves, force them to go to the enemy."[73] In 1652, the desertions occurred every day involving not only the infantrymen but also the artillerymen, engineers and officers.[74] Four years later, only "an ensign of a Corsican company, climbed the walls of a low redoubt with the flag and with three soldiers passed to the Turks", then in 1657 the situation worsened further. In eight months, from July to February, the officers received their salary only once, and "they are therefore forced to break the bonds of loyalty due to the Prince by turning to Turks, or to give in the worst excesses so as not to die of dissolution." Among these acts, there were numerous thefts because "the misery is such that it pushes the officers to steal where and how they can."[75]

Naturally, this scenario worried the Senate, especially when the dissatisfaction turned in mutiny and betrayal. In May 1650, the Albanian soldiers assigned to a bastion of Candia protested at the delay in paying salaries, and declared themselves ready to cede the forts to the enemy. The provveditor and the officers were able to turn the menace. In this case the Senate applied a severe punishment and even ordered that no more Albanian soldiers would be sent to Candia, but it was clear that the danger could soon reappear. In fact, the situation was critical not only inside Candia, but also in the other Cretan fortresses, where the risk was even greater. At the beginning of September 1650, the provveditor of Suda discovered a conspiratorial plot planned by some soldiers who want to "[kill the] commanders and deliver the fortress to the Turks."[76] To avoid the repetition of this threat, it would have been appropriate to alternate the troops, moving them from Suda, Spinalonga and Gramvousa to Candia and from there to send new ones. Unfortunately, the lack of money necessary to pay the troops and move them from one garrison to another prevented it.[77] The same threat also arose in Spinalonga in early February of the same year. In the fortress, the seditious movement had started from an ensign of an Italian company who had stirred up some soldiers of his company and others "of the French nation". They had agreed to attack and kill the fortress provveditor and the superintendent.[78]

In 1659 the provveditor of Candia, Luca Francesco Barbaro, identified the two main causes of desertions. The first, of course, stemmed from the fact that the soldiers were not paid regularly, sometimes even before the capitulations they signed. Consequently, having to survive with only three ducats a month,

73 *Ibid.*, 19 September 1650. These kinds of escapes were particularly serious, not only because the desertion of the officers obviously resulted in lower effectiveness of the garrison, but also for the diffusion of news to the enemy, them being usually better informed. This drawback was surely the greatest in the periods when sorties were carried out or, as was the case of 1650, were planned military operations on a larger scale. In these actions, the escapes not only increased, because on campaign it was easier to desert, but they benefited the enemy who could obtain valuable information from the fugitives.

74 *Ibid.*, b. 548, 3 November 1652: "Even the officers who were partly paid flee as soon as they received something of the arrears."

75 *Ibid.*, b. 550, 4 February 1657.

76 *Ibid.*, b. 546, 10 September 1650.

77 *Ibid.*, b. 549, 24 May 1651. In this regard, a remedy was introduced proposing to send to Suda the eventual arrivals of new forces, who had already received their pay in advance.

78 *Ibid.*, b. 546, 28 February 1650.

and the ration of bread or biscuit "the soldier ... eats or bets his salary in a single day resorting just to bread and water and then he becomes desperate".[79] It should also be added that, rather than gambling, the money just received was often used to pay debts. The second motivation lay in the current legislation on treatment to be reserved for deserters. The latter, if they returned voluntarily to the company, were not subjected to punishment, indeed the pardon would also extend to the convictions preceding the desertion. This provision, originally established to try to recover the deserters, was still in force, achieving only the effect of decriminalising the desertion. A dissatisfied soldier could leave his place and, if he did not find a better situation in the enemy camp, or had suffered ill-treatment, he could return to Candia without receiving punishment. Therefore, Barbaro proposed to revoke this provision, as in addition to being harmful by encouraging desertions, it did not bring benefits because very few returned. However, the provveditor left open the possibility of reintroducing the pardon for short periods so that it could continue to act as an incentive to return.

The following year, on 4 March 1660, the provveditor in charge changed with the arrival of Marco Bembo, and with the money he brought with him the whole city had a recovery. However it should be noted that since late May, namely in about 10 months, the garrison had lost 595 soldiers due to illness.[80] On 21 April, the provveditor could inform the Senate that the desertions had ceased. It was not a miraculous fact, because they finally resumed regular distribution of fresh bread instead of biscuit. The city experienced a moment of particular wellbeing, and the number of sick people fell significantly, as evidence of the benefits of better food.

Desertions represented a constant problem for the defenders until the end of the war, provoking several threats, as occurred in October 1667, when a German deserter offered himself to trigger an unexploded Venetian mine under the bastion of Panigrà.[81]

Obviously desertions, mutinies and switches from one side to another were not exclusive to the Venetian side. Apart from the thousands of Morlachs, Cimeriots, and Greeks from the Mani peninsula who fought under Venice, the Ottoman desertion represented a concrete problem too. Already during the siege of Chaniá, in 1645, the defenders tried to establish contact with some Albanian soldiers of the opposing side to induce them to desert. They were ready to escape, but the fear of reprisals against their families at home prevented the agreement.

The conquest plans, developed by the Sultan's complacent ministers, did not take into account the many aspects that made the Cretan war a completely new test for the mobilisation capacity of the Ottoman army. In this period, the traditional Ottoman military organisation was in the process of

79 *Ibid.*, b. 551, 8 March 1659.

80 *Ibid.*, b 552, 21 April 1660. The spiral represented by the continuous oscillation between relative well-being and misery that moves along with the long-awaited sending of money from Venice, was always ready to start again. It was a realisation that the failure to get new money would have plunged the garrison into a critical state. 1660 was also the year chosen to make the long-planned landing in Crete and the attempt to reconquer Chaniá.

81 Brusoni, *Libro* XII, p. 166.

transition. The *devşirme* system still provided the manpower for the janissary corps, but increasingly the standing army was enlarged by the enlistment of provincial troops for whom enrolment meant attaining the privileges of the corps, particularly enlistment in the *esame* (muster rolls), an entitlement to janissary pay and benefits. This transformation provoked several drawbacks in the course of Ottoman history, but affected the army very little during the Cretan war. The field army employed on the island rarely numbered more than 60,000 men, and this figure was reached in the first and in the last campaigns. From 1650 to 1666 the Porte rarely maintained in Crete more than 20,000 men, including the *timar* holders appointed after 1648. The shortage of permanent and professional troops affected mainly the navy, which several times offered special benefits for the volunteers who accepted to serve there. Several volunteers came from the *kapikulu*, and only oarsmen and sailors were recruited through this system. This act could well represent a belated official recognition of a trend already well under way.[82]

Manpower availability posed always a major obstacle for the Ottoman navy as it was mobilised for a campaign. Demands for the galley fleet were particularly heavy, and occasionally the Ottomans were called upon to dispatch two fleets simultaneously, one against Cossack raiders in the Black Sea, and the other to the Mediterranean. A number of the oarsmen were prisoners-of-war inducted into the ranks of the galley slaves of the *miri forsalan*, but according at least to contemporary chronicle,[83] the government consistently resorted during the early 1650s to the abusive practice of forcible conscription among guileless youth from the Anatolian hinterland who were seized from the streets of Constantinople and drafted into service as novices. The sultan's one-fifth share in war booty provided only a small part of the huge and, as the war dragged on, growing need for able-bodied seamen. For example, the 800 prisoners presented to the Sultan at the conclusion of the successful season of naval campaigning in 1654 would have been sufficient to man only four galleys for the incoming year.[84]

The unexpected stalemate in the face of the tenacious enemy resistance revealed not only the difficulty of the Ottomans in maintaining too long contingents in campaign, but also problems relating transport and supply, with the risk of exposing the troops to the Venetian reaction that could drive them out of the island. The naval blockade of the Dardanelles conditioned the supply of ammunition and food for many years, as well as the transport

82 As outlined by Virginia Aksan in her essay 'War and Peace', in *The Cambridge History of Turkey*, 2006; vol. III, p. 88, the *timar* system had already caused some concerns: "Furthermore, while historians have insisted on the strict distinction between *timar*-holding *sipahis* and janissaries, the blurring of the boundaries probably began far earlier than is generally conceded. The *timar* system appeared and performed adequately in the 1593–1606 Long War between Habsburgs and Ottomans, in part because a decline in the monetary value of such assignments, triggered massive reform from the government. This reform could well represent a belated official recognition of a trend already well under way. Quantitative data are hard to come by, as surviving statistics about the janissaries took into account only those stationed in the capital or posted to the numerous garrisons across the Ottoman territories, but not the *timariots*."

83 Mustafa Naima, *Tarih*, vol V, pp. 200–202, and Von Hammer Purgstall, cited work, vol X, p. 198.

84 See R. Murphey, *The Ottoman Resurgence in the Seventeenth-Century Mediterranean*, cited work, p. 192.

of reinforcements and the setting up of new contingents for the continuation of the siege. In February 1646, some informers of the Republic reported that inside the new-conquered Chaniá there were no more than 7,000 soldiers. This figure had been achieved by forcing 1,000 of sailors to spend the winter on the island, but there had been violent protests among the garrison for the delay of salary and for the bad treatment received. The statute of the janissaries and the prerogatives of the other professional soldiers established that each year the troops on campaign would be alternated, while the contingents assembled by the provinces could return home at the end of operations. For the 1646 campaign, which ended with the conquest of Rethymno, 4,000 janissaries and *sipahy* were sent to Crete, with a further 4,000 men of artillery, engineers and diggers. This force landed at Chaniá between March and June; many of them had spent months on the ships anchored in the ports of Greece or Anatolia to escape the Venetian navy. As if the adversities were not enough, a fire burst out at Constantinople in January 1646, destroying the neighbourhoods near the harbour in three hours and severely hitting the organisation for collecting supplies and sending reinforcements. A year later, the threatening presence of sailing ships out of the Dardanelles caused chaos in the capitals population, causing the looting of bazaars and the escape of many inhabitants to the Asian shore. In Anatolia, protests and rebellions broke out against local governors, who acted as independent princes. Disorders spread throughout the empire, triggering an endemic civil war that lasted until 1656. After the conquest of Chaniá and Rethimnon, the Ottomans spent more than a year approaching the capital and all this prudence was due not only to the traditional Ottoman indolence, but to all the problems which exacerbated the already dramatic scenario, such as the scarcity of troops available and the shortage of materials and food. In May 1647 the Venetians obtained such useful information by deserters, who reported that the Ottomans were not more than 12,000 roughly divided as follows: 8,000 infantrymen and 250 horses in Réthymnon, 2,000 in Chaniá while the remaining 2,000 were destined to the fleet for assaulting Suda Island.[85] As evidence of the shortage of troops, even the conquest of smaller forts, such as the small castles of Mirabello, Ierapetra and Milopotamo, required much longer than normal. According to the reconnaissance executed by the defenders, the *serasker* could deploy 12,000 men, but only 5,000 were 'people for arms' and a further 300 as horsemen, while the remaining were retailers and servants.[86] In May 1648, after spending nearly six months transporting new troops to Crete, *Deli* Hüseyn could deploy 40,000 soldiers and 20,000 auxiliaries.[87] To the left of the siege ring were encamped the Asian troops under the *sançakbegs* of Kanghri and Adana, and on the other side there was the European camp. But the heavy casualties suffered in the assaults soon prompted the demand of more reinforcements. They arrived shortly, often exhausted by the dangerous crossing. In September, the need for new forces became so urgent that the expected arrival of 462 miners was long awaited by the commander, as it was a decisive rescue. The internal situation of the

85 ASVe, *Senato, Dispacci di Provveditori*, b. 495, 1 May 1647.

86 *Ibid., Collegio, Relazioni*, b. 80, *Relazione di Niccolò Delfin, ritornato dal Reg di Candia*, 1648.

87 Von Hammer-Purgstall, vol. IX, p. 299.

government grew heated and all the actors of the tale blamed each other for the failure of the campaign.[88] In Constantinople, the government failed to restore order and keep it for a long time, while the accusations between the soldiers were now turning into open struggle. In fact, the horsemen of the *sipahy ulufely*, who were traditionally enlisted from courtesans' and courtiers' sons, constituted a privileged corps less willing to withstand the hardness of a siege, which therefore fell on the janissaries and other foot soldiers. The deposition of Sultan Ibrahim I further hardened the *sipahy* in their position, unwilling to give up their privileges, especially now that their prerogatives were contested. Before the end of 1648, the army was driven by a wave of violence never before seen, on 26 October, in the infamous At-Meydan hippodrome massacre, more than 2,000 sipahy were eliminated along with their commanders. In turmoil, the turbulent foot soldiers of the *kapikulu* even demanded the dissolution of the *ulufely*, replacing them with a new corps formed by mounted janissaries. The disorder, however, achieved some benefit, as 2,000 *sipahy*, dismissed after the 24 October sedation, was granted reinstatement in the corps after agreeing to go as volunteers to Crete.

By mid July 1649, for the second assault on Candia, *Deli* Hüseiyn deployed 30,000 soldiers and 15,000 auxiliaries, of whom one third were represented by *lagimçi* (miners). The need to find volunteers who agreed to take part in a war at such a remote location, coupled with the difficulty of transporting soldiers to the routes threatened by the Venetians and their allies, compelled the government to resort to any means at its disposal. It was the *serdar* Hüseyin who proposed to Grand Vizier Tarhonçu Ahmed the repartitioning of the island in 15,150 *zeamet* and *timar* (appointments with 70,000 and 20,000 *akçe* of income) as a reward to the volunteers who agreed to engage for three years campaigning in Crete, and at a later time to enlist a substitute fully equipped as a horseman. The division of territory would have virtually deprived the state treasury of any benefit, but ultimately proved to be useful for the continuation of the siege, since it was possible to maintain a garrison of almost 16,000 men, who could permit at least the possession of the territory conquered until then. If necessary, these tribute *sipahy* could be joined with the garrison formed by the *kapikulu* soldiers quartered in the fortified encampment of Yeni Kandie. The Ottoman army found more soldiers among the peoples who traditionally provided mercenaries for a fixed-term engagement. In the first year of war, many Bosnian and Albanian volunteers joined the troops of the Ottoman governors of the provinces close to Dalmatia. In 1648, 5,000 *arnavut* (Albanian

88 To the various factors that caused the intermittence of the Ottoman military engagement, the exceptional contingent climatic conditions must also be added. Torrential rains in 1646 and an exceptional drought in 1647 destroyed the surplus of the crop causing a serious lack of food, especially in a city like Constantinople that consumed 500 tonnes of bread every day. In 1647, an invasion of locusts destroyed the crops in Moldova. This devastation also prevented the two subsequent harvests. Still, in the two-year period 1659–60 the territories on the coasts of the Aegean and the Black Sea found themselves facing "the worst drought in a millennium", it did not snow during the winter and the spring was exceptionally dry. The damage to crops and populations was enormous and devastating. The bad climatic scenario also affected the enemy, but to make the situation worse, in July 1660, also due to the extreme heat, a fire which broke out in Constantinople grew out of control and destroyed two thirds of the city. See G. Parker, cited work, p. 204.

and Bosnian irregular infantrymen) were recruited in order to suppress the uprising of Scutari and Durazzo. Then, in 1651, the Grand Vizier increased the engagement prizes to form a border corps for repulsing the incursions of the Morlachs in Venetian pay. In the same year, some high commanders, accused of inefficiency and nepotism, were also removed. Perhaps the more resounding case was the replacement of the janissaries' *aga* Momie Hüseyn (Hüseyn the mummy). In 1652 a further 2,000 *sipahy ulufely* were sent to Crete for a three-year service, then more volunteers were enlisted in the states of Tripoli, Algiers and Tunis, not only to join the Sultan's navy but also to form infantry units to be used in the Archipelago and especially in Crete. The need for men forced the government to unusual measures, as it did in January 1649, when it offered grace to the notorious chief of the Anatolian brigands, Haideroglu, if he agreed to go to Crete along with his men. This type of offer was not only reserved for criminals, but was also to the followers of the rebel *celali* leaders captured after the battle of Karahisar on October 1648 and Boulgourlü on July 1649. The definitive turning point that allowed the state to regenerate the army took place in 1656, when Köprülü Mehmed was appointed as grand vizier. Under him, sanctions were applied to the governors who did not respect the contingent's request established in the *osur*, while all forms of insubordination were rewarded with the utmost punishment. The rotation of the troops forming the contingent in front of Candia began to be executed every three years and the number of professional soldiers was increased to 6,000 janissaries, *cebeci* and artillerymen. The Grand Vizier proceeded to a drastic reform of the major provincial governorship, and even though he had to face revolts in Egypt and Syria, he persisted with his goal of returning to the Empire its old power. Despite the war against Venice, Köprülü Mehmed did not hesitate to intervene in Transylvania against Prince György II Rákóczy and subsequently opposed the Austrian Habsburgs in the region, not fearing to open a second war front. He tried all means of circumventing the blockade of the Dardanelles by despatching troops and supplies from the ports of Smyrna, Alexandria of Egypt and North African ports. To reject the feared Venetian incursions on the Anatolian coast, he called 40,000 *serhaddkulu* reservists and built new forts in the Dardanelles and along the coast to prevent enemy landings. When he succeeded his father, Köprülü Ahmed found both the army and navy in a condition certainly better than his predecessors did, but there was still a lot to do. The war of 1663–64 against the Habsburgs had provided him with the valuable experience of managing a large army, and this proved to be useful in selecting a good number of experienced officers, many of whom were at his side during the final assault on Candia. The last campaigns were planned with great care, trying to transport all the siege materials very rapidly. In order to infuse his men with courage, he distributed money to the troops and presented Kaftans of Honour to the 300 officers who had come specifically from Constantinople. The first ships had landed in Chaniá before the end of 1666. On 3 November, a force of 4,000 janissaries and *cebeci* landed together with the same grand vizier Köprülü Ahmed; then in January, despite the constant threat of the Venetian galleys, the Egyptian contingent under Ramazan *Beg* had landed, followed by other ships with soldiers, ammunition and all sorts of weapons. In mid-April 1667 other reinforcements landed on Crete with artillery and ammunition aboard the fleet of *kapudan pasa* Kaplan Mustafa. Now the army numbered about 40,000 soldiers with 18,000 artillerymen, diggers and miners. By the middle of June, further reinforcements had come almost uninterruptedly from every part of the empire, sometimes even on board French and English ships. On the eve of the new siege, Köprülü Ahmed could deploy more than 70,000 men of all specialities with over 300 guns and mortars. The huge effort sustained by the besiegers consumed in a relatively short time immense quantities of materials of all kinds. In 1667 the Ottomans consumed 20,000 tonnes of gunpowder, rising to almost 30,000 the following year, and then double in 1669, in the last eight months of combat. The bad state of the communication routes did not facilitate the transportation of supplies between Chaniá and the Ottoman camp, and so from the winter of 1667 and the following spring, the Ottomans fortified a seaport four miles from Candia. From this improvised port, named Çanakliman, Köprülü Ahmed assured the supplies for the besieging army, but the Venetians fleet soon discovered the port and the provveditor Lorenzo Corner crossed the sea with seven galleys at the entrance of the bay, preventing the landing of supplies. Further reinforcements continued to arrive in 1667 with the Ofen (Buda) *paşa* Hüseyin, and the beglerbeg of Sivas, who before the end of the year landed with new contingents to Crete. At the beginning of 1668, to overcome the shortage of artillery projectiles, Ahmed melted 20 large cannons and 10 mortars, produced according to Venetian calibre to reuse the 30,000 projectiles fired by defenders. In spring, the Grand Vizier could deploy just 20,000 able men, of whom only 14,000 were soldiers, but at the beginning of the summer the flow of reinforcements and supplies began to grow and before the end of June thousands of Egyptian janissaries and *sipahy* entered the trenches. With them arrived 800 Rumelian (European) janissaries, 1,500 *cebeci*, 1,000 artillerymen, 1,000 Armenian pioneers and miners, 500 Syrian *sipahy* and further 4,000 *sipahy toprakly* from all provinces of the Empire. Along with these troops landed also 20,000 quintals of gunpowder, 15,000 mortar bombs, 80,000 artillery projectiles ranging from 40 to 80 pounds, 20,000 grenades, 600 sacks of match for musket, and then leather, lead, iron, canvas, timber and utensils of all kinds, since the war had devoured everything and every material to fuel the siege had to be transported from outside. Even the North African states, called the year before by the Grand Vizier, helped to transport of reinforcements and material to the besiegers. In 1668, vessels ftom Tripoli carried from Izmir to Chaniá 4,000 *okka*[89] of edible fat, 1,000 *okka* of olive oil and vinegar, 2,600 *okka* of wheat, and 1,000 *okka* of cream, in addition to the indispensable biscuit for the army and the crews of the ships for a further four weeks. Finally, the trial of force obstinately pursued by Köprülü Ahmed prevailed on the admirable courage of the Venetians, unable to prevent the arrival of supplies and avoid the city's fate being sealed.

89 *Okka* or *oka* was an Ottoman measure of mass, equal to 400 *dirhems*. Its value varied, but it was standardised in the late empire as 1,2829 kilograms.

V

War on the Sea

Commanders and Crews

The long Cretan war showed that the Venetian fleet, if effectively conducted, represented a formidable war instrument capable of moving its threat to the Anatolian coasts, very close to the capital of the Ottoman Empire, and almost provoking collapse of the supply network for the enemy army engaged in Candia. The skill of Venetian naval officers in this period was certainly one of the highest in the history of the Republic. Despite the disappointing outcome of the war, enterprises and victories in over 24 years of struggle on the seas are the most obvious demonstration of the extraordinary qualities of Venetian captains and crews. The case of the families Foscolo, Barbaro, Corner, Mocenigo and Morosini, who provided all excellent military leaders – both on the sea and on the field – shows that, despite the declining interest of the Italian aristocracy in the military career, there was still a tradition capable of facing up to the most demanding challenges. Despite the unpromising beginnings, during the war Venice was able to turn out a large number of motivated and prepared officers. This is even more remarkable if we assume that one of the most important characteristics of the Venetian ruling class resides in the high turnover to which aristocrats were subjected within the political and administrative Republican system. It was rare that a nobleman had been holding public office for a long time, and even in the navy, as well as in the army, command posts did not last long, even as the officers were required to cover other offices in the state machine and their service could finish before the three years time set. This meant that Venice did not have a large number of professional officers who made military life their final choice. Moreover, at the beginning of the 17th century any European fleet had a corps of professional naval officers. The United Provinces appointed professional navy officers only after 1625, while in England it was only in the half of the century which a modern corps officers, paid by the government, was formed.

Any analogy with Western navy disappears when observing the composition and formation of the Ottoman naval officer class. Constantinople's option to avoid at all costs the challenge with the Venetian fleet, did not contribute to the formation of a naval officers corps prepared and for the first part of the war the Porte did very little to improve the captain's tactical skill, forming crews of volunteers attracted by the engage prizes or the employment in the *kapikulu,* and resorting on many occasions to promote captain of a galley some enterprising janissary or *sipahy*. In the reports concerning naval battles, Ottoman crews often demonstrate poor preparation, which resulted in bad coordination between the units in battle formation. All this turned easily into crisis under the blows of a resolute adversary who decided to exploit the offensive impact. The fate of Ottoman ships appeared, as a contemporary witness wrote, similar to that of a undefended herd of sheep attacked by a pack of wolves. The best preparation of the North African corsairs or some governor of the coastal provinces was of little help when faced with such a disastrous condition of the whole Ottoman navy. All this was accompanied by the many defeats suffered, which annihilated the morale of the entire fleet, to transform it into an instrument used only for the transport of men and supplies for the continuation of the siege at Candia.

By observing the careers of the *kapudan paşa* in charge between 1645 and 1669, it is possible to note that had been placed indifferently men with or without naval experience. Before 1656, namely until the appointment of Köprülü Mehmed as grand vizier, only two of the 12 *kapudan paşa* who directed the fleet could be regarded as true sailors. In the Ottoman Empire, high-level careers obeyed even more particular dynamics than in Venice. The appointment of Circassian Koca Dervis Mehmed in 1652 is the starting point for a high-level career begun in 1649 with the appointment as beglerbeg of Bosnia, where he was replaced at the end of the year due to the poor results achieved in Dalmatia. Equally bizarre, Bosnian Kara Musa's career, *kapudan paşa* from the spring of 1646, who led the fleet out of the Dardanelles, but only to retreat to Chalkis pursued by Tommaso Morosini's ships. When the news about the immobilised fleet arrived to Constantinople, the Sultan's anger was such as to threaten the revocation of all trade permits with the West, but by the curious and regrettable, political scenario, Kara Musa was on the point of obtaining the appointment to grand vizier, if his death in combat, occurred on 27 January 1647, had not prevented him. Corruption at all levels allowed men without talent to occupy many key positions, including that of admiral, despite the Venetian menace being so close to the shores of the empire. A typical feature of the Ottoman society was the donation that all the officials had to pay to their superior after promotion or appointment. Originally it was a precious but symbolic gift; then, especially under the reign of Ibrahim I, it became normal to pay in money to get any assignment. The most striking case was the one involving the *kiaya* of the Galata arsenal, Weli Ammaroglu, who in February 1648 literally bought the appointment of *kapudan paşa* by corrupting the grand vizier Sofi Mehmed. For many years, the fleet's official class was involved in intestinal fights that raged at every level, with all the corollary of malpractice and bribery. When the purge under the vizierate of Köprülü Mehmed hit major and minor officials alike, in summer 1656, after the disastrous defeat suffered in the Third Battle of the Dardanelles, the order to execute all the navy captain involved in the catastrophic action did not astonish. Even the relatives of the *kapudan paşa* Kenan were arrested, and indicted for any military and civil assignment. A year later Topal Mehmed, responsible for failing to regain

Tenedos (today Bozcaada in Turkey), was strangled by the slave oarsmen of his galley after order of the Grand Vizier. In order to understand the operations of Ottoman admirals, the psychological condition in which they acted should not be underestimated. The prestige of the office and the opportunity to earn conspicuous earnings could mean little compared to the risks carried by the post. Moreover, for many commanders, it was necessary to operate in a context – the sea – with which they had little familiarity, using subordinates who occupied those positions thanks to the support of someone in the government or through corruption, and finally without considering that the appointment as fleet commander could represent a way to be eliminated more easily. This was the outcome for the brave *deli* Hüseyin, promoted as *kapudan paşa* in the spring of 1658 by Köprülü Mehmed and then executed before the end of the year. The action of the *kapudan paşa* was therefore by definition insecure and exposed to serious risks and this placed him in a condition in which, in order to avoid criticism, it was necessary to expose himself to the risks of war on the sea, considering that his direct Venetian antagonist, the *capitano generale da mar* (captain general of the sea), did not hesitate to give an example by fighting like any sailor or soldier. This viaticum was twice fatal to the Ottoman admirals. In addition to the already mentioned Kara Musa, killed in action in January 1647, in May 1649 Voynok Ahmed *paşa* lost his life cut in two by a cannon shot while attempting to conquer the Venetian fortress of Suda island. Even when they were good commanders, the problem remained how to confront aggressive adversaries like the Venetians. The Algerian Hosambegzade Alì, *kapudan paşa* from 1650 to 1651, known in the West with the curious nickname of 'Mazzamamma' (who killed the mother), was probably the best Ottoman seaman of the first part of the war, but destiny gave him opponents such as Alvise Mocenigo, Lorenzo Marcello and other commanders destined to formidable careers. Among his own officers, Alì could count only on one experienced captain, Mustafa *beg*, namely the Venetian renegade Nicolò Furlan. The unfavourable outcome of the 1651 campaign, closed with the defeat suffered between the islands of Eubea and Naxos, caused his removal. However, his qualities as a commander were known to all, and this allowed to Hosambegzade Alì to resume the command of the fleet 10 years later, when he achieved some success in controlling the routes which carried supplies to Crete. However, it was not long before Ali died at Chios in May 1661, infected by the plague epidemic contracted in Crete the previous year and replaced by his son Abdulkadir. Like his father, the new admiral was a good seaman, but in the new phase of government inaugurated by the Köprülü viziers, his experience seems emblematic. The new *kapudan paşa* moved the fleet from Chios to Rhodes, but having learned about the plans of the Venetians thanks to the capture of a merchant vessel which carried letters sent by admiral Giorgio Morosini to Venice, he sailed to Crete. On 24 August 1661, the fleets spotted each other, but a violent storm separated them. On 26 August, when the sun was rising, the Venetian fleet again sighted the Ottoman ships, which were in great disarray off Milos island, and attacked them. The Venetian side reported the loss of a galleon with 110 Ottoman prisoners who were liberated, but Abdulkadir lost about 4,000 men killed or captured, six sunken galleys, and two more galleys captured by the Venetian and Maltese squadrons. Despite this failure, the *kapudan paşa* resumed the route to Athalia, where the rebel governors with their followers were concentrated, and after landing the artillery, he besieged the city. The rebels surrendered and this success served to dispel the bad mood of the Grand Vizier for the defeat suffered at Milos. As few before him, Abdulkadir preserved his life, but was dismissed and replaced by the Grand Vizier's son-in-law Merzifonlu Kara Mustafa.

Despite the deep differences between Ottoman and Venetian high admirals, some similarities can be found by focusing both ranks. The Venetian equivalent of the *kapudan paşa* was obviously the *capitano generale da mar*, whose activity was equally conditioned by the unpredictable dynamics of politics. About the captain general, the aforementioned Cardinal Pannocchieschi wrote: "He is not only the master of the ships subject to waves and winds, and in the field his command becomes limited."[1] Different views of other observers would not confirm this statement and allow us to consider the role of the Venetian high commander in detail. In the early years of the century, English ambassador to Venice Henry Wotton, describes the captain general's position as a kind of dictatorship, while Amelot de la Houssaie, secretary of the French embassy in Venice, noted: "His power is absolute over all other generals and captains, who seems to be a dictator or at least a sovereign … His authority extends not only to the fleet, but still to all ports, islands and fortresses, where they obey his orders without replying.[2]

Surely, the captain general's authority had grown over the centuries: "Sometimes the Senate does not allowed him (the Captain General) to undertake anything without the government's consensus, but as distance greatly delayed affairs, and all resolutions were taken when the opportunities were expired, he received the freedom to do whatever he considered necessary at the moment",[3] provided that he served the interest of the homeland. It is no coincidence that to make his dignity even more relevant, the captain general was automatically assigned the charge of *procuratore*, even though it could happen that the campaign's performance would affect the appointment. In spite of this, while having the power of life and death over everyone and not receiving precise orders at the beginning of each campaign, the captain general, such as the *kapudan paşa*, did not have a margin of unlimited autonomy. He had to deal with the overseas authorities, with the same prestige and experience as the *provveditori generali* of Crete, Dalmatia, and the Three Islands (Zakynthos, Corfu and Kefalonia), were closely related to the local scenario and jealous of their prerogatives. The captain general also had to settle in the war council with the endless dissensions between allied commanders, almost inevitable, according to the contemporary historian Andrea Valiero: "Deplorable events that have always affected the Republic, but always common events among people who must eat the same dish. And even though the Senate continually

1 Pannocchieschi, cited work, p. 277.

2 Amelot de la Houssaie, *Histoire du gouvernement de Venise*, vol. 3 (Paris, 1705), p. 36.

3 M. Casini, 'Immagini dei Capitani Generali da Mar a Venezia in età barocca', in *Il Perfetto Capitano*. Immagini e realtà (secoli XV–XVII), edited by M. Fantoni, Rome 2001, p. 233.

excited all the commanders to the union of souls, evil was recognised without remedy".[4]

The rivalry between Venice and its allies was more than once caused by delays, mishaps and failures. The questions of precedence inherent in the complex ceremonial existing in relations between the states were challenged by the prejudice of officers who were unwelcome to some powerful Allies. Often, the Venetian government complained of these bitter rivalries, also gaining the support of some allies, but even among the Venetians harmony did not always rule, and in some cases incomprehensible behaviour occurred which could only be explained by the need to avoid the susceptibility of some important family, with the result of excluding someone from a position of command who had been proven to possess qualities useful for direction of the fleet. For example, a disagreement is known of, one of open hostility, between Francesco Morosini and Antonio Barbaro. The latter, according to many of the contemporaries, despite being considered one of the best Venetian seaman, was forced to resign his career in the fleet due to the hostility of the captain general. This scenario badly affected the fleet as well as the defence of Candia and other war operations. According to the opinion of some historians, the dedication of the aristocracy to careers in the war fleet has to be observed with caution. The captain general represents a special case of captain-prince. Consequently in the constitution of Venice, in which power was theoretically shared in equal form among the members, the captain general was at the same time a member of the highest sovereignty and servant of that sovereignty. The dual value of the captain general's capability, as well as the need to pay his war costs, are factors explaining why in choosing the candidates, the appointment was not always conferred according to the candidate's technical ability, since no specific experience would be required, but according to the political pressures, the position of prestige within a faction, personal wealth and the waves of enthusiasm following a victory. For instance, in 1645 it is possible to observe of Giovanni Cappello that he was "Senator of no great experience in maritime affairs", but ultimately elected as captain general "... for the goodness of his costumes, and for the severity used in other Republic's supreme offices."[5] However, Cappello did not succeed in achieving any success, and even after failing to prevent the loss of Chaniá, in 1646 he remained inactive at the fall of Rethymno. For replacing Giorgio Morosini as captain general in 1663, first Angelo Correr and later Battista Nani were chosen, but both refused, declaring themselves unfamiliar with the matter of war on the sea. Nani himself, the well known historian of Venice, considered captain general Alvise Mocenigo, one of the major heroes of the conflict, completely inexperienced as fleet commander. Emblematic is the case emerging from an anonymous relation dated 1664, which depicts Antonio Barbaro as one of the most tenacious and best soldiers of the Republic, but then adds that being poor and unpopular to some Senate members, he would not advance in the fleet's hierarchy, notwithstanding no one deserved more than him the dignity of captain general, a rank that, in

4 Valiero, p. 248.
5 M. Casini, cited work, p. 231.

46. "The Queen of the Mediterranean Sea", the galley, represented the main framework of the Venetian and Ottoman fleets during the Cretan war. (Venetian galley, after an Italian drawing by an anonymous artist, second half of the 17th century)*

fact, Barbaro would never reach. That the captain's election was subject to the changing orientation of the Senate, can be seen in the events of June 1656. After the Third Battle of the Dardanelles, the younger members rejected the Senate candidate, "the mediocre poor" Antonio Bernardo, and voted for the young and now famous Lazzaro Mocenigo, provoking the anger of Francesco Morosini, the other important candidate who aspired to command the fleet. The reciprocal suspect between the Venetian ruling class was ambivalent. In fact, Morosini often received reproaches from the Senate's members, because of his attitude to military matters. Political rivalry involved every level of the society, and against Morosini appeared also anonymous sonnets which criticised the aggressive and bellicose manner of the Republic's future hero.[6]

Political ability dominated the choice of captain general and it was essential for him, considered the diplomatic capacities required by this role. Firstly, the Venetian captain general represented the *Serenissima*'s sovereignty; secondly, he had to face in the war councils the aforementioned endless contrasts between the allied officers, the Venetian captains and the *provveditori da mar*. Finally, and above all, his leadership was subjected to serious inquiries by the Senate, which often opened proceedings on his conduct and exposed him to public opinion. Numerous examples can be done concerning the ambivalence of the supreme commander's reputation. Captain general and hero Leonardo Foscolo never managed to reach the highest Venetian dignity, the election to Doge, perhaps because of the widespread suspicion of his having diverted money. Giorgio Morosini was accused of corruption

6 *Ibid.*, p.232.

47. The galleass was an invention of the Venetians, who introduced it at the battle of Lepanto, and it was later imitated by other navies including the Ottomans', who called this ship *mavuna*. (Ottoman *mavuna*, copy after Hyeronimus Beck's *Exaratae turcarum imperatorum imperatorum, capitaneorum. Immagina, habitus, ludos, caerimonias*... Österreichische Nationalbibliothek Vienna, early 17th century)*

too in 1651, but more than any other Francesco Morosini had to defend himself from suspicions of misappropriation and other accusations until the strong attack by Antonio Correr in 1670, who accused him of having unduly surrendered to the enemy in Candia in September 1669.

The Cretan war was the last conflict in which galleys along with the galleazze/*mavuna* maintained their numerical supremacy over sailing ships. This feature has contributed to formation of the opinion that the Cretan war was conditioned by the serious technical delays of the Ottoman and Venetian navy. On the other hand, if we look at these figures with more attention, we discover that between 1645 and 1669 there had been great innovations. As a historian (Guido Candiani) pointed out, all the battles fought exclusively by sailing ship took place after 1646. If the major clashes were fought in the second part of the war, none of them happened without the presence of sailing ships, and three major battles of 14 saw the sailing ships as exclusive players. Therefore, it is evident that the height of collaboration between oared and sailing ships was achieved during the Cretan war. Before, in the Mediterranean, the sailing ship had often been an obstacle for combined actions with the galleys because of its slowness in manoeuvring, and the need to be constantly towed to face the enemy with such variable winds. Moreover, that is not to underestimate a decisive cultural factor, namely that Venetian galleys had always proved to be excellent and suitable instruments for sailing in the Mediterranean. They offered the indispensable quality, agility and manoeuvrability for performing along the coasts. Under this point of view, for the Venetian seamen it was difficult to abandon a weapon always considered as fundamental for that kind of war. In the past, the ability of Venetians and Ottomans to have a large navy and plenty of sailors had allowed them to build an empire with bases and ports of strategic importance. This allowed the galleys – the traditional weapon of both fleets – to supply water and food easily, as they had a maximum of four to five days of autonomy. Although the conditions on board were very hard and the captains tried to preserve provisions as much as possible, in summer every oarsman consumed at least seven litres of water per day, without which he could hardly serve at the benches. For this, an almost uninterrupted line of ports from the northern Adriatic, or from Anatolia, to the Aegean, allowed an easy supply and the escort of the merchant navy and sea control. As long as crews were available in abundance, the galley was the point of balance between military necessity and economic assessment, at least in a proportion believed reasonable by the government. Although to impose a naval blockade it was necessary to have the firepower that only the sailing vessels could guarantee, and without the support of the rowing units, success was not guaranteed. Moreover, as long as their armament was considerable, the effective firing distance of the guns of Dutch or British sailing ships was lower than the big galleys' guns – especially those of galleasses – could reach. The most important advantage of the galley compared to the sailing ship was obviously mobility, which was allowed by the 'human engine'.

The oarsmen represented more than 70 percent of the crew on a galley or on a galleass/*mavuna*. These men were subjected to a harsh treatment, though less brutal than some literature has handed down to us. Unlike other Mediterranean navies, Venice employed a very limited number of convicts and slaves to fill the benches of its galleys; on the contrary, the Turkish fleet used prisoners and slaves at all times, buying them in large numbers from the Tartars and other Caucasus populations.

Despite all possible caution being used, life on the galleys remained at the limit of endurance. In addition to the inherent risks of the fight, the oarsmen lived in a small space and were constantly exposed to the elements and tormented by parasites, lice, and bedbugs, which, according to numerous testimonies, were almost inevitable guests in every galley. Usually, each bench housed three oarsmen who shared a quilted leather mattress on which they sat and slept, and two barrels of water. A simple method to impose discipline and to avoid desertions was to punish the oarsmen of the same bank from which one had fled. A Tuscan archive source dated 1679 shows with some detail the mortality rate among the galley's oarsmen. On a total of 920 men assigned to the galleys of the order of Santo Stefano, in 10 years of cruises 508 oarsmen lost their lives. The causes of the deaths were varied, but the large majority, 419, died in Leghorn hospital, and only 78 in perished in navigation. According to the Tuscan source, the annual death rate was six percent of the total force. It should be pointed out that this ratio was recorded during a period in which the Medicis' squadron supported a few battles. Indirectly, it is possible to note that in Tuscany the percentage of volunteer oarsmen – or *buonavoglia* – was very low, and unlike in Venice, where regulation prescribed a minimum of six volunteers in each galley. The rate of death confirms this percentage. In fact, the deaths between the volunteers were only 33, against 248 deaths

48. This sea corselet belonging to the Grimani family is a mid-17th century piece from Brescia, now preserved in the collection of the Palazzo Venezia in Rome. The surface is bronzed and steel wheel -worked. Defensive armour such as this was usually worn on board ship by high officers of the Christian fleets.

among slaves and 225 among the convicted.[7] However, it should not to be ruled out that different treatment conditions determined the rate of survival. Another interesting data comes from the Venetian archives and show a more detailed scenario. This data confirms that galleys were extremely sensitive to outbreaks of epidemics among their crews, especially among the oarsmen, who due to the very harsh conditions of their service, such as exposure to heat during summer and cold winds and rain in autumn and winter, combined with malnutrition, were very susceptible to various diseases. The following examples provide an impressive account about the effects the epidemic outbreaks could have on galley crews. In June 1653, immediately upon the arrival of galley *Trona* in Zadar, its captain and 40 rowers became so sick that they were soon admitted to hospital. The galley was anchored in the port until they were cured.[8] Even more striking was the case of galley *Civrana*, which in December 1655 arrived in Zadar after a long and hard winter voyage. Upon docking, 48 of its rowers, who had fallen sick during this single voyage, were immediately dispatched to hospital. Moreover, the galley had already lost 55 crewmen during the previous campaign season and the overwhelming majority of them were oarsmen. The crew was reduced to barely 99 men or 40 percent of the full strength, making the galley completely incapable of sea service.[9] Probably one of the most dramatic example dates from the campaign season of 1658. At the beginning of the year the Republic had dispatched four newly armed galleys to the Adriatic, yet as early as August the state of these galleys was deplorable. A total of 168 crew members were dead and further 113 were hospitalised, bringing total losses to 281 men, or almost 25 percent of the crews, lost during a single campaign season.[10]

Though this last example may seem rather extreme, it was not that extraordinary. Some data compiled from several muster records of galleys serving in the Adriatic. It shows that the galley crews were, on average, at 75–83 percent of their full strength. An extensive loss suffered during a single season, such as those during 1658, could partially be attributed to a more demanding campaign, but probably even more to malnutrition, inexperience, and maladjustment of the newly formed crews to the conditions of life aboard the war galley. In 1658, general provveditor Antonio Bernardo offered to the Senate the following explanation for the deplorable state of the aforementioned galley crews:

7 ASFi, *Mediceo del Principato*, F. 2130, *Negozi diversi attenenti alle Galere*, cc. 234–235.

8 ASVe, *Provveditori da Terra e da Mar*, b. 474, c. 44.

9 *Ibid.*, b. 478, c.80.

10 *Ibid.*, b. 483, c. 207, in Split, 25 August 1658; attachment: *Nota delli morti et infermi delle Galere.*

> From this derives their fall, if not for the change, from the comfortable life, according to the conditions of each one, to the hard life on the galley; coming under a warmer climate, not they are accustomed to the torment of the oar, nor of the sea; and to this the soul afflicts these oarsmen, which prostitutes them to abandon desperately themselves, as if they were lost.[11]

Possibly, galley crews formed exclusively by Venetian subjects from the *Terraferma* compared to those armed with population from Dalmatian islands provide arguments in favour of the hypothesis that inexperience and maladjustment to the conditions of the sea service could have terrible consequences on the state of a galley crew. Galley *Bergamasca*, armed with a crew from inland Bergamo, who had had little or no experience in sea service, by May 1647 had lost a majority of its crew and was docked in the Zadar harbour. By contrast, two Dalmatian galleys, *Brazzana* and *Arbessana*, armed in 1646 (named after the island communities of Brač and Rab), responsible for manning these galleys, remained in service for the entire duration of the war and gave a very good account of their service. During the war there was never recorded a sharp decrease in the strength of the crews of these two galleys, manned with islanders well accustomed to the conditions and hardships of sea service.[12] Even though, when in 1653 galley *Brazzana* was rearmed because its worn out hull was no longer seaworthy, it lacked 118 crew members, this was a consequence of almost seven years of uninterrupted service. Moreover, since the galley served so close to its home, many of the missing crewmen should be considered as deserters or licensed.[13] The same

11 ASVe, *Provveditori da Terra e da Mar*, b. 483, dated 25 August 1658; attachment: *Nota delli morti et infermi.*

12 Venice continued to draw on its Dalmatian resources and in March 1657 even planned to arm an entire new galley with crewmen from Zadar and its district. Governor-general Bernardo informed the Senate of the strong opposition of the local population to this initiative: since up to that time, some 500 men had left for the Levant and only a few had returned. In spite of general provveditor Bernardo's doubts, the Senate decided to press forward with this plan. Over the following months, Bernardo managed to conscript prospective members of the crew for the new galley, but only after conceding to the demands of the local population that the galley was to serve only in the Adriatic. This new levy had completely exhausted the provincial resources and when in October 1657 a new order for the conscription of 150 rowers came to Zadar, Bernardo was forced to send armed boats to collect the necessary conscripts. The boats returned with only four men because the population had fled at the first sight of Venetian flags. The next attempt to gather reinforcements for the crew of the captain general in March 1658 also yielded a similar result; at the first news of the arrival of Venetian ships sent to collect conscripts for galleys, the remaining inhabitants of the islands and the Zadar countryside took cover and the prescribed quotas of the crewmen simply could not be gathered. In ASVe, *Provveditori da Terra e da Mar*. b. 482. c. 140 and b. 482, c. 158.

13 Concerning this topic, see also the excellent work of Domagoj Madunić, The Adriatic Naval Squadron (1645– 1669), cited work. The author focuses the Venetian Adriatic scenario with good detail. Concerning the recruitment of oarsmen in Dalmatia he adds: "In addition to the two Dalmatian galleys that for the entire duration of the war served almost exclusively in the Adriatic, hundreds of Dalmatians also ended up serving aboard galleys in the Levant. The seat of the Venetian administration in Dalmatia, the town of Zadar, and the islands of its littoral were burdened with one of the heaviest duties: to provide rowers for the galley of captain-general of the sea. At the beginning of the war, levying of men for this duty went without any serious problems. Every few years, when the new general provveditor set forth toward the Levant, some 100 or 150 men would be levied for his galleys in Zadar. However, since those who left for

data inform us about the composition of the crews, always with reference to the Adriatic Sea oared fleet at different times. On February 1646, the six galleys of the squadron mustered 1,324 crewmen and 424 missing. Oarsmen were 928 of a full strength of 1,200. Of these 883 were *zentavoli* 'volunteers', five were convicts, plus 40 others. On July 1659, the same six galleys claimed 286 crewmen missing, of which 55 were oarsmen. The volunteers were now 671 and convicts 448, a further 26 were Ottoman prisoners. On March 1660, now with three galleys, the squadron needed 211 crewmen, including 71 oarsmen. The volunteers were 398, convicts 123, Ottomans two, plus six others. Finally, on February 1668 the 3 galleys mustered 539 oarsmen and 61 missing. Now the volunteers were 224, convicts were 285, and Ottoman prisoners 58, plus five others.[14]

During the war, the Ottomans easily managed to replace losses, while the Venetians suffered a shortage of men, especially after 1648. The tremendous sinking at Psara, which occurred in March, caused the loss of 18 galleys alongside with three quarters of the oarsmen and the rate of recruitment was not able recover the light fleet from the disaster, affecting the overall numbers of galleys available, which rarely exceeded 35 units.

The harshness of life on the benches did not oarsmen being used in other tasks, perhaps with the promise of a reduction in punishment, whether they were condemned, or a prize. In 1649, at the siege of Risan, the oarsmen participated by digging trenches and mines, transporting materials from the galleys and unloading the artillery onto the beach. This type of aid was certainly easier to obtain by the Venetian commanders, on the other hand the high number of slaves and prisoners of the Ottoman galleys led on several occasions to mutiny, some of which ended with the desertion of the entire galley in a Venetian port. The strong presence of prisoners of war among the oarsmen of the Ottoman galleys must have remained constant throughout the war. In March 1668, Francesco Morosini liberated 1,000 Christian oarsmen who were on the galleys led by the corsair Durac Bey, defeated by the captain general before the Ottoman attempt to assault the island of Standia, a few miles off Crete. Once the oarsmen landed to Candia, they were mixed with other soldiers to form new battalions for defending the mine galleries: little better a destiny than the one they came from.

---

the Levant almost never returned, the first difficulties in finding men for this service began to appear by 1650. When the next order to gather 150 men for this duty arrived in Zadar in July 1651, Governor-general Girolamo Foscarini informed the Senate that he was approached by representatives of the community of the Zadar islands. They inquired if it would be possible for them to replace those selected for galley service with Ottoman prisoners or slaves bought from the Morlachs. After pondering the issue for some time, Foscarini decreed that only freemen could serve aboard the galley of captain general; however, prisoners could be used to staff other galleys with the substituted freemen transferred to the galley of the captain-general. How effective was this policy is unknown, yet by 1655, when the next contingent of 150 rowers was requested, general provveditor Zeno informed the Senate that the manpower pool of the islands was almost completely exhausted. Zeno wrote to his superiors that the situation was such that at the first rumour of this order, the remaining men eligible for service were ready to either hide or flee, some even to the Ottoman territory."

14 D. Madunić, cited work, p. 220.

Plate A

Venetian Crete, 1645 (L–R): Cretan militia horseman; Venetian *provveditor*; *Oltramontano* musketeer

(Illustration by Bruno Mugnai, © Helion & Company)

See Colour Plate Commentaries for further information.

Plate B

The *Armata*, 1653–57 (L–R): Venetian *sopracomito*, or galley commander; Venetian *bombardiere*, galley artillery NCO; Venetian sailor

(Illustration by Bruno Mugnai, © Helion & Company)

See Colour Plate Commentaries for further information.

The Mine, 1667–69 (L–R): miner; Dutch engineer; Italian infantryman

(Illustration by Bruno Mugnai, © Helion & Company)

See Colour Plate Commentaries for further information.

Last Defence, 1669 (L–R): pikeman of an Italian regiment; French volunteer and servant; *Oltramontano* grenadier

(Illustration by Bruno Mugnai, © Helion & Company)

See Colour Plate Commentaries for further information.

First Conquests, 1645–50 (L–R): janissary in campaign dress; janissary *aşçı başı*; janissary *odabasi*

(Illustration by Bruno Mugnai, © Helion & Company)

See Colour Plate Commentaries for further information.

Plate F

***Azab*, Levend and Corsair, 1648–1669 (L–R): naval *azab* in combat dress; *beg*, galley commander; *topçu levend*, naval artilleryman**

(Illustration by Bruno Mugnai, © Helion & Company)

See Colour Plate Commentaries for further information.

Guarding the Straits, 1653–59 (L–R): *sipahy ulufely* cavalryman; Köprülü Mehmet, Grand Vizier; *serhaddkulu* infantryman

(Illustration by Bruno Mugnai, © Helion & Company)

See Colour Plate Commentaries for further information.

The Trench, 1667–69 (front–back): two *kapikulu* infantrymen, *cebeci*; *serrhadkulu* infantryman, *azab tüfekçi*; *sipahy toprakly*, Syrian *timar*

(Illustration by Bruno Mugnai, © Helion & Company)

See Colour Plate Commentaries for further information.

The traditional cautiousness of the Venetian government is evident in the composition of the fleets launched since 1648. Apart from the early and final years of the conflict, which saw some significant forces thanks also to the allied and auxiliary fleets, the Venetians often found themselves lacking means. Many of the captain general's relations agree that with a few units it would have been possible to achieve a full success, not only in the large Dardanelles battles, but also in cruises against merchant shipping in the Aegean or Libyan Sea. The relationship between rowing units and sailing ships became less and less in favour of the latter, only increasing when the auxiliaries, or *ponentine*, as Venetians called their galleys, they were present with the *Armata*. The allied squadrons sometimes reached a considerable numerical consistency. In September 1645, in the frustrating expedition against Chaniá, participated 21 auxiliary galleys, of which six were from Malta and five each from the ecclesiastical State, Naples and Tuscany. Because of a disagreement with the Knights of St. John, the Genoese galleys had abandoned the fleet that was meeting between Civitavecchia and Messina. With their presence, the fleet would have deployed a total number of units never reached throughout the war. Subsequently, the auxiliary fleet never exceeded the total of 20 galleys of 1667, when six Maltese and Papal galleys, plus four each from Naples and Sicily anchored off Standia. Their participation interrupted a three-year interval during which no auxiliary units had taken part in joint actions with the Venetian fleet. During the 24 years of war the Maltese sent their galleys in 13 campaigns: six units until 1647 and then seven from 1656; the Pope sent his galleys 10 times up to a maximum of five ships; the Grand Duke of Tuscany sent his squadron in 1645, then only two galleys in 1659 and three in 1660. In 1658 10 rented sailing ships sailed to Crete with the economic support of some Roman aristocratic families.

The number of improved vessels increased exponentially over the years and the same tendency, although more irregular, was also recorded in the Ottoman side. The impulse to produce these type of ships derived directly from the war, especially when the Ottomans attempted countermeasures to break the naval blockade of the Dardanelles. In fact, in 1649, though having passed the Venetian fleet with their galleys and *mavunas* – taking advantage of the absence of the enemy ships engaged to get water – the Ottomans had suffered the defeat off Foça and so, from 1651, the Sultan's fleet launched an important plan of sailing ships for trying to break the siege. In the spring of 1651, 10 new sailing units were launched in the Galata shipyards, thanks to the recruitment of European technicians. The new ships entered in service in June of the same year with another five purchased from Western private ship owners. In fact, in those years, was recorded the largest increase in spending by the Ottoman treasures, totalling 687,200 *akçe*: the highest in the whole war and the highest even in absolute terms, as it produced a budget deficit of more than 500,000 *akçe*.[15]

At the half of the 17th century the Dutch were considered the best shipbuilders, and immediately after them, the English. Relations between

15 Von Hammer-Purgstall, vol. X, p. 296.

the Republic and London were, however, poorer than those which existed for years with the United Provinces of the Netherlands. For this reason the *Armata Grossa* engaged many ships and sailors from those regions, who demonstrated on several occasions their skill in sailing and fighting, especially the artillerymen. In the 1651 campaign, culminating in the naval battle of Paros, most of the sailing ships and crew employed by the Venetians, both for public and rented ships, came from the Netherlands. On that occasion a sailing ship had been hired in Hamburg's Hanseatic Republic, the *Rad des Glückes* (Wheel of Fortune) with 40 cannons, enthusiastically mentioned in the reports for the effectiveness of its artillery.[16] The technological development of northern European navies was never matched by Venice, who was able to arm the first vessel completely set up in the city arsenal only in September 1667: *Giove Fulminante* (*Lightning Jupiter*), was immediately sent to the Aegean with the rest of the fleet.

However, it would not be right to argue that the technological gap was passively endured by the Venetians, who in 1660 – while buying large vessels and enlisting foreign crews – began to design the first ships divided into three classes. A first-class public ship, according to the arsenal regulations, could embark 506 soldiers among officers, privates and musicians with 13 drums and fifes, plus 165 crewmen. During the war, the Venetians never stopped experimenting with new weaponry solutions for galleys and galleasses, and despite the delay in setting up large ships, the Venetian Navy could be regarded as one of the major fleets of the world and probably the first in the Mediterranean.

Duel in the Aegean Sea

Of the 27 years of the Cretan war, at least 16 were marked by particularly demanding naval campaigns carried out following the same pattern: the Ottomans were trying to supply their army in Crete, while the Venetians tried in all ways to stop this flow of supplies, isolating the besiegers from their bases. In the early years of the conflict there was a limited number of battles between the two fleets and the Venetian debut was far from satisfactory. Apart from the enterprise of captain of the Candian Guard Giorgio Morosini, who with three galleys managed to reach some relief to the besieged Chaniá, in the first year the Ottomans were able to transport undisturbed supplies to fuel the conquest of the island. The attempt made in September 1645 to attack the enemy fleet at Chaniá with the galleys fleet led by Captain General Giovanni Cappello, was rejected by the Ottomans, who on that occasion blocked the access to the port by linking masts to floating barrels and in this way thwarted the attempt to drive an incendiary vessel into the port. Before the end of the year, the only success achieved by the Venetians was the capture of a merchant vessel off Milo by Lorenzo Marcello

16 ASVe, *Provveditori da Terra e da Mar*, b 328, *Dispacci*, relation of the sailing ship's captain Francesco Barbaro.

49. Lorenzo Marcello became captain general after the death of Girolamo Foscarini. He held several assignments in the fleet, participating in the war from 1645. His first and last campaign as captain general ended on 26 June 1656 with a resounding victory in the Third Battle of the Dardanelles, during which Marcello was killed in action. (Fresco by Sebastiano Mombelli, Ancestors' salon, Ca' Marcello, Levada, Padua. With the kind permission of Dr Jacopo Marcello)

and Alvise Mocenigo. It was the commander of the sail ship Tommaso Morosini who argued to counter the Ottoman strategy preventing the convoys from getting to Crete. For achieving this objective, the fleet had to be sent to the eastern Aegean for blocking the access to the Dardanelles. The channel was actually the Achilles' heel for the Ottomans, and the intuition of the Venetian *procuratore* anticipated the validity of this by centuries. Indeed both the Russians in 1877–78, the Italians in 1912 and finally the Allies in 1915 would plan a similar strategy to force the Porte out of the war.

In May 1646, a large Ottoman fleet composed of 76 galleys and five *mavunas* was repulsed into the Dardanelles by Valier and Contarini's sailing ships. In the summer of 1647, a new squadron formed of 23 galleys, two *fruste* and 26 great and small vessels raised anchor from Constantinople and other ports in West Anatolia. On 25 August, the Ottomans were intercepted in front of the island of Chios by 16 Venetian sailing ships. This time, the Ottomans deployed about 20 French, English, and Dutch vessels which were in Smyrna. In both encounters, the lack of wind and the absence of galleys to tow the sailing ships allowed only a small fraction of Venetian units to enter into action. The encounters evolved into gun duels lasting many hours, but did not cause significant damage to the fleets. The same problem would occur again in the following years, proving that the sailing ships were unable to act with the hoped-for efficiency in the eastern Mediterranean. Before the end of the summer 1647, Venetian sailing ships managed to block the *kapudan paşa* in the port of Nauplia, but in early September Ottoman ships, evading the surveillance overnight, put out to sea and off Metelino joined the main fleet coming from Chios. Finally they reached Chaniá, where landed 9,000 men with many supplies.[17] In the autumn, the galleys sent by the new captain general Giovanni Battista Grimani, cruising the waters between Gramvousa and Candia, caused much damage to Ottoman traffic, highlighting its vulnerability due to the absence of alternative ports to Chaniá and Réthymnon. In 1648 the Venetian campaign was compromised by the death of the valiant Captain General Grimani, in the storm off Psara on 17 March, where nine sailing ships and 18 galleys were destroyed.

The Ottomans were barely able to exploit the enemy disadvantage, refuelling the garrison on the island, but avoided challenging the Venetians as well as refusing to plan actions against the strategic enemy outpost in the Aegean Sea.

17 Von Hammer-Purgstall, Vol. X, p. 79.

50. The rock of Moraiti on the islet of Suda, not far from Chaniá, was often the scene of ambushes carried out by the Venetian galleys on the traffic directed to the harbour conquered by the Ottomans in August 1645. The preservation status of the walls and rooms of the fortress is fortunate considering that, like other examples of Venetian and Ottoman rule in Greece, it was in danger of being demolished during the colonels' regime. (Author's photo)

The order issued by the *kapudan paşa* to his captain had to be very peremptory and possibly instilled in the crews poor faith in their own capabilities. The major drawback occurred at the end of April, when the sailing ship captain Jacopo Riva moved his squadron to the Dardanelles, in order to close the sortie from there. Here the Venetians repulsed the attempt of *kapudan paşa* Ammaroglu Veli to overcome the blockade with 40 galleys, five *mavunas* and an unspecified number of sailing ships with 5,000 soldiers for Crete. This failure resulted in the death sentence for the Ottoman commander.

The Ottomans had avoided any encounter against the enemies, but on 12 May 1649 they could not escape the challenge fought in the great battle in front of the Ottoman Port of Foça. Here, the Venetians achieved the first important naval success of the war. The battle was fought by 19 Venetian sailing ships, of which two were poorly armed, against 72 galleys, 10 *mavunas* and 11 sailing ships under the new *kapudan paşa* Haidar Oldì. The Ottomans were sailing under the forts erected to defend the cove. Ignoring the doubts of his captains, who did not want to operate so close to the coast against the enemy forces, Riva gained a very important victory, sinking or capturing 10 sailing ships and four *mavunas*, but only two galleys. However, Jacopo Riva, now appointed as captain general, complained that if he could have only a dozen galleys more, the victory would have been even greater.

If, on a tactical level, sailing ships did not yet guarantee the same results as oared ones, the strategic contest showed, that the presence of the sailing ships became more and more effective. With rented armoured merchants and small galleys squadrons' support, in the spring and summer 1649 the Venetians managed to block the Dardanelles channel almost uninterruptedly. The blockade was not only intended to cut off the main supply line of the Ottoman army in Crete, but also to paralyse Constantinople's trade with the rest of the empire, especially with Syria and Egypt.

Venetian strategy was slowly gaining some success, however, the Ottomans reacted and found other solutions to circumvent the blockade. On 5 May 1650, *kapudan paşa* Hosambegzade Alì declared that under the current conditions, the fleet could not leave the port; therefore, he relocated the ammunition and the 3,000 men destined for Crete, embarking them at Çeşme on the corsairs' vessels waiting for them outside the Dardanelles. In turn, the Venetians intensified their monitoring in the Aegean and captured several merchants between spring and summer. The following year, in May, the *kapudan paşa* thought that the time had come to get out of the straits and in mid-June headed for the eastern entrance of the Dardanelles with 53 galleys, six *mavunas* and 47 sailing ships. Before the end of the month, with this new squadron, the Ottomans came out on the open sea, taking advantage of the fact that the Dardanelles had remained unattended due to the problems with captains and crew of the Dutch vessels hired by Venice, who complained of delayed payments and the wear on their ships in the winter. Hosambegzade Alì moved his fleet to Chios to join the *bey* squadron and then sailed to Crete, loaded with supplies and troops to land at Chaniá, now with a force of 55 sailing ships, of which at least 37 were armed, including eight vessels provided by North African corsairs. Having resolved in part the controversy with the Dutch crews, the Venetians moved to catch the convoy with 28 sailing ships, six galleasses and 24 galleys. On 7 July 1651, the two fleets came into contact a few miles north of Santorini. The new captain general Alvise Mocenigo had arranged the fleet with a vanguard with 17 sailing ships under Francesco Barbaro and another eight sailing ships, along with the galleasses, in reserve with the galleys. If large sailing ships had not been placed in the front row in the past, this was done in the forthcoming encounter and to facilitate the complex manoeuvre, the galleys had towed the sailing ships to the assigned position. On that occasion, the sailing ships proceeded independently, applying a tactic that in the northern seas had yielded good results with the introduction of the frigate. This type of sailing ship, smaller but well-armed and still able to manoeuvre with more agility than the largest vessels, had been set up at the beginning of the century by Dunkerque-based French corsairs, and soon imitated by Dutch and English. However, the Venetian commander expected too much from his sailing ships, because only five vessels managed to keep the route as expected, while the other 12 lost contact and some even had to be towed. When the Ottoman wooden ships, which manoeuvred to try to flee towards Crete, were again sighted in the morning of 8 July, the five most advanced Venetian units moved boldly to engage the whole enemy fleet, but three of them soon found themselves in danger. Meanwhile, the Captain General was desperately trying to send other ships to their rescue. At the end, two of the fastest ships came to support the small avant-garde, but the others, too heavy and slow in the manoeuvre, remained upwind. In another sector, galleys and galleasses were studying the enemy, until Mocenigo, who manoeuvred upwind also, decided to take the initiative and close with the enemy, supported by four of the eight sailing ships remaining in reserve. The Venetian gunners opened the fire at a distance and for a while, the Ottomans replied, but then they turned away, taking advantage of a strong wind decay and towing their sailing ships with galleys. The 9 July was spent with the Venetians engaged in repairs and

51. Lazzaro Mocenigo was one of the most brilliant and daring Venetian naval officers of the war. (Portrait of Mocenigo as captain general, by Francesco Maffei; Naval History Museum, Venice)*

52. A stern decoration fragment of Lazzaro Mocenigo's galley. On the last day of the Fourth Battle of the Dardanelles, the galley was heavily damaged by the explosion of the ammunition depot, hit by the Ottoman batteries stationed on the banks of the Straits. (Naval History Museum, Venice)

grouping the fleet; then, at dawn on the following day, they rediscovered the Ottoman fleet in navigation north of the channel between Paros and Naxos island. This time the confrontation between the two fleets was inevitable and the commanders deployed their forces according to the classic naval battles scheme of the Mediterranean, with a centre and two wings ranging from galleys to galleasses or *mavunas* and sailing ships. Mocenigo had under his authority a good number of skilled captains, including some of the best commanders of the century: his nephew Lazzaro, the promising Lorenzo Marcello who directed a squadron of galleys, and the still unknown Francesco Morosini as captain of the galleasses. However, the early stages of the battle demonstrated how certain tactical choices, which proved decisive, occurred almost by chance. Some of the Venetian sailing ships once again encountered problems of manoeuvrability, confirming that homogeneity of speed remained haphazard for them, so that they had to be towed to the assigned place. While the Captain General was engaged in these operations, two of the three left-wing galleys, including the one commanded by the impulsive Lazzaro Mocenigo, moved forward to attack the isolated Ottoman galleys. Before the Venetian commander could recall the two galleys in formation, the *kapudan paşa* sent from the centre six *mavunas* and a dozen galleys, which with stiff rowing flanked the enemies. The two Venetian galleys, immediately supported by the galleasses, turned to present the artillery of the ircastles against the Ottoman ships. The Venetian guns fired a first volley and then approached further to unload the musketry and the smaller pieces. The clash rampaged violently around the ship of Lazzaro Mocenigo, targeted by the *kapudan paşa*'s galley along with two *mavunas*, to which were added some galleys who tried to board the enemy ship. Venetian Mocenigo's crewmen defended themselves with great energy, and using canisters and hand grenades they inflicted heavy casualties on the opposing crews. The arrival of two other galleasses forced the Ottomans to retreat, towing the flagship, which had nearly lost its stern. Along with the galleasses, another galley with two sailing ships also intervened on the left side of the clash, whose volley killed the unfortunate Ottoman crews. The contribution of both these vessels was impressive, as relayed in the Venetian relation about the battle: the guns of the Hamburg sail ship *Ruota della Fortuna* "slaughtered the enemy crews", while the Dutch *Acquila d'Oro* destroyed the stern of the *kapudan paşa*'s galley and captured the commander's standard as it fell in the water.[18] In the meantime, the opposite wing of the Ottoman side was trying to isolate the enemy right side. The action was carried out by 15 of the most powerful sailing ships with a part of the North African units, towed by *bey*'s galleys. Alvise Mocenigo saw from his galley the Ottomans' attempt against his right wing. Considering that the fight on the other side had turned to his favour, he sent seven galleys supported by one galleass which towed many ships. The conditions of the sea and the bad wind made the task of the oarsmen very hard, so that the Captain General ordered the tow ropes to be given up, to continue the action with only the galleys. Just one sailing ship, recorded in the source as a frigate, maintained the wind well and with the galleys invested the Ottoman ships with the fire of its long-range guns. In this way Alvise Mocenigo managed to stop the enemy plan and one by one the *beylere* galleys cut the ropes to find safety, abandoning the sailing ships to their destiny. With their bows towards the Venetian squadron, the Ottoman vessels suffered the heavy fire of the Venetian gunners. The three ships closest to the land drifted to the coast where they became stuck in the rocks, while the other seven crews left the hulls and hurled themselves into the sea in panic. Alvise Mocenigo managed to keep the squadron united and continued the action against the remaining enemy ships, but some crews defended themselves with great obstinacy. The Captain General's galley engaged in combat a Tunisian sail ship that had a corps of janissaries aboard. The Ottoman professional soldiers rebutted the heavy enemy fire without fear. Nevertheless, the Tunisian ship could not compete with the more manoeuvrable galleys, which targeted it, avoiding falling within the range of its guns. After a few minutes of violent fire, the North African sail ship surrendered and with the hull pierced at several points below the waterline began to sink. Those who could swim were thrown into the sea, while the Venetians, at the shout of *San Marco! San Marco!* boarded the enemy ship and with fierce rage slaughtered all the unfortunates they found aboard. On another Ottoman sailing ship, engaged by a galleass, a fire began to develop until it exploded, damaging the bow of the Venetian unit and killing several gunmen and soldiers concentrated on the bow castle. In the evening, at the end of the battle, 16 Ottoman sailing ships and one *mavuna* were lost, but all the galleys had been saved and some of them had been able to tow away from the battle five of the transport vessels. The second important naval battle of the Cretan war had been an overwhelming Venetian victory.[19]

---

18 ASVe, *Senato Mar*, R. 446, c. 22.

19 Regarding the battle, see ASVe, *Proveditori da Terra e da Mar*, f. 936, *Dispacci*, Alvise Mocenigo's relation dated 17 July 1651.

Alvise Mocenigo was able to exploit, with optimum results, the cooperation between sailed and oared ships. The best quality of the crews and the ability of the Venetian captains increased the difference with their enemies and once the initial danger from the galleys was counteracted, the discipline and the skill of Mocenigo's crews had prevailed over the Ottoman numerical superiority. The ability of his gunners allowed the Venetians to obtain the decisive advantage first on the left wing and then on the right, in spite of the inertia of the Ottoman centre, weakened by the move ordered by the *kapudan paşa*. However, it has to be emphasised how the Ottomans had provided a fleet of sailing ships from virtually nothing, and how it was the first time that they were confronted with such experienced opponents. The poor co-ordination and co-operation between sailed and oared ships caused a crisis of Ottoman deployment on the left and to the escape of the *beylere* galleys; the presence of well-armed ships of Algiers, Tunis and Tripoli, with some skilled sailors in their ranks, did not dampen the negative impact of the lack of experience of the Sultan's navy.

The victory of Paros confirmed the naval supremacy of Venice, but without affecting the permanence of the Ottomans in Crete, who were able to supply troops using the Peloponnese ports at least once to bring reinforcements and resources in order to consolidate the occupation of the island. Between 1652 and 1657, the Ottoman fleet attempted to restore communications with Crete, trying to overcome in one way or another the blockade – now only in force from spring to autumn – by the Venetian ships. In 1652 the new *kapudan paşa* Dervis Mehmed managed to get around the barrier in the straits, using only the *beylere* galleys and other units already in the Aegean, similar to the plan ordered two years before by his predecessor. In 1653, Dervis Mehmed was able to anticipate the arrival of the Venetians in the Dardanelles, then in 1654 the Ottoman fleet's action led to the first of the battles fought at the western entrance of the straits. The deployment of the fleets and the execution of the battles were conditioned by the particular nature of the canal, which restricted the movements of the ships and was characterised by a strong current, which could at some points exceed five knots, flowing from the Marmara Sea to the Mediterranean. All this favoured navigation for the ships coming from the east, forcing the Venetians to anchorages where it was difficult not to be dragged westward. The Ottomans could also benefit from the presence of artillery batteries on the two sides of the canal, with which they covered their ships and hindered the action of their opponents. To avoid being preceded a second time, the Venetian fleet arrived at the Dardanelles in the last week of April 1654 with 16 vessels supported by two galleasses and eight galleys. Captain general Alvise Mocenigo, aged 72, allocated to this task the *capitano delle navi* Giuseppe Dolfin, while he was cruising the water north of Crete to intercept the enemy trade with the galley fleet.

At dawn on May 16, *kapudan paşa* Murad left Constantinople with 40 galleys, five *mavunas* and 30 armed vessels and transport ships, while 22 *beylere* galleys with 14 North African sailing ships as escort waited for the main fleet on the other side of the Dardanelles, at the Venetian rear. Some northern African units had managed to return the channel in the night to join the Murad Paşa's main fleet. The large number of sail units had been collected to join the convoy by some obliging Dutch and English merchants. The Ottoman

53. The Florentine artist Stefano Della Bella (1610–1664) transposed effectively on paper the violence of a naval battle of the mid 17th century. The fighting rarely ended with the sinking of ships, the surrender of crews being more often the outcome. Another dangerous occurrence in these battles were fires, which could easily spread from one ship to another. (Author's archive)

numerical superiority was even greater in relation to armaments embarked. In fact, according to the Venetian commander Dolfin, only six of his vessels were actually able to oppose the Ottoman units of the same class. Perplexed about the actual force of his fleet and fearful of the use of oar units in such a narrow space – where the fire power overwhelmed manoeuvrability and speed – Dolfin recommended to his captains to act with caution, taking care to counteract and above all to avoid isolation and stay without the support of other units. The Venetian commander placed the ships on three columns: on the right, toward the Asian shore, seven vessels and more seven to the left, towards the European coast, while two sailing ships and the two galleys remained in the centre. Each galley was assigned to a specific vessel, with the task of giving mutual support and protection. Dolfin agreed with the second in command, the *capitano in golfo* Francesco Morosini (who had the same name as the most famous future captain general and Doge) to not lift their anchors before passing at least half of the enemy fleet, in order to find themselves windwarded and with the advantage of the current. The first ship in each column had to keep the position as much as possible, narrowing the sea to the opponent; each crew received detailed commands from their commanders, but the course of the battle showed that it was difficult to perform the original plan. The Ottomans advanced in the canal with their ships in a line at the front, driven by a light tramontane, followed shortly by the rowing units, led by the *kapudan paşa*. The battle suddenly began in the centre, with the boarding of the Dutch sailing ship *Aquila d'Oro – Gouden Adelaar* (Golden Eagle), commanded by the vice-captain of the sailing ships Daniele Morosini. The sails of the Venetian ship were caught on those of an Ottoman *sultana*, while the crew engaged in a fierce fight in which the Venetians prevailed. The success was short-lived because four other Ottoman vessels assaulted the *Aquila d'Oro*, forcing the crew to abandon it after burning it with the sultana. A few minutes later the *Orsola Bonaventura*, an armed merchant hired in England, also caught fire. Dolfin's choice of placing the ships along the canal extension to cover all the navigable sea provoked a dangerous fragmentation of the fleet, which remained involved in a series of isolated duels. This situation favoured the Ottoman numerical superiority, and the insidious Dardanelles current worsened the situation by pushing the sailing ships to the Asian shore. The French vessel *Apollon* ended up in a delicate situation when, after ploughing the seabed with its keel, it was likely to remain involved in the *Acquila d'Oro*'s out-of-control blaze. The tragic end of the two Venetian sailing ships forced the anchored units on the left side to leave their moorings and move down the canal. The manoeuvre evolved into an escape that also involved the Venetian units on the opposite side. In vain Dolfin and Morosini tried to restore order. Now, at the centre of the channel remained only two galleasses and the commander flagship *San Zorzi Grande*, otherwise known as *Sint Joris*, a 54-gun sailing ship rented in the Netherlands.

After a courageous resistance, the galleasses also lifted their anchors and, continuing to fight, they were drawn by the current out of the straits. The eight galleys who had taken their position next to the sailing ships tried to manoeuvre themselves to engage the enemy. Padua's galley cut off the trailer that secured it to the sail ship to get stern to stern, but the manoeuvre failed and the Venetian unit was involved in the fire of two enemy vessels, and was then attacked by five galleys that prevailed and captured it. As he saw helplessly crushing his plane, Dolfin was engaged by four Ottoman sailing ships, two at each side, which were targeting him without pause. Together with the *San Zorzi*, the galley of the captain of the Gulf Morosini suffered serious damage, losing two-thirds of the crew, including the commander, and was finally rammed by a *sultana* which broke it in two halves. After two hours of fight with guns and musketry, Dolfin anchored by stern, seeing that the current was pushing his ships toward the shore and with the risk of being under the threat of batteries and opposing infantry on the shore. At that moment, seeing the bow of the enemy flagship rotating in the centre of the canal, Murad Paşa sent two *mavunas* and six galleys against Dolfin to invest the enemy from behind. For hours, Ottoman oar ships targeted the Venetian vessel, which replied with all available weapons, using chained ball and canister. Far from the rest of the fleet, while the Ottoman brigandines carried aboard new troops to support the crews engaged against the Venetian commander, Dolfin's flagship lost one mast and then the rudder, but the crew defended with desperation and finally Dolfin managed to evade the engagement. Despite 12 shots below the waterline, the Venetian flagship came out of the straits dragged by the current, fortunately finding a passage between friendly and enemy units involved in the confused fight and finally joined the rest of the fleet. A Venetian galleass sailing ship risked getting lost when it was frontally attacked by two sailing ships which alongside the *bey*'s galleys entered into the straits to close the enemies in a noose, but it was saved by the arrival of the galleys of the Dolfin's fleet. A different destiny touched the sailing ship *Casa di Nassau*, encircled by two Tunisian ships, which stranded on the Asian shore and was captured with all crewmen including the commander, the nobleman Francesco Molino. An Ottoman sailing ship was launched in pursuit of *San Zorzi*, but at this point the parties turned in and it was the turn of the Ottoman ship to risk capture. The intervention of the *beylere* galleys and the Barbary sailing ships saved the *sultana*. The fight lasted for six hours, during which Venetians suffered the loss of 3,000 men and five ships, while on the Ottoman side were lost two vessels, one *mavuna* and three galleys, plus an unspecified number of soldiers and sailors. Murad Paşa was satisfied by the outcome of the battle and led the fleet to Mytilene and Chios, where he spent a few days for repairs. On 24 June, the Ottoman fleet left the ports in the night, with no lights, and in early July reached Crete, carrying precious supplies and the salaries for the army. During the sailing, Murad Paşa had attempted to attack the Venetian possession of Tinos, but being aware that Alvise Mocenigo's galleys were about to reach him, he resumed the route to Chaniá.[20] However, in 1654 the Ottomans had been close to defeating the Venetian fleet and this could have proved decisive, at least for the continuation of the blockade strategy. If the coordinated action of the *kapudan paşa* and that of the *beylere* with the North African corsairs had been done in a less chaotic and more determined way, Dolfin's ships would hardly have escaped from the trap and probably Venice could not have continued to maintain the blockade of the Dardanelles. Dolfin complained the outcome of the battle, accusing the captains and crews of the hired foreign sailing ships – who, except the Dutch, had performed very badly – and recommending to license all as soon as possible.[21]

The outcome of the campaign of 1654 much grieved Captain General Alvise Mocenigo, who died shortly after in Candia. Giuseppe Dolfin paid for the failure with removal from the rank.

Despite the failure, the challenge reopened a year later, when the Venetian fleet came again in front of the Dardanelles, anticipating once again the exit of the Ottoman ships. The Venetians now deployed 27 sailing ships, four galleasses and six galleys, placed in such a way as to avoid the mistakes occurred one year before. Instead of dividing the fleet into three separate squadrons, Lazzaro Mocenigo, *capitano straordinario delle navi* of fresh appointment, chose to keep the units grouped at the centre of the canal, deployed in four successive lines, so that they could more easily control the approaching enemy ships, awaiting the critical moment where the Ottomans, descending the channel, would turn to either shore and choose the right time to lift their moorings and to attack the enemies from behind. Mocenigo hoped to get the timing and the speed which had been missed at Dolfin in 1657, converting the Ottoman first advantage of the current into a factor in favour of the Venetians' side. The vessels were anchored in the centre, while galleys and galleasses were placed on the right, forming an autonomous squadron close to the Asian shore, where the current was less strong and where probably ships would not pass. Refreshed by the partial success of the previous year, the Ottomans – now under *kapudan paşa* Zurnassan Mustafa - arrived in the morning of 21 June 1655, sure to force the blockade, even though they could not have the North African sailing ships, forced to stay in their waters by the presence of an English squadron. Zurnassan Paşa disposed of 30 sailing ships, including three armed merchants hired by Dutch and English privateers, who advanced occupying the whole channel. Behind him there were eight *mavunas* and 60 galleys, who were committed to engage the enemy oared ship with good prospects of success, considered

20 This decision proves the poor morale of the Ottoman crews. In fact, when they sighted some enemy sails on the horizon they left the island, abandoning the infantry landed on the beach; see Valiero, p. 209.

21 ASVe, *Senato, Dispacci di Provveditori*, b. 328, Dolfin's relation, 27 May 1654.

the huge numerical superiority. According to the information held by the Venetians, the Ottoman fleet had on board 8,000 trained janissaries and *sipahy* for Candia; fifteen *paşa* each with one battalion of 600 naval infantrymen with whom to launch a landing offensive against the Venetian bases in the Archipelago. This time however, events took a different course than the one hoped by the Ottomans. Instead of removing the moorings and losing the order of the deployment, the Venetian ships remained at anchor waiting for the order of Mocenigo. The day before, the Venetian commander had inspected the ships one by one and urged captains and crews to carry out the task they were waiting for. In turn, Antonio Barbaro, commander of the oared ships, aboard a *felucca*, had visited the ships under his orders reminding everyone to abide by the orders and to behave with discipline, promising the certain victory. According to the provisions received, the first line of sailing ships – under Antonio Zeno – remained at anchor while the enemy fleet proceeded towards the open sea. As expected, the Ottoman ship turned to the European shore. Slowly, at reduced sail, the Ottomans advanced in a line of rows within the range of the guns and proceeding one after the other, preparing to receive the shots of Mocenigo's ships, which fired without stopping. Anchoring decisively favoured the precision of the Venetian fire, while the Ottoman artillery caused only minor damage. Some *sultanas*, hit beneath the waterline, avoided the blow and swerved, being caught with the ones that followed, and creating a tangle that would make the Venetian fire even more deadly. *Kapudan paşa* with galleys and the *mavunas* tried to overcome their opponents by circling all the way to the Asian shore. Taking advantage of the confusion of the fight, several Ottoman oared ships took the exit from the channel. The units in the rearguard were instead invested by the Venetian galleys and galleasses, and after a short but violent fight, in which one *mavuna* and three galleys were lost, they drove to traverse the channel and return to Galata. Until that time, the battle had taken place according to Mocenigo's plans, who ordered departure from the anchorage, but a sudden drop in the wind slowed down the vessels' manoeuvre. Despite the intervention of the galleys, which towed the sailing ships, the decisive moment was vanishing. Some of the sailing ships left without towing were dragged by the current, and three of them were isolated in the middle of the channel where they were attacked by Ottoman vessels. Mocenigo arrived to help two ships, while on board the Dutch sail ship *David Golia* a fire began which burned it, together the three *sultanas* that had approached. Another *sultana* was captured by Mocenigo on board the sailing ship *San Marco*, while two other Ottoman vessels beached close to the European shore. The rest of the Ottoman sailing ships were saved thanks to the intervention of the *bey* galleys, who towed them out of the straits. This time the battle ended with a clear result for the Venetians, who had lost a sailing ship and 126 men, while the Ottomans lamented the loss of nine vessels, 1,000 deaths and 358 prisoners.[22] Also, and these were the most important result, most of the transport had been forced to re-enter Constantinople, depriving the troops in Crete of supplies, and the

22 Regarding the account of the battle, see ASVe, *Provveditori da Terra e da Mar*, f. 1328, Lazzaro Mocenigo's relation dated 24 June 1655, and Brusoni, *Libro* XII, pp. 277–279.

planned attack against the Venetian bases in the Aegean had been annihilated. In fact, only the oared fleet had passed through the blockade to reach Foça. Implacable, Lazzaro Mocenigo pursued his enemies and closed the exit from the bay with his sailing ships. By the end of the summer the Ottoman fleet had only delivered some modest relief to Crete only with 12 galleys. The tactics devised by Mocenigo proved to be more than adequate to halt the enemy fleet, but did not block the oared units and did not solve the problem posed by the *beylere* fleet, which, acting out of the straits, was not affected by the blockade of the Dardanelles, allowing the *kapudan paşa* to mitigate the consequences of the failures and to keep open a vital supply channel for the occupation corps in Crete.

In 1656 the war council under Lorenzo Marcello, newly-appointed captain general, attributed the cause of the partial success of the previous year to the insufficient number of oared ship in support of the vessels, and therefore it was decided to allocate the whole fleet for the blockade of the Dardanelles. In the spring the Venetians anchored at the entrance of the channel with 28 vessels, seven galleasses and 31 galleys, now under the direct command of the captain general. In the middle of June, the signs of an outbreak of the enemy fleet became more and more evident. Like Mocenigo the year before, Marcello also deployed the fleet at the centre of the channel, but this time in a wider formation even more compact. Along with sailing ship, there were also five galleasses in the centre, while the other two with the galleys were in the back as a mobile reserve. On 26 June, the Ottomans came out of the harbour with an impressive deployment of more than 100 ships, including four large vessels with more than 60 cannons. Drawn by the strong current, the Venetian fleet was shifting towards the European coast, namely to the side that the Ottomans used to sail out of the channel. Foreseeing the trap, *kapudan paşa* Kenan Sinau ordered a deviation towards the Asian coast, a route never attempted before. On this side the coast of the channel is much more jagged and on that occasion the strong Tramontane wind pushed the Ottoman ships towards a cove at the headland of Kephez, where they remained bottled up and were forced to anchor, waiting to be towed by the galleys. To make the situation even more unfavourable for the Ottoman ships, the wind turned in favour of the Venetians and at that point their fate appeared sealed. Most of the Ottoman galleys managed to approach the ships to tow them out of the cove, but the arrival at full speed of the Venetian fleet, with the sailing ship *San Marco* conducted by Lazzaro Mocenigo – who had remained with the fleet as a volunteer – induced the galleys who were now in the centre of the channel to cut the tow ropes in order to find safety and leaving the sailing ships to their destiny.[23] Other galleys, in turn, remained bottled up between the sailing ships in the cove while all the Venetian units moved at maximum speed against them. From the battery on shore, the artillerymen tried to aim their batteries against the enemy to cover the fleet, but the Venetian galleys caught the Ottoman galleys

23 *Ragguaglio della Vittoria Navale conseguita a' Dardanelli. Dall'armata della Serenissima Repubblica di Venetia*. Venice and Rome, 26 June 1656, in Archvio di Stato di Roma, *Effermeridi Cartari-Febei*, b. 75, vol I, c. 12.

by surprise. Meanwhile the current continued to push the ships towards land, one against the other. Panic spread, and many crews abandoned their ships to escape and safely reach land. Under the frightened gaze of the grand vizier Sadjbagi Mehmed, who followed the battle from the shore, was materialising the most disastrous defeat from the Lepanto era. The arrival of the five galleasses, deployed since the beginning together with the sailing ships, gave the shot of grace to the remaining hopes of the *kapudan paşa*. Dropping their anchors a short distance from the *sultanas*, the Venetians began to target their bows and sterns, while with the fire of musketry massacred the crews, struggling to manoeuvre in a desperate attempt to regain the wind. The Venetian galleys, skilfully exploiting their manoeuvrability and speed, captured a large number of enemy ships. It was during a boarding of one of these *sultanas* that Captain General Lorenzo Marcello was fatally injured.

The news of the death of the brave admiral was kept hidden so as not to distract the crew in their task, namely fighting to achieve complete victory. Between 26 June and the following day, the Ottomans lost all their vessels, five *mavunas* and 45 galleys. Apart from the death of the Captain General, the only significant Venetian loss was the sail ship *San Marco*, commanded by the bold Lazzaro Mocenigo, stranded on the shore and then burned by his crew.[24]

The news of the defeat came to Constantinople the same day and caused panic in the population; the court itself with Sultan Mehmed IV abruptly left the Topkapi palace. The outcome of the battle was even worse since, this time, the oared fleet too had been destroyed, while in the other battles it had managed to avoid the naval blockade sailing to Crete. The defeat had dramatic consequences for the continuation of the struggle and put access to the Marmara Sea and the capital in peril. In the beginning of July, the situation became even more critical, because the Venetians, now master of the northern Aegean, occupying the islands of Bozcaada and Limnos with two landings, with the aim of a permanent presence in front of the straits. The success achieved, and the death of Lorenzo Marcello, led to the election of Lazzaro Mocenigo as captain general in March 1657, but now the Venetian commanders had to deal with a strategic situation different from the past, because the Ottomans, learning from the disaster of one year ago, decided to concentrate their naval forces out of the Dardanelles before the arrival of the Venetian fleet and finally they completed the ambitious plan of fortification of the channel. The grand vizier Köprülü Mehmed, just appointed, wanted to make the straits inaccessible to the enemy fleet by building new castles. Already in the past, *walide* Kösem had supported this project with all his authority, remembering the raid of Saint Stephen's Knights in 1609, but the treasury did not have the money needed for the construction of new batteries and the resistance of the communities of the surrounding villages, worried about the close presence of the garrisons, contributed to the failure of the project. The distance between the two canals was remarkable and many doubted that it could be effectively defended with the firing of the guns.

24 Regarding the battle, see in ASVe, *Provveditori da Terra e da Mar*, f. 1222, *Dispacci*, fleet provveditor Barbaro Badoer's relation, dated 30 June 1656, and Brusoni, *Libro* XIII, pp.298–300.

54. The stretch of sea between the Asian coast of the Dardanelles and the European stronghold of Kilidol Bahr, is well recognisable by its round tower. All the villages surrounding the channel were forced to provide all material needed for the construction of new castles in the straits. After 1656, in order to hinder the Venetian naval blockade, artillery emplacements were built on both sides, reinforced with infantry and cavalry. (Author's photo)

However, all the difficulties disappeared in face of the Grand Vizier's will. The fleet received the order to spend the winter at the entrance of the Dardanelles and the crews were employed to build the new fortifications under the direction of architect Moustafa Aga and commander of the Dardanelles garrisons, Frenk Ahmed Paşa. The two new castles formed a regular square of which each side had a length of 356 metres; one of them received the pretentious name of Kilidol-Bahr (Key of the Sea), the other was called Seddol-Bahr (Dam of the Sea), as opposed to those built under Mehmed II, on the Asian coast, bearing the most modest names of Koum-Kalaasi (Sand Castle) or Çanak-Kalaasi (Ceramic Castle) because of the ceramic factories that stood in the vicinity.

The energetic resolution of Grand Vizier Köprülü Mehmed to sail from Constantinople was apparent already in early March, when a squadron formed by 36 galleys and four *mavunas* allowed a fleet to concentrate between Mytilene and Chios that with the *beylere* galleys and the African corsairs could guarantee an effective escort for the merchants sailing from the Peloponnese ports or Smyrna to transport the salary for the army and all the supplies needed to keep the island under control, maintaining the siege ring at Candia. The unlucky Kenan Sinau had paid the defeat of the previous year with his life, but the new *kapudan paşa*, Sidi Ahmed, was not judged as fit by the Grand Vizier, who replaced him with veteran Topal Mehmed, an aged and limping man, and for this nicknamed by the sailors 'the lame'. Everything had been done to provide the new commander with a fleet capable of sustaining the challenge. Köprülü Mehmed allocated to the Galata arsenal the funds for the construction of 60 new galleys; he recruited sailors in all the provinces and enlisted oarsmen offering high prizes, considering the scarcity of slaves and prisoners of war that afflicted the fleet; for reinforcing the crews, he assigned 3,000 janissaries and 2,000 volunteers, who had signed on condition that after the campaign they would have been incorporated in the *kapikulu* cavalry.

Despite the initial strategic success achieved with early entry into the archipelago, in mid April the *kapudan paşa* failed to recapture Bozcaada, alarmed by the information about the coming of the Venetians as imminent. Warned about the activity of the enemy fleet, on 1 May Captain General Lazzaro Mocenigo sailed from Candia with 19 galleys and six galleasses; during sailing, he captured some small enemy transports off the Spalmadori Islands, in Chios Channel, and spotted the enemy fleet sailing in the direction of the Samos. Two days later the Venetians attacked 14 corsair units, capturing the flagship of the Algerian squadron. Taking advantage of the lack of wind and firing with chained balls at the masts, the heavy bow guns of the galleys and the large calibre of the galleasses forced the North African corsairs to shelter near the coast, where nine ships struck the rocks. Among the prisoners, the Captain

General interrogated an Ottoman *çavus* who had been sent to Chios with money and the order to join the North African fleet of *bey* Houssein of Algiers with the one of the *kapudan paşa*. Mocenigo also captured 346 prisoners and seized Egyptian merchandise for about 300,000 silver plasters. Then the Venetian galleys arrived at Sığacık bay, taking possession of the fort, where 30 cannons were found, among which many had the coat of arms with the lion of St. Mark, dating back to the conquest of Cyprus. In less than two months Mocenigo had captured 44 ships and a stronghold on the Anatolian coast. The Captain General had in the meantime sent the commander of the sailing ships, Marco Bembo, to the entrance of the Dardanelles to intercept the supply convoy that was assembling in Galata and to maintain the pressure on the capital of the Ottoman Empire. The Ottomans also knew that Venetian intentions were not limited to maintaining the blockade, but to extend the threat directly to Constantinople. The idea of tracing the straits and reaching the Bosporus to impose peace with the cannons of the fleet had been announced by Lazarus Mocenigo as a last attempt to put an end to the war once and for all.

The plan was audacious, but this time the target seemed to be achievable, considered the low state of the enemy fleet. Bembo had 20 sailing ships and seven galleys, but when the battle was engaged he could deploy only four galleys, so a smaller force than the one employed the year before and which had been so effective. The fleet dispersion was caused by the early Ottoman exit and the arrival of Northern African units in the archipelago. Complicating the situation for the Venetians was the lack of winds and the insidiousness of the currents, which diminished beyond expectationthe supply of water carried out to nearby Gökçeada island by the other galleys. By mid July, Ottoman crews were ready to sail to the straits, aware of having to endure a battle that could prove fatal not only to the fleet but to the Empire. The launch of the naval campaign had been followed from the beginning by the Grand Vizier in first person, who had landed in the Dardanelles. New batteries had been placed on both sides of the channel supported by infantry corps ready to intervene, while the cavalry travelled back and forth across the shoreline inspecting each ravine. The Venetian fleet stationed at anchor in front of the European coast, between the village of Büyük Kipos and the Kafirbucaçi bay, to facilitate the return of the galleys with the supply of water. The command of the Ottoman squadrons was entrusted to Çerkes Othman, lieutenant of the *kapudan paşa*, who had been in the Aegean since March. At dawn on 17 July, the Ottoman fleet moved from Galata and entered into the channel. A few hours later the two fleets met. Othman Paşa sent the 18 *sultanas* in line, followed by two *mavunas* and 30 galleys, while eight other *mavunas* had the task of engaging the enemies. These were the first units to enter into action, but once again, the accurate fire of the Venetians, who had anchored their ships, broke the impetus of the Ottomans. One *mavuna* was captured, four had their crews decimated, while the last three, each with a corps of janissaries on board, turned rudder and dwindled; the crews landed on the Asian coast and peacefully watched the battle.[25] Meanwhile, Genç Mehmed *sancakbeg* of Alaiye, who commanded

25 Von Hammer-Purgstall, Vol. XI, p. 68.

an infantry unit on the beach, threw about 60 soldiers onto two feluccas and assaulted the four enemy galleys that towed the captured *mavuna*, recovering it from the enemy with a daring action.[26] The sacrifice of the Ottoman *mavunas* enabled at least 13 sailing ships, one *mavuna* and six galleys to sail to the European coast and come out from the channel. Another five sailing ships tried to follow the same route but were intercepted by the Venetians and were lost. Mehmed Köprülü, who from the shore had witnessed the poor conduct of the janissaries, embarked on a felucca to approach the shore and intimidated them by threatening the use of weapons, to get them to return aboard the ships. Meanwhile, the 28-galley squadron of the Captain General had just entered the channel and was preparing the attack the Ottoman oared ships. Seventeen of them tried to avoid the encounter to put themselves under the protection of the artillery on the Asian side, near the village of Küçük Kipos. Another 15 Ottoman galleys avoided their enemies and then headed to the Asian coast where their crews landed on the beach. Inflexible, the Grand Vizier ordered the infantry to fire on the fugitives, then pointed the battery to protect the ships that were in front of Büyük Kipos. The 17 galleys, which thanks to their oars and the favourable wind had taken refuge under the batteries of the other village, were pushed by the current to the Asian coast and finally dropped anchor beneath the Koumtorni Castle, where, protected by the batteries positioned on the ramparts, they organised a resistance and passed the night there. The following day they repulsed a new Venetian attack. The second day passed with the Venetians trying to complete the destruction of the Ottoman ships, these latter anchored close to the shore under the protection of the coastal batteries.

The Venetian accounts concerning the battle agree to recognise that Ottoman sailors and soldiers had courageously fought and had manoeuvred with precision and promptness never seen before.[27] In addition, the presence of such a large number of batteries on both sides of the channel made difficult for the Venetians to carry out the attacks. Moreover, the shortage of galleys in the Venetian deployment, partially offset by the arrival of the Mocenigo squadron, did not allow a complete victory. During the Fourth Battle of the Dardanelles, took place the famous and controversial naval assault on Constantinople: a sort of final act of the war, led by Lazzaro Mocenigo with a squadron of 12 galleys. The reports on this fateful day do not agree on some details. It is not fully confirmed that the Venetians tried to attack the Ottoman capital and some testimonies reported that Mocenigo's galley was hit while trying to prevent seven enemy galleys from retreating back along the channel, protected by the coastal batteries, on the third day of combat, infuriated by changing winds, opposing currents, and harassment of the Ottoman artillery placed on the two shores. However, the episode marked a turning point in the war and the failure of the action, the result of which would have to be evaluated strategically, provoked a strong psychological

26 *Ibid.*, p. 69.

27 *Relazione della battaglia navele seguita nel canale de'Dardanelli fra e armate Veneta e Ottoman ail dì 26 giugno 1656*, Biblioteca Nazionale Marciana, Venice, ms. cl. VII, 580.

sense of impotence in Venice, which considered the option of leading the war close to the enemy's shores the key for defeating him.

The Fourth Battle of the Dardanelles was the last major battle of the Cretan War. The renunciation of the naval blockade strategy was not interrupted by the death of Lazzaro Mocenigo, as some historians have reported, but for another two years, the sailing ship squadron, supported by a dozen galleys and galleasses, came back to the straits, without engaging in any battle comparable to those of previous years. There were troops spread across the two shores, and new batteries had been built while others were getting ready. In the spring of 1658, penetrating the straits had become almost impossible. In September 1659, returning from Bursa to Edirne, the Sultan visited the new fortifications and ordered as many guns to be placed as possible. For the rest, the Ottomans continued to avoid any chance of confrontation until practically the end of the war.

Already since 1656, supplies and troops were mostly embarked in alternative ports such as Smyrna, Thessalonika, Methoni and other ports of the Peloponnese. The large convoys escorted by the fleet continued to sail between Anatolia, Greece and Crete, but another reason removed the effectiveness of Venetian strategy. In fact, the Ottomans turned to an ever-increasing number of little ships, more suited for evading enemy surveillance along the Aegean routes. The widespread use of xabecs, pinks and other small sailing ships continued until the last months of the war. Thanks to their agility and speed, these ships could not only escape the enemy galleys but also land on Crete in areas devoid of ports and therefore unguarded. Any major engagements occurred after the Fourth Battle of the Dardanelles and the Ottomans continued to avoid oared naval battles, considering the new strategy as the best for supplying their army in the island. The absence of encounters between the fleets was also due to the substantial difficulty the Ottomans had of deploying their ships, because between 1661 and 1664, the plague epidemic decimated the crews.

It was the new captain general Francesco Morosini, who succeeded to Mocenigo, who changed the strategic direction and the naval blockade that had directly or indirectly affected the fleet's action in the previous years. He replaced the old strategy with another marked by raids against enemy ports, in order to destroy the supply centres collected by the Porte to circumvent the blockade, without giving up the hunting along the Cretan routes of the convoys that carried troops and supplies to continue the siege. At this stage, the campaigns turned into exhausting cruises that in some respects recall the World War II battle between Doenitz submarines and the Allied fleet. Assuming the impossibility of preventing access to the ports of Crete to the Ottoman ships, the new strategy ended in a folding of the fleet on Candia, until, in the two final years of the war, the Venetian fleet was transformed into a tool to support the city under siege.

However, along with support for defenders and amphibious campaigns, but often subordinate to these latter, the Venetian fleet tried to interrupt the enemy transports, which arrived at Crete from all over the area, without achieving significant success. The Venetians attempted to close the access to the main enemy port, Chaniá, sometimes sailing in the Eastern Mediterranean to intercept the traffic between Alexandria and Crete. However, in the previous phases before the last three siege campaigns at Candia, the Ottomans still managed to land strong contingents of troops and large quantities of materials and supplies. In January 1667, under the constant threat of the Venetian fleet, the Egyptian contingent, led by Ramazan Beg, landed in Chaniá. The Ottoman commander was captured along with other officers after the attack of the galleys led by Grimani and Molino, lurking in the waters in front of the port and ready to intercept every enemy ship. But the new grand vizier Köprülü Ahmed did not lose heart and resorted to the mobilisation of all available ships, also to foreign merchants, paying very high indemnities to the ship-owners who at their own risk accepted to supply the army on Crete. At the end of the campaign of 1667, in order to increase the flow of supplies, the Grand Vizier turned peremptorarily to the Barbary regencies. Mehmed Aga, sent by the Grand Vizier to the North African states, informed him about the answers obtained. The paşa of Tunis promised to send 10 sailing ships, a further 10 from Tripoli, while Algiers declared itself ready to provide the entire fleet engaged against the French who had landed at Giger. Before the end of May, the Ottoman fleet managed to land all transport in Chaniá and other ports on the island. At the beginning of summer 1668, under these favourable auspices, the siege could resume with renewed energy and fresh resources. Raising morale even more came the news of the victory of Nio, against two corsairs paid for by the Venetian government, of which one – the cavalier Giorgio Maria Vitali, killed in the fight of 15 June – was considered by the Ottomans as one of the more fearsome. The author of this victory, the *kapudan paşa* Kaplan, known as 'the Panther', was generously rewarded by the Grand Vizier and honoured with the privilege of an inscription in his honour on the bastions of Leros island. In the autumn of 1668, it became clear that the Ottoman naval strategy was providing the resources for the continuation of the siege, which in fact did not end until the surrender occurred the following year. Before the end of 1668, 'the Panther' managed to land 1,000 Egyptian janissaries, 1,500 *cebeci*, 1,000 artillerymen and miners, 4,000 *sipahy* and *silihtar*, and 2,000 tonnes of gunpowder, 15,000 bombs for mortars, 80,000 artillery projectiles of great calibre, 20,000 hand grenades: practically everything needed for a siege of great proportions. Despite the abundance of resources and without an immediate emergency, the Grand Vizier did not allow rest to the crew of the fleet. After the victory of Nio, the squadron of Tripoli, formed by six sailing ships, had captured a Venetian merchant and in early July requested to the *kapudan paşa* permission to return home. Instead, the corsairs received the order to escort the supplies convoys sailing from Smyrna. The North African sailing ships crossed the southern coast of the island off to Ierapetra, whose small port, despite being expanded, remained inaccessible to larger ships and obliged the Ottomans to make a long and dangerous unload. Anyway, from that location, the besiegers could easily reach the north coast by a pass at the narrowest point of the island and communicate with the coastal road from the bay of Spinalonga to Candia. The naval campaigns of both contenders were now completely subordinate to the continuation of the siege and coincided with the needs of besiegers and besieged: material and, above all, men whose tremendous tribute of life reached in 1669 a daily average of 90 dead or wounded for the Venetians and probably one and a half times this figure for the Ottomans.

In July 1669 the Venetian and Allied fleets were protagonists of an extreme attempt to break the siege ring at Candia, the decision for which was made after the failure of the French sortie on 26 June. Allied generals gathered as soon as the auxiliary squadron returned to Candia. Captain General Francesco Morosini had already discussed with admiral Rospigliosi, appointed in 1668 as commander-in-chief of the allied fleet, the preliminary agreement for a joint action and both agreed to convene a war council on 7 July, postponed three days later because of the momentary indisposition of the French general Duke Annes de Noailles. The war council was held in Morosini's residence under the presidency of Rospigliosi and, in addition to the French commanders – Noailles and Admiral de Vivonne – also participated the *generale delle armi* Sant'André-Montbrun and the Venetian general Francesco Battaglia. Two proposals were examined: landing from the ships as many men as possible for attempting a new sortie, or using the fleet to bombard the enemy trenches in front of one of the most exposed bastions, destroy the batteries and with them the approaches and other siege works.

The choice fell on the second option, which to everyone seemed to promise some chance of success. However, Rospigliosi noted that for a long time the Ottomans were preparing for an attack from the sea and consequently had erected new trenches or adapted, transforming already existing ones. For the same reasons one year ago, the idea of a naval bombardment had been abandoned. Though there was the possibility of destroying some piece of artillery with the naval bombardment, almost certainly the defensive works would have suffered little damage, and on the contrary the action would have cost the fleet high casualties in relation to a possible success, as a fight between ships and repaired batteries behind the embankment had always been unequal, since just one cannon on the ground was much more effective than one 40-gun vessel. Despite these considerations, which also had a lot of weight, the majority of the members of the council favoured the bombardment with the fleet, and Rospigliosi had to surrender.

It was then decided to take action as soon as possible and on the sector of the Sant'Andrea's bastion, because on that side the ships could approach the coast much more than towards the Sabbionera, where the depth was less. The chances of success of a bombardment became ever smaller every day, as the Ottomans reinforced their coastal batteries. It took another two weeks before proceeding. The delay was attributable to the rough sea, considering that only with a perfectly calm sea could the fleet hope to hit the targets on the beach. Finally, on 23 July, there was no wind blowing, and the more experienced captains expected to move the next day. Rospigliosi had issued two orders: in the first he prescribed to galleys the towing of 15 French vessels, 14 Venetian vessels alongside the six galleasses and the moving of them to the assigned positions. The second order indicated the signs that – both day and night – the movements had to be carried out, and when exactly to open fire.

Each captain had received a map with the place assigned and the battle order was accurately indicated for each squadron. On the afternoon of 23 July, all the allied ships gathered in Candia's harbour and the next morning, before sunrise, they began to move to the assigned places. The Ottoman soldiers stationed in front of the bastion of Sant'Andrea must have witnessed an impressive spectacle when they sighted the manoeuvring of the 58 ships deployed in front of the beach. The Papal admiral proceeded first with the flag of the Holy Cross with the written *dissipentur omnes inimici ejus!* The fleet advanced in one line to anchor at musket shot range from the beach. As the fleet advanced, the Ottoman artillery violently opened fire and inflicting serious damage to the allied ships, especially since their crews could not react until towing and deployment were progressing. At 7:00 a.m., the impressive line of ships stretched from the Gioffiro River to Sant'Andrea. On the far right wing there were four Venetian sailing ships and then five Maltese and Papal galleys, then two other Venetian sailing ships, including the flagship of the *capitano delle navi* Iseppo Morosini, and finally four Maltese and Papal galleys. This part of the fleet had to bombard both the sectors near the river and the communication lines with the trenches in front of Sant'Andrea, to prevent the Ottomans from sending troops of reinforcements to the threatened bastion. Not far away, the centre of the fleet was formed by three Papal galleys and two Maltese, including the admirals of Rospigliosi and the Maltese Knight Accarigi, diagonally staggered, side by side with two galleys alternate with two Venetian sailing ships. The task of this squadron was to hit the enemy's trenches and especially the batteries on the side and rear. For this reason, the bows and sides of the ships were not parallel to the coastline, but facing south-east.

The left wing formed the main core of the deployment and was therefore very strong. It consisted of three squadrons: the one on the far right, with six galleys and seven French sailing ships; the central squadron deployed six Venetian galleasses; the left one with seven French galleys and eight vessels, including Admiral de Vivonne's galley and Vice-Admiral de Martel's ship. The galleys were alternated with the vessels, instead the galleasses formed an autonomous squadron. The fleet faced the tough task of engaging the Ottoman batteries and damaging or possibly destroying trenches and logistical structures of the enemy in the shooting range. The Papal captain's galley signalled the start of the bombardment one minute after 7:00 a.m., hoisted a red flag and fired the first shot. The thunder of more than 1,100 guns immediately erupted throughout the line, whose powerful effect immediately forced the Ottoman artillery into silence. The servants secured their guns behind the gabions and retreated into the trenches as the projectiles flew over their heads. Any movement on the beach was sighted by the ships; only a cavalry unit was seen moving back and forth between the heights of the camp near the Gioffiro River and the trenches of Sant'Andrea, certainly in order to supervise an attempt to land from the fleet. Inside the besieged city, everyone observed the great and terrible spectacle offered by the fleet. For the first time, after so many months, the fire of the Ottoman artillery against the curtain silenced; no enemy was shown behind the trenches and the batteries; no cry, no musket ball, no grenade, no mines exploded against the defenders. The absence of wind caused the first problems, and in a short time there was a thick cloud of smoke that wrapped the ships, making it impossible to point at the target. Despite the low visibility, the bombardment was not interrupted but continued without pause by pointing

55. Don Vincenzo Rospigliosi, *generalissimo* of the Allied fleet in 1668 and 1669, was Pope Clement IX's nephew. He belonged to a Tuscan family which had counted several knights in the order of St. Stephen and St. John, as was he himself before being appointed as commander in chief. His experience in naval warfare, however, was not sufficient to avoid the unsatisfactory conclusion of the last campaigns. (Author's archive)

the pieces toward an approximate direction. After three hours of continuous bombardment, a tremendous roar was heard in the sector where the French vessels were deployed, and planking, men and equipment of a ship flew in the air. It was the sailing ship *Thérèse* of 58 guns with 293 crewmen which had disintegrated due to the explosion of the gunpowder arsenal. The end of the French sailing ship was certainly caused by an accident on board and not by the Ottoman artillery, because at that moment the batteries on the beach were silent. The French ship sank in a few minutes and only seven crewmen were rescued. The explosion also seriously damaged French commander de Vivonne's galley, which was alongside the *Thérèse*. He was thrown into the benches of the oarsmen with some injuries, and like him all the crew were hit by the debris and the blast of the explosion. The galley lost a part of its stern and began to sink, forcing Vivonne to move onto the galley of Admiral Rospigliosi. Here, the French admiral immediately asked to suspend the bombardment. A few minutes later, the action of the ships had to be interrupted to allow a sortie from Sant'Andrea. According to the pre-established plan, defenders had to hoist a flag as a signal. But noting that ammunition was running out, Rospigliosi gave the signal of withdraw, considering that there was nothing more to do. But the critical moment of the whole enterprise began right then, as it was to move the fleet off again by towing the sailing ships, and making the operation more difficult, the wind had begun to change towards the land. The situation worsened because the sortie had been cancelled. The garrison in the city believed that the besiegers were aware of the plan and had prepared some mines to explode in front of their approaches. Real or not, soon the Ottoman artillery took advantage of this interruption to return to the batteries, point out the pieces of the fleet and open fire at will. As before, the allies could not reply to the firing of the guns and began to suffer serious losses, much more sensitive because of the imprudence of suspending the action instantly, rather than suspending it gradually, placing too much confidence on the effect of the sortie. One hour later the fleet managed to get out of the enemy guns' range, but another sailing ship was lost. Regarding the losses suffered by the allied fleet during this bombardment, there are notices only for the six Venetian galleasses and the French sailing ships. The casualties amounted to 28 dead and 56 wounded for the Venetians, 421 dead and 219 wounded for the French. Possibly similar figures can be applied to the rest of the fleet. It must be added, however, that all the ships were seriously damaged in the action; many had lost oars, and masts or their top sections, and almost all had been hit under the waterline. In spite of the great means employed, the result of the action was extremely minimal. A few days afterwards an Ottoman deserter reported that the losses in the besieging camps rose to more than 1,200 men, but apparently it was an exaggerated figure and this soon became apparent to the allies when pressure on the Sant'Andrea's bastion resumed with the same energy. Much more serious was the effect on morale, which was to the advantage of the Ottomans, since even the last hope of the defenders had vanished. The enterprise in which the largest fleet had been used had failed, and as a result there was only the certainty that not even the naval superiority of the Allies could have prevented the catastrophe: the fall of Candia was only a matter of time.

The Adriatic Theatre

The war theatre of the Aegean Sea had attracted the larger part of the resources, and therefore in this area occurred the major engagements. For this reason, the sea front of the Adriatic is less investigated and considered as irrelevant for the strategic context. Nevertheless, as Jan Glete rightly pointed out, "Warfare at sea is essentially a contest about the maritime lines of communication,"[28] and therefore, if the Ottomans had to find an alternative to the isolation in which the Venetians relegated them until 1657, the latter had to face the threat coming from the enemy corsairs based in Albania and in the Ionian island of Lefkada.[29]

The loss of control or even disruption of maritime lines of communication through the Adriatic would have undermined the Republic's ability to supply its armies and fleets in the Levant, and consequently its ability to wage war at all. Therefore, as far as the Venetian Senate was concerned, when the new war with the Ottoman Empire began in 1645, ships of the Adriatic squadron were expected to fulfil two important tasks. The first was securing the sea lanes of communication in the Adriatic from Ottoman attacks. The second, equally important task, was providing support to the Venetian land forces, especially in defence of strategically important Dalmatian fortified towns. During the war, their tasks consisted of a wide range of duties: from rushing in emergency deliveries of supplies and reinforcements to the endangered towns during Ottoman attacks, to providing additional firepower to the Venetian regular and irregular forces fighting along the coast, either in small skirmishes or during major offensive operations. These tasks were not different to those requested of the fleet in the Aegean Sea, but in the Adriatic the strategic context was strongly conditioned by the characteristics of the environment and the shortage of harbours and ports large enough to recover great fleets. However, the main strategic problem the Republic faced in the Adriatic was not a lack of good port towns but rather the fact that there were too many of them along the vital line of communication towards the Levant. The capture of any Dalmatian town by the Ottomans and the establishment of a major hostile naval base in the middle of the Adriatic Sea would create a dangerous threat to the Republic's control of maritime

28 Jan Glete, cited work, p. 1.

29 See also D. Madunić, cited work, pp. 1–37.

lines of communication with Crete and also with the Ionian domains of Corfu, Kephalonia and Zante. Such a threat would have to be matched by deployment of additional naval forces in the Adriatic, forces that would thus not been available for the Aegean theatre of operations. Grave consequences for the Republic's ability to wage war overseas which would have resulted from the loss of even just one port on the Dalmatian coast.

In 1645 and 1646 Venice had deployed just a small naval force in the Adriatic, which proved to be insufficient to face the Ottoman offensive against the domains in the eastern Adriatic Sea. Aware of this shortcoming, in July 1646 the Senate appointed Gabriel Zorzi, provveditor of Pula in Istria, as *Provveditore Straordinario in Golfo* (Extraordinary Governor of the Gulf) charging him with the command of all the naval forces serving in the Adriatic. Additionally, the ordinary provveditor in the Gulf was also granted a seat on the war councils alongside the major fleet commanders. However, in this, like in all other affairs, he was to be subordinated to the general provveditor of Dalmatia based in Zadar.[30] By introducing this new post of the operative commander through which general provveditor in Zadar could direct and coordinate actions of the fleet with the operations of the Venetian land forces and also with the main fleet, the Senate both greatly increased command and control over its forces in the region, and significantly eased the burden of directing the Republic's war effort in this battlefield. By July 1647, the Republic had concentrated in the Adriatic a respectable naval force consisting of seven galleys and more than 30 *barche armate* (armed boats) with a clear tendency to increase its strength even more. Until the end of the war this post was occupied, and governors of the Gulf cruised the southern Adriatic area between Ancona, Kotor and Ulcinj in search for Ottoman corsairs. In this period, provveditors in the Gulf had under their command separate squadrons numbering one or two galleys accompanied by several smaller vessels, *fuste*, *galeotte* or armed boats.[31] The base of operations of this squadron were the islands of Korčula and Hvar, the shipyard and arsenal of which provided necessary infrastructure for this force managed by the main arsenal of Zadar and, naturally, Venice.

Tactical deployment of the Adriatic squadron did not change much during the entire war and was above all determined by the operational tasks sketched above. In June 1646, Venice deployed in the Adriatic seven galleys and 30 armed boats overall. At the beginning of a campaign season in early spring, the Adriatic squadron would split into several smaller task forces, each consisting of four to eight units, and would deploy to the guard posts along the coast. The areas of deployment of these task forces were the following: the north littoral, stretching from Novigrad via the Island of Pag to the southern border of the Zadar district; Šibenik and its littoral; the coastal area between Trogir, Split and Omiš; the waters off the islands of Hvar and Korčula; the Bay of Kotor task force under the command of the extraordinary provveditor of the Gulf, with no specific base assigned, but

30 ASVe, *Senato, Rettori*, 17, f. 171–172, dated 19 July 1646.

31 *Ibid.*, *Provveditori da Terra e da Mar*. b. 475. C. 122; sent from Zadar, 27 April 1654

charged with cruising the Adriatic in search for Ottoman corsairs. The actual number of ships deployed at each particular post changed from year to year, and depended, above all, on estimation of the level of danger of an Ottoman attack. For example, during the years 1653–1656, when Split seemed the most threatened target, up to 20 units were positioned in its waters.[32] Similarly, in 1657 before and during the siege of Kotor, the Republic deployed the major part of the Adriatic squadron, with six galleys, three sail gunships and about 20 smaller armed boats.[33]

Once it became clear that a war with the Ottoman Empire was imminent, the Adriatic naval squadron went through rapid expansion similar to that of the Republic's land forces in the region. In March 1646, the Senate informed general provveditor Lunardo Foscolo that 12 hulls of armed boats were ready to be sent to Dalmatia, while at the same time, the magistrates of the Arsenal had been ordered to prepare a further 20, all destined for service in the Adriatic. A few months later, in December 1646, a further 10 armed boats were dispatched to Dalmatia.[34] Besides sending such bulk reinforcements of hulls, the Adriatic squadron was also gradually strengthened by issuing armed boats to individual captains who were commissioned by the Senate with recruiting new extraordinary companies of *Oltramarini*, destined for service in the Adriatic. With these reinforcements, by 1647 the number of *brigantini* and armed boats in Adriatic squadron rose from 20 to more than 40 units. Between 1646 and 1660 the number of these smaller warships serving in the Adriatic squadron was maintained at around 40–50 units.

After 1655 the composition of the Adriatic force began to change and over the years armed boats and *brigantini* were completely replaced by their larger counterparts, namely *fuste* and *galeotte*. This change was a result of a shift in the nature of warfare in the Adriatic. Although successful Venetian land offensives in 1647 and 1648 and destruction of all major Ottoman strongholds south of the Dinaric mountains decreased the direct danger to Dalmatian coastal towns, nevertheless, starting from 1654, a growing number of Ottoman corsairs begun to appear in the Adriatic posing a new threat to Venetian Adriatic domains. Small and agile, armed boats and *brigantini* well suited the needs of the first several years of the war when the navy was used mainly as the support for the operations of the Venetian land forces. Yet, the change of the Venetian strategy in this battlefield from active offense to passive defence, combined with increased activity of the Ottoman corsairs in the Adriatic, shifted the focus of duties of the Adriatic squadron. Its main priority became securing navigation through the Gulf. Armed boats, smaller than Ottoman *fuste*, were not well suited for the task of facing these ships. Although two to three armed boats could easily overcome one Ottoman *fusta*, the smaller number of oarsmen made these Venetian ships much slower than the Ottoman units and thus usually unable to catch them.

32 *Ibid.*, b. 474, c. 16; in Split, dated 4 March 1653, in the attachment: *Notta di Militie che sono in Spalato, Clissa, et Almissa con le Barc' Armate.*

33 *Ibid.*, *Senato Mar*, R. 481, c. 118; from Zadar, dated 14 August 1657; and c. 127, from Kotor, dated 11 September 1657.

34 *Ibid.*, *Senato Mar*, R. 104, c. 324, dated 24 December 1646.

However, the Venetian galleys, when fully manned, were in terms of speed and combat strength far superior to the Ottoman ones, yet, these warships were rather cumbersome tools for pursuing Ottoman corsairs. This was in the first place due to the fact that the galleys required very large crews, and the chronic problem of manning enough sailors for its warships, which had troubled Venetian navy in previous decades, was only amplified during wartime and in the end caused reduced manoeuvrability of these units. Finally, due to the needs of naval operations in the Levant, the number of galleys in the Adriatic was always limited and they had to be supported with smaller warships, in this case armed boats, which only slowed them down. All these problems were presented to the Senate in June 1660 by Governor-General Andrea Corner.[35] As the solution to the problem, he advised replacement of the worn-out armed boats with *galeotte*, the number of which at that moment was already slowly rising.

For the entire duration of the war, from early spring until the late autumn, ships of the Adriatic squadrons were in constant service at sea, either searching for Ottoman corsairs or guarding posts exposed to Ottoman attacks. Like any other tool or instrument that is in continuous use, Venetian warships were prone to deterioration and breakage and consequently in need of repair and maintenance. Since the Republic had at its disposal the facilities of the Zadar arsenal, the majority of necessary repairs were undertaken there. When, due to prolonged use, some vessel was beyond repair, it was disarmed either in Zadar with its usable parts stored in the local arsenal, or sent to Venice for the same purpose. The extent of dilapidation to which patrolling the Adriatic in search of Ottoman corsairs could reduce the Venetian naval forces, is illustrated in a letter from Governor-General Girolamo Contarini from October 1662. Contarini informed the Senate that almost one half of the small galleys or *fuste* under his command were unusable and that a shipment of 14 hulls of *galeotte* was necessary in order to replace worn out vessels.[36]

In contrast to the Aegean Sea where these ships were used chiefly in naval engagements against Ottoman vessels, in the Adriatic theatre of operations these ships mainly supported the Venetian land force defending Dalmatian coastal towns. The Republic put its trust in these floating gun platforms and their firepower to guard the entries into the bays of Dalmatian towns and to prevent the Ottomans from closing these entries and cutting off besieged towns by placing gun batteries along the shore.[37] The first two of such sailing ships (one armed merchantmen and one galleon) were hired in haste and dispatched to Dalmatia in September 1647, during the dramatic days of the

35 *Ibid.*, *Provveditori da Terra e da Mar*, b. 487, c 31, 6 January 1660.

36 *Ibid.*, b. 489, c. 34 sent from Split, 22 October 1662; attachment: *Nota da nuovi arsili di galeotte con gli armizzi et armi che occorrano.*

37 A very interesting description of this defensive doctrine, and discussion of the problems of defending Dalmatian towns and keeping the sea access to the besieged town open, is included in the letter of general provveditor Antonio Bernardo: "No other factor can contribute to the safety of these towns, as much as the protection of some warship accompanied by galleys, with them it is possible to accommodate bringing of the help where the most vigorous attacks are undertaken". In ASVe, *Provveditori da Terra e da Mar*, b. 481. 69, in Šibenik, 10 December 1656.

siege of Šibenik.[38] Even though these ships arrived too late to participate in the town's defence, they made a fine impression on Governor general Foscolo who requested them for the planned, but never realised, expedition to Albania in winter 1647–1648. Nevertheless, although the Senate approved this request, in January 1648, when it became clear that the entire operation was compromised, in order to cut expenses, these ships were recalled without seeing any action.[39] The sailing ships were employed in the Adriatic again in 1657. Alarmed by the news of massive Ottoman preparations that were steadily reaching Zadar, in 1656 general Provveditor Antonio Zeno included four "ships of war," armed with guns in the list of required reinforcements necessary for the defence of the province.[40] The first galleon arrived as early as June 1656, followed by two more in May 1657. This time the reinforcements arrived on time and Governor-General Bernardo made a good use of them during the defence of Kotor that year. Influenced by this positive experience, for the campaign of 1658, the Senate destined four vessels for the defence of Dalmatia. Meanwhile the Ottoman attention had turned to Transylvania, so these ships saw no action in 1658. It seems that the threat of years 1656–7 left a lasting mark on the Venetian command, because until the end of the war news of Ottoman preparations for an attack on Kotor were cautiously matched by a dispatch of sailing ships to the Adriatic, as occurred in 1663, when two vessels were sent for guard duty in the Bay of Kotor. The service record of this type of warships in the Adriatic remained meagre, especially in regard to their high cost, and could be considered as far from satisfactory for the Republic's interests. Yet the service record of the Venetian light galleys deployed in the Gulf was rather different.

The Venetian navy, light galleys particularly, provided crucial firepower support both during offensive operations, such as the assault against Skradin and Novigrad in 1647, and during the defence of besieged towns, such as Split and Kotor in 1657. The full extent of galleys' effectiveness against costal targets was proved during the Venetian siege at Ulcinj in March 1663. The Adriatic naval squadron, consisting of three galleys and one *galeazza*, after blockading the port and silencing the defending artillery, continuously bombarded the port for almost 24 hours, destroying six Ottoman *fuste* captured in the port and the arsenal full of naval stores as well. Galley crews also participated in the attack on Knin and were even employed as an additional workforce on Dalmatian fortifications, as happened in 1656. Though the Ottoman corsairs in the Adriatic did manage to capture a considerable number of prizes, for the entire duration of this conflict the squadron maintained firm control over maritime lanes of communication through the Adriatic Sea. It secured a constant flow of men, equipment and supplies to the Levant. Additionally, unchallenged control of the sea and the efficient cooperation of the Republic's naval and land

---

38 Contract of hire of two armed merchantmen *Sant'Angelo* and galleon *Corner*, for 1,200 and 1,900 *ducats* respectively. ASVe, *Senato Mar*, R. 105, f. 267, dated 2 September 1647.

39 *Ibid.*, *Provveditori da Terra e da Mar*, b. 465, c. 324, dated 3 October 1647, and *Senato Rettori*, 105, f. 81–92. The only benefit from these two ships in Dalmatia, was that Foscolo used the guns to arm the new fortifications erected in Trogir; ASVe, *Provveditori da Terra e da Mar*, b. 465, c. 360.

40 *Ibid.*, b. 479, 101, sent from Zadar, 18 March 1656.

forces was one of the key factors that contributed to the success of the Venetian arms in this battlefield. It gave the Republic's land forces a tactical and strategic edge that greatly compensated for their numerical inferiority. Without the ability to bring reinforcements and supplies to Dalmatian towns threatened by an Ottoman attack quickly and without obstructions, the Republic would hardly be able to defend its Adriatic possessions. For example, during Venetian attacks on Skradin or Novigrad in 1647, gunfire from Venetian ships was determinant in breaking the Ottoman defences. Also, during the siege of Kotor salvoes from Venetian ships frustrated the Ottoman assaults on the town walls. In addition to these major operations, the participation of smaller units of the Adriatic squadron, armed boats, small galleys and *fuste* supported often decisively Dalmatian village militias and Morlachs irregulars in countless skirmishes fought along the coast against the Ottoman raiders coming from the sea or land.

As the events of the Cretan War demonstrated, Venice lacked the power to put a stop to or interrupt the Ottoman threat in the Adriatic. Notwithstanding all, lack of capacity of the northern Ottoman harbours of Ulcinj, Bar and Levkas to host medium or large size fleets rendered these frontline bases just a minor threat. Here the Ottomans were successfully checked by a task force consisting of one or two galleys and several smaller warships patrolling the waters of the northern Albanian coast under the command of extraordinary provveditor of the Gulf. Similarly, the port of Herceg-Novi, due to its position in the bay of Kotor, was also rather easily neutralised by Venetian blockading force of no more than few armed boats. Without help from the main Ottoman fleet or squadrons from the Barbary Coast, these frontline Ottoman bases were too weak to threaten the Venetian dominion of the Gulf. Their activity was successfully controlled by the limited forces allotted to this area by the Venetian high command. In addition to these frontline bases, the Ottomans also had at their disposal two other respectable naval bases in the Adriatic Sea: Vlore and Durres, both capable of providing a shelter for large size fleets. However, in this war the Ottomans failed to utilise the strategic potential of both ports as they never dispatched a squadron of their sail fleet to either of these harbours. The only time when the Porte arranged for deployment of substantial naval forces in the Adriatic occurred in 1657, yet neither one of these ports was given a role in the Ottoman plans for that campaign. According to the reports received in May 1657 by Antonio Bernardo, Governor-general in Dalmatia and Albania, from his confidants and spies, the fleet of the *bey* of Tunis, consisting of 14 galleys and 18 large sailing ships, was ordered to sail to the Adriatic. This fleet was not heading for some Albanian port, but instead for the independent and neutral port of Dubrovnik (*Ragusa*), the sole port in the middle Adriatic that was capable of hosting fleets of significant size. The Porte planned to use Ragusa as its main base of operations for the coming campaign season and combined land and sea attacks on Split in Dalmatia and Kotor in Venetian Albania. Fortunately for both Adriatic republics, an unexpected storm stranded this fleet on the coast of Sicily and thus it never made it to Ragusa, its *rendezvous* point with the army of the *paşa* of Bosnia.[41]

Amphibious Operations

The fight for Crete was marked by a considerable number of engagements, both on the sea and on different land fronts, sometimes culminating in combined land and naval actions. This last type of operation – a direct consequence of the naval strategy of the contenders – constituted a novelty in the warfare in the Mediterranean of the 17th century, which further refined the tactics introduced by the Dutch at the end of the 16th century.

For the Venetian strategy, the amphibious actions served to move the front of the war into other direction. Francesco Morosini, and before him Lunardo Foscolo, had performed with effectiveness with their sudden landings, forcing the enemies to counteract the menace, but definitely losing the initiative. In this sense, to deprive the Ottomans of the initiative could mean their defeat or at least neutralise them. The major landings were executed in the last years of the war, but the Venetians had undertaken wide-ranging actions against the enemy ports already in the first months of the war. At the end of June 1645, as a retaliation for the Ottoman landing in Crete, Venetian galleys had bombarded the port of Patras. One month later the fleet had penetrated the ports of Koroni and Methoni in the Peloponnese, destroying the enemy ships at anchor and capturing hundreds of prisoners. In March 1646, Giorgio Morosini landed on Bozcaada island, but a few weeks later the Ottomans regained possession of it with an equally effective amphibious action. Similar actions took place in Crete itself, not always with favourable outcomes, as happened in September 1646 during the landing led by Count de Neuchesses, near besieged Réthymnon. The troops, recruited in France and organised in a single regiment under *sergente generale* Dumesnil, had been sent to Crete without their knowledge, and after a few minutes deserted en masse, returning to the ships. One year later, however, the galleys led by Giovanni Battista Grimani achieved a remarkable success destroying the Ottoman warehouses at Mirabello in Crete. On 12 May 1649, the same day of the naval battle of Foça, the Venetians scored one of the most daring actions of the war, disembarking an infantry unit which seized the enemy stronghold and dismantled the artillery which protected the Ottoman fleet in the harbour.

In the following years the amphibious actions were concentrated against the ports where the Ottomans collected supplies for the army on Crete and in other ports in the Aegean islands. In July 1650, the provveditor of the fleet Lunardo Mocenigo assaulted the port of Monemvasia and bombarded the fortress, capturing 17 enemy ships loaded with supplies ready to be sent to the army on Crete. In autumn 1651 Captain General Lunardo Foscolo landed in Samos, Leros and Kos, where he destroyed the forts, seized the supplies

41 *Ibid.*, b. 481. c. 97, dated 8 May 1657; as late as June, the Paşa of Bosnia was still waiting to hear news and confirmations concerning arrival of this fleet: and c. 101, dated 9 June 1657.

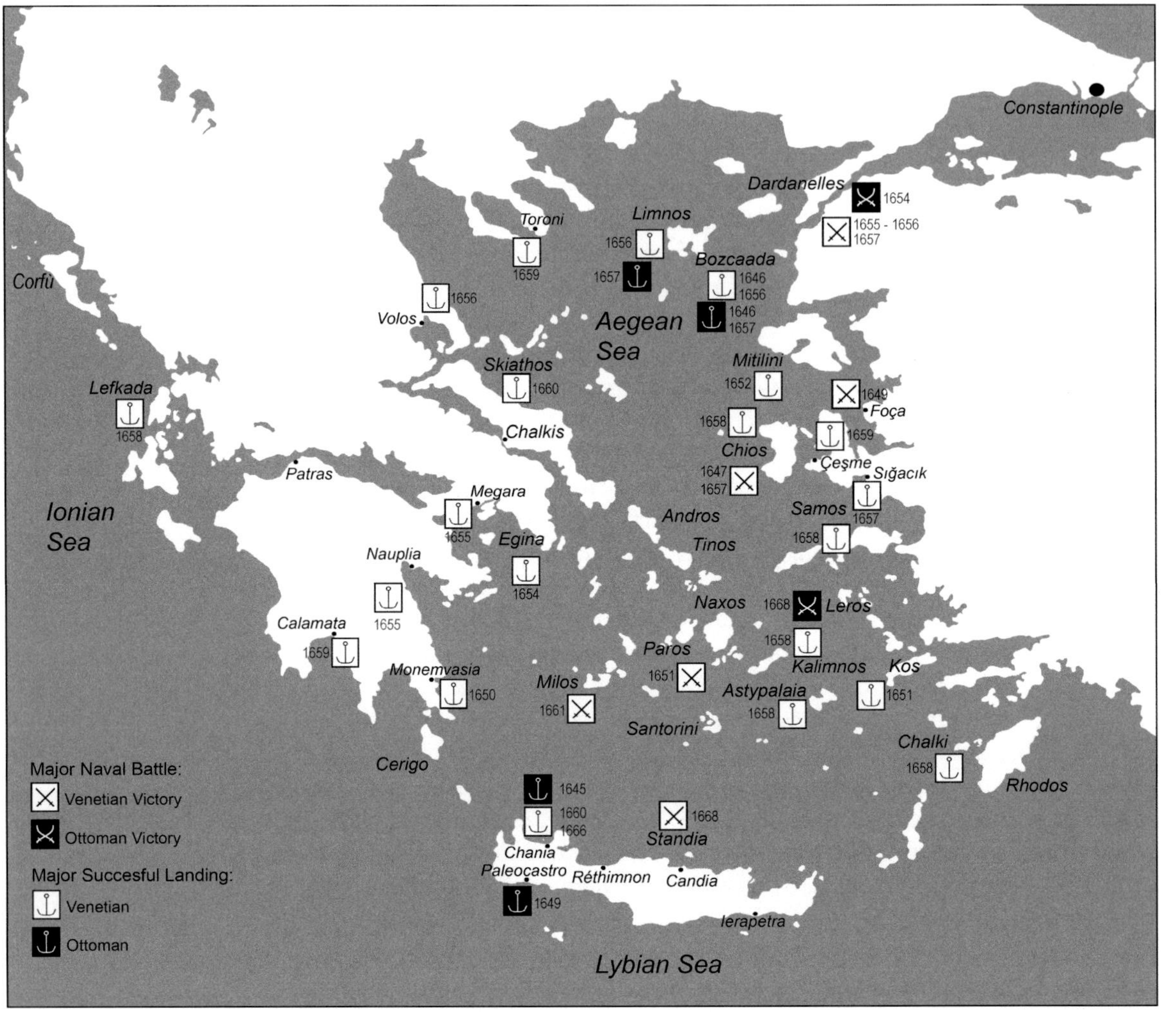

56. Naval battles and amphibious operations, 1645–1669

and enlisted oarsmen for the galleys. One year later Foscolo assaulted Mytilene, but had to renounce for a new assault on Monemvsia. In spring 1654 Francesco Morosini, future architect and specialist of the amphibious war, led several spectacular actions in the Aegean, patrolling the coast of the Peloponnese and disembarking in Aegina, where the Venetians sank 26 enemy ships loaded with wheat intended for Chaniá. The major landing operations were directed by the *generale dello sbarco* (general of the landing) Alessandro Dal Borro and impressed the contemporaries for the effectiveness and speed with which he conducted the action. The landing continued in the following campaigns, facilitated by the absence of the enemy fleet, involved to extricate themselves without success from the Dardanelles. The following campaigns continued under Antonio Barbaro, who at the end of June 1655 landed in Nauplia and held it under siege until the middle of September, after destroying the port. Then the Venetian fleet turned to Megara, despite the incoming autumn, where Barbaro found large quantities of supplies and strong resistance from the inhabitants. But the Venetians prevailed and the whole countryside was burnt and subjected to very severe looting. The

57. The Venetian fleet, under Francesco Morosini, assaults the port of Volos in the Aegean Sea, May 1655. (Detail from the cycle of frescoes on Francesco Morosini's enterprises, Museo Correr, Venice)*

frequency of the combined actions of the oared fleet and landing troops experienced an increase in the 1656 campaign, with the conquest of Limnos and Bozcaada in front of the Dardanelles and the devastation of Volos on the western shores of Greece. This landing, executed on 12 May 1655, was considered the masterpiece of general Alessandro del Borro and Captain General Francesco Morosini. The assault was part of the plan of operations against the ports where the Ottomans stored the supplies destined for Crete, in order to avoid the blockade of the Dardanelles. The port is located in the centre of a large gulf and the waters in front of it are difficult to access. However, Morosini led the galleys inside the gulf forcing the enemy resistance. At Volos the Venetians destroyed large quantities of food and other materials ready to be shipped. The death of the talented Tuscan commander, who in 1656 died of a disease in Corfu, did not interrupt the sequence of landings. In 1657 it was the turn of Siğacik, assaulted by the lieutenant of Dal Borro, Count Ossalco Polcenigo; then in 1658 new landings and looting took place in Evia, in Kalimnos and Samos under the direction of Francesco Morosini. Then, one year later, it was the turn of Toroni in the Chalkidiki peninsula, Çeşme in Anatolia, where the fortress was completely destroyed, and Kastelorizo, 90 miles east of Rhodes. This last landing was performed together with the galleys and the infantry of the Maltese knights. The assault on Chios was the most important action of the naval campaign in 1659, which consolidated definitively the amphibious address of the Venetian strategy, directed against the islands of the Aegean in order to destroy port facilities and depots set up by the Ottomans. The galleys of Francesco Morosini penetrated into the harbour and landed 800 soldiers, who conquered the fortified city after a fight that lasted several hours. The assault on the island of Skiathos in 1660, was another of the landings in the Aegean during the campaigns of

Francesco Morosini, who anticipated four months the largest action direct to the reconquest of Chaniá. In this operation the infantry played a major role, but there were not infrequent cases where the cavalry took part in the action, whose animals were transported on the galleys, making living conditions on board even more difficult. In all these actions the contribution of the light fleet was decisive and demonstrated how the galleys, with their limited draft, performed the required tasks perfectly, operating as modern landing craft.

Each amphibious action was planned according to criteria that took into account the extent of the landing, the distance of the objective from the beach and naturally the strength of the enemy defences. In a council of war held on 30 July 1668, in the presence of Admiral Vincenzo Rospigliosi, recently appointed commander-in-chief of the Allied fleet, it was decided to assault the fort of Santa Marina on the island of San Teodoro, located a few miles north-east of Chaniá. In July 1650, the *provveditore all'Armata* Luigi Mocenigo had subtracted San Teodoro to the Ottomans, who had conquered the island in June 1645, in the first action of the war. The Venetians had not long remained there and before abandoning it they had razed the fortifications to the ground, but the Ottomans had returned and after having restored part of the defences had installed a garrison. From that position they could signal to the port of Chaniá the presence of enemy ships and for this reason the Allies decided to intervene again. The war council planned the landing for the following 3 August and in the accurate instructions for the landing written by Captain General Francesco Morosini describes the modalities with which an amphibious operation was carried out. Having reached the shore, the galleasses were arranged at the wings and at the centre and with the galleys formed an arch covering all the space necessary to deploy the landing troops:

> All the galleys and boats of the Papal fleet will move to the right to disembark 250 soldiers at once, and the ships will be accompanied, for protection purposes, by the two remaining galleys. The same will be done to the left with all the ships' boats of the Maltese fleet under the protection of the two remaining galleys of the Order, to put 280 men of their troops on the ground. The two Venetian galleys will be joined by boats and boats to disembark 300 soldiers of the Republic. These six aforementioned galleys must not cooperate in the bombardment of the enemy, but only to protect the landing of the troops and, in the event that the enemy tries a sortie against them, their the galley will protect the retreat. The landings will have to get out the range of the fort and in places that offer space to the troops to deploy in formation. For the beginning, a special signal will be given from the galley of S.E. Admiral Vincenzo Rospigliosi. Similarly, galleasses and galleys in charge of the bombardment against the enemy will not open fire until the first shot has taken place from the Papal flagship, and they will continue the fire until the attack columns have approached the enemy, to avoid the risk of be offended by our shot. Only if the Papal captain will restart the shot, the other ships will be able to shoot again. As soon as the troops are on the ground, two assault columns will be formed of Papal, Maltese, and Venetian troops, who will be placed under the command of the respective officers.

This document reported other interesting details, such as the use of a marksmen's screen in front of the columns. This light infantry had to advance in open order, preceding the battle corps to "no more than half a musket shot" as normally they entrusted this task to the *Oltramarine* soldiers; on that occasion were employed the mercenaries of the *colonello* Angelo Maria Vitali, a famous corsair enlisted in Venetian service. All the infantry had to set off after a signal, in that case a big red flame at the flagpole of the master tree of the Papal flagship. The instructions written by Morosini closed with the indications to the commanders of the objectives:

> The infantry will move against the land front of the enemy's defence. The columns destined against the left side will follow two directions: the Venetian one will precede and them stop themselves right in front of the centre of the battlefield, while the Maltese, who will follow the first, will deploy in front of the half bastion on left. Papal columns will move towards the same objective in front of the right-hand bastion. The Venetian Colonel Andrea Facile, who is responsible for the operation on the field, will take care that the assault columns take the right path without exposing themselves in advance to the enemy fire and, when siding in the vicinity of it, keep themselves covered. It will then be attempted by a fire of musketry to compel the enemy to leave the place and, if it is successful, a certain number of engineers will move from each column to the curtains, will readily excavate at their bases, and with mines of 500 pounds of gunpowder will try to destroy them. Another special squadron, composed by 10 men for each Papal, Maltese and Venetians battalion, chosen among the more experienced and brave, half of grenadiers and half of musketeers, will protect the engineers' work by throwing grenades beyond the wall, and then climbing and firing from the top inside the enemy defence. When the breach will be open, three columns, one for each of Papal, Maltese and Venetian soldiers, will move, with God's help, to the assault, while the other troops will still remain in good order in front of the enemy place, ready to face a possible reverse; which usually happens when soldiers, as normal, begin to loot. Especially nobody will have to get other things that are not weapons and even these only for as long as it will appear necessary to gain honour and glory to the service of the Princes.[42]

The landing engaged less than 900 men in all, and it was resolved with an easy success, considering that the Ottomans had left the island before the assault. For the landings against more important targets, the Venetians deployed more than 3,000 men, as happened at Bozcaada and Limnos in 1656 under Alessandro dal Borro, who had two French regiments, *Labauda* and *Chevalier de Rosis*, plus other Italian, *Oltramontane* and *Oltramarine* companies. Speed was at the heart of the success, as the Dutch had clearly shown against the Spaniards in the Low Countries, but when the available forces were limited, the Venetian commanders tried to exploit the element of surprise, and above all to conceal the strength of their forces. In 1657, during the amphibious assault to Sığacık, the General Count Ossalco di Polcenigo had only 2,000 men, but he deployed

42 W. von Bigge, cited work, pp. 88–90.

58. Paleocastro, a fortress in south-west Crete on a jutting rock with a little haven for galleys. It was conquered in May 1649 by the Ottoman navy under Voinok Ahmed, who was able to elude Venetian surveillance and land with 7,000 soldiers and ammunition for besieging the fortress; the surrender of the little garrison soon followed. (Author's archive)

them in such a way as to appear in a much higher number and the expedient had the desired effect, so much so that Venetian commander received a special mention from the Senate. The Venetians became masters of the amphibious war in the Mediterranean, so that, except for the landing of 1645, in comparison the Ottomans were able to complete the landings only operating from coastal bases close to the objectives, as occurred at Gramvousa and Paleocastro in 1646, and Tenedo in 1658. In the other amphibious operations, thanks to the inability of the fleet to guarantee the protection of the troops, there collected always humiliating failures.

Less spectacular than the raids, but equally important for the conservation of the fleet, landings took place in large numbers for the supply of water. The so-called *acquate* always presented great difficulties and required a lot of time, while the water transported always ended after a few days. Furthermore, supplies were a source of significant risk when they occurred in regions controlled by enemies. For this reason, the water supply sorties carried out in Crete by the Venetian and their allies in July 1668, were punctuated by bloody fighting, which engaged several hundreds of soldiers from both side. On 14 July 14, the Maltese and Papal squadron sustained a violent battle in which 20 soldiers and two Knights of Malta were killed. Six days later, a new battle occurred when the commander of the Allied fleet, the *generalissimo* Vincenzo Rospigliosi, landed in the bay of Kissamos with his own galleys with a reinforcement of Maltese and Venetian galleys. Despite the deploying of a protective line formed by two infantry battalions, the Allies had to fight for four hours against the infantry and the enemy cavalry, until they requested the intervention of the galleys which, anchored at musket fire range, targeted the enemies barricaded in a nearby cloister. An even more violent battle took place on the island of Tenedo in August 1657, when, again following a sudden attack, the Venetians were surprised by the Ottomans who had recently landed a corps of troops to reconquer the island. Despite having already landed a contingent of 2,500 soldiers, General Count Polcenigo underestimated the risk deriving from the hills near the shore, and above all he did not deploy pikeman, but only musketeers. The violent assault with sabres and knives launched by the Ottoman infantry, lying in ambush behind the hills, caused panic in the infantry, which fired a volley, "and fled to the galleys, under the bow of which they were killed from three to four hundred."

The landings could be exploited not only for raids against enemy ports, but also as a means of conquering large-scale land targets. This idea soon made

59. After Paleocastro, the attempt to land at Suda Island in June 1649, was another rare amphibious action attempted by the Ottoman fleet after the landing of 1645. (Author's archive)*

its way into the Allied war councils, as it represented the natural escalation of the amphibious war tactics so brilliantly undertaken by the Venetian galleys. The idea was to prepare a strong landing to take away from the Ottoman control the largest Cretan port, Chaniá, sealing the flow of supplies to the island. This address was advanced for the first time in October 1658, by generals Gremonville and Villanova, during a war council with Captain General Francesco Morosini. Some spies inside Chaniá reported that the city was almost unguarded, and the larger part of the garrison were composed of convalescent soldiers. In the following spring Venice began to collect troops, using the infantry already assigned to the navy. However, Ottoman intelligence, for its part, informed Catrezoglu Ali Paşa – who had replaced Dely Hüseyn as commander in Crete – about the enemy plan. In turn, informed of the enemy movements of troops, the Venetians changed their plan and for that time the opportunity failed. The occasion reappeared in 1660, when Venice was able to assemble a considerable force, thanks to the renewed support of the Holy See and France. This time the operation seemed to be crowned by the best auspices, because at the beginning of that year a disastrous fire had destroyed the Ottoman shipyards at Galata and seriously damaged the Ottoman arsenal.

The Dutch had successfully introduced large-scale amphibious operations during the war of independence against Spain, during which they achieved a series of spectacular victories. The example of this sister republic of northern Europe pushed to emulation and comforted the convictions of those who, in Venice, insisted on the need to attack the enemy naval bases.

60. Alessandro dal Borro, subject of the Grand Duke of Tuscany, was a veteran of the Thirty Years' War who had served in the Imperial and Spanish Armies under Ottavio Piccolomini. (Painting attributed to Charles Mellin, Gemäldgalerie, Berlin)*

But embarking on a large landing operation directly to Crete, moreover close to an enemy army, concealed many dangers. Firstly, the Dutch operated from close quarters and could rapidly supply the landed contingents. In the Archipelago this could not always happen, as the recent past had demonstrated. It was necessary increase the network of storage but, except for Corfu, no other Venetian island hosted ports or deposits able to assure a flow of supplies of considerable proportions, without considering that the other Venetian islands in the Aegean were also far away from Crete. For this reason, it would have been necessary to upgrade some ports such as Cerigo, Tino or Paros to create a network of connections able to support the logistical effort necessary for the amphibious forces.

But any investment in this direction would have required a lot of time and much money, and in any case, even if equipped with well-provided bases, everything had to be transported from the mainland anyway. Thus, launching an amphibious offensive meant moving in a context much less favourable respect the Dutch in the Low Countries. Some large-scale actions attempted in the past against targets in Ottoman territory had ended in disastrous results. The landing of the Spaniards in Algiers in 1541 had failed, causing nearly 12,000 casualties and the loss of a large number of ships. In 1599, the landing of the Tuscan knights of Santo Stefano in Chios, had ended with the capture of the whole infantry landed. More recently, also the attempt made by the Venetians in 1650 had ended in a failure, even though it was evident to everyone that it was an ill-organised and even worse conduct operation. These and other failures were well alive in memory and sufficient to discourage the most hesitant.

However, the Senate authorised the campaign and in 1660 the Venetians resolutely took the plan to expel the Ottomans from Crete with a landing comprising numerous contingents, such as to make this operation much more complex than any previous experience. In the summer of 1660, 11,200 infantrymen and 1,200 horsemen were concentrated in Cerigo, landed in the following September near Chaniá. Six years later, in the last attempt to conquest the island's enemy ports, 8,295 foot soldiers and 1,008 horsemen. In both cases it was necessary to deploy the fleet complete, including the auxiliaries, to ensure protection for the troops who took a whole day to land and then disembark the supplies on the beach. The places of landing were carefully chosen, avoiding the risk of encountering awaiting Ottoman troops. The fleet constantly guaranteed protection during the landing and considerable resources were transported to the beach, but both these operations failed. In 1660 the failure was attributed to a series of unfortunate causes, but the result was unfavourable due to the serious strategic errors committed by the Venetians. In the first campaign, too much time was lost to collect troops destined for landing, waiting almost to the end of the summer before assaulting Chaniá. Then, politics contributed to burying the enterprise by accepting the interference of the Allies in the designation of the commanders, and finally the resistance of the Ottomans was underestimated, without considering that they were numerically higher than the adversaries. The general command was entrusted to the very young – barely eighteen years old – Prince Almerigo d'Este, brother of the Duke of Modena. The Prince was universally esteemed as a brilliant and clever captain who had served with distinction in the French army in Lombardy and Piedmont. However, his lack of experience in a war theatre like the Cretan one was not even compensated by capable lieutenants, mostly settled at the higher ranks thanks to the support of France or the Pope. Among the officers there was a profound distrust which made cooperation between the units difficult. The force assembled included soldiers recruited in every corner of Europe: French; Germans; Corsicans, naturally together with *Oltramarini* and Italians from the *Terraferma* domains or from the states which granted to Venice the permission to recruit mercenaries. With them, soldiers from the Papal States, Modena, Parma, Malta and Piedmont; finally, among the auxiliaries of the fleet there were Maltese, Papal and Tuscan sailors. The campaign was marred by the continuous protests of the soldiers and their officers, culminating in Cerigo with the refusal to embark if they had not been paid in advance four months of salary. The question was composed only after the payment of two months, authorised by the Venetian government. This event persuaded the Captain General to keep the 70,000 ducats sent from Venice and destined for the garrison of Candia. Doing so, Morosini wanted to be sure to dispose of money for the payment of landing troops.[43]

The fleet gathered north of the island of Suda, a few miles east of Chaniá. Here, the Allies expelled the Ottoman troops who besieged the Venetian fortress and, on 24 August, landed on the beach between the monastery of Caloiero and the fort of Calami. From these positions, the Ottomans targeted the galleys approaching the shore; the Maltese Knights landed first, having obtained the privilege to form the vanguard. Then, alongside the Maltese infantry battalion, they assaulted the enemy batteries, followed by the Papal troops and the knights of Santo Stefano. The action was fast but bloody and cost the life of the Maltese vice-commander, the knight Grimaldi, while the general of the landing troops, the Marquis of Correa, had a foot injured. Even the Ottomans lost their commander, Hasan Paşa, and all 12 guns, triumphantly transported to the Venetian ships. The success achieved did not pacify the climate and new disagreements arose between the Allies. The Maltese contingent, declaring polemically to be without commander, made an immediate return to Suda and did not participate in any action for almost two weeks. Other encounters occurred in the following days for the conquest of the Ottomans quarters near Chaniá. The joint action of the galleys and landing troops quickly broke the Ottoman resistance at

43 ASVe, Senato, Dispacci di Provveditori, b. 552, 21 April 1660. This fact was particularly unfortunate for the garrison of Candia because they were afraid to again face misery and starvation.

61. The assault at Chios was the most important action of the naval campaign of 1659, which consolidated definitively the amphibious nature of the Venetian strategy, directed against the islands of the Aegean Sea, to destroy port facilities and depots set up by the Ottomans. Chios was the most important Ottoman base in the Eastern Aegean, where the Porte had situated its merchants for supplying Crete. On 12 June the Venetian galleys penetrated the harbour and landed 800 soldiers, who conquered the port after a fight that lasted several hours. (Detail from the cycle of frescoes on Francesco Morosini's enterprises, Museo Correr, Venice)

62. The assault on the island of Skiathos in 1660 was another of the landings performed by Francesco Morosini, who with this action anticipated the largest landing planned: that of seizing Chaniá, for expelling the Ottomans from Chaniá. In these operations the infantry played a major role, but there were not infrequent cases where the cavalry took part in the action, whose animals were transported to the galleys, making living conditions on board even more difficult. (Detail from the cycle of frescoes on Francesco Morosini's enterprises, Museo Correr, Venice)

63. A rare image of Venetian infantry dating the Cretan war, depicted without the mediation of the Mannerist painting style in vogue in those years. The illustration represents the amphibious assault at Sığacık, in Anatolia, in spring 1657. The infantry appears dressed in a completely red uniform, except the NCOs, officers and musicians, who wear azure blue or yellow coats and breeches. Note the mounted officer distinguished by the azure sash and the coat with "Lombard style" sleeves.

Caloiero, Apicorno and Calami, allowing the Allies to have a sufficiently large bridgehead. The news of the landing was in the meantime also received by the Ottoman commander, Catrezoglu Ali, who had his command inside the fortified camp of Yeni Kandie. He ordered to send a reconnaissance of cavalry and then alerted the garrison of Réthymnon. The Allies estimated that the Ottomans had no more than 2,000 soldiers inside Chaniá, to which 500 or more were escaped from the conquered village. The Allied plan foresaw that once landed it would have had to arm the local population and employ it to guard the routes between Chaniá and the Ottoman garrisons on the island, to secure the shoulders of the army before starting the siege of the city. To call and organise this militia, however, spent other precious time and the result was lower than expected, since up to 6 September there were put together no more than 1,800 men. The sea voyage had hurt the horses, which began to die in large numbers due to the climate and unsuitable forage. Captain General Francesco Morosini went ashore to become personally aware of the campaign's progress and to meet the Prince Almerico, camped near the village of Cicalaria, where he was unwell.

At that point, the Venetian commander became aware of the general confusion in which the landing corps was operating. Morosini learned about the riots aroused among the soldiers who were always asking for more money. Then he was informed about the unavailability of the French contingent, which – without horses for officers and baggage – was still on the beach, declaring that it could not march. Among the subordinate officers reigned discord, while together with Prince Almerico also the *sieur* De Bas was feverish, and had returned to Suda leaving the command to the Chevalier de Gremonville, a soldier very little estimated by Morosini. Days before the cavalry commander, Marquis de Garenne, had fallen into combat. He was a skilled officer whose lack would have bad consequences. The situation was worsened by the accidental burning of the biscuit deposits and the unexpected arrival of the Ottomans, 6,000 in number on foot and on horseback, who had managed to overcome the passage of Malaxi, without contest. This crossroads was guarded by 600 Cretan militiamen under the orders of the Corsican colonel Aldrovandi, whose men had left their assigned places to loot the surroundings. The Ottomans slowly approached the encampment of Cicalaria, but did not move to the assault and this prudence was providential for the Allies, because most of the units fled away to save the loot they had collected. At the same time the French infantry lost 150 men in a sudden enemy sortie from Chaniá. The Allies re-established the situation thanks to the intervention of the Maltese battalion and the Venetian infantry of the galleys, which under Nicolò Zane engaged the Ottoman vanguard and finally repelled the enemy assault after a battle lasting seven hours. The war council of the following day evaluated as vanished the option of a regular siege at Chaniá and decided to embark the troops for an assault against the Ottoman fortified camp in front of Candia. According to the war council argument, it was reasonable to expect that *Yeni Kandie* was almost undefended and therefore, together with the garrison of the besieged city, it would be easy to defeat the enemy, conquer the enemy encampment and perhaps the whole eastern territory up to Sitia.

In 48 hours the troops returned aboard the ships and sailed to Candia, where they landed behind the enemy camp on 12 September. Prince Almerico was still in poor conditions, and in fact the operations of landing were directed by the De Bas and the adjutant of the Prince, the Count of Mileto. Morale was very low, as can be inferred from the Venetian historians: "Several disorders had occurred due to some commanders, or poorly practiced, or too malicious … and when they saw the face of the Turks immediately proposed to retreat inside Candia."

Despite the desperate situation, the troops moved against the Ottomans, and with the support of the fleet's artillery and one battery with eight guns easily overran the advanced enemy defences. In his *History of the Cretan War*, the contemporary historian Girolamo Brusoni gives an account about that day: "There was no doubt that Candia Nuova would fall … if the greed of a few Officers and Soldiers had not, with their eternal infamy, changed a glorious victory into a dreadful day."

Encountering a weak resistance, the allied troops began to loot quarters and houses abandoned by the Ottomans. As the first soldiers come out, arms full of loot, almost all the units disbanded and rushed in turn to plunder every place. At that point, the narration becomes confused and the dynamics of the events are not clear, however it seems that an uncontrolled voice about an enemy counter-attack spread among the troops causing their flight. As soon as the Ottomans realised that their adversaries were fleeing to the ships, they took courage and pursued the disordered mass, capturing more than 1,000 and killing them as many. In vain, Prince Almerico and Captain General Morosini tried with the reserve troops to arrest the fugitives. The

64. (top) Ottoman landings at Bozcaada and Lemnos executed in the summer of 1657 allowed the recapture of the two major islands in front of the Dardanelles, both conquered the year before by the Venetian fleet.*

65. (below) In 1658 a plan was designed to land a corps of troops at Chaniá, to wrest the port from the Ottomans and force them to leave Crete.*

66. (top left) The monument to the memory of Prince Almerico d'Este in the church of Santa Maria Gloriosa dei Frari in Venice. The young prince was the commander of the landing operations in 1660 against Chaniá and then in front at Yeni Kandie, both actions failed due to serious strategic mistakes and the indiscipline of the troops. The contingent under Prince Almerico consisted of soldiers recruited in France, Italy, Dalmatia, Greece, Corsica, and Germany. (Author's photo).

67. (above) French Officer, c.1660. For the landing at Chaniá in 1660, the Venetian army was mainly composed of contingents recruited in France. It may be surprising that French officers had gone to such a rugged theatre of war with the fashionable dress of that age, but several contemporary accounts confirmed it. This illustration is very interesting because it shows one of the first examples of a ***justaucorp***, here probably worn over a waistcoat that outlines shirt and breeches richly adorned with bows and laces. (Print after a drawing by Sébastien Leclerc; Musée de Louvre Collection, Paris)

68. (left) The Marquis Francesco Villa de Ghiron, commander of the landing at Chaniá in spring 1666. The Marquis had served in the of Duke of Savoy's army against the Spaniards in Lombardy and was considered an excellent officer. The campaign was accurately planned, but failed due to lack of collaboration among the command staff and the unexpected Ottoman resistance.

young prince, shivering with fever, dismounted to lean against a tree, feeling himself faint and thus disappeared from the sight of his officers, who struggled to look for him, making the situation even more confused. The unfortunate Prince died a few weeks later in Paros, further aggravating the pain for the failure of the campaign, while in Venice and Paris diplomats vented their frustration by accusing each other, or, as the historian Pietro Diedo wrote: "All tried to make known that the unhappy outcome was followed more by defect of direction, than by forces, which the Turks were not invincible, while, despite the mistakes of the captains, if our troops were not disordered for looting, they would have achieved a great victory."

The attempt to recover Candia with a landing was repeated six years later, relying this time on more reliable troops and officers, subjecting the units to intense preventive training. The Marquis Francesco Villa de Ghiron assumed the command of the army. He was an experienced and authoritative captain placed by the Duke of Savoy. The Venetians prepared this operation with care, gathering men and materials as early as December 1665. The army was composed of Italian and *Oltramarine* infantry, to which were added new regiments hired in Germany, Savoy and Switzerland. Cavalry was also well cared for, transporting the horses first to Zakynthos and then to Paros, to acclimatise them and avoid the deaths that had plagued the Allies six years earlier. The infantry numbered 7,728 rank and file, the mounted troops were 786 men among cuirassiers and *cappelletti*, and finally 72 dragoons. Villa de Ghiron accurately described the composition of the army in his relation about the campaigns of Crete:[44]

Infantry:

1st Brigade, Colonel Friesheim (4 battalions)
Regiment Friesheim (German), 14 companies: 738 men
Regiment Frigerio (Italian), 6 companies: 292 men
Regiment Wertmüller (Swiss), 5 companies: 320 men

2nd Brigade, Colonel Sagramola (4 battalions)
Regiment Sagramola (Italian), 5 companies: 327 men
Regiment Doglione (German), 4 companies: 246 men
Free Company Brusasco, Gelmi, Heraut (mixed): 214 men

3rd Brigade, Colonel Arborio (4 battalions):
Free Company Venturi, Lignon, Umberto (Italian): 253 men
Regiment Ersan (De La Cerverie) (Savoy), 7 companies: 273 men
Regiment Arborio (Savoy), 8 companies: 297 men
Regiment Pietro Antonio Furietti (Italian), 9 companies: 465 men

4th Brigade, Colonel Count Martinoni (4 battalions)
Regiment Negron (Bavarian), 5 companies: 295 men

44 *Les Memoires du Voiage de Msr le Marquis de Ville au Levant, ou Histoire Curieuse du Siege de Candia* (Amsterdam, 1670), pp. 69–83.

Regiment Marrone (Italian), 6 companies: 309 men
Regiment Michiel'Angelo Furietti (Italian), 9 companies: 559 men

5th Brigade, Colonel Buttis (5 battalions)
Free Company Piacentino, Bricheras, Sbrogliavaca, Bellini, Villeneourve (mixed), 311 men
Regiment Restori (Italian), 6 companies: 274 men
Regiment Spada (Italian), 5 companies: 282 men
Regiment Conti (Italian), 5 companies: 274 men
Regiment Zacco (Italian), 6 companies: 258 men

6th Brigade, Colonel de la Motte (4 battalions)
Regiment de la Motte (mixed), 20 companies: 593 men
Regiment d'Anclam (mixed), 6 companies: 320 men
Regiment Bianco (Italian), 6 companies: 282 men

Reserve:
Regiment Evangelista (Italian), 6 companies: 295 men

Cavalry:
Cuirassier regiment Sforza-Bissaro (Italian), 5 companies: 270 men
Cuirassier regiment Corradini (German), 4 companies, 143 men
Cappelletti regiment Varsama (Albanian), 6 companies, 186 men
Cappelletti regiment Rados (mixed), 187 men

Dragoons:
Companies Carboniers and Forest (mixed), 72 men

Contrary winds delayed the departure of the army to the end of February. The fleet anchored hidden by the island of Suda as six years before, and from there landed near to Chaniá on 26 February 1666. The plan had been discussed for a long time and at the end the proposal to assault the enemy encampment of Yeni Kandie, which would have required considerable forces, was abandoned, while the conquest of Chaniá, defended by a garrison drastically reduced due to the plague epidemic penetrated into the city, seemed to offer better chance. However, the war council assumed also the lack of help from the natives, abandoned to itself six years earlier. The landing operations took place rapidly and within one day, the troops had taken position around Chaniá without encountering resistance. Events took an unwanted turn in early March when, badly interpreting an order of Villa, Sergeant General Wertmüller led reconnaissance with the cavalry but came into contact with the enemy *sipahys*. The inexperience proved fatal to the Venetian cavalry, who pursued the enemy, but moved too far and were surrounded and isolated by Ottoman cavalry and infantry, who came out from the city to perform the most classic of traps. The Venetians lost 300 horsemen and this failure worstened relations between Villa and his officers, who in increasing numbers insisted on lifting the siege and assaulting the enemy at Candia. On 5 March, eight days after the arrival on Crete, some of the troops returned to the ships and headed to Candia, where they arrived on 10 March. The rest of the contingent remained in front of Chaniá, trying to conquer the city by starvation, but the besieged garrison refused the surrender. Finally, these troops too moved and joined the rest of the contingent in mid April. The Venetians had built a fortified encampment between the Gioffiro River and Yeni Kandie; then, on 19 April, after reorganising his troops, now reduced to 7,000 infantrymen and 556 cavalrymen and dragoons, Villa launched an unsuccessful assault on the Ottoman fortified camp, which ended after one day of fighting. The Venetians kept their positions close to the enemy, but the Ottomans remained barricaded in their encampment for over a month, until 1 June, when Marquis Villa ordered the retreat and with this outcome disappeared the last Venetian attempt to expel the Ottomans from Crete.

VI

Field Campaigns: Sieges

Because the defence of the Venetian fortresses on the island marked the strategic context of the conflict, the only actual field operations of the Cretan War were thereore concentrated in the sieges, culminating with the final assaults on Candia. In this respect, the Cretan War is little different to other contemporary European warfare. In fact, open field battles were very rare and – except for those that occurred in 1660 and 1666 during the Venetian landings in Crete – no great battles were engaged on the island or other fronts. After the landings, the most important field clash in Crete happened on 19 June 1647 at Messarea, when the Venetians, with 700 cavalrymen and 200 Albanian infantrymen reinforced by 2,000 Cretan militiamen, assaulted the much more numerous Ottoman vanguard encamped while marching to Candia. The battle resulted in a defeat for the Venetians, who from that date concentrated every offensive act in the sorties from the besieged city.

Other engagements, though they could be considered just skirmishes, occurred in the spring of 1650, when the Venetians decided to make an attempt to reconquer some Cretan fortresses. For this campaign arrived from Venice 5,000 infantrymen and 400 horsemen among cuirassiers and light cavalry.[1] Sure that the enemies were dispersed and almost demoralised, the Venetians conducted the campaign in a very inaccurate way. Their attempt to reconquer Ierapetra, on the south side of the island, failed, despite the reinforcements sent from Candia. The operation continued with exhausting slowness and the Ottomans, perhaps even warned by deserters, were able to send reinforcements to prevent the Venetian landings. The campaign ended in a disastrous outcome when the contingent led by provveditor Francesco Barbaro was surprised and annihilated by the Ottomans. On that occasion, ambushed by the enemy, the Venetian cavalry overwhelmed the infantry and caused a general rout. The other major engagement of that disastrous campaign which occurred near Sitia, ended with the flight of the Venetian infantry. Other open field actions took place in Dalmatia and Bosnia, in the strategic context of the campaigns conducted between 1646 and 1649, but with the exception of the battle fought near Knin, in March 1654, which

1 ASVe *Senato Dispacci* di *Provveditori* b. 546, 2 May 1650.

69. Walloon general Gilles De Haes entered Venetian service in 1645 and become *Governatore delle Armi* of Crete in late 1648, having served on the fleet as general of the landing. (Illustration after *Gilles De Haes, homme de guerre du XVII siècle*, by Charles Rahlenbeck, Bruxelles, 1854)*

involved a total of 5,140 Venetian and 11,000 Ottomans, sieges represented the major episodes of war even in this war theatre. After all, other field clashes occurred in Dalmatia were simple factions, if not just raids and lootings, conducted by small contingents of cavalry and infantry on the rugged terrain of those regions.

In the context of the debated analysis ofwar between Western armies and Ottoman ones, the Cretan War represents a field of investigation less studied. In his challenging study *Rethinking Military History*, Jeremy Black has pointed out the problematic aspects of the interpretation of the success of Western European armies based solely on technological and cultural factors, namely the adoption of more modern firearms and the scientific approach to military matters. He warns that the experience of several non-European war theatres has shown that the Europeans, indeed to be effective, were frequently forced to adopt local tactical methods.[2] The triumphal outcome of the campaigns of 1647 and 1648 in Dalmatia, when the Venetian regular forces went from one victory to another and routed Ottoman relief forces in open field encounters, can be taken as a good argument in favour of the more general statement, that by the mid 17th century, due to the development of new fighting techniques, European forces had become tactically superior to the Ottomans, at least where the encounters between deployments of similar size was concerned. However, this tactical superiority of the Venetian forces by itself does not provide any kind of guarantee for the successful defence of the Dalmatians' and Albanians' domains. Moreover, as the outcome of the battle of Knin in March 1654 has demonstrated, when allowed to exploit the terrain and their cavalry superiority, Ottomans were yet capable of defeating European enemies. In the Cretan war, the Venetian commanders considered the contingents of Italian and *Oltramontani* infantry the core on which rested the defence of the towns in Crete as well as in Dalmatia. Instead, the borders' surveillance and the offensive actions in enemy territory were performed mainly by irregular forces supported by a limited number of professional troops. In these actions, Venetian forces operated little differently to the Austrian *Grenzer* or even their Ottoman enemies. For more than two decades, the irregular forces prevented a major cost in blood for protecting the Venetian overseas domains in the East Adriatic Sea.

2 Jeremy Black, *Rethinking Military History* (New York: Routledge, 2004), pp. 84–85.

It can be taken as a real novelty if compared to the previous Ottoman–Venetian conflicts and an important step in the development of Venetian and Ottoman defensive system in the Balkans, as well as for the introduction of new tactics in the open field and in siege warfare. Thanks to the experience gained in the sieges, the combatants developed tactics that three and a half centuries later would return in the battlefields of the First World War. However, if in the naval war the 27 years of conflict brought great improvements and transformations in the fleets, at first view the technological progress of the infantry and cavalry appears on the contrary almost non-existent. In fact, the equipment of the soldiers did not record substantial changes, and compared to the first years of the war was dictated more by the changes in fashion than by the needs of war. The Venetian infantry as well as one of their allies continued to carry large bandoliers for ammunition and baldrics for their swords, while limiting as much as possible their use in tunnel warfare, but judging from the sources there were no real transformations such as happened in Europe after 1670, when the changed conditions of the battlefield led to a drastic reorganisation of infantry equipment, with the introduction of the sword belt, the ammunition pouch and the increase of the musketry compared to the pike. Moreover, these innovations had been conveyed by the siege war, which required less equipment for the soldiers. If the limited use of troops on horseback inhibited the evolution of cavalry equipment, for the infantry there were other factors that determined this immobility. First of all, there were the economic conditions that discouraged the reconfiguration of equipment. The heterogeneity of the contingents coming from all over Europe, often already equipped, favoured for obvious reasons the preservation of original equipment.

Secondly, the need for the Venetian commanders to employ field troops on several fronts, both to garrison the fortresses as well as for landing troops, and therefore the wide variety of scenarios, did not encourage so many changes. But if we observe this phenomenon from another perspective, we realise that the apparent lack of development of individual armament was, on the contrary, a form of adaptation to a type of war which, as related by the eyewitness, was completely different from any other known experience. The last three years of war absorbed most of the Venetian resources in the defence of the island's capital, where thousands of soldiers arrived each year, and before which the fleet also became a support to the Candia garrison's resistance. From 1667, the conflict turned into a terrifying war of attrition, in which certain tactics developed by the combatants were not very different from the ones introduced in the trenches of the Great War. The use of the pike and other weapons in the siege war, when viewed from the perspective of a close encounter, appear less anachronistic than one might think at first. The fact that no one in Crete decided to introduce the bayonet becomes more understandable if we take into account that in the close fights swords and other individual short weapons were more useful, as the infantrymen of the First World War also experienced. Pikes and other polearms, such as the *brandistocchi* and *corsesche* widely employed by the defenders, were the logical answer to the contingencies of the trench war. Furthermore, the ratio of musket to pike was already quite high in the Venetian infantry at the beginning of the conflict. Even the Ottomans, who made little use of polearms, still used a large number of individual cold weapons like sabres and knives and then they were already fully equipped for this kind of war.

Sieges

The only actual field operations of the Cretan War were concentrated in the sieges, culminating in the final 28 months of assault on Candia. The experience of Crete allowed the Ottoman army to achieve considerable progress in the siege war, such as to overcome in many ways the knowledge of their enemies. An advantage for the Ottomans consisted in the production of large calibre artillery, a tradition already consolidated at the beginning of the century and although these were less precise than those of their Western enemies, this handicap had little influence in the bombardment of a town's fortifications. But the most evident progress in sieges was obtained by the Ottoman engineers, who were the first to employ, even imperfectly, the parallels technique. With this, it must not be inferred that they were the actual inventors of this system of approach, perfected autonomously by the great French engineer Vauban, who realised this kind of approache for the first time in 1673 at Maastricht and then, in the regular distribution on three orders, in 1697 at Ath. It is unlikely that the relations on the siege of Candia provided Vauban with the crucial insight for the development of parallels, but it remains unlikely that this technique had been taught to the Ottomans by the Venetian Andrea Barozzi, the engineer who, in hatred of his fatherland, in 1667 deserted to the enemy. Before this date, to approach the enemy walls, the Ottomans used simple trenches, straight or winding depending on the shape of the terrain. During the first sieges, the trenches were already drawn parallel to the front of attack, to provide cover to the troops, but without any pre-established rule and so as a result were linear or tortuous. To proceed to the successive parallels, other approaches were either linear, tortuous or zigzagged, for each sector was built as a system of parallels which finally connected to each other. On the other hand, the method for protecting the flanks with the backward refolding of the approaches was not yet known. The trenches built in the early years of the war were particularly narrow and shallow compared to Western standards, and then broad approaches were implemented up to 3.5–4 metres with a depth of 2.5–3 metres, but later in larger size. The execution of the earthworks was not entrusted to the fighting troops, but instead to diggers – the *musellim* – flanked by volunteers and other workers recruited on the island. The soldiers took possession of the trenches at a later time to organise the defence, but later it was necessary to support the engineers with soldiers to counter the Venetian sorties, which burst into the trenches without encountering resistance. This problem had already become evident in 1645 at Chaniá, with the sortie launched by the defenders in the late evening of 17 July and it was only because the action was carried out to facilitate the entry into the city of the reinforcements that the approaches suffered limited damage. Four years later, a sortie from Candia carried out by a single Greek company of Marco Lombardo's regiment, assaulted the Ottoman trenches behind the fort of San Demetrio, chased away the Ottoman engineers and took away all the tools. The occupation of the trenches was entrusted to the janissaries and other foot troops, who after taking possession of a sector

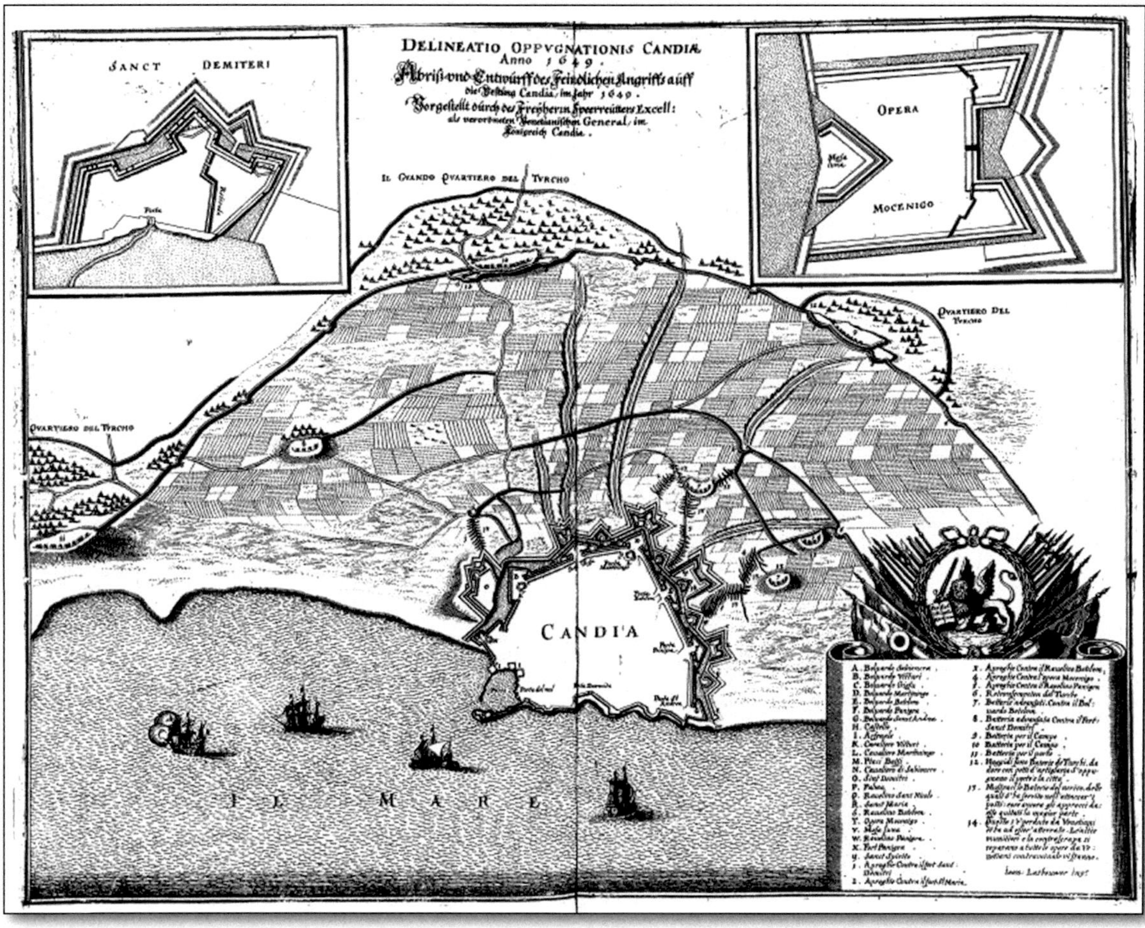

70. The ancient walls of Candia were renewed between 1538 and 1539 by Michele Sanmicheli. At the beginning of the war the work was still unfinished; technical delays and a chronic shortage of money had prevented several improvements and many sectors remained obsolete compared to the updates introduced by Dutch engineers.*

settled there permanently, building in the walls of the trenches shelters for groups of six men, which served as housing. Although in Candia the terrain near the fort of Sant'Andrea was mainly rocky, and the one on the opposite side, Sabbionera, clayey and crumbly, in both sectors the Ottomans made approaches with bundles, gabions and sandbags, with which they built in time of the ingenious protections, following the scheme of the traditional trenches. As soon as the walls of a fortress had enough bricks to be climbed, the Ottomans launched assaults with squadrons of volunteers armed only with sabres or daggers, who preceded the infantry and this latter in turn, after performing a general discharge, advanced as quickly as possible against the target. During the second siege of Candia, begun in July 1649, the besiegers devised other attempts to overcome the city's defences. On 27 July, the Ottoman approaches had arrived near the arrow outside the crown of Santa Maria and about 500 soldiers, each with a bag of earth, jumped out of the trenches and threw them on top of each other over the palisade, thus forming in a short time a very high trench that dominated the Venetian defence. The cavalry contingents from Anatolia arrived in campaign with the typical equipment of the Asian warriors. Obviously, bows and arrows proved to be of little utility against the ramparts. In this regard, Girolamo Brusoni cites one of his correspondant, who informed the historian about the Ottoman army at Chaniá, where he saw "many bows, spears and a few of firearms".[3] Evidently, in 1646 the Ottomans began to replace the most obsolete armaments with firearms, because at the siege of Réthymnon they appeared better equipped. On many occasions the Ottomans proved to be particularly insidious as marksmen, taking advantage of the shelters offered by the trenches or other prepared defences. One of the preferred tactics was to position several well-hidden riflemen a few metres from the opposing positions to target who, carelessly, leaned out of the parapets. This method allowed the besiegers to kill many enemies and in July 1648 with this method killed the Neapolitan general Vincenzo Della Marra, recently appointed general commander at Candia; one year later they scored a similar target, killing general Rodolfo Colloredo with a shot in the nape.

Regarding the artillery, the Ottomans placed the batteries without a pre-established scheme. In this period nobody, included the Ottomans, had yet experimented with rebound shot and therefore there were few limitations as to where to place the artillery, which was simply limited to looking for the highest sector of the terrain. In the 17th century, the artillerymen tried to obtain the superiority of fire by the number of guns and the availability of heavy calibres. The Ottomans attributed great importance to artillery fire, especially in their siege tactics. To make certain of advantage, where the terrain did not offer dominant points, they built elevated platforms with batteries on the top with as many pieces as possible. Using large contingents of diggers, large elevated platforms were erected in reasonably short periods. In the summer of 1667, a great platform was built on the eastern shore at Candia. On the top a battery was placed to hit the port, employing eight months of work and 1,000 workers. During the sieges, the Ottoman artillery tended to place the cannons very close to the fortifications, advancing to an echelon until exposing the shooting of the enemies. That is the reason because at Chaniá they covered the advance with the smoke of fireworks, and built false encampments deploying bands of instruments with drums to deflect the defenders. On that occasion, the Ottomans placed a battery of three heavy cannons not far from the Réthymnon gate on the eastern side of the city, but without causing serious damage. Then they built two forts, one of which was manned by the North African corsairs in front of the Sabbionera gate on the western side, to provide a shelter for the artillerymen assigned to the battery. Other batteries were set up close to the bastion of Sant'Atanasio and the platform of San Dimitri, and finally a third battery was placed in front of the half-moon of San Costantino, with which they continuously targeted the access route to the Réthymnon gate.

At Candia, the besiegers re-proposed the same tactic during the first assault on the city started in May 1648, when they managed to place two cannons a few metres from the tip of the bastion of Jesus, to target the ramparts and provide cover to the *musellim* who were advancing towards the palisade in the ditches. After 1668, the Ottomans employed an increasing number of large-calibre mortars to shoot inside the city. Explosive projectiles and other incendiary devices were also used, using hollow metal balls whose

3 Brusoni, *Libro* II, p. 45.

71. A drawing from the *Novissima Praxis Militare*, by Johann Scheither, eyewitness of the siege at Candia in 1668–69 as an officer of the Brunswick-Lüneburg infantry. Underground encounters were a constant during the last three years of siege and involved hundreds of men on each side, who faced each other in the darkness of the tunnels engaging in fearful fights.

use was very risky and caused frequent accidents. However, it remained difficult, due to the lack of precision in shooting, to silence the opposing artillery and the besiegers, even with the continuous use of cannons, rifle and hand grenades, managed to advance only slowly and with high losses. The Ottomans experimented late the breaching shot and for collapsing walls they concentrated from the beginning on the underground mine. The first mines of the Cretan war exploded at Chaniá on 7 August 1645 under the bastion of San Demetrio; at Candia, three years later, the first mine exploded on June 15 against the crown of Santa Maria, a sector where the besiegers turned the most violent assault and in which they were able to penetrate in early July. While in Chaniá, the Venetians had prepared few tunnels to counter the enemy progress, in Candia they had set up an efficient underground network from which they greatly hampered the enemy. Ottoman mines were generally powdered, but sometimes they used, as in the Middle Ages, another means consisting in creating excavations at the base of the walls to be wrecked, propping them with lumber, and then producing the collapse after setting fire to the framework. The mines were not only used to open breaches, but the besiegers extended them in such a way as to generate a ferocious underground war, culminating in the last three years of the siege in terrible close encounters. From the spring of 1667 to the late summer of 1669, at Candia exploded 1,364 mines, and more than 40 encounters of great proportions took place in the underground galleries. In the tunnels, the Venetians deployed up to 2,000 men, of whom 800 were organised in listening groups, who constantly watched the enemy works. Diggers and soldiers under an officer or a chief engineer composed each group. They operated against the enemy miners ready to intervene each time they discovered a gallery. The defenders tried to cut the tunnels and destroy them with a countermine or to flood them with water. The Venetians thwarted many enemy mines in this way, but each time the Ottomans restarted the work to get closer to the objectives from another direction, or digging deeper. In 1672, Captain Johann Scheither calculated in his *Novissima Praxis Militari* that in this way a single layer of terrain was dug more than 40 times by the two sides. In the first years of the siege it reached a depth of two or three metres, then in 1668 it was considered normal to go down to more than 20 metres below; a depth reached with relative ease thanks to the dry season and to the soft ground in the sectors distant from the sea. Regarding explosives, the charge of the Ottoman mines was always powerful, to obtain the most disruptive effect possible; depending on the target to be hit, starting from 10 or 15 barrels of powder up to more than 60. To regulate the charge on the effect to be achieved there was no pre-established rule and each miner acted according to his own criterion. In the Ottoman camp the most skilled miners were reputed to be the Armenians, who in fact demonstrated on more than one occasion great skill even in the opinion of their enemies.

Years later, Luigi Ferdinando Marsigli interviewed some Armenian miners who had participated in the siege of Candia, and obtained precise information on the technique they used in the mine warfare:

> To measure the distance from the wall they wanted to demolish, they sent an experienced and daring miner with a stone tied to a string, and who, at night, from where they had decided to start the tunnel, threw the stone to the wall and then he cut off the superfluous string, and the one that measured the distance dragged it to the nearby trench, calculating the quantity of the feet.[4]

The interlocutors of Marsigli confessed that the work in mine was very risky, as well as the excavation phases of the tunnels, always exposed to the danger of being intercepted by the enemies who, in the underground tunnels, were constantly lurking ready to seize the decisive moment to break in and kill everyone they met. However, the Armenian miners confessed that the rewards paid by the Ottoman commanders were very generous, because the risk was certainly worth that price.

Though the Ottomans achieved great progress in the war of mines, and generally in the art of siege, the countermeasures introduced by the Venetians were in many ways even more ingenious. The different experiences that matured during the conflict led the defenders to devise different solutions depending on the case, giving a significant impulse to the development of tactics adapted to the new reality of the siege war. The strong presence of trenches and other prepared defences contributed to the development of the most suitable weapons for the destruction of the enemy's works. So, the Venetians formed groups of soldiers trained to use explosives, which led to the creation of real grenadiers in modern sense. The presence of soldiers equipped with grenades began to become relevant from 1650, to become in the last three years of the conflict a stable element of the defence. In the sortie, the Venetians usually deployed one grenadier for every 10 musketeers. Also on the Ottoman side grenades and explosive projectiles were used to be thrown against the defences.

It is widely believed that the Venetians succeeded in delaying the fall of Candia by carrying out victorious sorties to destroy the enemy's trenches and approaches. In fact, apart from the large sorties carried out in the last two years of the siege, the defenders almost never launched large assaults. This

4 Marsigli, p. 141.

decision was not to preserve the troops, but because the intricate network of the trenches greatly impeded manoeuvres and made almost impossible to deploy the cavalry. In order to destroy superficial repairs, such as the approaches in front of San Demetrio and Sabbionera, the defenders preferred to conduct sorties with storming parties equipped with grappling hooks and hooked poles to remove the sandbags or gabions with which they were built.

Though the final siege of Candia represents the most important episode of the war and in the last three years the most violent and devastating fights occurred; the Venetians began very early to introduce the countermeasures devised by modern military science. Chaniá and Réthymnon had fallen in a short time – after 54 days the first and 24 the second – due to insufficient fortifications and the limited number of soldiers; while in Candia the Venetians had sufficient time to strengthen the garrison and improve the defences.

Alarmed by rumours of an imminent Ottoman assault, in early spring 1645 the Senate had sent in the island three Dutch engineers: Frans van Wert, his son Johan and their pupil Hyacintus van Bor. In Europe everyone appreciated the expertise of the engineers of the Netherlands and the speed with which they built extraordinarily effective fortifications with little expense. Their defensive works were designed to advance the line of defence with simple earthworks and to delay the enemy's impact by means of ditches complete with scarp and counterscarp at the base of bastions and external defences. At Crete, the three technicians reinforced the curtains and designed some projects for the improvement of the other strategic places, starting from the island of Suda, just opposite to Chaniá, where they fortified the cliff of Moraiti; precaution that proved to be useful, considered that twice, in 1646 and 1649, the Ottomans failed to conquest the fortress. The lack of time did not allow completion of all the devised improvements, but the work of the three engineers served at least to show the way to follow in future. In September 1647, after witnessing the death of his son at Chaniá, Frans van Wert was killed during a reconnaissance outside Candia. For the meritorious work carried out in Crete, the Senate granted a pension to his family and dedicated to him a solemn oration. In the four months preceding the first Ottoman assault, the walls of Candia were surrounded with additional defences: crown works; horns; crescents; arrows; ravelins, built under the supervision of the *governatore delle armi* Prince Camillo Gonzaga. The aim was always to move the centre of gravity of the defence outwards and multiply the flanking shot between the bastions.

On the eve of the siege, the contemporary reports relate a very dramatic scenario. In late summer 1647, the plague had penetrated into Candia. The conditions of life inside the town appear desperate, under the crossed grip of "the rabid disease, the horrendous influx of infirmity, the famine of everything, the extreme lack of money."[5] Camillo Gonzaga found on his arrival in Candia a desperate and terrible scenario. With courage, Gonzaga try to remedy these evils, first of all the plague, ordering the removal of the

5 ASVe, *Collegio, Relazioni*, b. 80, *Relazione dell'Ill.mo N.H. Nicolò Dolfino, provveditore dell'Armi in Regno*, 1648.

72. Candia: bastions and fortifications in 1667. A: Sant'Andrea; B: Panigrà; C: Betelem; D: Martinengo; E: Gesù; F: Vitturi; G: Sabbionera. 1: ravelin of Sant'Andrea; 2: ravelin of Santo Spirito; 3: external work of Panigrà; 4: ravelin of Panigrà; 5: Moceniga halfmoon; 5b: Morosini arrow; 6: ravelin of Betelem; 7: crown of Santa Maria; 7b: arrow of Santa Maria; 8: ravelin of San Nicolò; 8b: arrow of San Niccolò; 9: Palma; 10: Crevalcuore; 11: fort of San Demetrio; 11b: ravelin of San Demetrio; 12: Molina; 13: port.

corpses from the houses and separating the sick from the subjects still in good health. The forces available were divided into eight corps. Each of them, under the command of a colonel, consisted of 600 men, except for the eighth corps which deployed 1,500. Each corps had been assigned to a specific bastion, while the eighth one, as well as the most numerous, acted as tactical reserve. The task of the latter, consisting of regular soldiers and *feudati*, would have to intervene in the most threatened sectors. The *proli* present in the city had been divided between the first seven corps.[6] Since the

6 *Ibid.*, *Senato, Dispacci di Provveditori*, b. 545, 26 May 1648.

73. For more than 20 years the port of Candia represented the only link between Venice and the defenders, whose resistance was effective thanks to supplies sent by sea. (Author's photo)*

bastions had to be manned 24 hours a day, the soldiers had to sleep directly on the ramparts under improvised shelters or tents.

Inside Candia, the war council esteemed that the strategy of the besiegers was "to avoid any offensive act but wait until the length of the siege and tiredness forces the town to surrender."[7] Instead, encamped a few miles from Candia, in early April the Ottomans performed ambushes and engaged duels of musketry, which caused the first casualties. The encounters grew in intensity, then one artillery battery was placed on the hill and every day more and more violent fights took place: a clear sign that the Ottomans had received the reinforcements necessary for a regular siege, which started on 1 May 1648.

The Ottomans competed the circumvallation in front to the curtain between the external defences of San Demetrio and Santa Maria, and from there moved the approaches against the bastion of Gesù. Meanwhile, they placed new batteries, which daily targeted the external defences. The Venetians replied with counter-batteries in the most useful places, while new spaces for placing the artillery were built in the most threatened sectors. On 25 May some parties of Greeks and *cappeletti* assaulted the enemy approaches in front of Palma and routed the Ottoman diggers. This failure did not stop the besiegers who, on 10 June, assaulted the arrow of Santa Maria where they were involved in the explosion of the first Venetian *fornello* and were finally neutralised by the musketry. Three days later, a new assault against the external defence of Gesù was performed by the Ottoman infantry, who encountered a strong resistance and was finally repulsed with heavy casualties. In the same day, Prince Camillo Gonaga resigned his charge, in contrast to the Venetian government, accused not to guarantee the necessary aid to the garrison, but perhaps because he presaged an imminent defeat. The command of the defence was transferred to captain general Alvise Mocenigo, who arrived in Candia on 22 June. With him, landed also soldiers and crews from eight galleys, two galleasses and two sailing ships to reinforce the garrison reduced to 3,500 soldiers and a few militiamen.[8]

7 *Ibid., Collegio, Relazioni*, b. 81: Relation by Camillo Gonzaga.

8 *Ibid.*, b. 82.

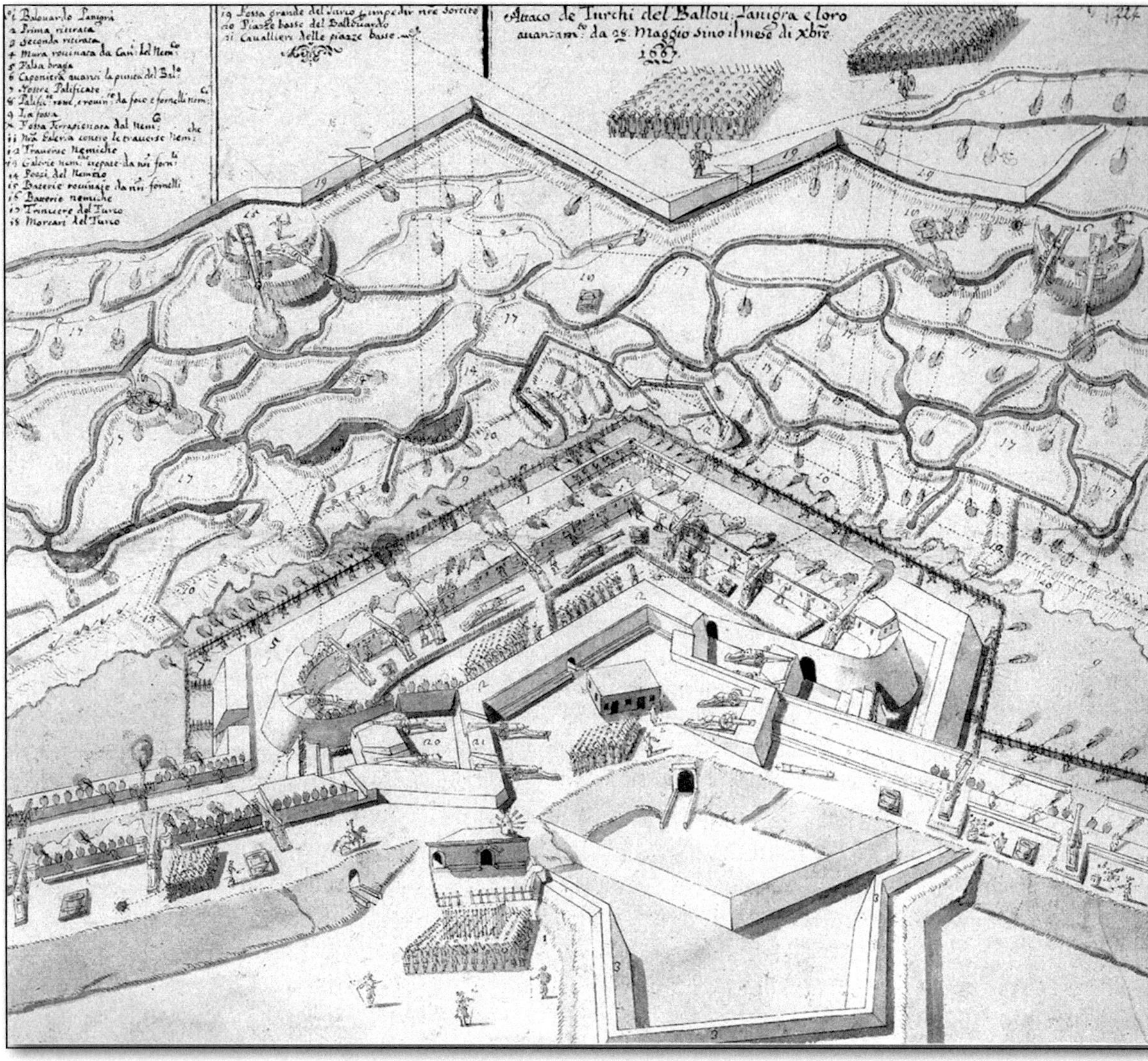

74. The bastion and the external defence of Panigrà, as they appeared during the Ottoman assault in the summer of 1667. (Author's archive)*

In early July, the Ottomans had penetrated into the ditch and now occupied the palisade in front of Santa Maria and Gesù. The Venetians opposed a strong defence and neutralised every enemy attack with mines, grenades and musketry fire. The Ottoman commander, Dely Hüsseyin, understood that the assaults would have been repulsed each time, if he could not neutralise the mines prepared by the enemy. For this reason, he concentrated the offensive on the curtains, targeting them with every type of artillery and intensifying the underground offensive recruiting more miners in Crete. However, at the end of the summer, the defences were still standing, and the besiegers had lost hundreds of men without being able to overcome the moats.

For the defenders there were critical moments, such as the loss of the Palma sector on 4 July 1648, despite the order to defend it at any cost. The situation worsened the next day, when the Ottomans had entered into the crown of Santa Maria, from where they began to bombard Martinengo's curtain with all the available artillery. Count Livio Noris held the command there, but after the explosion of a mine on the left corner of the bastion – and the destruction of an ammunitions depot – he ordered the 500 Italian, Croats and Greeks soldiers to withdraw, who, without firing a shot, left their posts in disorderly fashion. It was the providential intervention of Captain General Alvise Mocenigo to save the situation, who led the people in arms for a counter-attack. For his behaviour, Noris was arrested along with the officers under his orders and sentenced to death, the sentence then commuted to perpetual prison by the *provveditore all'Armata* Lorenzo Marcello. Another critical moment came on 6 August, with the Ottoman assault against the bastion of Martinengo. After having approached on the eastern side and having advanced the cavalry in front of the bastion of Sant'Andrea, the besiegers went to the assault with 1,000 men against Martinengo, which was occupied until the retreats. Immediately, they began to dig trenches to protect themselves from the shooting of the Venetian artillery placed on the bastion's elevated platform: "which caused a horrible slaughter".[9] The defenders sent the Cretan *feudati* squadron to the counter-attack, along with some companies of the infantry regiment de Remorantin and after two hours of fierce fighting, the Venetians retook control of the area.

The underground battles were just as bloody as the one 16 June, infuriated for almost four hours in the tunnels under the fort of San Demetrio. Here, the Ottomans had tried to overcome the obstacle constituted by the fosses using the tunnels conquered by the defenders and in the middle of July, they began again to advance with five different approaches against Martinengo, three against Gesù and two against Vitturi bastion, opening new galleries under the curtains. On 26 July, some signals revealed that the Ottoman *lagimçi* were working under the curtain between Gesù and Vitturi and before the end of the month, the Venetians successfully triggered four countermines prepared by the French engineer Odoardo Vaudeblanch. This sector of the walls,

75. The impressive network of tunnels dug by the Venetians in the sector of Sant'Andrea, despite the rocky terrain and proximity to the sea, with the countermine prepared before the end of 1668.*

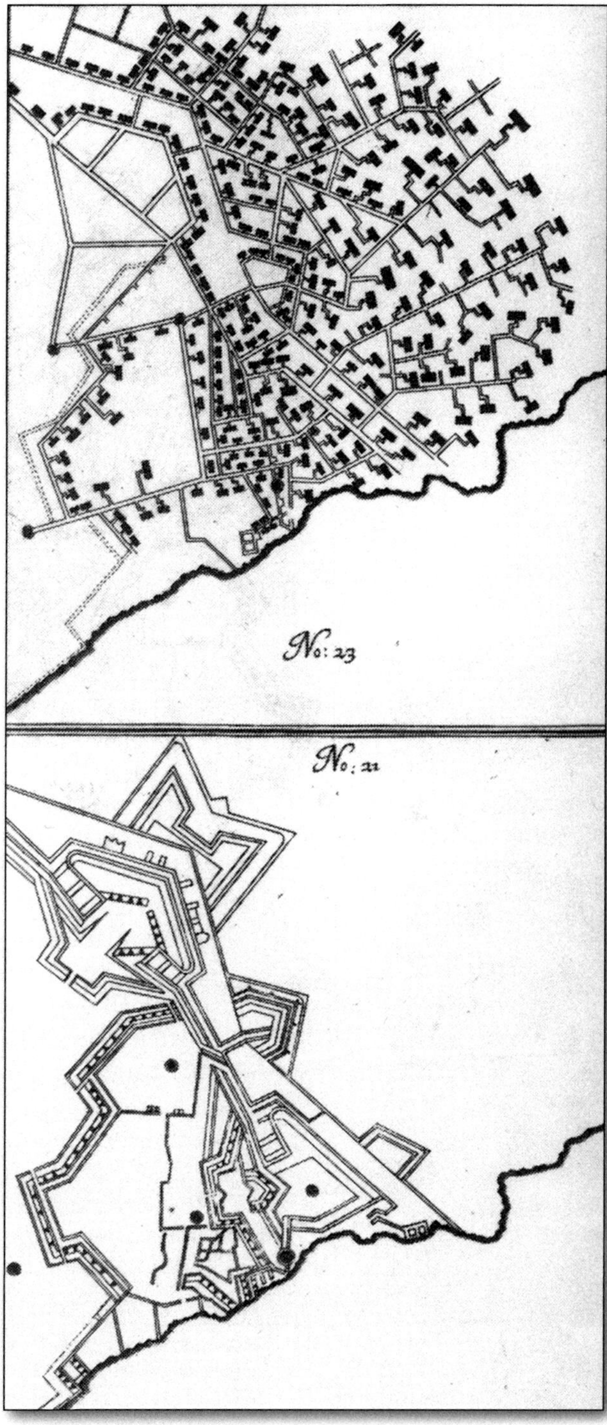

9 Brusoni, *Libro* IX, p. 208.

protected by too narrow a fosse and close to some buildings, constituted a weak point of the defence and if the besiegers were able to cause their collapse they could certainly use the ruins to easily climb the wall. For this reason, the defenders destroyed all the buildings in the area, including a church. Other important successes came to the Venetians in the underground duels, as happened on 4 August under the fort of San Demetrio, when they managed to defuse a mine of 26 barrels with all the accessories ready to explode. The Venetian miners obtained other important victories in September, and in the following month, when on 3 October they triggered a *fornello* that destroyed the Ottoman approaches in the counterscarp of the beset San Demetrio fort. On 10 October, the incessant rains flooded trenches and tunnels, ending the operations for that year.

In mid July, the defence of Candia had been taken on by Walloon General Gilles De Haes, who took the charge two months after the city's investment, with great expectation of the inhabitants and soldiers. De Haes organised the resources available with great skill; he distributed the troops assigning to each nation a sector to defend and appointing for each bastion a commander with a lieutenant. He also assigned to all civilians a place where they must present themselves every evening, and finally entrusted tasks to clergymen and Jews too. The hyperactive De Haes also recruited a considerable number of women to support the engineers in the work in the tunnels and to dig the earth necessary to repair the breaches. He divided the women in companies, entrusting each to a responsible person and assigned to them a pre-established sector, paying a reward for each day of work. Under the Walloon general new tunnels under bastions and curtains were prepared, so that they met each other and organised continuous turns of work, rightly considering these measures as the best methods to improve the defence. To protect the weaker points of the wall, De Haes employed large quantities of faggots, gabions and mattresses and ordered the excavation of new retreats in the most threatened bastions and ravelins. Then, he continually targeted the enemy's approaches with the mortars, causing much damage to them. and finally he made new counter-batteries, increasing the height of the platform where possible. In the first siege, the Ottomans had concentrated the pressure on the southern side of the city, investing the fort of San Demetrio, the opera Palma, and the crown of Santa Maria, and relentlessly bombarding the port and the bastions Vitturi, Gesù and Martinengo; but all the countermeasures introduced by the Venetians proved to be effective.

However, the struggle had caused heavy damage to the defences, which need urgent restoration. In early 1649 two French engineers, Jean Bellonet and Philippe Besseti de Verneda.[10] arrived in Candia as specialists of the siege warfare. They demonstrated great expertise in the improvement of the ravelins and in repairing the breaches opened in the curtains. Employing

10 The family Verneda supplied Venice with more two engineers, Jean, son of Philippe, and Jacques, nephew of this latter. For their service to the Republic, the Senate granted to Philippe and his descendant the title of *Cavaliere*. In 1668–69 Jean participated in the last campaigns of the siege of Candia, where, with a scientific approach, he established the minimum number of soldiers necessary to preserve the town.

large quantities of land, Verneda managed to obtain excellent results, quickly erasing the damage produced by the Ottomans, while Bellonet directed the building of new *bonetti*, namely the elevated quadrangular embankments with which to protect the corners of the ravelins and other external defences. The fortifications on the west side of San Demetrio were extended, reinforcing this sector with three new ravelins in the direction of the countryside, very tall and complete with ditch, counterscarp and palisade. The flanks of the fort, which had suffered heavily from the Ottoman artillery fire, were repaired by Verneda with parapets of earth, but for lack of time the ditch remained incomplete. However, both sides were secured with palisades, which continued the line of the ravelins and terminated in the counterscarp. Both French engineers improved the network of countermine already expanded in the previous year, starting the tunnels far beyond the walls and perfecting the explosive devices to be used, including a special delayed petard invented by Bellonet.[11] The work of both the technicians proved its usefulness in the subsequent siege campaign, when in the night of 17/18 July 1649, the besiegers resumed the assaults against the same objectives of the previous year, to which they added the ravelin and the bastion of Betelem, the crescent Moceniga and the ravelin in front of the bastion of Panigrà. Every day, at dawn, the Ottoman artillery began the bombardment of the city, while the approaches resumed to move forward threateningly. In order to continue the siege, reinforcements were needed which arrived on time, in August 1649, on British and French ships. Twenty thousand Ottoman soldiers and miners disembarked near Réthymnon, together with large quantities of ammunition and provisions. The siege could then resume.[12]

In 1649, the underground battles reached an even greater intensity, forcing Deli Hüseyin to employ an increasing number of diggers, but without ever prevailing over the formidable Venetian resistance, now supported by new skilfully prepared traps. With a tactic that involved assaults against a sector of the enemy front, followed by a retreat, the defenders drew the enemies over previously prepared countermines and detonated them at the appropriate time. At the end of July, the Venetians had with this method nullified the enemy progress against San Demetrio and other sites. The chronicle of the events is punctuated by the detailed narration of Girolamo Brusoni:

> The following month, going to meet the Turkish approaches against the Mocenigo crescent, they [the Venetians] prepared four large countermines that exploded one after the other on the side nearby Panigrà, destroying the enemy's works and killing many of them. And it was so much the fright for the Turks in the nearby trenches, from seeing so many dead and so many ruins, that they fled without knowing where to save their lives.[13]

According to some prisoners, the explosions had buried the whole crew of a galley. The charges of the Venetian countermines became so powerful

11 Brusoni, *Libro*, IX, p. 211.
12 ASVe, Provveditori da Terra e da Mar, b. 495, c. 55.
13 Brusoni, *Libro* IX, p. 210.

76. **Arnavut Abdi Abdurrhaman, first lieutenant of the janissaries' *aga* in 1667, was another of the Ottoman officers present at Crete destined to have a prestigious career. After the Cretan war, he was appointed as *beglerbeg* of Hungary. Abdurrhaman is described as a clever official who governed the province with skill and honesty. He was killed in action in 1686, while directing the defence of Buda against the Imperial army.**

that they even managed to knock the guns off the ground. On 18 August 1649, a Venetian countermine exploded under the trenches in front of Betelem with such violence that it threw onto the ramparts "a villain of the country still in agony, one whom the Ottomans employ to dig out the approaches, which seemed truly admirable". At the end of the month, after countless bloody assaults, the Ottomans had penetrated into the counterscarp between Panigrà and Betelem, while they were pressing against the work of Santa Maria, and from that position, they advanced against the ravelin of Betelem, managing to occupy it on 1 September. In the night, this conquest, which had been the greatest result achieved in a month and a half of continuous fighting, returned under the control of the Venetians thanks to a surprise assault led by engineers Bellonet and Verneda, descended into the ravelin with the favour of darkness: "... through dangerous and rough passages".[14] On 9 September, the Ottomans were on the verge of taking control of another external defence, when they started a tunnel from the counterscarp of the Moceniga half-moon to break into a shaft occupied by the enemies, but a powerful countermine exploded further down burying all the Ottoman miners. After this action the Venetians took possession of the half-moon again, but now, due the shortage of men to defend the position, they decided to use it for a new trap by preparing a gigantic *fornello*. However, this time the Ottomans did not advance, and avoided the trap. The last countermine of the 1649 campaign exploded on 13 September under the counterscarp of San Demetrio, where the Ottomans had managed to penetrate at the end of a violent battle that lasted one day.

The countermine technique devised by the defenders was simple and ingenious and was designed to strike in depth as well as to defend the superficial defences threatened by enemy approaches. For this purpose, underground chambers were prepared, ready to be filled with explosives. The direction of the works was entrusted to an engineer who knew the network of tunnels in his sector. Johann Scheither, infantry officer of Brunswick-Lüneburg, eyewitness of the fighting at Candia in 1668–69, left an exhaustive description about the preparation of a countermine:

> In Candia most of the mines were of the Italian type, known as *fornello* [literally: stove] consisting of a chamber, large or small according to need, where there were placed on the ground sturdy poles or boards well connected with nails, to

14 *Ibid.*, p. 216.

> preserve powder from moisture. Then, the powder had to be introduced into bags or barrels; the primer was also used, using boxes of wood, nailed together and internally wide 2 or 3 inches and long up to 16 feet. Lastly, the entrance, or mouth of the mine, was closed with brickwork by propping up the back side of the chamber with wooden beams contrasting one with the other.

Before the ignition of the mine, sentinels were stationed at the entrance of the gallery, while in turn the miners took their places in the tunnels, to catch the slightest noise revealing the presence of the enemy, ready to sound the alarm if someone approached the countermine. In this regard, Scheither added: "The defenders diligently watched that the enemy did not reach the already prepared mines, get to know, or take away the powder, as sometimes happened, so when someone wanted to trigger the mine we remained with the empty hand."[15]

The most common option for counteracting the enemy mines was to introduce smoke, bees, hot pitch, or boiling water into the mine. Countermines – supported with timbers – could also be dug underneath the attacker's mine and fired in an effort to collapse the mine above. Many times, Ottomans and Venetians ended up colliding in the tunnels giving rise to frightful close combat, or they entered the gallery to intercept the enemy progress, lighting a fire to fill the sector with smoke, or seal it by collapsing and burying all who were there. The Ottomans devised several expedients to free the tunnels from the enemy threat. In summer 1668, they thought to have found the final solution, thanks to an English 'chemist', inventor of a mixture made with poisonous substances to be spread inside the galleries with smoke. But the Venetians reacted promptly to this menace, and shortly thereafter they found a way to neutralise the poisons by burning juniper boughs and inundating the gallery with the alcoholic spirit *acquavite*.

Eyewitnesses had described the fighting of the first two years by calling the war theatre "a triple hell". The landscape, devastated and enveloped by the smoke of the explosions, had been compared to the Phlegraean fields, while the smell of gunpowder could be detected miles away. On 2 October Hüseyn ordered the suspension of the siege, but ordered the troops to remain for a few days in the trenches, and then abandoned them before the end of the month. In two years of siege, more than 20,000 Ottoman soldiers and engineers had fallen at Candia. Casualties were also high for the Venetians, complaining of no less than 6,000 soldiers killed or wounded, alongside an unknown number of civilians.[16]

The years between 1649 and 1667 are considered a long period of quiet instead, between besieger and besieged, the duel reopened occasionally. The defenders planned offensive acts to hinder the restoration of the fortifications, the besiegers to maintain the pressure on Candia operating from the fortified encampment built a few miles from the city, who took the name Yeni Kandye (new Candia). The Venetians launched sorties of some importance in 1652

15 W. von Bigge, cited work, p. 66.

16 Valiero, p. 223.

77. (above, and left) Two sketches of Jacques Courtois (1621–1676), active in Italy and known as il Borgognone. He was a renowned painter of battles who accurately reproduced the soldiers after real models. In the essential lines the figure in the foreground shows the typical officer dress of the 1660s. Note the spontoon, the plumed headgear and the wide decorated bandolier (Private Collection, Rome)

and 1654, followed by two more in 1659 and in 1662 with about 1,000 soldiers against *Yeni Kandye*. On the other hand, in April 1660, the Ottomans, to the number of 5,000, appeared in front of the walls, immediately targeted by the Venetian artillery.

The relative low number of engagements did not mean the end of dangers and deprivations. The Ottomans were long forced into isolation due to the naval blockade, but the Venetians faced a no less gloomy and problematic period.[17] Though the enemies depended on the supplies coming from the homeland, the Venetian garrison too had to wait the arrival of resources and reinforcements from the outside. Not only soldiers and food, because the besieged city needed everything: from wooden boards to nails, from sacks of canvas to cordages for the arsenal, to medicines for hospitals. Some 972 miles of sea separate Venice from Crete, a distance that we could now travel by air in a few hours, while in the 17th century it required weeks, and perhaps

17 The best summary of what for long periods of time would be the routine of Candia, was written by Giorgio Morosini in 1650: "I consider that in the present time this square is much more fought by the internal discomfort that from the outside violence, while not only is deprived of food, but also the means necessary to procure it..." ASVe, *Senato, Dispacci di Provveditori*, b. 546, 31 March 1650.

more, depending on the weather. Since the supplies necessary to Candia did not come entirely from Venice, but were bought directly by merchants closer to the island, it is not surprising that the sense of insecurity about the supplies would be increased.[18] The merchants, not always operating in optimal conditions, could allow the load to get wet and this meant the strong possibility that it would rot and become unusable, especially in the case of biscuits or flour.[19] Obviously, the problem assumed a great importance, conditioning also the strategic conduct of the war. In 1658 some loads arrived in large part ruined, the waste amounted to 100,000 pounds. To understand the magnitude, we can compare this figure with the monthly consumption of biscuit required by the city of Candia, when bread was not available, ascending to 300,000 *lire* a month.[20] Similarly, the load of a merchant arrived in Candia from Venice the following 25 March, carried a total of 203,000 *lire* of biscuit, but 14,967 were damaged.[21]

In this regard, the year between the first sieges of Candia and the subsequent assaults of 1667–69, constituted the period of an actual 'war of materials' pursued in a new and unexpected way. In the first sieges, had been sent between 70,000 and 100,000 ducats each month; more or less the same figures as the last 28 months of siege. The economic effort involved real financial availability to pay the suppliers, who as always had to be paid on delivery.[22] There was another way to pay the suppliers, that is, to pay the goods in exchange letters, but this method exhausted its potential already in 1649 for the difficulties encountered in collecting the money in Venice. Possibly, behind the choice to procrastinate the payment, there was the will not to allow the spread of the debt accumulated for the defence of Candia.

---

18 Cretan provveditor Giorgio Morosini, in 1650 wrote: "I cannot trust to the uncertain and casual help with which the town was miraculously supported until now, and much less in the provision of biscuits, which are obliged to the need of the fleet, the fortresses, and all other parts, and occurrences." He was referring exactly to this situation of indeterminacy. Morosini added: "Great point is this, Most Serene Prince, that the preservation of a fortress, even of a kingdom defended so long with the waste of so much blood, and with the profusion of endless treasures, we have to depend on this from contingencies and chance and I can truly say that I have twice seen the freedom and security of everything precipitating between the extremes of poverty." ASVe, *Senato, Dispacci di Provveditori*, b. 546, 31 March 1650.

19 The biscuit was a kind of twice-baked bread, which, if kept dry, was edible for a long time. It was the main food of the sailors and was sent to Candia to be there sent to the fleet, but it was also used by the city itself in case there were no grains to make bread. This latter, at some periods, became so precious that they were considered as exchange currency, as referred by Francesco Barbaro in 1660: "Bread runs in place of salary for the soldiers, benefit for the people, and everybody uses it buy everything", in *ASVe, Collegio, Relazioni*, b. 80, dated 23 June 1660.

20 It is the Venetian *libbra grossa*, heavy pound, of 0.476 kg. The other measure of weight was the *libbra sottile*, light pound, of 0.312 kg.

21 ASVe, *Senato, Dispacci di Provveditori*, b, 546, 26 March 1658.

22 In fact, at the beginning of June 1650, the Venetian government bought grain on credit from a French vessel, 10,000 measures, however, it was possible to pay only 3,000 immediately. The remaining was also delivered on the promise of receiving the rest before the end of the month. With the aggravation of the economic shortage and the upcoming winter, in November, the situation became more complicated. Three ships loaded with grain arrived in Candia, but did not enter the port, refusing to deliver the load without first being paid. Otherwise they threatened to go elsewhere to sell their cargo, including to the Ottomans. See in ASVe, *Provveditori da Terra e da Mar*, b. 546, 8 June and 5 November 1650.

78. Captain General Francesco Morosini was 48 years old when in summer 1667 he assumed the command of the operations in Crete. He successfully climbed the military hierarchy starting as sopracomito (galley captain), when he was only 20. In Candia he began a duel with his opponent Köprülü Ahmed, which lasted until the surrender of the town. The Venetian commander was older than his counterpart, but all in all they were both quite young compared to the average age of the respective general staff.

With the supplies, also soldiers and horses sailed to Crete. The ships were often overflowing with people who were travelling crammed like animals, when not directly in the company of the same. In this way, the condition of many of the casualties suffered by the garrison of Candia began during the journey. When in 1650 the Senate authorised the concentration of troops to recapture some of the Cretan fortresses in possess of the Ottomans, about 5,000 infantrymen sailed from Venice. They arrived in three different groups between March and June, and by the end of the month they were all in Candia, but now were less than 4,000, because 1,000 arrived sick or dead. The first to arrive were 1,005 infantrymen, among them Italians, including part of a regiment of Parma, and *Oltramontani*, landing in Crete between 3 and 20 March. When they left Venice, their number was 1,204. The main losses were the *Oltramontani*, who out of 439 infantrymen lost in the sailing 109. It was much better for the troops who arrived between 11 and 13 April, because out of 701 infantrymen only 13 were missing. However, it was only a brief improvement, as the last group, which arrived in June, sustained the previous level of losses: of the 984 departing from Venice, 734 arrived, of which 251 were not able to take service.[23] These figures are indicative of the fact that it was the length of the journey, combined with the poor confidence with the sea, that was the main problem, because the companies that arrived from Dalmatia in the same period did not have losses. Two years later, of the 240 infantrymen from Oltramonte, who left Venice and arrived to Candia in May 1652, another 40 died during the journey and another 70 passed directly to the hospital. Probably the ship that carried them was too small and, consequently, the journey was particularly uncomfortable.[24] Similarly, of another 190 infantrymen, again departing from Venice, 25 died during the sailing and most arrived sick at the destination. Travel conditions worsened in the summer due to the hot weather, the length of the journey, the narrowness of the environments on board and the scarcity of water. The concern of the supervisors regarding these situations is evident, and the blame lies on the excessive length of the travel, without breaks, from Venice to Candia: "and it can always make sure to lose a third of the troops when they are sent in this way". Instead, when the soldiers boarded in Corfu, their transfer was much shorter and easier. The 200 Italian infantrymen who departed in May 1652 from Corfu landed at Candia "all healthy and in very good order." [25]

Dispatches from Candia concerning the arrival of the troops continue to enumerate the sad accounting of losses caused by the sea voyage. Between May and June 1662, of the 1,076 men in 12 companies who travelled with Prince Philipp von Pfalz-Sulzbach, recently appointed as *governatore generale delle armi* in Crete, only 994 soldiers arrived at their destination.[26] Of these, 282 were very sick and passed directly to hospital. This contingent formed six Italian companies and another six of *Oltramontani* and the respective percentage shows clearly that the largest number of deaths and sick belonged to the latter, evidently not accustomed to the climate of the Mediterranean and for sailing on board ship. Even with the progress of the conflict, it was impossible to find a solution to avoid losses of soldiers due to transfers by sea, even before seeing only one enemy.[27] This is only a part of the problem, because Venice enlisted soldiers throughout Europe, and for them the difficulties of travel began well before their arrival in the Lagoon.[28]

23 *Ibid.*, 31 March and 16 April 1650.

24 *Ibid.*, b 548, 23 May 1652.

25 *Ibid.*, In the correspondence between Venice and the military comman in Candia there is the proposal to use Corfù as a logistical centre for the troops destined for Crete. In this way, it would be possible to allow a pause of a few days in order to let the soldiers rest and reduce the losses and sickness. Unfortunately, we do not know whether this advice was accepted or not, even if it does not seem to have been very successful, because Corfu is rarely mentioned in the following years as a seaport for the troops sent to Crete.

26 *Ibid., Dispacci di Capi da guerra*, b. 9, *Principe Palatino Filippo Sulzbach*, 6 June 1662.

27 *Ibid., Dispacci di Provveditori*, b. 554. 18 July 1664. In 1664, Antonio Priuli, just arrived in Crete as an extraordinary provveditor, accompanied by twelve companies, 724 infantrymen in overall, noted that many soldier had fallen ill and died during the travel or were transferred to hospital on their arrival in Candia.

28 Troops recruited in northern Europe spent months even to arrive in Venice. The Walloon and Flemish troops embarked in Amsterdam, otherwise they sailed via rivers and often needed special passports to facilitate their travel, in particular to cross the Meuse, and for the subsequent

The ever-present danger of a surprise attack by the Ottomans, encamped a few miles from the walls, was the greatest threat against which it was necessary to remain vigilant. In particular, the increase of the external defences had practically doubled the number of soldiers needed to garrison bastions and external defence. These included a huge number of posts, the main ones are shown in the following table, together with the number of soldiers required daily to form the guard:[29]

Fort of San Dimitri:	1,005
Opera Palma:	365
Crown of Santa Maria:	490
Half-moon Moceniga:	170
Opera Panigra:	264
Ravelin Santo Spirito:	145
Redoubt Sant'Andrea:	72
Ravelin Betlemme:	125
Ravelin San Nicola:	125
Ravelin Panigrà:	125
Total men:	**2,886**

Despite the necessity of horses being relatively urgent in Candia, nevertheless the remounts destined for the cavalry were sent several times by sea. In 1657, of the 145 horses expected to reform the squadrons of *cappelletti* light cavalrymen, only 120 came to their destination and in very bad condition. In this case, the problem was not only the hardness of the travel, but also because "the soldiers on board had no interest in dealing with horses and as a result they almost never governed them."[30]

The Venetians faced minor difficulties in recruiting miners and diggers. Apart from Cretan subjects (until their numbers became insufficient), the enlistement of workers turned to the three Ionian islands. Later they also turned to the inhabitants of the Aegean islands under Ottoman rule, as occurred in 1667 when Captain General Francesco Morosini urgently recruited 2,000 *guastatori* in the face of the imminent Ottoman siege.[31]

The other constant concern of commanders and provveditors in Candia was ammunition supplies, the lack of which would inevitably have caused the surrender of the city. Ammunition meant not only gunpowder and projectiles, but also guns, mortars, weapons, matches, lumber for guns

river journey they needed of Dutch and Spanish passports. See Bibliteca Nazionale Marciana, VII 1912, *Capitoli per una leva di truppe fiamminghe col Sergente Generale Gritti,* 1648.

29 ASVe *Senato, Dispacci di Provveditori*, b. 563, miscellany from 1650 to 1669. Since the turn on duty lasted generally two days, after which the soldiers were transferred to another sector, and then rested one day after two or four turns, the optimal size of the garrison was to be at least 4,000 men, but this number was reached only rarely, thus forcing the soldiers to garrison the positions for several days.

30 ASVe, *Senato, Dispacci di Provveditori*, b. 550, 7 October 1657. Because of a misunderstanding, the horsemen had been held in Venice and in their place, with the remount, had been embarked infantrymen.

31 *Ibid., Senato, Mar*, R. 133, cc. 159–160.

79. Grand Vizier Köprülü Ahmed assumed command of operations in Crete at the end of 1666 and the following spring ordered an assault against the bastions of Panigrà, Betelem and Martinengo. After continuous failures, in June 1668 he concentrated his efforts on the sectors closer to the sea, which effectively constituted the weak points of the Venetian defence. The impressive network of trenches excavated by his men earned the grand vizier the nickname of "the excavator". (*Theatrum Europeum*, Frankfurt am Main, 1670)

carriages, metal accessories and various tools needed to maintain the artillery park and arsenal in an efficient status, because Candia was had no workshops or personnel for the maintenance of artillery. The siege required an ever-increasing number of artillery pieces for the additional defences that increased considerably over the years. Compared to the sieges of 1648 and 1649, in 1669 the artillery continued to increase, mainly due to the use by the besiegers of a huge number of guns and mortars, with the consequent need to face the enemy fire with new counter-batteries. In the early sieges, the type of cannons used by the defenders was very varied. In the dispatches are mentioned culverins, cannons, falcons, *petrieri*, *sagri*, *aspidi* as well as mortars and fireworks. Moreover, different calibres were represented within the categories which could vary significantly. The culverins showed calibres ranging from 50 to 14 lb, but the most common were those of 30, 20 and 16 lb. Similarly, the guns presented calibres of 60, 50, 30, 20 and 16 lb, with a predominance of 20 and 50 lb. Such an impressive amount of artillery and the enormous heterogeneity of the calibres required an amplified logistical effort, since it was necessary to provide projectiles for each type. The artillerymen needed both iron and stone projectiles, hollow bombs with various fuses and canisters. In 1667, this problem was partly solved, as the variety of gauges was drastically reduced.

In addition, the conditions of efficiency of the guns varied considerably between one case and the other. In 1652, of the 24 culverins on the ramparts of Candia, 11 were useless and 10 others in bad condition. In the same period, of the 110 guns present, 21 needed repairs.[32] In early 1667, at the eve of the final series of sieges, the artillery inside Candia amounted to 405 guns and mortars, and in 1668 this number grew until to 461 pieces of various types. However, the main part was useless and only 184 could be considered in perfect condition, while 105 were otherwise unserviceable or needed maintenance. Of the remaining ones, another 60 were considered dangerous and 113 as "damaged, fissured or offended by the enemy in the handles, and the most worn out in the bottom or destroyed."[33]

The consumption of gunpowder and projectiles by the artillery was added to the consumption of balls and gun powder for muskets. In the first siege of

32 *Ibid.*, *Senato, Dispacci di Provveditori*, b. 548, 15 April 1652.

33 *Ibid.*, b. 563, 19 October 1668. The enemies had possibly damaged the weapons described as "offended in the handle" or worn out. The cut of the handle and the breaking of the touchhole were typical actions for neutralising the artillery, compromising the use of the piece or its balancing on the carriage.

Candia, 1648, were fired daily up to 120,000 musket balls, in addition to the continued fire of about 130 guns.[34]

Of course, the problems concerning supplies and reinforcements were even greater for the Ottomans. In spring of 1651, a little more than a year after the end of the last siege at Candia, the besieging army could deploy about 12,000 men.[35] This number allowed them to keep the siege ring, but not to resume the fighting. In 1654, the Ottoman army appeared so inoperative as to be defined as "sleeping" by Andrea Corner.[36] It was obvious to everyone that there were not enough forces to try a new attack and that the Ottoman commanders were expecting new help.[37] Even the artillery was few in number and in poor condition. The network of informers and spies set up by the Venetians along the route from Constantinople to Crete reported information that was not always certain, but which revealed the level of the enemy's preparatives for Crete. Some informers referred of 1,000 infantrymen already ready at Monemvasia to be transported to Chaniá with the galleys, and a further 10,000 who were expecting the fleet in Constantinople. In 1652, the Venetians believed that in Crete there were only 16,000 infantrymen and 1,500 horsemen, a number very close to reality.[38]

80. On the funeral monument of Count Josias von Waldeck, commander of the Brunswick-Lüneburg corps in Crete, are depicted some figures of soldiers and officers during the siege of Candia, where Waldeck lost his life along with 1,680 soldiers of the contingent sent by Duke Georg Wilhelm in 1668. (Richard Knoetel, *Die Grosse Uniformenkunde*, Rathenow, 1890)

In 1667, when Köprülü Ahmed resumed the siege, he understood very well the risks of the enterprise, in which twice the brave Dely Hüseyn had failed, perfectly aware that a defeat would have been fatal. The Grand Vizier waited almost three months before embarking at Isdin on the southern coast of Anatolia and arriving in Chaniá on 3 November 1666. Two months more passed while the Grand Vizier's residence was being built, in sight of the walls of Candia, from where he personally inspected the Venetian fortifications and reviewed the troops. Köprülü had now three new encampments in front of the city's land sides. He discussed the situation with the *serdar* Ahmed Paşa, who until then had commanded the besieging army. The Grand Vizier gathered the war council daily and made direct acquaintance with the *alaybeg* and other officers, who – according to the custom – kissed his garment and received from him the

34 *Ibid.*, b. 495, 8 May 1649.

35 *Ibid.*, b. 547, 24 April 1651.

36 *Ibid.*, b. 549, 16 May 1654.

37 According to the historian Robert Mantran the approximate conduct of the preparations and the lack of dynamism of the Ottoman army, combined with the long years of conflict, could confirm the relative importance attributed to the conquest of Candia by the Ottoman side after 1649. See 'L'impero ottomano, Venezia e la Guerra' in *Venezia e la difesa del Levante*, Arsenale Editrice, Venice 1986, p. 232.

38 ASVe, *Senato, Dispacci di Provveditori*, b. 548, 21 March 1652.

81. François de Vendôme, Duke of Beaufort (1616-1669). After having contrasted the French monarchy during the Fronde, Beaufort reconciled with Mazzarino and in 1658 was named general superintendent of navigation and chief of the navy.*

testimony of interest of the Sultan and his for the endurance suffered until now. The Grand Vizier surrounded himself with a few trusted officers: the commander of the janissary, Ibrahim Paşa, with his lieutenant Arnavut Abdurrhaman; the beglerbeg of Rumelia, Pehlivan Mohammed Paşa, an elderly soldier who had participated at the sieges of 1648–49; the governor of Anatolia, Merzifonlu Kara Mustafa, his adoptive cousin, destined to succeed him to the office of grand vizier and in 1683 to lead the army which besieged Vienna. On 25 May 1667, the war council deliberated the directives for the imminent assault and the plan that prevailed was to invest the bastions of Panigrà, Betelem and Martinengo. The idea of concentrating the efforts against the bastion Vitturi and the external defences of San Demetrio was discarded, because both sectors, actual barycentre of the defence, would have made more difficult the besiegers' progress, and would have exposed them to dangerous counter-attacks to the flanks. It was then decided to concentrate the assault on the south-west side, leaving in the other sector some drums with a few guns and a cavalry screen to secure the access to the encampments. The Ottoman army was divided into three corps that simultaneously had to assault the three bastions. On the left, there were the European troops under the Rumelia's *beglerbeg* and the janissary's *aga*; behind them, the Grand Vizier was encamped in the ruins of Yeni Kandie, dismantled by his order, because everyone understood that the conquest of the city was now nearly achieved. At the centre was deployed the Egyptian contingent under Ahmed Pasha, in front of the Betelem bastion and the Mocenigo crescent. Finally, on the right, towards the Martinengo bastion, the Anatolian troops led by Kara Mustafa took up position. Three large corps, European, African and Asian, were gathered together to launch the assault at Candia's bastions. The fights were immediately violent. At dawn, the Turkish batteries began to target the city, while the ring trenches began to spread all around the walls. The first Ottoman mine exploded on 5 July under the tip of the Panigrà bastion – which managed to damage the wall – but caused the collapse of some galleries burying 100 miners. Failure did not discourage the Grand Vizier, who intensified the work, directed by Mustafa Pasha, the talented commander of the Anatolian miners. He was killed in action at the end of the July by a Venetian fire pit. From July to September 1667, the Ottoman *lagimçi* did detonate 152 mines, to which the defenders replied with 182 countermines and explosive shafts, most concentrated in the Panigrà sector. On 26 October the Ottomans succeeded for the first time to settle in the bastion, where they planted five banners, but three Venetian mines, each containing 70 barrels of powder, blew up the rest of the defences together with all the enemies who were penetrated there. Throughout this period, the

82. General Annes de Noailles, commander of the French field contingent, arrived in Crete in June 1669, and succeeded as high commander after the death of Beaufort. The defenders had many expectations of these reinforcements; however, after the failure of the great sortie executed on 29 June, their departure hastened the surrender of Candia. (Engraving by Françoise de Poilly, *Gabinet des Etampes de Musèe de Louvre*, Paris)

defenders intermittently launched sorties with parties formed by 50–60 musketeers, supported by grenadiers and pioneers, directed against the enemy approaches. The struggle grew in intensity, culminating in violent duels of musketry, to which were added grenades and the projectiles of the guns that thundered without pause. Concerned by the Ottoman progress against the crown of Santa Maria, Captain General Francesco Morosini, who had taken command of the defence at the end of June, decided on 3 October to launch a general sortie with 1,000 infantrymen drawn from the Italian regiments Maron, Cremasco, Marini, Restori, Imberti; the Swiss regiment Wertmüller and the *Oltramarini* under Colonels Georgio Maria and Rados.[39] Two lines of trenches were overwhelmed and for two days, the Venetians engaged the besiegers in a bloody close combat. This was the first large sortie launched by the defenders, who had never performed with more than 100 soldiers. Most of the sorties carried out by the Venetians almost took place to destroy the besiegers' progress only in limited sectors and consisted of a combined assault of small corps of soldiers equipped with grenades, supported by musketeers and pioneers who were tasked with destroying the opposing approaches. Several times Francesco Morosini declared himself contrary to the large sorties, which required a large number of soldiers and the outcome was always inconclusive. Indeed, after an initial slowdown, new approaches began to advance and in a short time, the besiegers had recovered all the lost ground. On 11 November, Morosini launched a second large sortie having exploded four mines between the bastions Betelem and Martinengo, and invested the Ottoman approaches and killed three *agas*, the janissaries' commander, the one of the *cebeci* and the chief of the *serdengeçdi* (the volunteers who led the assaults).[40] Eight days later the Grand Vizier suspended the assaults and ordered the troops to prepare for the winter. In the first year the Ottoman casualties would rise to about 8,000 dead, of which 400 belonged to the janissaries; two *beglerbegs* and 100 officers had fallen, many more wounded and sick. The Venetian sources, citing a letter written by the Grand Vizier falling into their hands, tripled these figures claiming that Köprülü had only 23,700 men still able to fight. In all likelihood, the estimates put forward by the Venetians regarding the opposing losses were magnified for propaganda purposes, and in fact, they were circulated in the besieged city and in the European chancelleries to raise morale and consolidate the support that the

39 Brusoni, *Libro* XXV, p. 255.

40 Von Hammer-Purgstall, Vol. XI, p. 325.

Republic received on the international level. The macabre accountability of the losses, transcribed by Girolamo Brusoni at the end of each year, reports for 1667 the figure of 7,908 soldiers, miners and civilians dead, among which the provveditor of the kingdom Lorenzo Pisani, together with other important figures and officers. The torrid summer had caused the onset of many diseases, then the cold and wet winter that followed added new evils; the besiegers as well as the defenders suffered greatly, because the trenches were flooded, while in the tunnels they worked with water up to their waists. In early December, the Sultan sent a message to the army, saying that he would grant rest only after the conquest of the city and indeed the fighting resumed despite the cold season. The pressure against the sectors chosen in spring was intensified. On the first day of the new year a countermine exploded under Panigrà ravelin, followed one day later by a 40-barrel *fornello* against the Ottoman approaches to the outer defence of the same bastion, now reduced to a pile of rubble. The continuing failures persuaded the Ottoman commander to change tactics, because the mass assaults were always rejected with heavy losses. The cold weapon assaults decreased and were launched only against limited objectives, such as palisades, batteries or isolated *bonetto*. The besiegers also sought to coordinate attacks by taking advantage of the effect caused by the explosion of a mine. But the most drastic change was the decision to modify the plan of the siege. While until May 1668 the efforts of the besiegers had concentrated on the west side of the city, from the first of June, coinciding for the Ottomans with the beginning of the new year, the siege moved towards the sectors near the coast: the bastion of Sant'Andrea, to the north-west, and Sabbionera, near the port, at the north-east. Although in these areas the terrain did not favour the excavation of trenches, both the bastions were almost devoid of flank defences and the walls were weaker than in other sectors, and they did not have a deep moat or even a counterscarp. Furthermore, there was a natural approach on the Sabbionera side, consisting of the bed of a winter stream. From this position, with an appropriately built platform, the artillery could easily bombard the port. After each assault, the Venetians reinforced the bastions, but due to lack of time and money, restorations and improvements had concentrated on the most threatened sectors. Moreover, Sabbionera as well Sant'Andrea had never suffered major attacks. To improve the defence it would be necessary to build two half-moons, high and extended, reinforcing them with embankments and building a covered road: four months and 400 workers. The intuition of the Ottoman commanders about the weak point of the Venetian defence was supported also by the interrogations of the deserters and the carefully conducted reconnaissance. In mid June the siege resumed with unusual violence with the bombardment of the city with all the guns and mortars of the batteries. From the trenches, the Ottomans constantly kept the enemy positions under the fire of the musketry, and before the end of June one Ottoman marksman scored an important target, hitting the provveditor Bernardo Nani. A few weeks later, the German Colonel von Frisheim was killed; together with him, the Baron von Degenfeld and the brother of the Marquis Villa, who had returned to Candia as a volunteer with the Pope's troops, who had fallen fighting from the ramparts. With them, a large number of Venetian nobles dead or remained wounded: Balbi; Badoer; Grimaldi;

Corner;[41] Barbaro, not counting the Marquis de Montbrun, commander of the infantry after the departure of the Marquis Villa, was wounded several times, but each time returned to the bastions to lead his men.

A veteran of the wars against the Spaniards, aged 65, the Marquis had entered in the service of the Republic and after his experience in Crete he wrote that everything he had witnessed in 50 years of campaigns were child's play compared to the siege at Candia. The pressure exerted with close assaults and the massive use of artillery, associated with the implacable action of landmines, was the tactic that the Ottomans intensified since the autumn of 1668. Before slowly, and then with ever increasing vigour, the besiegers advanced against the two external bastions. Though the underground works diminished considerably, against Sant'Andrea the mines were prepared by digging in the rock. Before the end of the summer, the besiegers overcame the external defences in front of Sant'Andrea, constituted by *bonetti* and improvised arrows embankments. They passed the ditch and "... began to work with the sapper at the basement of the wall" despite the continuous fire of the Venetians, who had placed one battery with 18 guns for the defence of the bastion, supported by three others with more 18 guns of 50 lb. between the ravelin of Santo Spirito and the bastion of Panigrà. In the same sector, the Ottomans responded deploying eight batteries with 28 cannons and eight mortars, 8,000 infantrymen and 5,000 diggers occupied the trenches under the sight of the Grand Vizier. Now even the port was under the fire of the besiegers' artillery. It was evident that before the end of the year the bastion would have fallen, therefore inside the city the defenders worked feverishly to build a backward additional fortification, building a redoubt reinforced with an embankment, although without ditches, to which followed a second one built further backward, larger and stronger than the previous one and completed with a ditch. The fighting raged despite the arrival of rains and the cold season. At Sant'Andrea, the Ottomans penetrated through the open breaches on the sides of the bastion, fighting day and night, in an exhausting war of position, conquering one metre of land at a time, building repairs and contending with the enemy for the highest positions to target the place, while musketry and explosions resounded incessantly.

The Venetians tried to stop the enemy's progress by resorting to ever-new expedients. Since the terrain in Sant'Andrea was rocky and difficult to excavate countermine tunnels, they devised a new type of weapon, known as *fogata* (blaze). It was a superficial explosive chamber, filled with powder mixed with inflammable material, especially directed against the enemy trench heads.[42] The Ottomans replied, intensifying the artillery fire. Now the artillery positioned above the huge platform erected on the beach

41 The death of Caterino Corner, *provveditore generale all'Armata*, left a deep impression in the general staff. The valiant officer was inspecting the ravelin of Sant'Andrea when was hit by a heavy projectile that opened his stomach. Transferred to his residence, he survived for another three hours, exhorting his officers and other commanders not to surrender. Brusoni, *Libro* XXVI, p. 101.

42 W. von Bigge, cited work, p. 122. To destroy the Ottomans' approaches each proposal was examined, including the most bizarre, such as the one presented in 1649 by a Scottish sea captain, who proposed 'a wonderful device' to bring water from the sea to the ramparts and a 'special artillery', with which he wanted to clog the Ottoman guns. The research for new technologies

in front of Sabbionera could hit the port, forcing the Venetians to enter only at night. The conquest of the Sant'Andrea bastion put the Venetians in a risky position, because there the ground began to degrade, leaving to the Ottomans the highest position. In that sector the command was held by provveditor Caterino Corner while at Sabbionera commanded general Francesco Battaglia. This latter was killed on 26 September and replaced by the general of the *Oltramontani*, von Spaar.

More than once, the council of war more proposed to launch a sortie in force, but Francesco Morosini always opposed this action, because in his belief the sorties were always difficult and unsuccessful, because the Ottomans were always strong and well protected in their trenches. Moreover, it was difficult to reach contact with them, as well as to drive them away. In this regard, Scheither outlined: "taking a sortie from the city was like trying to run down a wall with the head". The defenders continued to launch sorties, however, carried out in order to infiltrate a team of a few dozens of men to hit the most advanced enemy approaches on the shoulders and flanks, avoiding the mass assaults of hundreds of soldiers, which inevitably ended up stopping in the intricate network of trenches. The most famous and certainly the most spectacular sorties of the whole conflict took place on the initiative of the French contingents present in the city. The first of these was an action undertaken with a chivalrous spirit by the volunteers who arrived in Crete in 1667. In practice, it was a daring act that had little chance of success, and that perhaps was even encouraged by the Venetians, anxious to get rid of the cumbersome presence of that bevy of unruly and demanding volunteers. The sortie took place on December 16, 1668, performed by 450 French *venturieri*, accompanied by 100 German soldiers. The French volunteers gathered in the morning at the Sabbionera bastion divided into four brigades. Each nobleman was accompanied by one servant who recharged the muskets. In the previous days, some deserters had warned the Ottomans about the preparations for this action, and the defenders guessed that the enemies were ready to receive the sortie. The action lasted just over an hour. The volunteers came out of the bastion in columns, and engaged a violent exchange of musketry with the janissaries, who, from their positions under repair, soon prevailed. Eyewitnesses report that the splendid contingent, though forced to retreat, made it in good order and "with great skill and talent", particularly on the part of the Duke de la Feuillade and the Count of Saint-Pol.[43] The sortie cost the French volunteers 180 dead and 40 wounded.

At the end of 1668, the casualties had been terrifying: the Venetians had lost 6,971 men, including 25 generals and colonels; on the Ottoman side, according to the Venetian sources, the losses rose to 36,839 dead and 6,667 wounded.[44] During the year the besiegers had carried out 18 general assaults and triggered 69 mines, to which the Venetians had replied with 47 great and little sorties, and 292 countermines, *fornelli*, *fogate* and fire shafts. Before

---

never stops and in 1667 Francesco Morosini examined a project for the development of flying bombs for destroying the enemy batteries.

43 Brusoni, *Libro* XV, p. 274.

44 *Ibid.*, *Libro* XIV, p. 227–230.

the end of the year, through a dispatch, the Sultan warned the Grand Vizier that Venice had sent a new ambassador to Larissa – where the great lord had moved to be promptly informed about the progress of the siege – to negotiate an armistice. Venetian Ambassador Molino proposed the return to the Sultan of all the recent conquests in Dalmatia, the demolition of the fortifications of Candia, and the payment of an annual tribute in exchange for the suspension of the siege. The proposal was tempting, and in the confidential letter, Mehmed IV expressed to Köprülü Ahmed his thoughts. In particular, the Sultan was worried about enormous war expenses. He expressed his fear that the Ottoman treasury would not be able to sustain that level of spending and continue the war for another year.[45] Fazil Ahmed wrote to the Sultan asking him to reject the Venetian offers, informing him that hundreds of metres of wall had fallen, and that victory was near. Köprülü closed his letter by writing that: "... after having conquered so many redoubts, dug countless trenches, triumphed over such a prodigious number of mines, Allah would grant his soldiers the grace to seize the city" and closed praying to him to not believe in lying relations and that the whole army and its commander were preparing to spend another winter in the trenches. The situation for the Venetians was becoming more and more critical every day.[46] Therefore, ambassador Molino sailed to Candia to meet the Grand Vizier, who welcomed him with the usual courtesy. Köprülü knew that Molino did not have a mandate to cede the city, but his presence served to impose silence on the murmur that stirred a part of the troops. In fact, a few days before, 500 menacing *sipahy* and janissaries, together with many officers, had gathered around the Grand Vizier's pavilion accusing him of wanting to prolong the siege and threatening to stone him. But Köprülü managed to restore the situation thanks to the intervention of his cousin Kara Mustafa, the janissary *aga* and the *koulkiaya* (the senior lieutenant general of the janissaries' commander) who, with a handful of soldiers devoted to them, had dispersed the seditious. The rescuers invited the Grand Vizier not to follow up on this episode, considering the scarcity of soldiers for continuing the siege, but after this fact, in a fit of rage, Köprülü exclaimed that with a modest increase in money, even the diggers recruited from the Constantinople's populace would have performed better than janissaries and *sipahys*, and that: "... like a rank of feeble mutineers, they are only able to make themselves strong of their prerogatives and privileges granted by the Sultan, who paid them 120 *akçe* a day, but who they serve no more than to ruin the empire."

45 R. Murphey, *Ottoman warfare 1500–1700*, cited work, p. 186. The letter reached the Grand Vizier at the end of the second, unsuccessful, year of assaults, the twenty-third of the war.

46 In those desperate weeks, the Venetians resorted to every means to persuade the Sultan to accept an armistice. In the same days, also the monk *Padre Ottomano* made his appearance in Crete. He is one the most enigmatic figures in Cretan history. This mysterious religious and his mother Zafira had been captured when the Maltese fleet assaulted the *Caravana* of the Cairo on 28 September 1644, the act which opened the war for Crete. The Maltese Knights educated him in a monastery on the island, convinced that he was the first-born son of Sultan Ibrahim I. Instead, the young captive was the Sultan's wetnurse's son. His arrival on the scene was demanded by the Venetain Senate, hoping to move Mehmet IV to milder sentiments.

83. Model of a Venetian 9 lb *Sagro*, after Tommaso Moretti's *Trattato di Artiglieria*, Venice 1665.*

84. Since 1667 the Ottoman artillery employed for the siege of Candia an increasing number of large-calibre mortars.*

85. A late-17th century Ottoman rampart musket, reproduced in the work of Cevad Ahmed Beg: *Etat Militaire Ottoman depuis la Fondation de l'Empire jusqu'à nos jours*, published in Istanbul in 1882.*

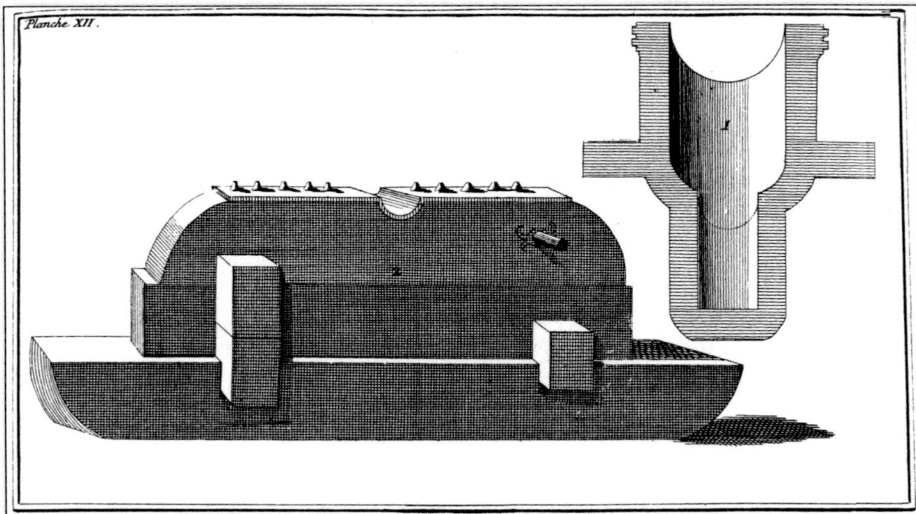

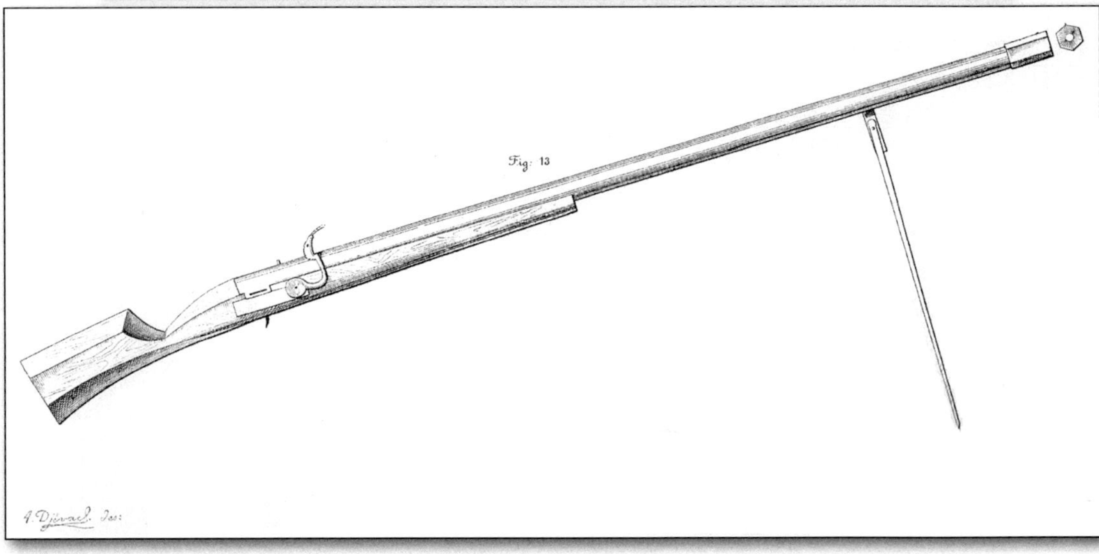

As happened the previous year, the siege continued in the winter with the usual artillery and musketry duels, alternating with the explosion of mines. The beginning of the new year opened with the explosion of a mine under the ravelin of Santo Spirito, triggered even though in the tunnels the water was high up to the knees. The smoke caused death by suffocation of the sentinels and many Venetian miners who were stationed there. In March, with the arrival of new Ottoman reinforcements, the intensity of the fighting increased, and the siege resumed the usual deadly trend. The Ottomans progressed with the tunnels under the Sant'Andrea bastion. Here, the defenders became aware of the enemies presence, and to neutralise the threat decided to trigger a large *contromina* prepared on the slope closest to the sea. The action was unsuccessful due to the lack of preparation of the engineers present in that sector.[47] In early March at Sant'Andrea, for the first time, the besiegers managed to penetrate into a bastion and to maintain it.

The bastion of Sabbionera opposed the most stubborn resistance, against whom the Ottomans concentrated 26 guns and eight mortars divided into seven batteries to breach the wall. The Venetians tried to neutralise the enemy battery with one *fogata*, which caused little damage to the enemy, while invested one elevated *bonetto* defence hold by the defenders.[48]

On 31 March 1669, the Venetians prepared a gigantic mine loaded with 200 quintals of gunpowder to destroy one of these batteries. The frightful explosion hurled pieces and artillerymen into the air; the rain of debris forced the infantry in the trenches to flight. The force of the explosion caused the collapse of a bell tower in the city, raised an enormous amount of debris that overwhelmed some 20 Venetian soldiers, and covered the ground killing the *defterdar paşa* (the administrative official of the army). Inside the city the conditions of the defenders worsened every day: the tattered and miserable soldiers were reduced to sleeping outdoors in the absence of neighbourhoods where they could recover; most of the officers appeared exhausted and reduced to pitiful conditions. The commanders tried to encourage the troops by taking a position on the line of fire and exposing themselves to the risks of the siege. On 10 May, the Marquis of Saint'André-Montbrun was wounded in the face by the explosion of a mine at Sant'Andrea, while his adjutant remained buried up to the neck from the debris. Three days later, the provveditor Caterino Corner was mortally wounded by an explosive projectile fired from an Ottoman mortar while he was in the nearby small ravelin of Santo Spirito. Morosini continued to employ the soldiers at his disposal in the best possible way, deploying Italian, Greek and the *Oltramarine* troops in first line and using the Germans and the freshest but less experienced contingents as a tactical reserve, as he had experimented with the soldiers of Brunswick, who "although universally beautiful" found themselves in trouble when they first supported an Ottoman assault against Sant'Andrea. The Venetian troops were arranged on several lines, in order to support each other and, if necessary, increase the intensity of the fire, with a

47 *Ibid.*, p. 288.

48 *Ibid.*

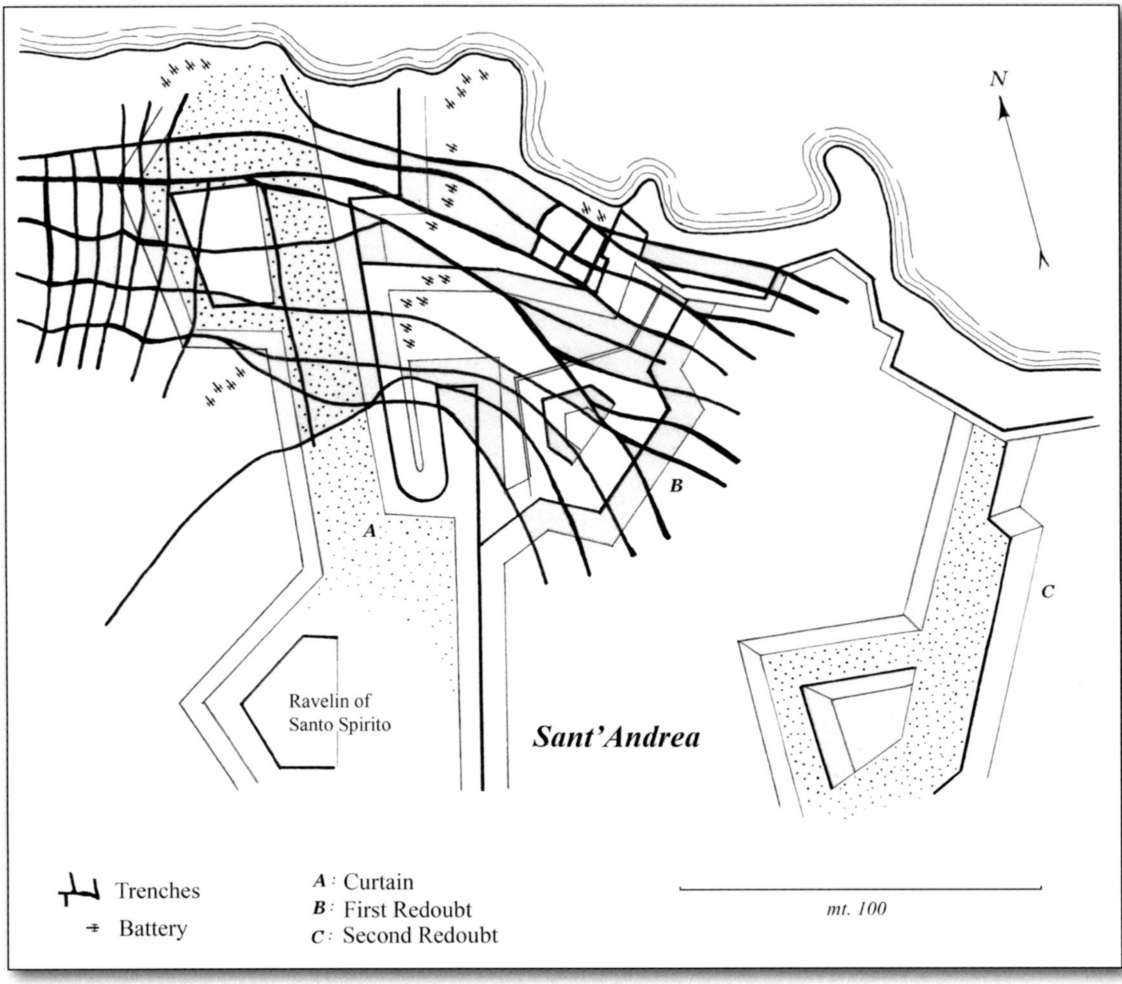

86. The bastion and the Ottoman approaches at Sant'Andrea bastion, on the west side of Candia, as they appeared in late August 1669. In this sector the fighting was extraordinarily fierce and in 1669, to prolong the resistance, the Venetians built two additional redoubts drawing back of about 50 metres, but presenting every time to their opponents a new obstacle to overcome. At the end of the siege, the Ottomans renamed Sant'Andrea the "Surrender Bastion".

small group of grenadiers and other soldiers armed with short pikes and other polearms ready to intervene in the most threatened sectors.

The diversity of opinions on the usefulness of the sorties provoked many arguments in the allied command. These differences of belief contributed to disagreements in the war council, a prelude to the negative outcome of the siege. The French *Grand Admirail* François de Vendôme, Duke of Beaufort and General Annes de Noailles insisted on launching a new great sortie employing their troops. Great expectations were placed in this sortie planned on 25 June, prepared with care and conducted by more than 3,000 French soldiers. The action was directed by Beaufort, who personally directed the troops against the enemy. For the assault, the cavalry was also employed in order to secure the flanks of the five columns deployed for investing the trenches and the batteries from Sabbionera to San Demetrio. Ramps were prepared outside Sabbionera and placed above the ditches to facilitate the exit of the troops. Two squadrons of galleys had to support the sortie by bombarding the trenches with their heavy guns. This time the Ottomans did not expect the sortie. The assault successfully progressed until the third order of trenches, but the sudden explosion of a munitions depot caused the rout of the troops, who thought

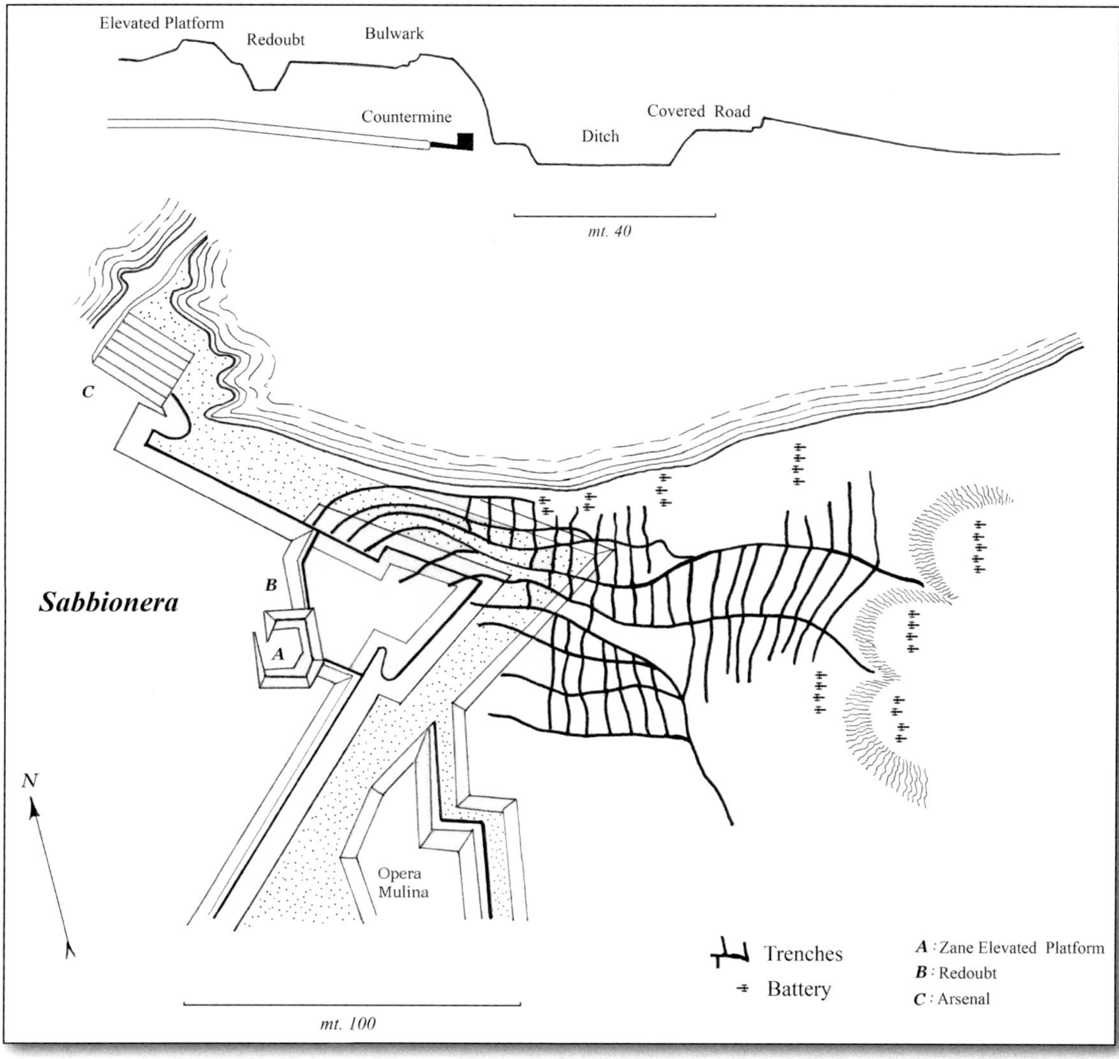

87. Sabbionera bastion on Candia's east side during the siege's last phase, with the Ottoman trenches as they appeared just before the surrender. The Venetians added supplementary defences, digging a redoubt and building an elevated platform inside the bastion. Ottoman progress in this area was modest in comparison to Sant'Andrea. The besiegers renamed the fortifications: Sabbionera was the "Red Bastion", Vitturi the "White Bastion"; Betelem "Bastion of the Jews", while the Martinengo was known as "the trap for the pigs".

it was a mine prepared against them. Meanwhile the Ottoman commanders reacted by sending reinforcements to Sabbionera who assaulted the enemy column on the flanks provoking panic in the disoriented French troops. The situation changed rapidly and after a few minutes, the French escaped in disorder towards Candia. The sortie cost 500 men, including the Duke of Beaufort. Yet not even this time could the defenders succeed in changing the outcome of the siege.[49]

In the summer of 1669, after the double failure of the French sortie and the bombardment of the Ottoman trenches by the fleet, the situation of the defenders appeared desperate. The bastions of Sant'Andrea and Sabbionera were reduced to a pile of rubble, but with incredible obstinacy the Ottomans continued to

49 According to Brusoni, de Noailles intended to launch a new sortie in early July with more than 10,000 men, asking from Morosini 4,000 infantrymen of Venetian troops, because they were more expert of the terrain outside Candia.The Captain General firmly refused the request, allowing the participation of a small corps formed by German infantrymen. Brusoni, *Libro* XVII, p. 309.

88. Sultan Mehmed IV reigned from 1648 to 1687. He succeeded his father Ibrahim when he was only 11 years old. Mehmet remained hostage of his officials and women of the Harem, but redeemed his lacklustre conduct in January 1669, rejecting the offers for an armistice proposed by the Venetian ambassador Francesco Alvise Molino. (Engraving by an anonymous artist, after the equestrian portrait published by Nicolas Visscher, Vienna 1683)

advance with approaches and mines, decreasing the intensity of the assaults but keeping constant pressure with the fire of the muskets and grenades. At Sant'Andrea they placed a battery of seven guns to hit inside the curtain and the first of the redoubts built on the bastion, now close to falling. The Venetian resistance continued to the bitter end, despite the failure of the French sortie, whose commander began to be less ready to follow Morosini's drawings, until ordering the re-embarkation of the troops in mid August. Meanwhile, illnesses and desertions magnified the gaps between defenders and besiegers. The city appeared semi-destroyed; the population – the few old men, women and children who still survived in the ruins – reduced to extreme poverty. The Ottomans tried to make morale falter by throwing tickets into the city containing the offer of surrender. On 10 August, Köprülü Ahmed ordered a violent assault on the crucial sectors of Sant'Andrea and Sabbionera; Morosini replied by blowing up a gigantic mine of 100 barrels, prepared long before under the second redoubt of Sant'Andrea, which annihilated hundreds of enemies in one giant blow. At Sabbionera, the Ottomans managed to conquer some platforms, but the tenacious resistance of Savoy and French soldiers, who were still in Candia, rejected every assault. In vain, Morosini asked the Duke de Noailles to let 3,000 men of his troops to remain, so that, by joining them to the others still able to fight, he could guarantee the resistance of the city until the arrival of the new reinforcements that Venice was collecting.

Once the French had left Candia,[50] the Maltese followed, and with these other contingents declared through their commanders the intention to abandon the defence. To the Captain General remained only 3,792 men with whom it was impossible to continue the resistance. After bringing together the war council one last time, he sent a message to the Grand Vizier and opened negotiations for surrender. But while the parties were discussing, the Ottomans and Venetians returned several times to engage in sudden and violent skirmishes. The Ottomans were persuaded that penetrating further into the city they could obtain more favourable conditions of surrender, which obliged the defenders not to cede in order not to be forced to negotiate in position of inferiority. On 3 September, the Ottomans placed one battery of 10 guns in front of the redoubt of Sant'Andrea, with which they suddenly opened fire against the palisade. Fearing that a new general assault would follow, the Venetians triggered a long-prepared mine, and

50 According to French Historians, the decision assumed by de Noailles to withdraw the French troops from Crete much angered Louis XIV. The King asked to prepare another expedition to Crete and appointed Maréchal de Bellefonds as commander, but the final surrender suspended the preparations. See John B. Wolf, *Louis XIV* (New York: Norton & Company, 1968), p. 225.

let the battery fly into the air. This explosion closed the last eight months of the siege. The Venetians declared the loss of 12,716 men, excluding more than 2,000 French casualties suffered in 1669. In this accounting the contemporary historians outlined the sacrifice of 280 Venetian patricians, a figure equal to a third of the Senate's members. According to the same source, overall Ottoman casualties from January 1668 were reported as 37,719 dead and 7,917 wounded. For a long time, the account of casualties reconstructed in a more than suspicious way by Venetian historians has been the only source for the Ottoman side, and only recently an official report compiled by the adjutants of the Grand Vizier was identified. It is a document as rare as it is precious, as it allows us to compare the numbers of Venetian sources with the actual casualties incurred by the besiegers in the last three years of the siege of Candia.[51]

Paşa:	15
Çorbaci (janissaries' officers):	84
Çavus (adjutants – warrant officers):	164
Janissaries	39,939
Azabs and other infantrymen:	69,850
Alay Begs (provincial levies officers):	799
Toprakly (provincial levies):	37,465
Serdengecdi and *sipahys* (volunteers and *kapikulu* cavalry):	49,635
Gureba sipahy ('foreign' *kapikulu* cavalry):	7,900
Topçu (artillerymen):	29,965
Humbaraci (bombardiers):	41
Lagimçi (miners):	29,965
Total dead and wounded:	**259,002**

In the last eight months of the siege, the fighting had reached a violence never seen before; the Ottomans had carried out 56 assaults, all against Sant'Andrea and Sabbionera, supported by the fire of 59 batteries. The mines were 472

51 The total figure of 259,002, given in the source, should be 265,822, a discrepancy of 6,820. Figures cited by Murphey in *The Ottoman Resurgence*, cited work p. 193, after Mühürdar's history, *Ottoman Casualties at the Siege of Candia, June 1667–9 September 1669*. The same figures are listed in the manuscript copy found in the Topkapy Palace Library: Ms. III Ahmed 3605, f. 57a. Some figures are controversial, such as the *cebeci* casualties, here considered as *azabs* alongside other infantrymen. According to Prof. Kahraman Şakul, these figures may be explained in another way. Murphey cites the Ottoman casualties registered in the Mühürdar's chronicle, which is quite detailed in terms of figures and overall numbers. These are impressive indeed. There is an obvious discrepancy between these figures and those given by European observers in late 17th century. The explanation is as follows: 1) Mühürdar explicitly says that every service group (*cebecis*, janissaries, timar cavalry, miners etc.) in the army were tasked with digging approach trenches (parallels), because the siege was too long and manpower was too short. In other words, conventional job descriptions do not really work in the final phase of the siege. 2) He also points out several thousands of *cebeci* soldiers were recruited from many places such as Larissa (modern Greece) and Istanbul. 3) Therefore, his figures for *cebeci* must be understood as the total number of casualties among the men who were recruited for serving in the *cebeci* corps and fought under the *cebeci* flag. That does not mean that they only served in the armoury in the army camp. Nevertheless, Prof. Kahraman Şakul still thinks that his overall figures are disputable.

with 45 underground encounters. Countermines of the defenders exploded 1,172 times, 96 times they assaulted the enemy trenches and spent 84,874 grenades of glass and 100,960 of metal. On 6 September, Francesco Morosini signed the surrender of the city, obtaining the evacuation of the garrison and the population who intended to leave the island, preparing to defend himself and his choice in the process that would inevitably be followed in the Senate. The Venetian garrison and Morosini disposed of 20 days for leaving Candia. According to the honourable terms, of the surrender, they could bring all the movable goods with him. In Venice, the news would come late, causing amazement, as after many years it was unbelievable that Candia could surrender. The definitive conclusion of the hostilities came one year and a half later, because the boundaries in Dalmatia remained to be defined. On 27 July 1671 the conflict between the Ottoman Empire and Venice ended, the fifth conflict fought until now by the two states, to which contemporaries could find no other comparison than the legendary Trojan War.

Appendix I

The Private Soldiers of the 17th Century

It is difficult to form a social and cultural picture of the soldiers who participated in the Cretan war, finding ourselves in an era where sources are more easily concentrated to illustrate the enterprises of the aristocrat officers and reserve only a few citations to the common soldiers. However, a vivid description of the soldiers who were in Candia comes to us thanks to Captain Johann Scheither, who in 1669 served as a captain in the infantry of the Brunswick-Lüneburg:

> Today most of the Christian soldiers are very different people in terms of religion, language, way of life, as well as for their style of dress and temperament, and not to be compared to the Ottomans in general. What is most striking and most valiant is that they have enough courage to do what is commanded and do not fear danger, no matter how great it may be. In Candia the Germans, then the Slavs and the Greeks, were esteemed better than others and therefore followed the soldiers of the other nations. The Germans can resist the cold and the discomforts a little better, while the others much more badly and scarcely in moments of shortage are content just to eat and drink, paying no attention to what will become of them. Moreover, the soldiers are for the most part so done, that above all they do not feel the fear of God, but they scrub with no scruples of sins and vices of all sorts and animalishly blaspheme. Insatiable in eating and drinking, they often spend the day and night in revels worse than the beasts, and count as their greatest happiness and life of Paradise when they have enough to gorge, and if their money is not enough, they give to the robbery and resort to other means. On the march and at the encampment they are accustomed so that they have much to do to give them orders and bans to keep them in campaign or in the regiments, otherwise they would sack the country and end up giving them the coup de grace.

The judgement of Captain Scheiter about the different quality of the troops finds confirmation in some contemporary sources, while is denied in others. For instance, in 1648, the Greeks are described as "not to be trusted" and sometimes as sick: "From the total taken away the sick and the Greeks who are

89. **Gerhard Ter-Borch,** *Soldier*, **c.1660.***

as unreliable as the sick."[1] In 1650 the judgment on them has drastically changed: "The Greeks support the deprivation better than any other nation and lend even more fruitful service no less in the military events than in the work."[2] In 1652 the judgment has even overturned disfavour for the *Oltramontani* who are considered the least motivated: "With regard to the quality of these troops," the Greeks are the soldiers who show good temperament, the Italians and the *Oltremarini* were considered as mediocre while the *Oltramontani* "they do not demonstrate the hoped for strength and vigour".[3] The consideration about the various contingents varied in a fluctuating manner, also according to the season since some nationalities suffered most in the hot season and others in the cold one.

In an indirect way, it is possible trace stories of private soldiers that allow us to understand something about the social origin of the men who composed the lower ranks and the dynamics that led some of them to enlist as soldiers. In the history of Brescia by Giovanni Treccani Degli Alfieri we find the story of some local prejudice, sought by the Venetian authorities for thefts and robberies that occurred in 1647. One of these criminals, Pietro Aurelio Porcellaga, already banned from his city, had been captured again, and considering the great need of men for the war against the Porte, it was proposed his ban was commuted by his presenting himself as a 'volunteer' to serve in Dalamatia for one year and after spending that period serving another five years of relegation in Zadar. Porcellaga could reduce his punishment if he found other volunteers, so – to grant him this opportunity – the sentence was suspended for one month. It was a method to find recruits used quite frequently in the Italian states, according to the dominant mentality that considered the criminals as the most suitable men to carry weapons, obtaining the dual purpose of purging society from dangerous subjects and at the same time offering a chance to redeem themselves with the honoured profession of soldier. However, the collateral effect was to fill the army with unruly subjects, with the risk of compromising cohesion inside the unit and the contamination of the other soldiers with the bad habits of these forced volunteers.

1 ASVe, *Senato, Dispacci di Provveditori*, b. 545.
2 *Ibid.*, b. 546.
3 *Ibid.*, b. 548.

The Morlachs

The emigration to Venetian territory of semi-nomadic populations, coming from the internal regions of the Balkans, already dated back to the previous century, when their settlement had been encouraged to repopulate large border areas exposed to the Ottoman incursions. They were mostly communities of Christian Orthodox shepherds from Bosnia and Herzegovina, Montenegro and even Albania, with a highly structured hierarchy, therefore suitable for fulfilling the dual role of settlers and soldiers, according to a pattern very similar to the contemporary Austrian *Militärgrenze*. In a few years, the war against the Ottomans produced a rapid increase of these communities in the Venetian region. The disappearance of the native population in the border areas had caused the end of the existence of an organised militia. The most depopulated areas were the districts of Šibenik and, to a lesser extent, Zadar, where due to the native population exodus, a large part of the countryside was practically left to the newly arrived Morlachs. From a few tens at a time, up to 430 Morlachs settled in the countryside of Pula in March 1647, dragging with them a herd of 4,500 animals.[4] In a few years they reached more than 5,000 families, from which it was possible to raise corps of irregulars on foot and horse.

In June 1647, the number of men fit to bear arms was around 1,000. By January 1648 this number rose to 2,000, and in May 1648, when the major phase of the migration was over, the Republic had acquired more than 4,000 combatants.[5] These 'noble savages', without discipline but brave and fierce warriors, as the Morlachs were generally described in the contemporary sources, who in "search for liberty" and to escape the "Ottoman yoke" fled to the Venetian side, managed to capture the imagination of those with whom they came into contact.[6] However, most interested in the Morlachs connection was the general provveditor Lunardo Foscolo. For him the Morlachs were above all a valuable military force, which enabled him to at least partially compensate for the lack of soldiers, and after 1649 the Venetian decreasing military commitment in Dalmatia, caused by the financial strains of prolonged warfare and pressing needs of other fronts, mainly Crete and the Archipelago.

Under Venetian rule, the Morlachs enjoyed a large measure of autonomy. They were governed and led into actions by their own leaders, elected by the male Morlachs and confirmed by the Venetian government. At the beginning of the war, the Republic formed 22 companies organised in the same structure as the *Oltramarini*, although the size of the Morlachs' companies depended primarily on the person of the *harambaša* (the chief or leader), his charisma,

4 In 1655, the relation of general provveditor Lorenzo Dolfin estimates the number of the Morlachs who had defected to the Venetian side at 28–30,000 people, *Commissione et Relatione Venetae*, 7, p. 116.

5 ASVe, *Provveditori da Terra e da Mar*, b. 466, cc. 416–428.

6 Among the many, the French traveller Pierre Michel De la Haye, in his essay on Venice, compared the Morlachs to the Native Americans, when he described them as "the Iroquois of these countries". Further reading: Domagoj Madunić, *Defensiones Dalmatiae: Governance and Logistics of the Venetian Defensive System in Dalmatia during the War of Crete, 1645–1669* (Central European University, 2012), pp. 212–245.

90. Stjepan Subotich, known as Sorich, in a 1688 dated imaginary portrait. In 1647, after being a famous and feared leader of the Morlachs, he answered to the Ottomans who, admiring his value, flattered him to return under their protection: "For fifty years I have been a slave of a tyrant, it will not be less disgraceful, if I will live the rest of my life ...under the rule of the most right Republic of the world."

skills and status among the communities, and could range anywhere between 20 to 200 men. In addition to these company level commanders, the Morlachs of Zadar elected one of their chief as overall leader with the title of *serdar*.[7]

Their contribution to the defence of Dalmatia was very important. Led by their leaders Stjepan Sorich and Nicola Mandusich, the Morlachs engaged the Ottomans in a fierce border war made of raids and ambushes, in which they rarely took prisoners. The bellicose temperament of these soldiers, equally ruthless with soldiers and civilians, was at times a problem for the Venetian authorities. In April 1648, taking advantage of an incident that occurred after the surrender of Klis, the Morlachs killed and robbed the inhabitants who were evacuating the city, and despite the attempt of the Venetian officers to stop the massacre, the Morlachs killed over 100 civilians. One year later, during the siege at Risan of Kotor, seeing that among the besiegers there were several Morlachs, the Ottoman officers responded negatively to the offer of surrender and free evacuation advanced to them by Lunardo Foscolo. They asked to the provveditor why Venice left its soldiers free to use such cruelty against the civilians by burning houses and crops: "and having understood that this was by impulse and made by private individuals against the intention of the officers, they replied that if the commander was not so good to be obeyed, he would never have been sincere".[8] The fierce hatred between the Ottomans and the Morlachs turned the war into a ruthless ethnic clash without mercy, so as soon as they could, the Ottomans repaid the Venetian borders with equally cruel treatment. In the summer of 1648, during the Foscolo campaign in the Lika, the Morlachs were repelled and pursued by the Ottomans to the border, losing two of their major commanders: Sorich was captured and killed after suffering the most painful tortures, while Mandusich fell in combat. His tortured body and his head were thrown into Venetian territory. After the campaigns of 1646–49, the border between Bosnia and Dalmatia experienced periods of relative calm, interrupted by the Ottoman raids against Zadar in 1650, the Venetian siege at Duare in the following year and the reciprocal looting near Trau and in the Lika in 1653. The absence of action, with the consequent decrease of the war spoils, together with the delay with which the salaries were paid from Venice, provoked various contrarieties among the

7 The title of *serdar* represents a direct link with the Ottoman legacy in the Morlachs society. See also D. Madunić, cited work, p. 215.

8 Brusoni, *Libro* IX, p. 226.

Morlachs. Some families crossed the border to settle near Sinj, in Ottoman territory, while others committed great wickedness. Venetian records about the Morlachs cited several affairs, such as when they enslaved several Venetian deserters and in addition committed thefts of children to sell them to the Ottomans. There were also acts of piracy against the communities settled in the islands of Brač and Hvar, so that the Adriatic seemed infested as in the war against the Uskok corsairs. Provveditor Girolamo Foscarini tried to intervene with energy to re-establish the order and prosecute the guiltiest, often protected by the silence of the clan chiefs. The need of men for war made prevail a mild attitude by the government, worried about losing the support of the fierce Balkan warrior-shepherds. The war in Dalmatia resumed a certain vigour in March 1654 with the Venetian campaign against Knin, which was attended by 1,600 Morlach infantrymen and another 300 on horseback.[9] The siege ended, however, with a severe defeat, during which the irregulars abandoned the siege to return to their homes, refusing any promise of money. Before the end of that campaign the chief Smiglianovich, colonel of a mounted regiment, was surprised by the Ottomans while loaded with loot and two days' march from the border, and was killed together with 100 of his men. Notwithstanding this bitter failure, the importance of the Morlachs as a fighting force grew even after 1654, when they remained the only available troops to protect the Venetian conquests away from the coast. In this regard, the general provveditor Antonio Bernardo was the first to improve the tactical employment of the Morlachs in defensive operations. Instead of simply using them to lay ambush to small and medium size Ottoman raids, as was usual practice with his predecessors, or allowing them to indiscriminately assault targets in the borderland, Bernardo perfected the use of the large-scale attacks over the Ottoman border with the goal of countering and defeating local *sipahys*, or provoking their return home from the main Ottoman army. Moreover, while his predecessor looked favourable at bloody engagements, Bernardo aimed to preserve the Morlachs as much as possible but not to engage with organised Ottoman forces. Bernardo rightly interpreted the strategic scenario, considereing that the Ottoman incursions never involved more than 6,000 men. The action of February 1659, when the *serdar* Janko Mitrović led a storming party of 2,000 Morlachs and *craine* from Zadar and Split, represented the last major raid of the war.

Starting from 1660, the Ottomans changed their tactics and launched their raids against Venice rather early, in February or March. By doing so, they managed to achieve the element of surprise and inflicted heavy losses to the Morlachs. After the departure of Antonio Bernardo, the offensive actions on enemy territory became less frequent and much smaller scale. Reasons were many: Venice, content with the turning of Ottoman attention to other objectives, began to restrain the Morlachs in order to prevent them from provoking the Ottomans and from forcing them to undertake new raids against Dalmatia. In addition, general provveditor Caterino Corner introduced a practice that Morlachs should pay for the munitions issued for

9 Brusoni, *Libro* IX, p. 257.

actions in enemy territory, which definitely could not have encouraged them to carry more raids. Furthermore, the long years of war and constant fighting demanded a heavy toll among the Morlach leaders. When in June 1663, general provveditor Girolamo Contarini reviewed the Morlach's of Zadar, he noted that they were "...all men of good stature, well equipped and armed, but badly provided with leaders, which cannot be remedied, since the best and braves have perished in the frequent encounters during this war."[10] The life expectancy among the *serdars* was between 2–4 years and no better for other prominent chiefs.

The Morlachs continued to serve as frontiersmen on foot and on horseback, opposing the Ottoman raids sporadically launched against the major towns. Significant clashes and raids took place around Split in October 1657, then in 1659 at Šibenik and Trogir, again at Šibenik, Trogir and Split in 1660 and 1665, near Zadar in 1662 and in 1666, and finally at Klis in 1669.

10 ASVe, *Senato, Dispacci di Provveditori*, b. 490, 1st June 1663.

Appendix II

Prisoners of War

With all its corollary of mourning and destruction, the long Cretan War represented a crossing point between two cultures that had long been intermingled, even before clashing. The case of the *Fondaco dei Turchi*, namely the building on the Canal Grande, since 1621 destined to be the emporium of the Ottoman merchants and which remained open throughout the conflict, demonstrates how for Venice as well as the Porte, business was as important as the war. During the Cretan War the warehouse remained operational, although in the last years of the conflict activity practically disappeared, and the only people who used the emporium were mainly Dutch and other Northern European merchants, Lebanese, Franks and other Christians of the Ottoman Empire.

Official assessments and data on Ottoman and Venetian revenue collections clearly tell only a part of the story. Whatever the amount of treasury coming from this unofficial commerce might look like during the Cretan War, it seems clear that private sector and mercantile interests benefited greatly from the flourishing trade both in legal supplies for the Ottoman fleets and illegal commerce with the enemy. The relationship remained open even when the conflict reached an intensity never recorded until then. The history of the war reports countless episodes of brutality committed by both parties, such as the slaughter of Gramvousa's defenders by the Ottoman side, or the merciless treatment reserved by the Knights of Malta to the Ottoman prisoners after the battle of Standia in 1668. In this context, it may seem strange to learn that trade relations between the two States never completely stopped.[1] Commercial relations served to keep open that diplomatic channel through which both sides tried to find an agreement to settle the current struggle. Commercial contacts between the two shores of the Mediterranean also served to deal with the question of prisoners of war. An idea of the economic value that slaves represented during the Cretan war is provided in many Ottoman as well as Western sources. The Ottoman records of Galata suggest that a minimum price for redeeming slaves was a little over

1 Already in 1648, during the first siege at Candia, the Venetian Senate thought to obtain financial support for the besieged city, with the commercial traffic that could be maintained with the countries subject to the Sultan. See ASVe, *Senato Mar*, R 107, cc. 33–34, 26 September 1648.

91. Much more than on the galleys, the Ottomans employed prisoners of war for forced works. In general the treatment of prisoners was bad, especially if they were not important people and unable to pay a ransom. In the spring of 1668 the Venetians freed over 1,000 prisoners held by the North African corsairs, and took them for the defence of Candia. (Illustration from the *Codex Vindobonensis*, late 16th century, Vienna)

7,000 *akçes*, while the more usual sum paid was 10,000 *akçes*.[2] The Ottoman historian Evliya Çelebi, writing some 150 years later, reports the payment of a ransom of 770,000 *akçes* equivalent to 4,000 gold pieces, for the release of a vice-admiral captured after a boarding off the Anatolian coast. While Evliya's figure is no doubt much exaggerated, facilitating prisoner exchanges was undoubtedly a lucrative business throughout the Mediterranean in this period. Contemporary Western accounts, such as the journal of the English sea captain Thomas Allin in 1669, confirm that a common price charged for the release of rank and file prisoners was in the range of 32–40 gold pieces.[3]

Both the Venetians and the Ottomans recognised the right of redeeming of prisoners. Negotiations in this kind of trade were a practice that the Venetians, like the Ottomans, exercised without interruption, leaving interesting information on the life and conditions of those who were prisoners in Venice or Constantinople. Information on prisoners' fates can be reconstructed through indirect data, such as the several reports about the

2 These prices are consistent with the information we have concerning slave redemption prices in the 16th century provided by Abdi Çelebi, who speaks of a usual price of 35 gold pieces paid for the release of Ottoman captives held in Malta. Abdi Çelebi notes however that in the case of high-ranking or socially prominent captives (such as himself) the ransom fee could be raised to as high as 200 gold pieces. See Murphey's *Ottoman Resurgenses*, pp. 191–192.

3 *Ibid.*

92. A Greek infantryman and sailor. The Greek communities subject to Venice provided a large number of soldiers to the Republic, which employed them both on ships and on land. In Candia the garrison was composed of either Italians, ***Schiavoni*** or ***Oltramontani***, but included always a significant number of Hellenic soldiers. In 1651, for example, the garrison consisted of 4,440 men of whom 1,005 came from Greece. Despite their presence, little is known about the clothing and equipment of the Greek infantry in the 17th century, but thanks to an ex-voto preserved in a church of the Mani Peninsula, dating back to the last years of the war, it is possible to light the darkness. The anonymous infantryman is portrayed on a silver relief and this unfortunately does not provide any details about colours, but the drawing shows some typical elements of traditional Greek costume, such as a floppy hat and wide breeches, mixed with clothing of Western origin. Several iconographic sources indicate that in late 17th century the "national" infantry dressed mostly in red. Like the ***Oltramarin***i troops, the Greeks were also light infantrymen armed with musket and sword.

The Greek sailor is reconstructed after an embroidered figure on a wedding pillow preserved in the Benaki Museum, Athens, probably manufactured in the Ionian Islands, and dating to the last quarter of the 17th century. The sailor wore a typical white cotton ***fustanella*** skirt, a short-quilted jupon with side buttoning on a white shirt, black headgear and stockings.

liberation of slaves by Venetians, Maltese and other Christian pirates; while in other cases the news about the episodes experienced by the prisoners are told by themselves, through the letters sent to solicit the payment of the ransom, or simply to inform the relatives who were still alive. A precious and touching testimony regarding prisoners of war was discovered many years ago by the historian of the Ottoman Empire Alessio Bombaci in the 'Ottoman Documents' preserved in the State Archives of Venice.[4] Some documents date back to the years of the Cretan War and reveal a world that is nothing short of surprising. One of these letters, dated April 1647, was written by an anonymous Ottoman prisoner, probably a provincial officer of a Bosnian *ösur*, captured during the campaigns of Lunardo Foscolo in Dalmatia, as can be deduced from some details mentioned in the correspondence. The prisoner informed his relatives that he had been captured along with 15 other soldiers and he had arrived in Venice in February of 1647. Nine prisoners remained in Venice, while he and four others had been transferred to Verona. He informed that two of his companions, the old Mosinaoglu and his brother Ömer had died; then he added that, Halil Beg of Vrana, possibly his commander, had been captured alive and was now imprisoned in Brescia; but in spite of everything he was consoled by the treatment received: "In Verona they (the Venetians) removed the irons and put us in a large room.

4 Collected in the book 'I Documenti Turchi' dell'Archivio di Stato di Venezia, edited by Maria Pia Pedani (Ministero per i Beni Culturali e Ambientali – Ufficio Centrale per i Beni Archivistici, Venice 1994), pp. 411–413.

They gave us a mattress and a blanket, and we are fed well." Some of the most interesting parts of the letter show the relationship between prisoners and their guardians: "The Venetians reproached us because the Cristian prisoners were beaten every day and badly fed" and therefore he recommended that this treatment should not happen again: "I learned that you bought a slave named Petron for 100 *akçes* to exchange with me." In the letters we learn that the change had been not possible, because the Venetian prisoner did not have great resources and therefore the author of the letter recommended to get a certain Ivan, slave in Livno, since he had a powerful friend, namely the governor Possidaria: "a very influential citizen of Zara [Zadar] and who would pay him at least 300". In the last lines, he revealed that many friends in Venice had tried to obtain his freedom, but the one who had captured him had not allowed it.

Appendix III

Weapons Technology and Chemical-Bacteriological War

At different times during the Cretan War, the Venetians successfully thwarted Ottoman strategy and nearly collapsed their siege operations on Crete. After a series of formidable victories, the fleet seemed to be on the verge of victory – or at least close to reaching an armistice with the Sultan – in 1657. In those years, the Venetian fleet deployed captains, sailors, and gunners of extraordinary value. In Venetian naval history and among even the best contemporary navies, this force was by far the most prepared. Thus, the Republic remained convinced that it possessed a powerful weapon that could easily prevail against the poorly trained Ottoman fleet. The war lasted more than 27 years and in this period the development of weapons produced a considerable effort directed above all to the improvement of the sailing ships. The Venetians, and the Ottomans too, intended to abandon their armed merchant vessel policy, especially hiring very expensive vessels from northern Europe. Additionally, the ongoing technical evolution rapidly compensated for the disadvantages that these large vessels faced in the Mediterranean against oared ships. The increasing ability to shake the wind rendered sailing ships independent from the oared fleet. This allowed both sides to adopt the linear tactics successfully introduced in the second half of the 17th century during the Anglo-Dutch wars.[1] With respect to northern European fleets, Venice and the Ottoman Empire faced a significant technological gap substantially filled during the war.

It is remarkable to note how the war of mining during the Cretan war developed principles and techniques that, in fact, remained current until the First World War.[2] However, another aspect of the brutal modernity of the Cretan

1 On this topic, see also the excellent essay by Guido Candiani, 'Vele, remi e cannoni: l'Impiego congiunto di navi, galee e galeazze nella flotta veneziana, 1572–1718', in: *Mutazioni e Permanenze nella Storia Navale del Mediterraneo*, secc. XVI–XIX, Franco Angeli, Milan, 2010), pp. 116–162.

2 Christopher Duffy remarks: "The defence of Candia was in every way worthy to be ranked with the epic siege of Ostend at the beginning of the century, both as a feat of arms, and an academy of fortress warfare for a new generation of engineers." *The Fortress in the age of Vauban and Frederick the Great, 1660–1789*, Siege Warfare, Volume Two (London: Routledge, 1985), p. 221.

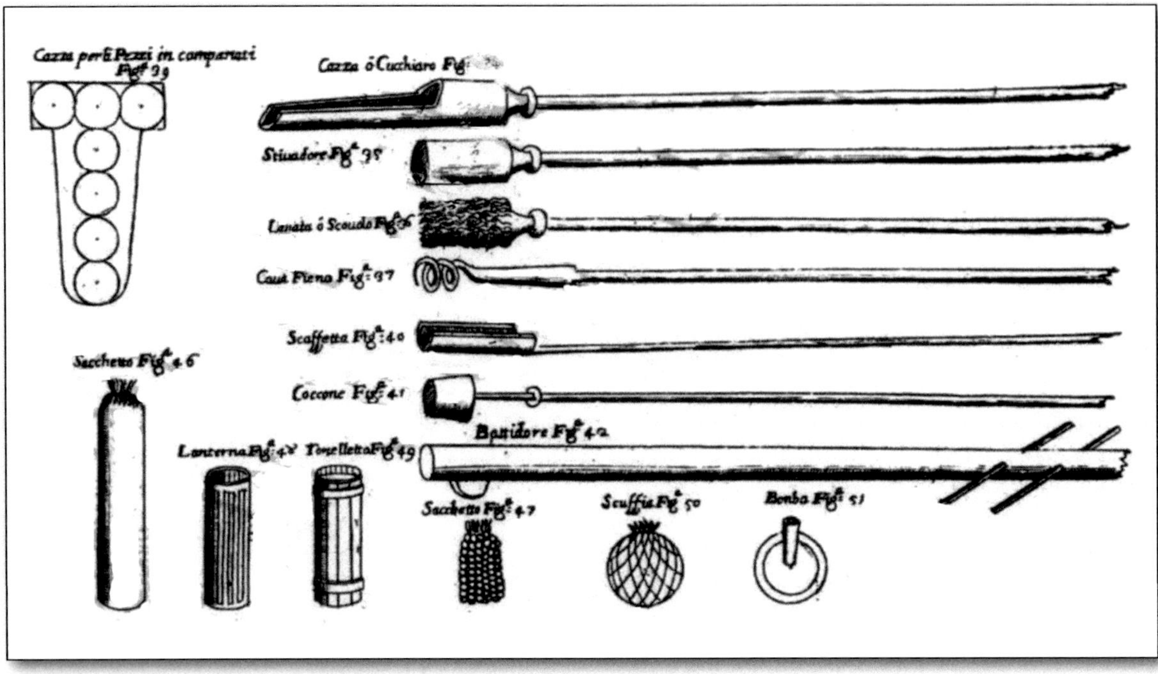

93. Artillery tools and projectiles of the Venetian 17th-century military treaty by Tommaso Moretti. The belief that the war for Candia had not affected weapons development and combat tactics is more apparent than substantial, and this is partly demonstrated by the high number of printed works that appeared in Venice. Although in the 17th century the lagoon city was one of the major publishing centres of Europe, out of 123 treaties written between 1600 and 1699, more than 10 percent were printed in Venice.

War can be found in the introduction of chemical and bacteriological weapons by both sides. The poisoning of wells and attempts to spread epidemics among the enemy was a common practice already in the Middle Ages, but with the Cretan War there was an actual scientific approach for the development of this kind of weapons. The first attempts of poisonings were usually directed against renegades and enemy leaders. From the beginning of the war the phenomenon of deserters who surrendered to the Ottomans took on worrying proportions. The Senate called for "exemplary punishment" for the traitors and instructed the 'secret services' to eliminate them, to stop "the scandal and the resulting political and military damage". In November 1653, after the flight of a deserter named Navagero, the bailo's secretary at Constantinople, Ballarino informed the government that a considerable number of renegades were gathering in the capital. Their presence made Venetian diplomacy dangerous and "fraught with bad effects"[3] and for this reason they had to be neutralised. Between 1653 and 1655 a secret operation began against the renegades, conducted through a friar, guardian of a Catholic convent in Galata, who had the poison delivered by a diverse group of local agents, such as the converted Jew Zacuri, the physician Giovanni Andrea Scoccardi,(alias the Danish pharmacist Skovgaard, graduated in Padua and a spy of Venice and the Hapsburgs in Constantinople), Mustafa Zanchi, another converted Jew resident in Constantinople, and the 'confidant' Gripari, who managed to provide for a good number of renegades the "passport to send to the other world", including Navagero and a corsair captain named Grillo. The Venetian secretary wrote that most of the traitors had been eliminated, justifying how the expense, although high, had been

3 ASVe, *Inquisitori di Stato*, b. 457, 31 December 1653.

repaid with the successful outcome of the operation. Four years later, still Ballarino, informed the Senate about the death by poisoning "in secrecy and with little expense" of Giuseppe Zacuti, the Jew's brother who supplied the poisons but who was causing considerable trouble in his relations with some Ottoman officials. Among the last attempts occurred at the end of the war, in 1664 there were the poisoning of some Italian artillery deserters and in 1665 against the *terçuman* (interpreter) Pace Fortunich, "who offended Venice with his presence."[4]

Other initiatives took the form of sabotage, sometimes inspired by the respective commanders, but more often undertaken individually by the regional commanders. In the early stages of the conflict many attempts were made to sabotage and other attacks on ships or soldiers, but all with poor results. On 22 March 1645, even before the war began, a Venetian merchant suggested an expedient to "destroy and annihilate the crews" with poison, while in April 1655, an agent named Giacomo Rizil offered to burn, through a Russian renegade, the Ottoman ships in Chaniá.[5] What had failed in wartime could be achieved in time of peace: on 25 July 1673, the provveditor of Split planned to secretly ignite some merchant ships of Ulcinj by means of a suitably corrupt Ottoman *reis*. Possibly, the most famous case of poisoning occurred after the war, was the one against the hated traitor Andrea Barozzi, the Venetian engineer, native of Crete, who in 1667 deserted to the Ottomans and would have informed them about the weak sectors of Candia. Barozzi had converted to Islam and after the war he had transferred to Constantinople. He had become a real obsession for the Venetian government, which had instructed its agents to eliminate him at any cost. For 10 years Venetian hired assassins committed themselves to hunt the "treacherous and very sad Barozzi"[6] wherever he went, and tried to kill him several times with false riots and increasingly strong poisons. Finally, in 1682, diamond powder mixed with a drink offered during a carnival fest in the residence of the French ambassador, put an end to Barozzi's life.

Poison and other ingredients were widely produced in Italy and also in the Ottoman Empire. However, the method considered as the best to eliminate enemies was to resort to contagion by imposing bacteriological weapons provided by the recurrent epidemics that had occurred in Crete since 1649. Probably the Venetians were the first to resort to these expedients, inspired by the news regarding the 'unctions', true or presumed, during the great plague of 1630–31. In 1645 Lunardo Foscolo, as general provveditor in Dalmatia, had a contract with the physician Michiel Angelo Salomone for preparing "a liqueur made from bile, bubos and sick coals combined with other ingredients", to infect hats and other clothing to be left in enemy territory.[7] The physician, enticed by the promises of generous compensation, prepared jars containing pestiferous substances. Foscolo informed the

4 *Ibid.*, b. 418, 1 December 1659.

5 *Ibid.*, *Capi del Consiglio dei Dieci, parti Segrete* f. 509 f. 45, 1655 and *Parti Comuni* f. 509, 1645.

6 *Ibid.*, *Inquisitori di Stato*, b 420, 5 August 1682.

7 Sick coals: a literal translation of *carboni d'appestati,* an ancient term which probably means some matter infected after exposing it close to sick people.

government about the effectiveness of the project and accurately described its details. However, the operation was postponed because the winter season was upon them, and it was known that the plague spread more rapidly in the summer. The idea was resumed in August 1651, but the absence of further news suggests that the operation was not carried out. The chemical war was practiced above all during the sieges, and once again, in 1646 Lunardo Foscolo urged the government to send him 1,000 pounds of arsenic to poison the water of the enemies besieging Novigrad. Then, in 1660, Francesco Morosini received 'toxins' to be spread to Crete with special sprinklers on the meadows grazed by Ottoman horses. In June 1646, Foscolo again urged the sending to Novigrad, then besieged by the Ottomans, of 'delayed poisons' to spoil the wells where the enemies supplied themselves. On 27 October, he finally received 1,000 lb of arsenic, but the surrender of Novigrad prevented him from pursuing the plan. Foscolo tried again between 31 August and 26 October, proposing to the government to poison 60 barrels of water with arsenic, to be sent with a trap to the enemy. His successors in Dalmatia often let themselves be seduced by the prospect of a decisive blow through the use of increasingly deadly poisons. The chemical warfare continued even after the war. On 22 March 1682, the provveditor Girolamo Corner proposed to poison the waters of some villages in Bosnia to prevent the repopulation of the borders.

Appendix IV

Succession of Officers

Succession of the *Kapudan Paşa* from 1645 to 1669

1645: Mascovich Youssuf (sentenced on 21 January 1646)
1646: Oglu Ammar
1647: Kara Musa Paşa (killed in action on 27 January 1647 off Chalkis)
1647: Kilavuz Fasli Paşa
1648: Ammaroglu Veli (sentenced)
1648: Voìnok Ahmed Paşa (killed in action on 29 May 1649 off Suda Island)
1649: Haidar Oldì
1650–51: Hosambegzade Alì, known as 'Mazzamamma'
1652: Koca Dervis Mehmed
1654–55: Kara Murad Paşa
1655: Zurnassan Paşa
1655–56: Kenan Sinau Paşa (sentenced)
1656: Sidi Ahmed
1657: Topal Mehmed (sentenced)
1658: Deli Hussein Paşa (sentenced)
1659–60: Ali Paşa
1661: Hosambegzade Alì 'Mazzamamma' (dead of illness at Chios, 15 May 1661)
1661: Hosambegzade Abdulkadir (son of the above)
1662: Merzifonlu Kara Mustafa
1664: Ibrahim Paşa
1666: Mustafa Paşa
1667: Kaplan Mustafa

Capitani Generali da Mar from 1645 to 1669

1645: Francesco Erizzo (the *doge*, died before he assumed the command)
1646: Giovanni Cappello
1648: Giovanni Battista Grimani (drowned on 7 March in the storm off Psará)
1648: Alvise Mocenigo
1652: Lunardo Foscolo (replaced due to illness by Alvise Mocenigo)
1654: Alvise Mocenigo (dead of illness on 27 December, at Candia-Heraklion)
1655: Girolamo Foscarini (dead of illness on 31 May, sailing to the Aegean Sea, replaced by Lorenzo Marcello)
1656: Lorenzo Marcello (killed in action on 26 June in the Dardanelles)

1657: Lazzaro Mocenigo (killed in action on 19 July in the Dardanelles)
1658: Francesco Morosini
1661: Giorgio Morosini
1664: Andrea Corner (after the renunciation of Battista Nani)
1667: Francesco Morosini

***Provveditori all'Armata* from 1645 to 1669**
1645: Francesco Molin
1646: Lorenzo Marcello
1647: Lunardo Mocenigo
1648: Antonio Bernardo
1649: Luigi Mocenigo
1652: Bernardo Morosini
1654: Francesco Morosini
1656: Barbaro Badoer (dead of illness on 16 August 1657)
1658: Antonio Barbaro
1659: Lorenzo Corner
1660: Antonio Barbaro (suspended in October 1660)
1661: Francesco Mocenigo
1662: Andrea Corner
1664: Pietro Diedo
1666: Girolamo Pesaro
1668: Caterino Corner (killed in action at Candia-Heraklion, 31 May 1669)
1669: Andrea Corner

Capitani delle Navi from 1645 to 1669
1645: Antonio Cappello
1646: Tommaso Morosini (killed in action on 27 January 1647 off Chalkis)
1647: Bernardo Morosini
1648: Jacopo Riva
1651: Luca Francesco Barbaro
1653: Giuseppe Dolfin
1655: Lazzaro Mocenigo
1656: Marco Bembo
1658: Girolamo Contarini
1662: Pietro Diedo
1664: Girolamo Grimani
1667: Alessandro Molin
1669: Iseppo Morosini

Appendix V

Naval Battles and Casualties

Foça, 12 May 1649
Venetians and Maltese: commander Jacopo da Riva
19 ships: *Ruota della Fortuna, Croce Dorata, Tre Re, Mercante Diletto, Principessa, Giacomo, Carità, Esperienza, Madonna della Vigna, Giove, Profeta Samuel, Amburgense, Sacrificio d'Abram, Orca Negro, San bartolamio, Francese, San Felipe* (Maltese), *Fregata Contarini.*

Casualties: 110 dead and wounded

Ottomans: Haidar Oldi, *kapudan paşa*
11 sailing ships
10 galleasses
72 galleys

Casualties: 9 sailing ships sunk and 1 captured; 3 galleasses sunk and 1 captured; 2 galleys sunk and 1 captured

Paros-Naxos, 7–10 July 1651
Venetians: Captain General Alvise Mocenigo
28 sailing ships: *Liocorno Bianco, Giovanni Battista, Aquila Negra, Arma di Venezia, Profeta Daniel,San Giobbe, San Zorzi Grande, Maria Elizabeta, Principe Piccolo, Margarita, San Pietro, San Zorzi Piccolo, Madonna della Vigna, Aquila d'Oro, Dragon, Sacrificio d'Abram, Difesa, Ruota di Fortuna, Croce d'Oro, Damian, Tommaso Francesco, San Marco Grande, San Marco Piccolo, Beneditione, Profeta Samuel, Fregata Grimani,* plus two more unidentified ships
6 *galleazzas*
24 galleys

Casualties: 35 dead and 50 wounded

Ottomans: Hosambegzade Ali, *kapudan paşa*
55 sailing ships
6 *mavunas*
53 galleys

Casualties: 5 sailing ships sunk and 11 captured; 1 *mavuna* captured; 965 prisoners

First battle of the Dardanelles, 16 May 1654
Venetians: Giuseppe Dolfin, captain of the sailing ships
16 sailing ships: *San Zorzi Grande, Aquila d'Oro, Concordia, Casa di Nassau, San Zorzi Piccolo, Aquila Coronata, Orsola Bonaventura, Anna Bonaventure, San Michiel, Spirito Santo, Apollon, Margarita, San Giovanni, Conte Sdrini, Genovese Grande, Pinco Tremartino*
2 *galeazzas*
8 galleys

Casualties: 2 sailing ships sunk (*Aquila d'Oro* and *Orsola Bonaventura*) and 2 galleys sunk; 1 sailing ship captured (*Casa di Nassau*)

Ottomans: Murad Paşa, *kapudan paşa*
Main fleet:
30 sailing ships
6 *mavunas*
40 galleys

Reserve fleet:
14 sailing ships
22 galleys

Casualties: 2 sailing ships, 1 *mavuna* and 1 galley sunk

Second Battle of the Dardanelles, 21 June 1655
Venetians: Lazzaro Mocenigo, captain of the sailing ships
25 sailing ships: *Capitana, Aquila Coronata, Profeta Samuel, Tomaso Francesco, Campo d'Oche, Principessa Grande, Tre Re, Croce d'Oro, Sacrificio d'Abramo, Lepre Rosso, Principessa Piccola, Corona, Gallo d'Oro, Ercole Grande, Re David, Isabella Maria, David e Golia, Pesce Triglio, Arma di Nassau, Lionessa, Arma di Lech, Sant'Antonio di Padova, Leon Negro*
4 *galeazzas*
6 galleys

Casualties: 1 sailing ship sunk (*David Golia*); 126 dead and 180 wounded

Ottomans: Murad Paşa, *kapudan paşa*
36 sailing ships
8 *mavunas*
60 galleys

Casualties: 11 sailing ships sunk; 1 *mavuna* sunk; 1 galley sunk; 358 prisoners

Third Battle of the Dardanelles, 26 June 1656
Venetians: Captain General Lorenzo Marcello

29 sailing ships: *Tomaso Francesco, Principessa grande, Tre Re, Croce d'Oro, Sacrificio d'Abram, Aquila Coronata, Profeta Samuel, Arma di Nassau, Lionessa, Arma di Lech, Leon Negro, Madonna del Carmine, Santa Caterina, Profeta Elia, San Bartolamio, Fama Volante, Ercole, Rosa Bianca, Speranza,Principe di Colognia, San Pietro, San Marco, Santa Margherita, Paramore, Fregata Contarini,* plus two more unidentified ships
7 galeazzas
24 galleys

Casualties: 2 sailing ships sunk (*Arma di Nassau* and *San Pietro*), 1 stranded and then abandoned (*San Marco*), 207 dead, 260 wounded and 94 missing

Maltese: don Gregorio Carafa
7 galleys

Casualties: 40 dead and 100 wounded

Ottomans: Kenan Sinau, *kapudan paşa*
4 great sailing ships
24 sailing ships
2 *pinchi*
9 *mavunas*
61 galleys

Casualties: 4 great sailing ships captured, 22 sailing ships sunk; 2 merchants captured; 4 *mavunas* sunk and 5 captured; 34 galleys sunk and 13 captured

Fourth Battle of the Dardanelles, 17–19 July 1657
Venetians: Captain General Lazzaro Mocenigo
29 sailing ships: *Aquila Coronata, San Zorzi Grande, Paramore, Profeta Elia, Rosa Moceniga, Zardin d'Olanda, Tamburlano, Principessa Reale, Principe di Venezia, Piccola Fortuna, Principessa Grande, Principessa Piccola, Gallo d'Oro,* plus 7 more unidentified sailing ships.
7 galeazzas
31 galleys

Casualties: 1 galley sunk; 190 dead, wounded and missing

Ottomans: Topal Mehmed, lieutenant *kapudan paşa*
28 sailing ships
10 *mavunas*
61 galleys

Casualties: 4 sailing ships sunk and 1 captured; 1 *mavuna* sunk; 1 galley captured

Appendix VI

Fleets

Naval forces for the sea campaigns from 1645 to 1657

		1645	1646	1647	1648	1649	1650	1651	1652	1653	1654	1655	1656	1657
Venetians & Aux.	galleys	61	48	52	24	26	30	24	28	22	22	24	31	32
	galleasses	4	4	4	5	6	6	6	6	6	6	6	7	7
	sailing ships	36	24	29	27	25	24	27	22	21	18	25	29	29
Ottomans	galleys	75	55	65	40	72	52	53	60	60	62	60	61	61
	mavunas	?	6	6	5	10	6	6	4	5	4	8	9	10
	sailing ships	40	?	37	?	20	19	55	18?	34	34	36	28	28

Naval forces for the sea campaigns from 1658 to 1669

		1658	1659	1660	1661	1662	1663	1664	1665	1666	1667	1668	1669*
Venetians & Aux.	galleys	36	37	38	35	30	24	24	22	16	45	30	23
	galleasses	6	6	6	6	6	6	6	6	5	5	6	6
	sailing ships	22	24	30	20	18	15	10	7	35	5	10	8
Ottomans	galleys	50?	50	?	70	60	35	36	30	38	?	36	36?
	mavunas	8	10	10?	?	?	?	8	9	8	?	?	?
	sailships	27	30	30?	?	17	?	18	18	34	54?	20	24?

Sources: Brusoni, Valiero, Nani Mocenigo, von Hammer-Purgstall.

* For the campaign of 1669 has to be added 15 French sail ships and 13 galleys arrived in June.

Appendix VII

Regiments and Battle Order

Italian and Corsican Infantry Regiments and Battalions

Year	Designation (Colonel)	Nationality	Campaigns	Licensed
1646	*Ornano*	Corsican	Crete	1646?
1646	*Bretton*	Italian	Dalmatia	1658?
1646	*Scotto*	Italian	Dalmatia	1653?
1647	*Grassi*	Italian	Crete	1647?
1647	*Sottovia*	Italian	Dalmatia	1649
1647	*Freccia*	Italian	Dalmatia	1648
1647	*Prestatori*	Italian	Dalmatia	1648?
1647	*Prete*	Italian	Dalmatia and Crete	1660?
1647	*Pellizzari*	Italian	Dalmatia	1650?
1647	*Cavaliere della Teloniera*	Italian	Dalmatia	1648?
1647	*Pallavicini*	Italian	Dalmatia and Crete	1649?
1648	*Peri*	Corsican	Dalmatia, Aegean Sea & Crete	1668
1652	*Farnese*	Italian	Aegean Sea and Crete	1657?
1662	*Bacigalupo*	Corsican	Crete	1662?
1665	*Villanova*	Italian	Aegean Sea and Crete	1667?
1666	*Pietro Antonio Furietti*	Italian	Aegean Sea and Crete	1668?
1666	*Michiel'Angelo Furietti*	Italian	Aegean Sea and Crete	1668?
1666	*Maron*	Italian	Crete, defence of Candia	1669
1666	*Frigerio*	Italian	Crete, defence of Candia	1668
1666	*Cremaschi*	Italian	Crete, defence of Candia	1667?
1666	*Sagramola*	Italian	Crete	1666
1666	*Zacco*	Italian	Crete	1666
1666	*Marrone*	Italian	Crete	1666
1666	*Restori*	Italian	Crete, defence of Candia	1668
1666	*Spada*	Italian	Crete	1666
1666	*Conti*	Italian	Crete	1666
1666	*Bianco*	Italian	Crete	1666
1666	*Evangelista*	Italian	Crete	1666

1667	*Marini*	Italian	Crete, defence of Candia	1668?
1667	*Imberti*	Italian	Crete, defence of Candia	1668
1667	*Zanetti*	Italian	Crete, defence of Candia	1668
1668	*Aldrovandi de Marè*	Italian	Crete, defence of Candia	1669

Oltramontane and French Infantry Regiments

Year	Designation (Colonel)	Nationality	Campaigns	Licensed
1643	*Coppet*	Swiss	Istria	1647
1644	*Furstenau,* 1648 *Sorgo*	German	Istria and Dalmatia	1649
1645	*Solms,* 1646 *Antonini*	German	Dalmatia	1648?
1645	*Prinz Philipp von Böhmen*	German	Crete?	1646?
1645	*Valletta*	Swiss	Crete	1646?
1645	*Burlamacchi*	Swiss?	Mainland?	1645
1645	*Beaucastel*	French?	Crete?	1645
1646	*Holzhab*	Graubund?	Dalmatia	1648?
1647	*Longueval*	Walloon	Crete?	1647
1648	*Wertmüller*	Swiss	Mainland and Dalmatia	1650
1648	*Remorantin*	French	Crete, defence of Candia	1649
1649	*Salis*	Swiss	Crete, defence of Candia	1649
1651	*Degenfeld,* 1653 *Herberstein*	German	Dalmatia and Crete	1662
1651	*Aspremont,* 1658 *Weiss*	Swiss	Dalmatia	1660
1653	*Büller,* 1654 *Glau*	Graubund	Dalmatia	1657
1653	*Keller*	Swiss	Crete	1655
1654	*Hanenyus*	German?	Dalmatia	1654?
1654	*Dansse,* 1661 *Locher?*	Swiss	Crete	1665?
1655	*Chevalier de Rosis*	French	Aegean Sea, Tenedos, and Lemnos	1658?
1655	*Labauda*	French	Aegean Sea, Tenedos and Lemnos	1658?
1660	*Gremonville*	French	Crete	1661?
1660	*De Bas*	French	Crete	1661?
1660	*Spaar*	German	Crete	1663?
1660	*Stalmocher*	German	Crete	1663?
1661	*Falkner*	Swiss	Crete?	1661?
1662	*Faret*	Swiss	Crete?	1662?
1665	*Doglione,* 1667 *Venturini*	German	Crete, defence of Candia	1667
1666	*Friesheim*	German	Crete, defence of Candia	1667
1666	*Wertmüller*	Swiss	Crete, defence of Candia	1668?
1666	*de la Motte*	Mixed	Crete, defence of Candia	1667
1666	*D'Anclam*	Mixed	Crete	1666
1667	*Degenfeld*	German	Crete, defence of Candia	1669

Auxiliary Infantry Regiments

Year	Designation (Colonel)	Nationality	Campaigns	Licensed
1648	*Mirogli*	Papal	Dalmatia	1651
1650	*Farnese*	Parma	Crete	1651
1652	*Sgamba*	Papal	Dalmatia	1652?
1653	*Facchinetti*	Papal	Dalmatia	1654?
1654	*Corsi*	Papal	Aegean Sea	1657
1660	*Masino*	Savoy	Crete	1660?
1660	*Masserac,* 1662 *Arborio*	Savoy	Dalmatia, Aegean Sea and Crete	1669
1660	*Aiassa,* 1665 *La Cerverie*	Savoy	Dalmatia and Crete	1669
1665	*Mattei*	Papal	Dalmatia and Crete	1668
1667	*Pistolozzi*	Tuscany	Dalmatia and Crete, defence of Candia	1669
1668	*Mirandola*	mixed*	Creta, Defence of Candia	1669

* Regiment formed by the Pope in association with the Dukes of Modena, Parma and Mantua.

Note for all the above tables: these lists have to be considered as incomplete. Due the absence of updated analysis in the archive sources, there are many problems identifying the unit when some authors relate the regiments or colonels without specifying whether it is a newly formed unit, or if the officer had replaced another commander. In addition, some units are registered as regiments even when they are individual battalions, such as the 500-man Papal *Mattei* Regiment, the 400-man Tuscan battalion under the Marquis Filippo Pistolozzi, or the *Cavaliere della Teloniera* musketeers battalion.

Hired Infantry Regiments

Year	Designation (Colonel)	Nationality	Campaigns	Licensed
1649	*Crossen*	Bavaria	Crete	1653?
1659	*Negron* or *De Baviere*	Bavaria	Crete	1660?
1661	*Sargan,* 1667 *Onolzpach*	Bayreuth	Crete	1668?
1668	*Waldeck* or *Leibregiment*	Lüneburg Celle	Creta, Defence of Candia	1670
1668	*Molesson*	Lüneburg Celle	Creta, Defence of Candia	1670
1668	*Rasfeld*	Lüneburg Celle	Creta, Defence of Candia	1670
1668	*Pallant*	Lüneburg Celle	Creta, Defence of Candia	1670
1669	*Harcourt*	Lorraine	Creta, Defence of Candia	1669
1669	*Bürhen*	Bavaria	Creta, Defence of Candia	1670
1669	*Kielmansegg*	Austrian	Creta, Defence of Candia	1670

Source: Brusoni; Valiero; Nani; Sansovino; Staudinger; Sichar; Bigge; Tessin.

Battle Order of the French Volunteers Corps for the Sortie of 16 December 1668

Commander: Duke de la Feuillade. Adjutant: de Tresmes

1st Brigade: Count de Saint Pol. Adjutants: du Pré; des Roches. Ensign: Derlingue.
Compagnie: de Chamilly; Jovency; Cavalier de Molets; Segeville; Tambonneau; de Chalain; Beau-Chevilliers; de Fourneaux. (230 infantrymen)
2nd Brigade: Duke de Caderousse. Adjutants: Dampierre; de Rouville. Ensign: Hongre.
Compagnie: de Refuge; Suze; de Torde; Flavigny; Bois-Commun; Eilncault. (175 infantrymen)
3rd Brigade: Duke de Villemaure. Adjutants: de la Montile; de Longuemer; Ensign: de la Coste.
Compagnie: de Bois le Corate; de Villemaure; Charmont; de Virginy (115 infantrymen)
4th Brigade: Duke de Chateu-Thierry. Adjutants: de Liomecourt; de Poncet; Ensign: de Gonor.
Compagnie: Saint Marcel; Mordivi; de la Forèt. (90 infantrymen)

French Expeditionary Corps, June–August 1669

Infantry Regiment	Strength	
	Brusoni	Bigge/Susane
Gardes Françaises	3 coy	3 coy
Espagny	4 coy	4 coy
Saint Valzer	4 coy	4 coy
Lignieres	4 coy	2 coy
Montaigu	4 coy	4 coy
Lorraine	4 coy	4 coy
Rozan	3 coy	3 coy
Bretagne	4 coy	2 coy
Conti	2 coy	2 coy
Grancey	4 coy	4 coy
Montpezat	2 coy	2 coy
Vendome	2 coy	2 coy
La Fere	2 coy	2 coy
Chateau-Thierry	2 coy	2 coy
Jonzac	4 coy	4 coy
Rovergue	4 coy	4 coy
Reformed officers	2 coy	2 coy
TOTAL	54 coy	50 coy

535 Foot Guards; 4.490 infantrymen and 232 reformed officers (Bigge and Susane); 7,000 of infantry, cavalry and seamen (Brusoni).

Cavalry	Strength
Mosquetaires du Roi	2 coy
Cavalerie Légère	3 coy

223 *Mosquetaires du Roi* and 328 meistres of *cavalerie legere*.

Commanders in Chief: Duke Annes de Noailles; Lieutenant-General: De Bret

Brigade Generals: Castellan (Guards); De Choiseul (cavalry); Mareschal de Camp: Colbert (infantry)

General intendant: Delacroix; general commissar: Jacquiere.

Note: the 10 companies (800 infantrymen) of the *Harcourt* Regiment joined the French contingent, but the Duke of Lorraine recruited them, and the regiment is already considered in the 'Hired Regiments' table (above).

Appendix VIII

Venetian Forces in Crete

Venetian Garrison's Strength in Candia, 1646–1669

December 1646	4,045
April 1647	4,125
July 1647	4,000
February 1648	3,750
March 1648	4,000
April 1648:	4,550
May 1648	4,680
March 1649	5,000
September 1649	6,720
January 1650	5,210
May 1650	5,920
July 1650	5,870
September 1651	4,430
April 1652	4,010
August 1652	5,186
October 1653	4,490
May 1654	4,472
January 1656	4,637
February 1656	4,631
January 1657	4,371
May 1658	4,396
December 1661	3,873
March 1662	3,451
July 1662	3.320
December 1662	3,100
May 1663	3,125
June 1664	4,478
June 1666	4,012
April 1668	4,866
June 1668	4,000
August 1669	3,521
September 1669	2,500

Source: ASVe, *Provveditori da Terra e da Mar*, b. 429, b. 446, b. 455, b. 463, b. 470, b. 484, b. 499, b. 508, b 522, b. 525, b. 599, b. b.642, b. 651, b. 698.

Nationalities Inside Candia

	April 1648	**May 1650**	**September 1651**	**February 1656**
Oltramontani	1,750	1,738	1,624	1,649
Oltramarini	506	278	301	246
Italians	850	896	502	887
Greeks	848	790	852	687
Corsicans	345	489	997	112
	December 1661	March 1662	December 1662	May 1663
Oltramontani	1,231	1,182	1,061	1,200
Oltramarini	253	257	239	259
Italians	784	779	781	760
Greeks	679	665	534	540
Corsicans	102	385	100	100

Source: ASVe, *Provveditori da Terra e da Mar*, b. 445, b. 470, b. 491, b. 520, b. 595, b. 645, b. 650, b 670.

Flag Commentaries

Composite image, p.253

The evidence relating to Ottoman naval flags confirms the use of various colours and symbols, but some peculiarities are more common than others. 1. A large red ensign with three white crescents belonged to *kapudan paşa*, who hoisted it at the stern. Other ensigns belonging to Ottoman warships show white or yellow crescents on a green or azure-turquoise background, unless for the latter it could be a loss of pigment in the original colour. 2–3. White flags with a black star and blue and red bands, or azure-red-white belonged more often to the Ottoman merchant ships. 4–5. Red and green flags with white crescents or red and yellow, especially with the *zulfiqar* sword, identified Algierian ships, while white and red (6–7) were hoisted by the Tunisian navy. 8–9. Green flags with open or closed crescents, or red-white-green bands (8–9) belonged to Tripoli. Several flags represented here are preserved in the church of Santo Stefano's Knights in Pisa and many of them date back to the Cretan War. Sizes vary, but the flying is approximately more than two metres. 10. Along with the flags, in the army as well as in the navy the *tugh* was the most important insignia for the commander's identification. The gilded metal *tugh* with a black horse tail is preserved in the naval museum of Copenhagen, war booty of the Admiral Cort Adler, who fought with the Venetian fleet between 1658 and 1659. This is the only known example of a naval *tugh*. 11. A Venetian galley's large ensign represented in the "Codice Bassan", dating to the second half of the 17th century: a carmine red background with a St. Mark lion and golden yellow embroidery; white cross on black squares in the corners. 12. A Venetian mast ensign displayed the same symbols but with a simplified pattern: a carmine red background with golden yellow edge, and St. Mark lion as for the previous ensign. 13. The great banner hoisted on the galley's stern of the Santo Stefano order of Tuscany had colours and symbols similar to those of the Venetian and Maltese fleets: a background like the previous ensign, charged by a red cross on white. 14. The mast ensign of the Tuscan knights was the reverse of the Maltese one: a red cross on white background. 15. The great banner of the Holy Cross is mentioned many times in the sources for the Papal navy flagship; the example shown is a reconstruction after the most common insignia used in the 17th century: a white background, both saints and Christ are in natural colours; a black inscription ("Dissolve all his enemies!")

1
2
3
4
5
6
7
8
9
10
11
PAX TIBI MAR CE
EVAN GELI STA MEUS
12
13
14
15
DISSIPENTUR OMNES INIMICI EJUS!

Composite image, p.255

1. Each janissary's *orta* was identified by a number and more or less all the *ortas* were involved in the conflict, but only in a few cases we know which of them fought in Crete in a determinate campaign. In Johann von Hammer-Purgstall's history of the Ottoman Empire, six *ortas* are mentioned for the 1648 campaign: 14, 16, 19, 38, 51 and 53. Each unit displayed a symbol which indicated their own encampment and it could consist in a flag or symbols drawn on the top of the commander's tent. (From left to right, above to below) 14 and 16: white background; 38: a red snake on white; 51: black *zulfiqar*, green-yellow band, flame and background in white; 16 (alternative) green-black; 19: red on white; 53: a black-yellow crescent; 53 (alternative) a black musket with grey barrel. (Reconstruction after L.F. Marsigli, Stato Militare dell'Imperio Ottomanno, 1720). 2. The Bavarian infantry regiment von Bühren, in Venetian Service between 1669 and 1670, received a flag with a St. Mark's Lion possibly used with the colonel's insignia, which unfortunately has been lost. The use of flags with the Venetian symbol, even by hired foreign regiments, must have been common in the Venetian army. Note that in this flag, the St. Mark's lion is unsupported by the hind legs on the sea, as always represented in other flags of the period, but it may be caused by deterioration of the colour. Approximate size 190x190 cm; a gold-yellow lion and cross, emerald green hills outlined in yellow, azure background (after the original preserved in Bavaria). 3. Venetian infantry ensign, unknown unit, represented in the "Codice Bassan", late 17th century. This flag exemplifies the Venetian field ensign of the period. Usually each company carried an ensign with the captain's heraldry in the centre: a golden-yellow lion and war trophies on a carmine red background, brown hills outlined in silver, the coat of arms of the Gritti family: a white cross on black-white outlined in yellow, golden crown. 4. Infantry(?) banner, unknown unit; 1660. Striped flags used by Venetian land or naval forces are mentioned in several contemporary sources: black-white-red-azure. Similar flags were also used for purposes of reporting, as happened during the sortie in June of 1669, when a white and azure striped flag was hoisted on the ramparts to indicate the order for the assault. Approximate size 170x190 cm. 5. Heavy cavalry company standard, 1659. Approximate size 70x70 cm. 6. Papal field ensign: a white cross on a white background, yellow-golden mitre and keys with red cordon. This flag shows the common pattern of the Papal colours of the period, and in some case the flag was charged with the Pope's coat of arms in the centre. Papal flags were also carried by the French contingent which arrived in Crete on June 1669, to conceal the formal participation of the Louis XIV's soldiers in the conflict against the Porte. 7. Maltese infantry ensign: a white cross on scarlet red. Maltese ensigns were also carried in 1668 by the French volunteers under la Feuillade.

1
14
16
S
38
51
16
19
53
53
2
6
3
7
5
4

Black & White Image Commentaries

Part I: Oars, Sails and Soldiers

2. The Ottoman landing at Gognà beach in front of Chaniá occurred on 24 June 1645; it was, the first action of the conflict and the largest amphibious operation of the Cretan War, which involved nearly 200 ships and 60,000 men. The action was directed by Mascovich Yussuf, and startled the Venetians, who lost valuable time beforehand to gather their fleet in Crete. The Cretan fleet of galleys had four ships and another 10 had been prepared a few months before the threat was foreseen, but these latter had not yet completed their crews. (*Theatrum Europeum*, Frankfurt am Main, 1670)

3. Ibrahim I (r.1640–48), here in an imaginary portrait, was the untalented sultan who began the war against Venice. Before being deposed, he bankrupted the state finances. Among the many anecdotes about Ibrahim's personality, contemporary historians related his insane passion for zibeline furs and fat concubines. (*Theatrum Europeum*, Frankfurt am Main, 1670)

5. The remains of the fortification on the island of Agios Theodoros a few miles from Chaniá, on which now lies a small church with a few houses. Here, in June 1645, occurred one of the most dramatic acts of the war: the Ottoman assault against the Venetian garrison under Captain Biagio Zulian. Unable to receive relief, the Venetian commander would have set fire to the ammunition depot, causing the explosion of the fort. The little island was later reconquered by the Venetians, who demolished the fortifications. The island was occupied again by the Ottomans, who maintained it until 1668. (Author's photo)

6. The *kapudan paşa* was the chief admiral of Sultan's fleet. Here he is portrayed with the peculiar insignias of his rank: brocade *ust kürkü* kaftan, and small size turban, inspired by the traditional headdress used by Ottoman and Northern African sailors. Like his Venetian counterpart, *kapudan paşa* personally participated in the engagements and during the war two were

killed in action: Kara Musa Paşa died on January 1647 in the battle off Chalkis, while Voínok Ahmed was killed in May 1649, attempting to conquer the fortress of Suda Island. (M. la Haye, *Recueil de cent estampes representant differentes nations du Levant*, Paris 1714)

7. The European revisers of these mid-17th century Ottoman miniatures identify the figure to the left as a janissary from Cairo, while probably, this is a marine *azab*. The meaning of the word *azab* – bachelor – coincides with the same term used by the Venetians for indicating the members of the galley infantry picket guards. *Azab*, *levend* and *mensugat* were the Ottoman naval infantry. The *azab* belonged to the Sultan's fleet, while the others were recruited from the governors of the sea provinces, the same who competed in the formation of the *beylere* galleys squadron. A vast iconography is available about the *levend*, which portrays them always with naked arms, like the figure to right, while there is very scarce information concerning the *mensugat* corps. Unlike the land troops, who gave up bows and arrows at the beginning of the Cretan War, around 1650 individual weapons of the naval infantrymen still included a percentage of archers. (Ottoman mid-17th century miniatures from the Rålamb collection, Stockholm)

8. On board ship the Ottomans employed a variety of firearms, including portable guns like the ones depicted in the illustration. Although these weapons had some effect, the absence of standard equipment was symptomatic of the technological gap in the Ottoman fleet. (Illustration from Cevad Ahmed Beg, *Etat Militaire Ottoman depuis la Fondation de l'Empire jusqu'à nos jours*, 1892)

9. The Janissaries' ceremonial dress comprised special ornaments to be applied to their *ak börk* headgear. The miniature model of a galley identifies the soldier in the centre as belonging to the janissary *orta* 56, originally assigned to the surveillance of the Golden Horn residences, and quartered close to the naval arsenal of Galata. This particularity created confusion among some authors, who identified them as "naval janissaries". Instead, all the *kapikulu* infantrymen could be used on board ship, as was the case during the Fourth Battle of the Dardanelles. As members of the *kapikulu*, the janissaries followed the complex court protocol, which also strictly regulated the pattern of the clothing. The *ak börk* hat, typical of the Janissaries, was worn during the ordinary service at the court and in parade. The *kaftan* and the *entari* coat could be of various colours, although the more common was azure-turquoise. The yellow leather shoes identifies these janissaries as belonging to the *yayabeg* category. (Illustration from the *Codex Vindobonensis*, late 16th century, Vienna)

10., 11. The Ottomans disposed a composite military structure, including several special corps such as the *dely* raiders of the *serrhadkulu* cavalry. These borderers were organised in troops of 40 horses, employed in recognition and intruding duties and garrisoned in the strongholds near the frontier. This cavalry played a major role against the Venetian domains in Dalmatia and

Albania, especially for counteracting the Morlachs' action in Bosnia. Though the Ottomans maintained a constant pressure on the border, launching several raids between 1650 and 1665, they caused only minor damage without gaining territorial conquest. (Hyeronimus Beck's Exaratae turcarum imperatorum, capitaneorum. Immagina, habitus, ludos, caerimonias… Österreichische Nationalbibliothek Vienna, early 17th century)

12. Köprülü Mehmed was appointed as grand vizier on 15 September 1656, in the middle of the severe economic and political crisis, aggravated by internal rebellion and external threats, which were dividing the Empire. He introduced severe and brutal countermeasures to restore authority and political stability to the state. He prevailed on the rebels in Anatolia and in 1658 achieved another important success with the end of the Venetian blockade of the Dardanelles. Under the energic leadership of Köprülü Mehmed, the Porte could continue the war for the conquest of Crete. (Mid-17th century Austrian print. (Author's archive)

13. The *Capitano Generale da Mar* was the most important military position in Venice, being the Doge's lieutenant in the navy and army. Occasionally in the history of Venice the same person held both offices, as happened for a short time at the beginning of the Cretan War when the aged Francesco Erizzo, Doge since 1631, became the high military commander, but his activity was curtailed by death in January 1646. (Engraving after the Doge's portrait by Bernardo Strozzi, Author's archive)

14. The captain general's carmine red ensign, after an illustration of Giovanni Grevenbroch, published in 1757. The Venetian high commander directed the fleet on board a "bastard galley" recognisable by three lights on the stern, the great banner of St. Mark with the golden ball, and two square flags hoisted onto the mainmast and foremast.

17. Carpenters and other craftsmen building vessels, from a Venetian 18th-century panel of a carpenter's workshop. Both the Ottoman and the Venetian arsenals held all the main activities such as gunpowder making and wood collecting. The works were organised in chain production as in a modern factory, where thousands of workers and sailors operated on different stages. In Venice, the average number of workers at the end of the Cretan war was 5,000, a considerable figure, as in the whole of Venice lived 100,000 inhabitants.

18. For Venice, the galley was not just a warship but also a symbol of the state power. Furthermore, galleys were also used for a multitude of ceremonial duties. Every arrival of a Republic's high official in the province represented a public event and part of the standard decorum was for them to arrive into the place of service aboard a galley. Whenever possible, additional effort was put into maintaining this protocol. For example in March 1651, during the stay of general provveditor Foscarini in Trogir, the new extraordinary provveditor of Trogir and Split also arrived into the area aboard a sailing ship.

This moved Foscarini, in order to "upkeep the dignity of this service in the town so close to the enemy" to relinquish his own galley to the extraordinary provveditor for his ceremonial entry into Split. (Captain general's galley, oil painting by anonymous artist, dated 1680; private collection, Venice)

22. Count Achilles de Remorantin entered in Venetian service in 1646 as a colonel of an infantry regiment recruited in France by himself. The rank of colonel had already appeared in the Venetian army in the 16th century. Starting from 1510, *colonelli* are already mentioned in charge of the command of corps which totalled more than 3,000 men, distinguished by captains, who led companies of 100 or 200 men. In 1539 had also appeared a rank similar to lieutenant colonel. In the same year, the Senate decreed that the command of a military corps could be issued only to captains who had commanded at least 100 men in time of war or already served as a lieutenant colonel. (Author's archive)

25. Venetian *corazza* (cuirassier), mid 17th century. All contemporary sources relate that the Venetian heavy cavalry employed metal plates more than their foreign colleagues. For this feature, the Venetian cuirassiers received the nickname "iron pots". Later documentary sources show that this trend survived a long time in Venice. The cuirassier depicted wears a classic leather coat under a three-quarter cavalry corselet manufactured in Brescia. The weaponry includes a heavy Walloon sword, a wheellock carbine and a pair of saddle pistols. (Author's illustration)

Part III: Judith and Holophernes: Diplomacy and Strategy in the Cretan War

38. Ferdinando II de' Medici, Grand Duke of Tuscany, here portrayed in Turkish dress. The Grand Duke was in order of importance the third major Italian ally of Venice. His effort developed with the occasional sending of the order of St. Stephen's galleys. The interest of the Medici in the Levant increased specifically under Ferdinand II, who had close relations with the rebel leaders of the Druze of Lebanon and planned a raid to Jerusalem to dismantle the Holy Sepulchre and transport it to Florence. (Painting by Justus Sustermans, Palazzo Pitti, Florence)

Part IV: *Campo di Marte dell'Europa*

40. Oarsmen received harsh treatment, although they were a human engine, and therefore of capital importance for the conduct of naval campaigns. To complete the ranks, usually Venice resorted to volunteers and convicts, joining them with the *leva da Mar* (sea levy) supplied by the domains, and only sporadically turned to slaves and war prisoners. During the war the Ottomans easily managed to replace the loss of oarsmen, while the Venetians suffered a shortage of men on several occasions. The tremendous sinking off Psará, in March 1648, caused the loss of 18 galleys and three quarters of the oarsmen. The rate of recruitment did not allow the light fleet to recover from

the disaster, affecting for a long time the overall number of galleys available, which never exceeded 28 units.

41. Ottoman sailors and oarsmen, after the *Codex Vindobonensis*, presented to the Emperor Rudolf II of Habsburg in late 16th century. Many historians insist that in the Ottoman galleys oarsmen were only slaves or prisoners of war, and certainly the Ottomans employed them in greater numbers than their adversaries, but the presence of volunteers was not irrelevant, equivalent to Christian *buonavoglia*. To control an unruly crew of enslaved oarsmen constituted a not insignificant risk. Between 1667 and 1668 the oarsmen of two Ottoman galleys mutinied: officers, sailors and soldiers jumped into the sea and surrendered themselves and their ships to the Venetians.

45. *Oltramarini* foot soldiers, second half of the 17th century. 1) *crovato* (croatian) or *scappolo* of a picket guard on galleys and galleasses; 2) Albanian *Cimerioto* irregular of foot; 3) Morlachs. This reservoir of recruits from the Eastern Adriatic domains proved very useful to the Venetian strategy. Specifically, their relatively low salary offered economic advantages. Additionally, these troops served in many tactical roles: as landing troops, light infantry, and scouts in sieges or open field. Obviously, the *Oltramarini* from Dalmatia and Kotor also fought on the domestic front during the conflict and participated alongside Italian and auxiliary units in several actions against the Ottomans in Bosnia and Albania. (Author's illustration with kind permission of the Web Magazine *History and Uniforms*)

Part V: War on the Sea

46. The "Queen of the Mediterranean Sea", the galley, represented the main framework of the Venetian and Ottoman fleets during the Cretan war. The galley, being primarily a warship, had a very small hold, capable of containing only the ammunition and provisions, particularly water and biscuit, and other scarce supplies. Consequently, it had no space to house the crew and the soldiers, who had to live outdoors. In practice, the only accommodation was that located in the sterncastle, reserved for the captain. The small tonnage – about 50 tons at full load – made it very fast: with wind in favour, a galley with a full complement of oarsmen, was able to reach 7–8 sea knots, but could only sail with calm sea and in the event of a storm had to reach a safe place as quickly as possible. The classic mid-17th century galley had two masts with Latin sails, and 24–27 benches, fewer than the Venetian *galera bastarda* and the Ottoman *orta*, usually reserved for the respective fleet commanders. Usually the ordinary Venetian galley needed at least 180–200 oarsmen, 50–60 men among sailors and other personnel including officers, 10 artillerymen and 48 *scapoli* (bachelors) or infantry pickets for guard and sentry duty. In the Ottoman galleys crews were of similar proportions, except for a higher number of soldiers. The armament was concentrated in the bow, where at the end of the deck there were large calibre guns. In general, the galleys were fitted with 50 or 30 pound pieces (in Venice the full weight of the ball was in pounds thinner: 50 pounds would correspond to the common

32 pounds). On the forecastle, with the main piece were placed two or four guns of different calibres, plus other minor pieces, usually falconets used as anti-personnel weapons. Compared to an Ottoman galley, the Venetian one was more efficient. In the second half of the 17th century innovations had been introduced in construction methods, the principal of which was the introduction of the rear galley pole. The arsenal technicians were perfectly informed in the study of construction techniques and naval architecture was built with a scientific approach to the project. The Ottomans did not use special paint for their galleys, while the Venetian sources show ships painted in red; on some occasions the captain general's galleys were in black. (Venetian galley, after an Italian drawing by an anonymous artist, second half of the 17th century)

47. The galleass was an invention of the Venetians, who introduced it at the battle of Lepanto, and it was later imitated by other navies including the Ottomans, who called this ship *mavuna*. During the Cretan War both sides continuously employed this type of ship, particularly effective in offensive actions, thanks to the high concentration of guns in the bow. Galleasses and *mavuna* were characterised by the presence of two castles – one forward and one aft – had from 32 to 46 oar benches and could carry up to 900 crew members, three fifths of whom were oarsmen. At the beginning of the war the Venetian galleasses were armed with 22 guns, of which two were 50 pounds, and four 30 pounds. Four of these large guns were colubrine, longer and more powerful than ordinary guns. Altogether there were eight culverins ranging from 50 to 14 pounds, plus another 14 guns of 30, 20 and six pounds. The galleys also had 12 *petriere* of six, three and two pounds and a number of small calibre weapons. In other galleasses, probably later, six pieces were arranged in the bow, namely two 50-pound colubrines, two 14-pound and two six-pound guns, as well as six *petriere* of various calibres. In the centre there were eight guns, two 30-pound and six 20-pound colubrine, with another eight *petriere*; and finally finding a place in the stern another eight guns, two 30-pound and two 14-pound colubrines alongside four six-pound guns. The armament of the Ottoman ship followed similar criteria, but while the Venetians used a growing number of modern iron cannon, in the Sultan's fleet were still used bronze weapons, including some guns dating back to the previous century. The Venetian galleasses, like the galleys, were usually painted in red. In the early 18th century, the galleass of the Venetian squadron commander appears completely black, but in other sources the colour would seem to be associated with subordinate captains' units. (Ottoman *mavuna*, copy after Hyeronimus Beck's *Exaratae turcarum imperatorum imperatorum, capitaneorum. Immagina, habitus, ludos, caerimonias…* Österreichische Nationalbibliothek Vienna, early 17th century)

51. Lazzaro Mocenigo was one of the most brilliant and daring Venetian naval officers of the war. In 1655, as captain of the sailing ships, he defeated the Ottoman fleet in the Second Battle of the Dardanelles; the next year, volunteering under Lorenzo Marcello as simply the captain of a vessel, he contributed to the success of his side by leading the assault against the

Ottoman fleet, and losing his right eye. On 15 May 1657, only with his galleys, he attacked and defeated off Chios island 14 Barbary vessels under the Dutch renegade Mehmet Bey. The portrait, painted after his appointment as captain general, shows all the attributes reserved for the highest military rank of the Republic. (Portrait of Lazzaro Mocenigo as captain general, by Francesco Maffei; Naval History Museum, Venice)

57. The Venetian fleet, under Francesco Morosini, assaults the port of Volos in the Aegean Sea, May 1655. The Venetian fleet applied the tactics of direct landing on enemy ports and costal strongholds long before the change of strategy devised by Francesco Morosini. The Venetian assault at Kos took place in 1651 under the command of Lunardo Foscolo and followed similar actions performed against Samos and Leros. At Kos the Venetians destroyed the port and sank eight transports destined for Chaniá, but failed to seize the fortress. (Detail from the cycle of frescoes on Francesco Morosini's enterprises, Museo Correr, Venice)

59. After Paleocastro, the attempt to land at Suda Island in June 1649 was another rare amphibious action attempted by the Ottoman fleet after the landing of 1645. Despite the great resources spent by the Ottomans, the Venetian garrison – led by Pietro Diedo – repelled the assault with their batteries, firing on the surface of the water, and thanks to the efficient fortifications renovated a few years previous by the engineers sent from Venice. In this action the Ottoman *kapudan paşa* Voynok Ahmed was cut in two by a cannon shot. After this valorous defence Pietro Diedo began a brilliant career, reaching the rank of provveditor of the fleet and captain of the sailing ships. (Author's archive)

60. Alessandro dal Borro, subject of the Grand Duke of Tuscany, was a veteran of the Thirty Years' War who had served in the Imperial and Spanish Armies under Ottavio Piccolomini. In 1654 he entered Venetian service as *generale dello sbarco* (General of the Landing). Dal Borro performed a series of successful operations in the Aegean Sea between 1655 and 1656, including the landing at Volos and the conquest of Lemnos and Bozcaada. Sadly, the already fragile health of the general worsened in a short time, and before the end of the year dal Borro died in Corfu aged 56. (Painting attributed to Charles Mellin, Gemäldgalerie, Berlin)

64. Ottoman landings at Bozcaada and Lemnos executed in the summer of 1657 allowed the recapture of the two major islands in front of the Dardanelles, both conquered the year before by the Venetian fleet. The proximity of targets to the mainland allowed the Ottomans to land troops while minimising the risk of being intercepted by the enemy fleet. The conquest was also facilitated by the conduct of the Venetian provveditors Loredan and Contarini, who surrendered almost without fighting. For this behaviour both officials were deleted from the nobility and sentenced to death in absentia. (Ottoman 17th century miniature depicting a siege scene, from the *Manuscript Cicogna*, Museo Correr Library, Venice)

65. In 1658 a plan was designed to land a corps of troops at Chaniá, to wrest the port from the Ottomans and force them to leave Crete. The court of Modena acted as base for the operation, helping itself to the collection of forces sending 600 soldiers and 200 oarsmen, who participated in the campaign of war between August and September 1660. (Illustration from *L'Idea di un Prencipe et Heroe Christiano*, Modena 1659)

Part VI: Field Campaigns: Sieges

69. Walloon general Gilles De Haes entered Venetian service in 1645 and become Governatore delle Armi of Crete in late 1648, having served on the fleet as general of the landing. De Haes did not come from an aristocratic family and he had climbed the military hierarchy beginning as private soldier. This exposed him more than once to unflattering opinions, although he was a clever and capable officer. In 1649, during the second siege of Candia, he directed vigorously the defence, successfully rejecting all the Ottoman assaults. However, on several occasions his temperament led him to collide with the Venetian provveditors, and the Senate suspended him twice from military service. From 1651 to 1652 De Haes was reinstated as commander in Crete, then in 1658 became military governor of Dalmatia, where he died a year later aged 60. (Illustration after *Gilles De Haes, homme de guerre du XVII siècle*, by Charles Rahlenbeck, Bruxelles, 1854)

70. The ancient walls of Candia were renewed between 1538 and 1539 by Michele Sanmicheli. At the beginning of the war the work was still unfinished; technical delays and a chronic shortage of money had prevented several improvements and many sectors remained obsolete compared to the updates introduced by Dutch engineers. The works continued until the eve of the siege in 1648 with the building of a new battery for the guns, and an accumulation of large amounts of earth to build an elevated battery, cover the bunkers and fill embankments. Visible in the illustration, made at the time of the first siege, are the external works in their original configuration before the enlargements that were continued until 1667.

73. For more than 20 years the port of Candia represented the only link between Venice and the defenders, whose resistance was effective thanks to supplies sent by sea. Although isolated from the rest of the overseas domains, the assiduous work of Francesco Morosini – in his role of governor between 1655 and 1657 – granted access to international trade with dispensation of fees in favour of merchants and encouraged privateers to sell stolen goods on site. In the same period, new galleys were built, something which had not occurred since 1648. Before the war 31,000 people lived in Candia, but at the surrender of the garrison only 4,000 inhabitants remained. (Author's photo)

74. The bastion and the external defence of Panigrà, as they appeared during the Ottoman assault in the summer of 1667. In the drawing Venetian soldiers armed with muskets are recognisable behind the palisade in the ditches and on the ramparts, while mixed corps of musketeers and pikemen are deployed

as a tactical reserve in front of the retreats. Panigrà was the theatre of one of the most spectacular mining battles, which took place in early March 1668. The Ottoman miners were advancing with a gallery under the ravelin and were preparing a huge mine, but the Venetians had noticed it and had prepared a countermine under the enemy. The Ottomans discovered the Venetian work and dug a new tunnel even deeper to place a second mine and finally triggered it. The explosion caused the collapse of the whole area, weakened by the overlapping tunnels, causing the deaths of hundreds of miners and soldiers of both sides. The Ottomans tried to trigger the first mine under the ravelin, throwing in all sorts of weapons, but their efforts were thwarted by the courage of a Venetian engineer who, despite the flames and smoke, prevented the threat. (Author's archive)

75. The impressive network of tunnels dug by the Venetians in the sector of Sant'Andrea, despite the rocky terrain and proximity to the sea, with the countermine prepared before the end of 1668. The veteran of the siege captain Johann Scheither wrote: "When a mine exploded, the whole town was shaken as it was an earthquake … which was produced by the fact that mines were excavated within the rock or very compact terrain and then men flew into the air along with rocks and earth with so horrible crash that was terrible to behold, and sometimes could see people do so many twists and turns in the air." Venetian countermines represented a nightmare for the Ottomans throughout the siege and even after the surrender of Candia, the fear of being victims of a trap made them hesitate for long time before entering the city. The events of the war left indelible traces in the Ottoman common people, and the impression became so strong that, when someone wanted to curse someone else, he wished him to go to the siege of Candia. (Illustration after the *Novissima Praxis Military*, 1672)

81. François de Vendôme, Duke of Beaufort (1616–1669). Having quarrelled with the French monarchy during the Fronde, Beaufort was reconciled with Mazzarino and in 1658 was named general superintendent of navigation and chief of the navy. In 1664, he directed the expedition against the pirates of Algiers, which concluded unsatisfactorily. Five years later Louis XIVappointed him as commander-in-chief for the expedition to Crete. The fleet left Toulon in early May 1669 and transported to Candia 7,000 soldiers and sailors with 15 sail ships and 13 galleys. Beaufort was the major supporter of the great sortie executed on 29 June, personally directed by him. The action ended with a defeat and the Duke was killed. His body was brought back to France with great pomp, and given official honours. (Engraving after the Beaufort's portrait by Jean Nocret, Château de Coucy, France)

83. Model of a Venetian 9 lb *Sagro*, after Tommaso Moretti's *Trattato di Artiglieria*, Venice 1665. The Venetians employed a large amount of artillery in Candia. In 1668 there were 340 pieces, of which about 90 were large-calibre guns or mortars and other 110 small weapons "still usable". The opinion of the eyewitnesses concerning the effectiveness of these weapons was not positive. On this subject Colonel von Bigge, quoting Captain Johann

Scheither, said that:

> The Venetians obtained poor results with their Artillery, [which] were largely useless, as far as is necessary for the maintenance and the manufacture of carriages, wheels, ammunition was in Venice. The gunners still present, mostly Italians and Greeks, were real beasts, and so inept that they would not listen, nor where to hit where they pulled, and sometimes did fire on us, bringing us harm and also shot dead a lot of our soldiers, so we had to beware their guns rather than those of the enemy. And when these men were playing us a shot of this kind, they laughed at our backs, nor was there ever an officer who intervened in this regard. To this end, they were forced, when they wanted to shoot, to make us a signal with a weather vane, so that we could take shelter from their shot. (With kind permission of the Querini-Stampalia collection, Venice)

84. Since 1667 the Ottoman artillery employed for the siege of Candia an increasing number of large-calibre mortars. Some reports related about pieces up to 300 pounds, shooting explosive or incendiary projectiles into the city. The Ottoman mortars were in bronze and mounted on wooden carriages reinforced with iron fittings in large quantity. To judge from contemporary evidence, the Ottomans did not use paint or protective varnish. (Illustration from L.F. Marsigli, *Stato Militare dell'Imperio Ottomano*, 1720)

85. A late-17th century Ottoman rampart musket, reproduced in the work of Cevad Ahmed Beg: *Etat Militaire Ottoman depuis la Fondation de l'Empire jusqu'à nos jours*, published in Istanbul in 1882. These heavy weapons, in some cases more than two metres long, were widely used at Candia to target the defensive positions and more than once the Ottoman marksmen killed important enemy officers.

Appendices

90. Stjepan Subotich, known as Sorich, in a 1688 dated imaginary portrait. In 1647, after being a famous and feared leader of the Morlachs, he answered to the Ottomans who, admiring his value, flattered him to return under their protection: "For fifty years I have been a slave of a tyrant, it will not be great think, if I will live the rest of my life …under the rule of the most right Republic of the world."

91. Much more than on the galleys, the Ottomans employed prisoners of war for forced works. In general the treatment of prisoners was bad, especially if they were not important people and unable to pay a ransom. In the spring of 1668 the Venetians freed over 1,000 prisoners held by the North African corsairs, and took them for the defence of Candia. (Illustration from the *Codex Vindobonensis*, late 16th century, Vienna)

92. A Greek infantryman and sailor. The Greek communities subject to Venice provided a large number of soldiers to the Republic, which employed them both on ships and on land. In Candia the garrison was composed of

either Italians, *Schiavoni* or *Oltramontani*, but included always a significant number of Hellenic soldiers. In 1651, for example, the garrison consisted of 4,440 men of whom 1,005 came from Greece. Despite their presence, little is known about the clothing and equipment of the Greek infantry in the 17th century, but thanks to an ex-voto preserved in a church of the Mani Peninsula, dating back to the last years of the war, it is possible to light the darkness. The anonymous infantryman is portrayed on a silver relief and this unfortunately does not provide any details about colours, but the drawing shows some typical elements of traditional Greek costume, such as a floppy hat and wide breeches, mixed with clothing of Western origin. Several iconographic sources indicate that in late 17th century the "national" infantry dressed mostly in red. Like the *Oltramarini* troops, the Greeks were also light infantrymen armed with musket and sword.

The Greek sailor is reconstructed after an embroidered figure on a wedding pillow preserved in the Benaki Museum, Athens, probably manufactured in the Ionian Islands, and dating to the last quarter of the 17th century. The sailor wore a typical white cotton *fustanella* skirt, a short-quilted jupon with side buttoning on a white shirt, black headgear and stockings.

93. Artillery tools and projectiles of the Venetian 17th-century military treaty by Tommaso Moretti. The belief that the war for Candia had not affected weapons development and combat tactics is more theoretical than substantial, and this is partly demonstrated by the high number of printed works that appeared in Venice. Although in the 17th century the lagoon city was one of the major publishing centres of Europe, out of 123 treaties written between 1600 and 1699, more than 10 percent were printed in Venice.

Colour Plate Commentaries

Commentary relates to the figures from left to right

A. Venetian Crete, 1645–48

Cretan Militia Horseman
In Crete the Venetians disposed cavalry and infantry militia mounting on paper to more than 10,000 men, which according to the Republic's plans could be increased up to 70,000. While the infantry was formed mainly of Cretan peasants, the "Creoles" and the Venetian owners constituted the *Feudati* (feudal) cavalry. These units, almost always with low grade and outdated weaponry, proved to be unreliable and useless, and then, before the siege of Candia, they were largely disbanded with a few exceptions. This horseman wears a mix of Greek items, such as the round black headgear and Western European clothing and accessories. (Reconstruction after a particular in the Crucifixion painting by Emanuele Tzanes, Cretan school, second half of the 17th century; Hermitage Museum, Saint Petersburg)

Venetian *Provveditor*
In the Republic of Venice, the title of *Provveditore* was awarded to government officials selected by the various councils through which the state was articulated. Each provveditor was responsible for a specific matter or government of provinces: therefore, they were the key figures of the Venetian power system, both in civil and military affairs. The double role makes them similar in many aspects to the Ottoman *paşa* and *beglerbeg*, although these latter were principally military leaders. The dress of the Venetian ruling class in the mid 17th century was strongly influenced by that introduced in the Low Countries. Officials and aristocrats usually employed black or dark grey for their clothing, as well as a neutral colour for accessories, such black or grey in different shades. The large plumed headgear is an echo of the Mediterranean roots of this Venetian provveditor. (Reconstruction after a portrait of a unknown Venetian Provveditor by Carlo Ceresa, 1648; Venice, Private Collection)

***Oltramontano* Musketeer**
In the mid 17th century the infantry constituted more than 80 percent of

the Venetian field army. At the early stage of the war, the defenders deployed in Cretan regiments or independent companies of Italians, Corsicans and *Oltramontani*, including Dutch, German, Swiss and French soldiers. The last three continued to be represented in the Venetian army, while the Dutch presence ended in 1646. Until this date, the United Provinces of the Netherlands provided Venice with many mercenaries. At the beginning of the war, there were in Crete at least 300 Dutch soldiers organised in independent companies, who fought during the defence of Chaniá and Réthimnon between 1645 and 1646. During the conflict no other mercenary infantry came from the Netherlands, but Venice rented in the Seven Provinces many ships and enlisted sailors and other specialists. (Reconstruction after a drawing of the *Codice Bottacin*, 1640, Padua and Cesare Vecellio's painting, c.1645, preserved in the Palazzo Ducale, Venice)

B. The *Armata*, 1653–57

Venetian Sopracomito, or Galley Commander
(Armour after Lazzaro Mocenigo's portrait, 1657; Oriental style *taschetto* helmet, North Italian manufacture, beginning of the 17th century, Stibbert Museum, Florence)

Venetian bombardiere, Galley Artillery NCO
(Reconstruction after an engraving from Pietro Paulo Floriani's treaty *Difesa et Offesa delle Piazze*; Venice, 1655)

Venetian Sailor
Gli abiti de' veneziani, di quasi ogni età con diligenza raccolti, e dipinti da Giovanni Grevenbroch; Venice, 1757. In the middle of the 17th century in the Venetian fleet there was no uniform in the modern sense, however, some specific instructions regarding dress were used in ceremonial occasions, in order to provide a fine and well-suited aspect of the crew. On these occasions, sailors and oarsmen were required to wear a special uniform consisting of a red canvass coat and cap. The oarsmen were also issued with sailcloth breeches, shoes, socks, and muslin quilting for the chained leg.

C. The Mine, 1667–69

Miner
During the defence of Candia, miners represented the major actors in the dramatic duel fought underground. The Venetians recruited miners both in *Terraferma* and other states where the technique of mining had been developed, and finally in Greece, such the 2,000 miners enlisted in 1667 by Francesco Morosini. Inside Candia, the defenders were organised into companies formed by diggers and specialists with the rank of NCO. (Reconstruction after Johann Scheither's Novissima *Praxis Militari*, 1670)

Dutch Engineer
In the half of the 17th century the term "engineer" identified different specialist

competencies, including fortification, artillery and explosives and these activities were performed in theory as well as in practice, placing him at an intermediate level between officer and NCO. The Cretan War represented a turning point for the codification of the engineers in a more modern meaning, giving them the role of specialist in siege tactics. Venice enlisted several engineers in the Low Countries and France from the first year of the war, such as the Dutch van Wert and the French Verneda and Bellonet, who greatly improved the original walls and bastions of Candia. The dress of this engineer shows the characteristics of the transitional period introduced in northern Europe and includes a single-breasted *pourpoint* jacket with trimmed short sleeves, worn over a pair of wide breeches. The small size of the jacket sleeves highlights the white cotton shirt, typical of these years. The dress could be completed with a cape tied at the back. (Reconstruction after Gerhard Ter Borch and a drawing from the *Speculum Militare*, Nurnberg, 1665)

Italian Infantryman

In the mining war the infantry preferably employed small arms, such as pistols and cavalry carbines and even the ammunition was reduced to a minimum to facilitate movement in the gallery. (Reconstruction after a drawing from Johann Scheither's Novissima *Praxis Militari*, 1670)

D. Last Defence, 1669

Pikeman of an Italian Regiment

During the sorties of the last three years of siege, the infantry used every kind of polearm useful to destroy the enemy approaches. According to the sources, for the sortie the defensive armament was strongly reduced, to facilitate the movement through the full trench-crossed terrain in front of the city; however, helmets were largely employed by the defenders, officers included. (Reconstruction after Johann Scheither's *Novissima Praxis Militari*, 1670)

French Volunteer and Servant

In September 1667 the Duke de La Feuillade collected on his own initiative for one corps of 600 volunteers for Crete, recruited among the aristocrat families' cadets and Louis XIV's army officers. About one year after, the Duke attempted to perform a sortie in force to destroy the Ottoman trenches. The action ended with a disastrous defeat for the volunteers; however, this enterprise had a vast echo and for Venice was useful to gain more support in the European courts. In the sortie, planned for the morning of 18 December 1668, the French contingent was divided into four brigades and supported by 100 German mercenaries. Each nobleman was assisted by a servant who reloaded the muskets and joined him in battle. This volunteer wears a fashionable *justaucorp* over an embroidered shirt, and *rhingraeve*-style breeches, embellished with ribbons and silk inserts. His musket is equipped with a modern Roman-style flintlock. The servant wears a coat with the Dampierre family's livery. (Reconstruction after van der Meulen contemporary drawings and Maurice Leloir's *Histoire du Costume*)

Oltramontano Grenadier
During the last three years of the siege at Candia, grenadiers became very important specialists on both sides. The defenders organised a team of intruders with a core formed by 10 grenadiers with musketeers and other soldiers with polearms as support. Grenadier tactics are often mentioned in the account by Johann Scheither, who participated in the defence of Candia in 1668–1669. Coats in red were traditional of the Venetian infantry since 1660s. The cloth cap is one of the options worn by grenadiers instead of the large broad-brimmed hat. (Reconstruction after the *Speculum Militare*, Nurnberg, 1665)

E. First Conquests, 1645–50

Janissary in Campaign Dress
Despite several contemporary Ottoman miniatures representing the Janissaries in full dress even in battlefield scenes, in action the *kapikulu* infantry replaced the sumptuous court clothing with more practical items. Eyewitness relations describe the Ottoman soldiers in battle wearing short quilted jackets, turbans or other headgear, such as the *tekke* cloth cap here represented. Some distinctive accessories, such as garters under the knee, were issued to the most valorous soldiers. The equipment comprised usually *tüfek* musket, sabre and one or more knives. Before moving against the enemy to engage them in close combat, the Ottoman infantry usually fired a series of volleys. The assaults, carried out with curved sabres and knives, were led by *serdengeçdi* (volunteers) chosen among janissaries and *sipahy* and usually accompanied by a gloomy background of encouraging screams. (Reconstruction after a 17th century drawing from the *Bull Collection*, Stibbert Museum Library, Florence)

Janissary _aşçı başı_
The *aşçı başı* – chief cook – was a distinctive rank of the janissary corps, comparable to a junior officer, in charge of managing the cousin of the *orta*-unit which he belonged. Several ranks of the janissaries derived their name from food terminology, like the commander of the *orta*, the *çorbacı* –soup maker. As a symbol of his rank, the *aşçı başı* carried a large ladle-like instrument for dishing soup or stew out of huge metal pots. His was a non-combatant rank and he usually wore elaborate dress consisting of a lined *kaftan*, gilded metal belt and other accessories hanging from his waist. The typical janissary's headgear, the *ak-börk*, identified him more than anything else. It was of tubular white felt, running down his back to below the shoulders. The origin of the headgear goes to the Ottoman mystic Hacı Bektaş who blessed the corps when it was first formed by placing his white sleeve on the head of a janissary. As a result, Hacı Bektaş became the patron saint of the corps. (Hyeronimus Beck's *Exaratae turcarum imperatorum, capitaneorum. Immagina, habitus, ludos, caerimonias*, and M. la Haye, *Recueil de cent estampes representant differentes nations du Levant*, Paris 1714)

Janissary *odabasi*
In 1657, the Swedish delegate in Istanbul commissioned a wonderful collection containing 20 large paintings with wooden frames, illustrating the *kapikulu* soldiers in full colour. Several paintings show the janissaries rank and file in parade. The *odabasi* was the non-commissioned officer of the Janissary *oda*, or "room": the tactical and administrative units which composed the *orta* or "battalion" of the *kapikulu* infantry. Each *orta* was identified by a number, but the series did not follow a rank order, because the first *orta* had the number 19, the second had 1 and the third 111. Furthermore, each *orta* had its ensign and symbol, and the latter could be tattooed on arms or hands of the unit's members. For the war each *orta* increased its battle force to 600 men, divided in 20 or more *odas*. This *odabasi* wears an aulic *dolama* kaftan of azure-turquoise wool and turban garnished with one metal *celeng* as distinction of bravery. Usually the rank was indicated by the waist sash and polearm, carried only in parade. (Reconstruction after drawings of the Rålamb Collection, 1657–58, Stockholm)

F. *Azab*, Levend and Corsairs, 1648–1669

Naval *azab* in Combat Dress
(After Mahmut Şevket Paşa's *Osmanlı Askeri Teşkilatıve Kıyafetleri*,1363–1876, vol. I; İstanbul, 1983)

***Beg*, Galley Commander**
The Ottoman galley commanders received the title of *beg* or *bey*. Like the Venetian *sopracomito*, the *beg* was identified by an ensign and decoration of his galley's stern, like the coverage on the quarterdeck. Green or azure-turquoise were reserved to *begs*, while carmine red with gold brocade were exclusive of the *kapudan paşa*. The coverage was replaced every year, because traditionally the crew received the old one as present. (*Turkish Navy Captain, Ottoman Costume*, 1667, Id. 81949; Wallach Collection, New York Public Library; late 17th century Turkish pistol, Askeri Museum, Istanbul)

***Topçu Levend*, Naval Artilleryman**
(Reconstruction after the *Combattimento fattosi dalle galeotte condotte dal capitano Ridolfi* ... 1664, engraving by Gaspar Bouttats; Anne S.K. Brown Collection, Rhode Island, USA)

G. Guarding the Straits, 1653–59

***Sipahy Ulufely* Cavalryman**
(Reconstruction after drawings of the Rålamb Collection, 1657-58, Stockholm; late 17th century helm, Askery Museum, Istanbul; mid-17th century mail coat, Badishes Landesmuseum, Karlsruhe)

Köprülü Mehmet, Grand Vizier
The grand vizier wears a fine silk *entari* waistcoat under a prestigious fur-lined *üst kürkü* kaftan with false sleeves. The *mucevveze* turban with yellow-

gold silk was the characteristic distinctive headgear of the grand vizier. (Reconstruction after contemporary sources)

***Serhaddkulu* Infantryman**
(Reconstruction after *Ottoman Costumes*, 1667, Id. 12502; Wallach Collection; New York Public Library and *Księga Osmańskiego Kostiumy*, c.1640–48; Biblioteka Narodowa, Warsaw)

H. The Trench, 1667–69

Two *Kapikulu* Infantrymen, *cebeci*
The *cebeci* were elite infantrymen of the *kapikulu*, who were also responsible for the custody of firearms and their maintenance. As specialists and marksmen, special weapons were also assigned to them, such as the heavy rampart musket served by a couple of soldiers. In action they wore the more practice campaign dress with some distinctive items of their rank, like the metal helm with the gilded metal "spoon" of the *kapikulu*. (Reconstruction after L.F. Marsigli, *Stato Militare dell'Imperio Ottomano* and Ahmed Çevad Beg, *Etàt militaire ottoman depuis la fondation de l'Empire jusqu'à nos jours*)

Serrhadkulu* Infantryman, *azab tüfekçi
The *azab* infantrymen were originally employed for garrison duty instead of the janissaries when they marched on campaign. Under certain aspects, the *azab* were similar to the Austrian *Landwher* or the Venetian *cernide* and *craine*, but compared to the latter were usually employed outside their native area. (Reconstruction after a drawing of the Bull Collection, Stibbert Museum Library, Florence)

Sipahy Toprakly*, Syrian *Timar
In war, each province's governor led a contingent formed of soldiers on horseback, known as *sipahy toprakly*. These corps could also be very numerous, as it increased their ranks with volunteers and with the holders of districts in which each province was divided, namely *zeamet* and *timar*. After the war, the *toprakly* of Crete totalled on paper more than 30,000 men. This Syrian *zeamet* wears a typical Mamluk *kaftan* with large sleeves and a *çicak* helm of local production. For trench warfare helm and other metal protection were widely employed as protective items also by the Ottoman soldiers, as related in several contemporary sources. (*Firdousi Schāname*, Berlin manuscript, early 17th century; Syrian *çicak* helm, mid-17th century, Arts Collection of the Castello Sforzesco, Pavia)

Select Bibliography

Archive Sources

Archivio di Stato di Venezia (Venice State Archive)

Capi del Consiglio dei Dieci
Collegio, Relazioni
Inquisitori di Stato
Provveditori da Terra e da Mar
Provveditori alle Fortezze
Senato Mar
Senato, Dispacci di Capi da Guerra
Senato, Dispacci di Provveditori

Archivio di Stato di Roma (Rome State Archive)

Cartari-Febei
Vera Relatione del Successo seguito nell'Isole dell'Arcipelago tra l'Armate della Serenissima Republica di Venetia & Ottomana; Effemeridi della cronaca anni 1646–1647, in Roma MDCXLVII
Vera Relatione delli felici Progressi dell'Armi della Serenissima Republica di Venetia, nel regno di Dalmazia; Effemeridi della cronaca anno1648, in Roma MDCXLVIII
Lettera di Ragguaglio dell'Impresa del Volo; Effemeridi della cronaca anni 1654–55, in Roma MDCLV
Ragguaglio della Vittoria Navale conseguita à Dardanelli dall'Armata della Serenissima Republica di Venetia; Effemeridi della cronaca anno 1656, in Roma MDCLVI
Lettera di Ragguaglio del Combattimento tra l'Armata Veneta e la Turca à Dardanelli; Effemeridi della cronaca anno 1657, in Roma MDCLVII

Archivio di Stato di Firenze (Florence State Archive)

Mediceo del Principato, Milizie in Levante and Negozi diversi attenenti alle Galere

Archivio di Stato di Lucca (Lucca State Archive)

Deputazione sopra le Milizie

Cretan War, Contemporary Sources

Brusoni, Girolamo: *Historia dell'Ultima Guerra tra Veneziani e Turchi* (Venice, 1673)
Nani, Battista: *Historia della Repubblica Veneta* (Venice, 1679)
Sansovino, Francesco: *Venetia Città Nobilissima et Singolare* (Venice, 1673)
Santa Croce, A.: *Frammenti istorici della guerra di Candia* (Bologna, 1647)

Siri, Vittorio, *Del Mercurio, overo Historia de' Correnti Tempi* (Casale, 1667)

Valiero, Andrea, *Historia della Guerra di Candia* (Venice, 1679)

Villa de Ghiron, Francesco, *Les Memoires du Voiage de Msr. le Marquis de Ville au Levant, ou Histoire Curieuse du Siege de Candia* (Amsterdam, 1670)

Military History: Ottoman Empire

Anderson, R.C., *Naval Wars in the Levant, 1559–1853* (Hartford, CT: Martino Publishing, 2005)

Bombaci, Alessio, & Shaw, Stanford J.: *L'Impero Ottomano, in Nuova Storia Universale dei popoli e delle civiltà*, vol. VI, part II (Turin: UTET, 1981)

Briot, M., *Histoire de l'Etat Présent de l'Empire Ottomane* (Amsterdam, 1678)

Cevad Ahmed Beg: *Etat Militaire Ottoman depuis la Fondation de l'Empire jusqu'à nos jours* (Constantinople, 1882)

Cianci, Bruno, *La Marina dell'Impero Ottomano, 1299–1923* (Bologna: Odoya, 2015)

Goffmann, Daniel, *The Ottoman Empire and Early Modern Europe* (Cambridge: Cambridge University Press, 2004)

Guer, Jean, *Moeurs et Usages des Turcs* (Paris, 1747)

Hammer-Purgstall, Joseph (Freiherr von), *Geschichte des Osmanischen Reiches*, vol. VII and VIII; (Pest 1827–33)

Mantran, Robert, *L'Empire Ottoman du XVI au XVIII siècle* (Paris: Fayard, 2005)

Marsigli, Luigi Ferdinando, *Stato Militare dell'Imperio Ottomanno*; vol. I–II (Amsterdam, 1732)

Murphey, Rhoads, *Ottoman Warfare, 1500–1700* (London: UCL Press, 1999)

Murphey, Rhoads, 'The Ottoman Resurgence in the Seventeenth-Century Mediterranean: The Gamble and its Results', in *Mediterranean Historical Review*, n. 8 – 1993

Panzac, Daniel, 'La Géostratégie navale de l'Empire Ottoman', in *Annali di Storia Militare Europea – 2: Mutazioni e permanenze nella storia navale del Mediterraneo, secc. XVI–XIX* (edited by Guido Candiani and Luca Lo Basso (Milan: Franco Angeli, 2010))

Panzac, Daniel, *Histoire économique et sociale de l'Empire Ottoman et de la Turquie (1326–1960)* (Paris: Peeters. 1950)

Streusand, Douglas E., *Islamic Gunpowder Empires: Ottomans, Safavids, and Mughals* (Philadelphia, PA: Westview Press, 2011)

Military History: Venice and Western Europe

Bilotto, A. Del Negro, P. Mozzarelli, C. (eds.), *I Farnese: corti, guerra e nobiltà in antico regime* (Rome: Bulzoni, 1997)

Bradford, Ernle, *Storia dei Cavalieri di Malta: lo scudo e la spada* (Milan, 1998)

Brunelli, Giampiero, *Soldati del Papa. Politica militare e nobiltà nello Stato della Chiesa* (Rome, 2003)

Camporota, Buonaventura, *Vita di Francesco Morosini Peloponnesiaco, doge di Venezia* (Naples, 1865)

Canale, Cristoforo, *Della Milizia Marittima, libri quattro trascritti e annotati da Mario Nani-Mocenigo* (Venice, 1928)

Candiani, Guido, *I Vascelli della Serenissima. Guerra, politica e costruzioni navali a Venezia in età moderna, 1650–1720* (Venice: Istituto Veneto di Scienze, 2002)

Casini, Matteo, *Immagini dei Capitani Generali da Mar a Venezia in età barocca*; in 'Il Perfetto Capitano, immagini e realtà' (Rome: Bulzoni, 2001)

Dalmasso, Gian Luigi, *I Piemontesi alla guerra di Candia (1644–1669)* (Torino, 1906)

Del Negro, Piero, 'La politica militare di Venezia e lo 'Stato da Mar' nel Sei-Settecento', in *Studi Veneziani,* Nuova Serie 39 (Venice, 2000).

Del Negro, Piero, 'Il leone in campo: Venezia e gli oltramarini nelle guerre di Candia e di Morea', in *Mito e antimito di Venezia nel bacino adriatico* (secoli XV–XIX), Atti del primo convegno italo-croato; Venice, Fondazione Giorgio Cini, 11–13 November 1997.

Del Negro, Piero, 'Il tramonto della tradizione militare italiana: il caso veneziano tra Sei e Settecento', in atti del seminario *Lo Spirito Militare degli Italiani*; Padova, 16–18 November 2000 (Padua, 2002)

Ercole, Guido, *Vascelli e Fregate della Serenissima* (Trento: Gruppo Modellistico Trentino, 2011)

Hale, John R., & Mallet, Michael, *The Military Organization of a Renaissance State* (Cambridge: Cambridge University Press, 1984)

Infelise, M. and Stouraiti, A. (eds.), *Venezia e la guerra di Morea. Guerra, politica e cultura alla fine del '600'* (Milan: Franco Angeli, 2005).

Madunić, Domagoj, *Defensiones Dalmatiae: Governance and Logistics of the Venetian Defensive System in Dalmatia during the War of Crete, 1645–1669* (Central European University, 2012)

Nani-Mocenigo, Mario, *Storia della marina veneziana* (Rome, 1935)

Pezzolo, Luciano, *Stato, Guerra e Finanza nella Repubblica di Venezia fra Medioevo e Prima Età Moderna*; in atti della conferenza "Navies and State Formation"; *Volos*, 9–12 September 2004

Prelli, Alberto, *L'Esercito Veneziano del Primo Seicento* (Venice: Filippi Editore, 1993).

Preto, Paolo: *Un aspetto sconosciuto del conflitto Veneto-Turco in Dalmazie e in Levante: la guerra chimica e batteriologica*; in 'Studi Storici Militari' 1999.

de' Quincy, Marquise, *Histoire Militaire du Regne de Louis le Grand Roy de France*, vol. I (Paris, 1726)

Rahlenbeck, Charles, *Gilles de Haes* (Gand, 1854)

Sichart, Ludwig, *Geschichte der Hannoverschen Armée*, vol. I–IV (Hannover, 1866–71)

Staudinger, *Geschichte des Bayerischen Heeres*; vol. IBiblioverlag, III (Munich, 1901–08)

Susane, Gen., *Histoire de l'Infanterie Française*, vol. I–V (Paris, 1876)

Tessin, Georg, *Die Regimenter der Europäischen Staaten im Ancien Regime des XVI. bis XVIII. Jahrhunderts, Teil I.: die Stammlisten* (Osnabrück: Biblio-Verlag, 1986)

Vaccher, Roberto, 'L'esercito veneziano e la difesa di Candia, 1645–1669 (Master's degree thesis) Università Ca' Foscari, Venice, Academic Year 2013–14

Military History: Generalities

Bigge, Wilhelm, Col., *Der Kampf um Kandia in den Jahern 1667–69* (Berlin 1899)

Childs, John, *Warfare in the Seventeenth Century* (London: Harper Collins, 2006)

Duffy, Christopher, *Fire and Stone: the Science of Fortress Warfare 1660–1860* (Newton Abbot: David and Charles, 1975)

Duffy, Christopher, *Siege Warfare: the Fortress in the Early Modern World 1494–1660* (London: Routledge, 1979)

Glete, Ian, *Warfare at Sea, 1500–1650* (London: Routledge, 2000)

Guilmartin, John: *Gunpowder and Galleys* (Cambridge: Cambridge University Press, 1974)

Faroqhi, Suraiya N. (ed.), *The Later Ottoman Empire* (Cambridge: Cambridge University Press, 2006)

Kohlaas, Wilhelm, *Candia 1645–1669. Die Tragödie einer abendländischen Verteidigung mit dem Nachspiel Athen 1687* (Osnabrück: Biblio-Verlag, 1978)

Lo Basso, Luca, *Uomini da remo. Galee e galeotti del Mediterraneo in età moderna* (Milan, 2003)

Lo Basso, Luca, *A vela e a remi. Navigazione, guerra e schiavitù nel Mediterraneo* (secc. XVI–XVIII) (Ventimiglia, 2004)

Diplomacy and Policy

Brewer, David, *'The Hidden Centuries', Turkish Rule from the Fall of Constantinople to Greek Independence* (London: I.B. Tauris, 2011)

de la Houssaie, Amelot, *Histoire du gouvernement de Venise* (Paris, 1705)

Detorakis, Theocharis, *History of Crete* (Heraklion: Detorakis, 1994)

Greene, Molly, *A Shared World: Christians and Muslims in the Early Modern Mediterranean* (Princeton NJ: Princeton Modern Greek Studies, Princeton University Press, 2001)

Pannocchieschi, Francesco, *Relazione delle cose di Venezia di Monsignor Francesco d'Elci Pannocchieschi, nipote e coadiutore di monsignor Scipione, Nunzio Apostolico in Venezia* (Pisa, 1656; Libro I)

Parente, Antonio, *Quando il carcere era galera e bagni erano penali* (Dipartimento dell'Amministrazione Penitenziaria, Rome 2002)

Romanin, Samuele, *Storia documentata di Venezia* (Venice, 1858)

Setton, Kenneth Meyer, *Venice, Austria and the Turks in the Seventeenth Century* (Philadelphia, PA: Diane Publishing, 1991)

Treccani degli Alfieri, Giovanni: *Storia di Brescia* (Brescia: Morcelliana, 1963)

Valensi, Lucette, *Venezia e la Sublime Porta* (Bologna, Il Mulino, 1991)

Zorzi, Alvise, *La Repubblica del Leone* (Milan: Rusconi, 1979)

Conferences, Essays and Exhibitions

AA.VV., *Venezia e la difesa del Levante, catalogo dell'esposizione del 1986* (Venice: L'Arsenale Editrice, 1986)

Blackmore, David S.T., *Warfare on the Mediterranean in the Age of Sail: A History, 1571–1866* (London: McFarland, 2011)

Madunić, Doagoj: 'The Adriatic Naval Squadron (1645–1669): Defense of the Adriatic during the War for Crete', in *Dalmacija* UDK (Zagreb, 2013)

Pedani Fabris, Anna Maria (ed.): *I 'documenti turchi' dell'Archivio di Stato di Venezia, con l'edizione dei regesti di Alessio Bombaci* (Ministero per i Beni Culturali e Ambientali – Ufficio Centrale per i Beni Archivistici, Venice 1994)

Ortalli, Gherardo (ed.), *Venezia e Creta, atti del convegno internazionale di studi; Iraklion-Chanià, 30 September – 5 October 1997*; Istituto Veneto di Scienze, Lettere a Arti, Venice 1998